AFTERNOON
OF A FAUN

AFTERNOON OF A FAUN

HOW DEBUSSY CREATED A NEW MUSIC FOR THE MODERN WORLD

HARVEY LEE SNYDER

AMADEUS
PRESS

An Imprint of Hal Leonard Corporation

Published in 2015 by Amadeus Press
An Imprint of Hal Leonard Corporation
7777 West Bluemound Road
Milwaukee, WI 53213

Trade Book Division Editorial Offices
33 Plymouth St., Montclair, NJ 07042

Due to limitations of space, acknowledgments of permission to quote from previously published materials are found on p. 383, which constitutes an extension of this copyright page.

Printed in the United States of America

Book design by Lynn Bergesen, UB Communications

Library of Congress Cataloging-in-Publication Data

Snyder, Harvey Lee.
  Afternoon of a faun : how Debussy created a new music for the modern world / Harvey Lee Snyder.
     pages cm
  Includes bibliographical references and index.
  ISBN 978-1-57467-449-1
  1. Debussy, Claude, 1862-1918. 2. Composers—France—Biography. I. Title.
  ML410.D28S68 2015
  780.92dc23
  [B]
                          2015027704

www.amadeuspress.com

To Carol
and to the memory of Claude Debussy
and to the good people of the twenty-first century
who still read books

It is in Music, perhaps, that the soul most nearly attains that great end for which, when inspired by the poetic sentiment, it struggles—the creation of supernal beauty. It may be, indeed, that here this sublime end is, now and again, attained in fact. We are often made to feel, with a shivering delight, that from an earthly harp are stricken notes which cannot have been unfamiliar to the angels.

—Edgar Allan Poe, "The Poetic Principle"

CONTENTS

DECEMBER 22, 1894

Always collect the stones that are thrown at you. They may help to build your monument.

—Attributed to Hector Berlioz[1]

The first thing you notice is his massive head—the prominent forehead and the bulge above each eyebrow, as if his enormous intellect were about to burst through the cranium. The brow juts forward, the way Jupiter's does in those drawings of gods in children's books. Scattered about the head are heavy-lidded eyes, large ears, the nose a bit too small for the monumental skull behind it. With his curly black hair and beard, average height, and solid build, he looks more like a bourgeois shopkeeper than the ardent, impoverished *artiste* that he is.

On this important evening, there are few empty seats at the Salle d'Harcourt. Some of his former Conservatory companions are here, and friends from the city's dense population of writers and artists. Some influential critics, too. His new *Prélude à "L'Après-midi d'un faune"* will be heard for the first time, and it's certain that many in the hall know the steamy Mallarmé poem that inspired it. The music will be judged harshly if it doesn't measure up. But can this composer, any composer, capture the mythic symbolism at the heart of the poem? Can music possibly simulate the opulent language, or evoke the languor, the torrid atmosphere of a sylvan afternoon, or portray the erotic ambitions of the faun?

Mallarmé will be in the audience. What will he think of it?

Backstage, amidst a flock of agitated musicians, Debussy greets the conductor, Gustave Doret, with a self-conscious smile that betrays his anxiety. Like all of Debussy's friends, Doret knows how thirsty for recognition the composer is. At twenty-one Claude won France's highest honor for young composers: the Prix de Rome. In the ten years since, he's written dozens of songs and piano pieces that have been heard in Paris but nowhere else in the world. A year ago the first performance of his String Quartet left some musicians aghast because it departed arrogantly from the Beethoven model. Nevertheless, it drew a few accolades from the critics, who more often condemn his music as if he had brought shame on the French republic. But this work, this *Faune*, is so very different. What will the critics report?

Earlier on the day of the concert, Captain Albert Dreyfus, a Jewish officer charged with selling government secrets to German agents, was convicted of treason and sentenced to life imprisonment. The cafés were buzzing with the news, and the Paris press reacted with triumphant, vindictive joy, reflecting a widespread opinion that the nation had staved off a grave threat. Among the crowd at the Salle d'Harcourt, few could imagine how French society would be riven by the Dreyfus case.

Even fewer suspected that tonight they would hear a ten-minute *Prélude* that would turn the music world on its head.

Orchestral works by Franck, Saint-Saëns, and several lesser names will challenge the ears and torment the derrières before attention turns to *Faune*.[2] For Debussy, who meticulously crafted his tone poem and conscientiously broke every rule of the Paris Conservatory, it will be a long evening. Will the audience be ravished by the beauty of his music or outraged by its heresies? The latter verdict would crush his craving for a better life, finer wines.

Doret takes the podium, faces the orchestra of the Société Nationale, and with a flourish begins the program with Glazunov's tone poem *The Forest*—far less exciting than the folk-flavored Russian music performed a few years ago at the Universal Exposition. Next, the Allegretto from the *Serbian Suite*, by Jules Bordier, a provincial composer and an early champion of Wagner.

Those in the audience whose lavish dinners have induced sleep are jolted awake by the first stormy bars of Duparc's brilliant nautical nightmare, "La Vague et la cloche," sung by the baritone Numa Auguez. . . . Now we hear *The Burial of Ophelia*, by Louis-Albert Bourgault-Ducoudray. An interesting man—but one wonders: Which of these composers will be remembered in a hundred years?

The music goes on and on . . .

Turbulent years, these last two. Debussy is living with a lithe, green-eyed woman named Gabrielle Dupont. Gaby shares his poverty as well as his bed, endures his moods, and often sits home alone while he spends his evenings at the homes of the *haute bourgeoisie* or with Mallarmé's intellectual friends. Earlier this year Gaby was stunned by his engagement to a middling soprano named Thérèse Roger, and stunned again weeks later, when he was forced to withdraw his proposal. Chausson and a few other disapproving friends felt morally obliged to break off relations with him. Gaby forgave; or perhaps she didn't, but she stayed.

More happily, Debussy had discovered Maeterlinck's play *Pelléas et Mélisande.* He was convinced that *Pelléas* would be the ideal libretto for the opera he longed to write, the kind of opera he had imagined and talked about ever since his insufferable residency at the Villa Medici in Rome. He has been working on the score for more than eighteen months now. He is almost obsessed with it. No one can explain where he found time to finish the String Quartet and *Prélude à "L'Après-midi d'un faune"* (Prelude to "The Afternoon of a Faun"). When inspiration comes knocking, you open the door wide.

Strong applause for young Mathieu Crickboom's virtuoso performance of the Third Violin Concerto by Saint-Saëns. The composer is a cofounder of the Société Nationale, and well liked here. Now Numa Auguez comes to the stage again to sing Guy Ropartz's "Prière."

The man in charge, Gustave Doret, is still in his twenties, just a child in music-years, and the baton feels a little insecure in his hand. He was surprised when Debussy asked him to conduct the premiere of *Faune*. It was an honor and signified great trust, as Doret had never conducted a concert as important as this one.

Only a few months ago, Doret came to Debussy's tiny apartment to hear the work for the first time. Sitting beside his friend at the piano, he was entranced, overwhelmed, by the way Debussy was able to tease out the flutes and horns from the instrument's unsuitable hammers and strings. Examining the orchestral score, Doret saw it was dense with neatly penciled changes and corrections. There would be problems with the tempo, which changes often, and hazards in the chromaticism—sharps and flats strewn across the pages. Debussy was concerned that his novel instrumental effects might not translate well from page to orchestra. Doret promised that the music would receive all the rehearsals it might need.

Nearing the end of the program now. An orchestral excerpt from César Franck's oratorio, *Redemption*, is well received.

The *Faune* rehearsals generated a feeling of intimate collaboration such as Doret had never known. At first the players didn't understand the music; it was so unlike anything they had ever performed or heard. It took them a while to feel comfortable with the innovative structure, the sinuous melodies, the near absence of rhythmic pulse, the dissonances that didn't resolve, the unexpected modulations, the harmonies that seemed to go astray, but with magical effect. Too often the composer, still striving for just the right timbres with new instrumental combinations, would bring revised pages to be learned. In the end, the musicians, familiar now with Debussy's musical language, were passionate about their mission: to communicate, to an audience unprepared for something truly new, the wonder of Debussy's music in all its ineffable beauty, its clarity, its charm.

Clarity! In this age of Wagner, Bruckner, Franck, and Brahms, the word is hardly used any more. Charm? Yes, that too.

Backstage, during a break, Debussy wraps his hands around Doret's. He can barely sustain a smile or utter a word of encouragement before the conductor returns to the podium. Now it's time. Doret waits for the audience to settle down. He gathers the attention of his players, raises his baton. The hall is completely silent as Georges Barrère, the flutist, unfolds the faun's peculiar melody, sliding down the scale, then up again as it expands and settles lazily around a thousand ears. The oboes, clarinets, and horns murmur softly while the harps throw fairy dust over all. The faun repeats his tune, now attended by shimmering strings . . .

Doret senses, as some conductors can, the reverential stillness behind him, an audience enthralled. Not a whisper, not a cough, hardly the blink of an eye, all ears tuned in unison to this perfect analogue of Mallarmé's honeyed dream of an afternoon.

The faun's unhurried tune is now in the flutes, now in the oboes and clarinets, down the scale, then up, again and again, each time with small variations, giving way to a frisky, playful arabesque as the elusive wood nymphs lead their pursuer on the chase. A new theme introduces a rhapsodic interlude expressing the amorous yearnings of the faun. The first theme returns, a bit more mellow, a bit fatigued; then, in the last measures, the faintest ping of ancient cymbals as the faun tries his tune once more. He quivers, yawns, and—lulled by the hushed woodwinds, the harp, the distant chimes, a plucked chord in the bass—he succumbs to sleep.

The audience erupts in applause and cheers. A complete triumph! *Encore! Encore!* The Société Nationale prohibits encores, but today Doret makes an exception for his friend's *Faune*. The clamor subsides. The orchestra gladly plays the work again, as they had come to love it and wanted the audience to love it, too.

A persistent thought tiptoes around Doret's mind: It's been a long time since Paris has heard a masterpiece of this caliber.

Leaving the concert hall, perhaps no more than a few people in the audience understood that they had been present at the dawn of a new modern music, a French music.

A new French music, fresh air in a stuffy room!

In the late nineteenth century, French composers, or at least some of them, tried, without much success, to shake off the dust of mediocrity. France's musical contribution to the late Romantic era had been "an empty and paltry thing, emotionally shallow," wrote the music critic Lawrence Gilman, "refined and adroit, but meager and unrewarding."[3]

The composers of Germany and Austria—Bach, Haydn, Mozart, Beethoven, Schubert, and many others—had dominated European music so thoroughly for more than two centuries that every music conservatory on the Continent and Britain was teaching the same dogma. The rules of harmony and counterpoint, the classic symphonic formalism, the instrumental anatomy and proportions of the orchestra—all were codified by seventeenth- and eighteenth-century Germanic music masters. The French antagonism toward Germany had simmered and boiled for eons, for reasons more political and territorial than musical. But in the decades between the Franco-Prussian debacle of 1870 and the First World War, the French were repeatedly reminded that they were a second-rate nation.

By the time of *Faune*, a late-Romantic French style had developed, characterized by elegance, impeccable taste, and unimpeachable craft, and by its formalism, graceful melodic contours, and orthodox use of harmony. Saint-Saëns was its consummate practitioner. Chabrier and Fauré had each made some progress in brightening the colors of the musical palette. But French music was laden with the sentimentalities of the older, establishment composers: Gounod, Delibes, Massenet, and Franck. As lovely and accomplished as French music could be, the repertoire was lightweight and culturally insignificant when compared with that of Brahms, at the height of his career; Liszt, a pioneer of harmonic indiscretions; and Wagner, whose musical adventures had overwhelmed and forever changed European culture.

While Debussy was still finding his way, said Gilman, the prevailing attitude of the French musical public could be judged by its reception of Franck's Symphony in D Minor, in 1889. The audience at the Paris Conservatory concert, well versed in the music of the day, "could make neither head nor tail of it."[4] Today we place Franck's work in the mainstream of Romantic symphonies. But in 1889 Franck was considered, not always admiringly, a pioneer of modernism. Today that would be taken as a joke.

In this light, we can imagine how puzzling *Prélude à "L'Après-midi d'un faune"* sounded to the same public five years later. Though the first audience applauded loudly and called for an encore, the critics were tepid, at best. One thought it was "too exquisite . . . flabby and insipid."[5] The *Figaro* critic wrote that music like *Faune* is amusing to write but not to listen to.[6]

In his twelve years at the Paris Conservatory, Debussy was taught the same dogma as all the other composers of his time. Then what inspiration, divine or mundane, sent Debussy down a path that was so different from his compatriots'?

Debussy was the sort of genius whose knowledge of a certain range of human endeavor—in his case, music, literature, and the visual arts—was so broad and penetrating, and whose mind was so nimble, that he could synthesize these various strands and weave something that was new and individual and, most of all, pleasing to many others.

He was inspired by sources that had rarely if ever been prominent in European music. Other composers of his time were musical descendants of Bach, Mozart, and Beethoven, or followers of Liszt and Wagner—great masters all, certainly. But this narrow band of antecedents, all grounded in the Teutonic musical tradition, fostered a homogeneity in the music of composers from Grieg in Norway, to Dvořák in Bohemia, to Tchaikovsky in Russia. By the last decades of the nineteenth century, their symphonies and operas, which defined the late-Romantic period, had come to sound tired, and the music of Wagner seemed to some composers like the path forward.

Young Debussy found his inspiration not in the works of Bach and Beethoven, but in the paintings and literature he loved, and in what we might think of today as "alternative" modes of music. The gypsy violins he heard in the cafés of Budapest, the Javanese gamelan ensemble at the 1889 Paris Exposition, the medieval liturgical chants and polyphony that had been lost in the dust of five centuries—he recognized these as musical languages that could enrich his own. He studied Chopin's harmony and pianistic technique and grasped the way Mussorgsky plumbed his Russian soul to find new realms of vocal expression. And though Debussy often made dismissive or disparaging comments about Wagner and was deeply troubled by the Bayreuth master's corrosive influence on the music of his era, he never denied that Wagner provided some useful techniques to employ in *Pelléas et Mélisande*, or that *Parsifal* contains some of the most beautiful music ever written.

Just as important to Debussy's development was his affinity for the infinite world of nature, including his own nature. In a 1911 interview, he articulated the way nature spoke through him:

> Who can know the secret of musical composition? The sound of the sea, the outline of a horizon, the wind in the leaves, the cry of a bird—these set off complex impressions in us. And suddenly . . . one of these memories bursts forth, expressing itself in the language of music. It carries its own harmony within itself. However much effort one makes, one could not find anything better, anything more sincere. Only thus does a soul destined for music make such beautiful discoveries.[7]

Louis Laloy, Debussy's first French biographer, believed that for centuries French composers were mostly ignorant of the art and literature of their own time. "It was reserved for Debussy," Laloy wrote, "to give us the composer-humanist, sensitive to beauty of every sort, knowing how to read and how to write."[8] By the time he began writing *Faune*, Debussy had been welcomed into the elite tribe of intellectuals—poets, playwrights, critics, and painters—who gathered around Mallarmé's table on many Tuesdays. Their colloquies about the artistic and philosophical currents of the day fueled Debussy's imagination and creativity for years. For someone with as little nonmusical education as Debussy, it was an ongoing seminar in contemporary aesthetics.

He challenged himself to convey in music what he saw in paintings and drawings. He found ways to make J. M. W. Turner's blazing light and wind-whipped seas resound in *La Mer*, and to make music as dark and mysterious as James Whistler's nocturnal paintings, especially in his own orchestral *Nocturnes*. He built dozens of songs and an opera on the verses of symbolist poets, and he incorporated their aesthetic philosophy into much of his instrumental work.

"The music of France had witnessed no such spectacle as Debussy," Gilman wrote. When he arrived, French music was "speaking mediocre rhetoric. He left it capable of speaking poetry."[9]

An essential element in this transformation was Debussy's lifelong instinct for originality, which was innate, unforced, natural. From his teen years at the

Conservatory, he followed a path never before taken, a path that was terra incognita even to his teachers. He didn't plan it that way. His music, as revolutionary as it was, did not spring from a rebellious nature, or from an ego seeking fame. The rebel and the ego were well served by his originality, but he was driven instead by dissatisfaction with the music the Conservatory was training him to write, a formulaic music that restricted his creative options. He followed a more perilous path than the one his teachers mapped out for him because, as he discovered early on, his response to natural beauty or poetry or love could not always be expressed in the language of traditional harmony or exclusively within the impregnable walls of Western aesthetics.

The spirit of rebellion was there, too, putting an edge on his quest for originality. Léon Vallas wrote of "Debussy's constant, almost exaggerated determination to react against all the symphonic mannerisms of his day, especially those that were traceable to Beethoven, Franck, and Wagner." Much of his music, said Vallas, shows "unmistakable evidence of a spirit of contradiction that is both instinctive and deliberate."[10]

A fellow student, Maurice Emmanuel, described how Debussy, sitting at the piano in Ernest Guiraud's composition class, would "shake the foundations of Conservatory harmony" with his forbidden series of parallel fifths and unresolved dissonances. "To Guiraud's accusations of 'theoretical absurdity,' Debussy replied that 'there is no theory. Pleasure is the law.'"[11] Some people mistook this progressive notion for hedonism, but he only meant that pleasing the ear is more important than following rules—a shocking idea at the Paris Conservatory.

The audacity of his originality came at a high price. Through most of his career Debussy was ignored or attacked by French academics for his rejection of tradition and for creating music that resisted conventional scholarly analysis. The old guard didn't understand it, fundamentally, and what isn't understood often breeds resentment. Baffled music critics marginalized him with their scorn, sarcasm, or very faint praise. Before *Pelléas et Mélisande*, these attacks and snubs limited the number of performances his works were given, even in Paris, and kept a lid on his income and his spirit. After *Pelléas*, of course, orchestral societies and concert pianists clamored for his music.

Debussy wrote primarily because for him, as he said, there was no greater joy than to express himself in the language of music. Much of his work was meant to entertain that small core of enlightened Parisians who enjoyed their music at private salons, rather than the bourgeoisie in their concert halls. The music he liked to write was not necessarily what played well to the crowds. But he strove always to provide pleasure to those who performed his music, especially the pianists, even the less skilled among them. He wanted musicians to delight in the technical challenges he set down for them and to relish the joy and understated wit that surfaces unexpectedly but often.

It took many years for Debussy's revolution to be seen for what it was: a benign form of musical anarchy, a reversal of the rules imposed by the German hegemony. It's not that Debussy didn't use the techniques or conventions of his predecessors; many of his works, even late in his career, employ major and minor scales, four-bar phrases, symmetrical melodies, and so on. But Debussy did not feel constrained by rules. If he wanted to suggest a kind of vagueness, for example, he used the ambiguous whole-tone scale, or a series of dissonant chords that refused to end in a refreshing consonance, or phrases that eroded the comfortable sense of rhythm or pulse. At first Debussy's occasional vagueness was considered a disagreeable stylistic flaw, but later it was seen merely as one of his distinguishing characteristics, pleasing to the modern ear.

The abolition of centuries of rules and traditions was Debussy's most important contribution to Western music. His great gift to composers was not to show them a new way to write, but to give them freedom to write in a new way, their own way. Igor Stravinsky could feel secure in the rhythmic explosions of *Petrushka* and *The Rite of Spring*. Béla Bartók could employ spicy harmonies from the folk music of Eastern Europe. Arnold Schoenberg, employing Debussy's gift of freedom, could destroy harmony completely and invent atonality. And so on through the generations.

With the passage of time, Debussy's innovations became commonplace in the classical music, jazz, and pop songs of our day. But innovation alone doesn't guarantee immortality. Debussy's music survives because he has given us so many tonal images of eternal freshness and sublime beauty that leave us with a powerful desire to hear more.

PART I

DEBUSSY'S BIRTH TO WAGNER'S SUNSET

CHAPTER 1

A CONFLUENCE OF CIRCUMSTANCE (1862–1884)

Our soul is bequeathed to us by a set of completely unknown people who, through their descendants, act upon us all too often without our being able to do much about it.

—Debussy[1]

The family name comes from Bussy-le-Grand, the ancestral domain of the Comtes de Bussy, in a part of Burgundy called the Côte-d'Or, where the hillsides produce some of France's greatest wines. The best-known of the counts of Bussy, Roger de Rabutin (1618–1693), distinguished himself as a young soldier, but his amorous passions took precedence over his military duties, and he was sent to the Bastille for several months by Cardinal Richelieu. He secured his lasting fame, and another visit to the Bastille, by writing a scandalous novel satirizing the noble ladies and gentlemen of the court of King Louis XIV.

Some historians tried to link Claude Debussy to the Burgundian aristocracy, but no—Claude's father, Manuel de Bussy, was less nobly descended from peasant stock, men and women who in the seventeenth and eighteenth centuries were laborers and farmers, locksmiths, tradesmen, and carpenters. Claude's maternal family too was of humble origin.

Manuel de Bussy enlisted at eighteen in the Second Infantry Regiment of Marines and served his seven-year term. He married Victorine Manoury in 1861, when both were twenty-five years old. The newlyweds moved into an old three-story house in Saint-Germaine-en-Laye, just west of Paris. Manuel ran the china shop on the ground floor, and upstairs, on August 22, 1862, their first child, Achille-Claude de Bussy, was born. Before his first birthday he had a baby sister, Adèle. Emmanuel was born in 1867, and Alfred followed three years later. Another son died in childhood.

The china shop failed after two years of Manuel's management, and the de Bussys moved to Clichy to live with Victorine's mother. In 1868, Manuel found work at a printing shop and moved his family to Paris. For most of his life Manuel struggled and repeatedly failed to earn enough to support his family in comfort and stability. He never held a job for very long, and Victorine sometimes worked as a seamstress to help make ends meet.

The eldest boy was called Achille (pronounced "ah-*sheel*"), but he was Chilo to his family. At his baptism his godparents were Manuel's sister Clémentine and her lover, a rich financier named Achille Arosa. As a young adult, Chilo preferred to be called Claude, signed his name Claude-Achille, and modernized the family name to Debussy.

He was a quiet boy—"dreamy" was a word often used—who found refuge in solitude. Unlike his three siblings, he never went to school. His mother, who had little education herself, kept him at home and taught him to read and write. But Victorine had no enthusiasm for motherhood. More than once she sent Adèle to Cannes to be raised by Clémentine. Alfred was in Clémentine's care until her death in 1882.

Clearly, the de Bussy clan was not an auspicious incubator of genius. Nothing in the historical record suggests that music was a significant part of the family life, or that the children were exposed to the ripe artistic and cultural climate of Paris. Manuel confidently believed Achille would follow in his footsteps: He'd be a sailor when he grew up. (Later in life, the composer of *La Mer* [The Sea] found this amusing.)

But before Achille was nine, he had the great luck to be favored by a sequence of political and familial circumstances that determined the direction of his life.

The Accidental Warrior

On July 15, 1870, the Franco-Prussian war erupted when, after years of minor conflicts between the two nations, Emperor Napoleon III rashly challenged Prussia's vastly superior army. Soon other German states aligned with the Prussians against the French. The German forces pummeled the ill-prepared Frenchmen in battle after battle; Napoleon and his army surrendered on September 2, and the emperor was taken captive. But French resistance troops continued the fight, against great odds. On September 19, the German armies surrounded Paris and held it under siege for four months. The siege was devastating not only for Paris, where many starved, but also on the flanks of the city, where German troops, lacking food and medical supplies, perished. In early January, Bismarck ordered 12,000 shells to be fired into the city for twenty-three days, hoping to shatter the morale of the stubborn Parisians. On January 25 came the harshest bombardment, and Paris surrendered three days later.

At the beginning of the war, Manuel de Bussy was unemployed, but in the autumn of 1870 he found a job in the civil service with an office at the Louvre. With enemy forces advancing toward Paris, Victorine took her children to the safety of her sister-in-law's boardinghouse in Cannes (where she gave birth to Alfred). Clémentine, a shrewd and enterprising woman, had prospered in her liaison with Arosa, and then as the wife of a Cannes innkeeper. She saw something in Achille—whether it was his intelligence, or his loneliness, or a latent creativity, we don't know. He had an indefinable quality, an unselfconscious show of intellect or spirit, perhaps, which even in his childhood was interpreted by a few sensitive adults as a sign of great possibilities. With uncanny intuition Clémentine engaged a local musician to give the boy piano lessons. After a month or so, the teacher concluded that Achille had no particular musical aptitude, and the de Bussys returned to Paris. (Unfortunately, the teacher was a violinist, not a pianist, and evidently not much of a talent scout.)

The war ended with the surrender of Paris. The Prussians occupied much of the city. The French government was in tatters. The nation was wretchedly humiliated. Whispers of rebellion swept the shell-pocked streets of the capital. Napoleon, blamed for his army's defeat, was stripped of his power and condemned to a comfortable exile near London. Ominously, the German and Prussian states united to create a powerful new German empire.

France held an election, and a monarchist republic was created, based at Versailles. On March 15, 1871, Manuel de Bussy left his civil-service job and joined the National Guard. Three days later a workers' insurrection, aided by Guardsmen and their guns, swept the socialist Communards to power in Paris. The Loyalist soldiers retreated to Versailles, regrouped, and launched attacks on the insurgents. The poor people of Paris, fatigued by war but now suddenly empowered, took to the streets, vandalizing and looting shops as they went. Fires erupted all over the city.

On May 3, Manuel, a poorly trained soldier, was hastily promoted to captain. (The fate of his first-born son, Achille, hovered nearby.) Early in the morning of May 8, with orders to capture the fort at Issy, Manuel's commanding officer was kicked by a horse and badly injured. He withdrew from the field and left his new captain in command. It was a once-in-a-lifetime chance for true heroism. De Bussy and his men charged, but when the Loyalist soldiers opened fire, the ragtag rebels fled, deserting their captain on the battlefield. Manuel was arrested. Before the end of the month, the Commune was brought down by the Loyalist army in fighting so fierce and savage that it's still known as "Bloody Week." An estimated 18,000 citizens and soldiers were killed, and 25,000 were imprisoned.

Thousands of captured Communards, including Captain de Bussy, were held for weeks or months at Satory, a military camp near the palace of Versailles, in inhumane conditions of crowding, squalor, and rampant disease. Many died or were shot by soldiers.

With Manuel in captivity and no resources of her own, Victorine de Bussy wrote to the authorities, pleading on her husband's behalf. She explained that with four young children and no job, Manuel had decided "to accept the rank of Captain in the National Guard so that his wife and children might eat."[2] This was the only reason he joined the Guard and fought, she argued, implying somewhat disingenuously that he meant no harm to the Loyalist forces. Nevertheless, Manuel was tried and found guilty on December 11 and sentenced to four years' imprisonment.

The Prussians, Communards, and Napoleon III would be incidental to Debussy's story but for one of those improbable accidents of destiny found only in the lives of the famous and the blessed. While awaiting trial, Manuel became acquainted with another prisoner, a young, little-known musician: Charles de Sivry, son of the late Marquis de Sivry. He talked about his mother, the grandly named Antoinette-Flore Mauté de Fleurville, an accomplished pianist who had studied with Chopin. Manuel mentioned to Charles, perhaps with a father's proud flourish of exaggeration, that his son played the piano. De Sivry was released from prison. Not long after, her interest sparked only by the report of a chance encounter at Satory, Mme Mauté asked to hear young Achille play. Confident that the boy had the makings of a virtuoso, she offered to give him piano lessons, free of charge. He must become a musician! she exclaimed, like the godmother in a fairy tale. (Of course, the story of Mme Mauté's discovery of Achille may be apocryphal, like many stories of long-ago heroes, but no other version of these odd events is more plausible.)

The Mauté Family and the Society of Young Poets

In her daughter's memoir, Mme Mauté is said to have enjoyed entrée to the artistic set that included many prominent French writers and even Richard Wagner. But her daughter's homage, and her family's pretensions, were later challenged by historical facts. Mme Mauté had no illustrious ancestry. Her father was a music teacher. Her first husband, Louis de Sivry, was not a marquis but the son of a hatmaker. Her second husband, Théodore-Jean Mauté (who invented the surname "de Fleurville"), the son of a grocer, was a landowner with a substantial income. There is no evidence that Mme Mauté ever studied with Chopin, but her pianistic abilities have never been questioned. From all accounts she was a strong, wise, loving, and generous woman. The poet Paul Verlaine described her as "a charming soul, an instinctive and talented artist, an excellent musician of exquisite taste, intelligent, and devoted to those she loved."[3] Verlaine knew her quite well.

By the time she met young Achille, Mme Mauté and Charles de Sivry had become players in a sordid drama that fascinated Paris's literary circles. In 1870, Charles introduced his friend Paul Verlaine to his half sister, Mathilde Mauté.

We must assume that Mme Mauté knew something about Verlaine when she gave her consent to their marriage. His reputation as a young poet was well known, and a musician such as Mme Mauté would surely have been pleased to associate her family with an admired man of letters. His family was respectable. He had attended an excellent lycée in Paris, where he would have acquired a first-rate education had he been paying attention.

By the time Verlaine met his future wife, he had passed up the law career that his father wanted for him. Instead, he passed long days and nights in cafés where he became acquainted with many of the writers, painters, composers, and radical thinkers of the thriving avant-garde. His essay on Baudelaire brought him to the attention of important literary figures. He took a job as a civil servant, but he didn't take it seriously. In 1869, he published a book of poems called *Fêtes galantes*, inspired by the eighteenth-century rococo paintings of Watteau and other artists—poems and paintings alike peopled with characters from the Italian commedia dell'arte.

Young Verlaine's personal life was awash with alcohol in all its forms and flavors, especially absinthe, a seriously seductive potion infused with herbs.

Verlaine wasted several years ricocheting from bars to brothels and very young men, but he awoke one day determined to turn his life around. His savior was to be Mathilde Mauté, a mild-mannered, innocent daughter of the Parisian gentry. She was only sixteen, and he was ten years older. Verlaine wooed her with his verses (later published as *La Bonne Chanson*) and married her in 1870. He continued to drink and sometimes abused her. He sobered up enough to be trusted with a rifle, defended Paris during the siege, and was appointed to a position in the short-lived Commune. When the insurrection was crushed, Verlaine feared retribution for his Communard connections, so he returned with his wife to the anonymity and comfortable safety of the Mauté family's fine house on rue Nicolet in Montmartre.

In September 1871, around the time that Mme Mauté began teaching Achille de Bussy to play piano, Verlaine received some poems from Arthur Rimbaud, a sixteen-year-old from Charleville, in the Ardennes. He was raised by a strict, shrewish mother. His father, a soldier, was rarely home on leave; after 1860, he never returned to his family. By sixteen, Arthur was writing brilliant, sardonic verses and longed to be anyplace but Charleville, where he was ridiculed for his outrageous behavior. On the last day of 1870, thousands of Prussian shells fell on Mézières, the little town across the river, and he watched with curious detachment as fire consumed the town and many of its people. In the aftermath, Rimbaud's poetry became more violent in its imagery, more complex in its syntax, more original in its astounding leaps beyond Baudelaire. Without a sou, he ran away several times and was forced to return home, dejected. In the summer of 1871, a friend agreed to send Rimbaud's poems to Paris acquaintances. The first readers were uninterested, but Verlaine saw the "terrifying beauty" in the writing. He received more poems and several letters describing the boy's difficulties at home, his poverty, and his powerful desire to be in Paris. Verlaine showed the verses to other poets, and soon the cafés were buzzing about the new prodigy. Rimbaud was provided with a one-way ticket to Paris, and a guest room was prepared at the Mauté house.

The nasty affair of Verlaine and Rimbaud has been thoroughly documented elsewhere, but it deserves here at least a quick sketch. Verlaine introduced Rimbaud to the young poets of Paris, who saw him as a peasant boy in shabby, ill-fitting clothes, with a child's face, lice-ridden hair, wild blue eyes, and a gift for writing with an energetic voice that was damnably original. They couldn't decide if he was Jesus or Satan. That he was a genius was not in question, nor was the stench of his unwashed clothing. It was clear that his radical poetry would challenge all the literary conventions. But as a guest in the Mauté house and subsequent others, it was also clear that the boy was a petty thief and possibly a madman.

A few weeks after Rimbaud's arrival, Mathilde gave birth to a son. For months, Verlaine lived a double life with Rimbaud, at the farthest fringes of society, and with Mathilde, with whom he was a drunken and sometimes dangerous man. He reportedly threw his infant son against a wall and threatened his in-laws' lives. Then he left.

For a while, the two poets traveled and lived in Belgium and London. Mathilde obtained a legal separation. When Rimbaud wanted to leave him, Verlaine shot a bullet into his lover's wrist and was imprisoned in Belgium for eighteen months. Two years after they first met, the poets' destructive relationship ended.

Perhaps Mme Mauté was grateful for a pleasant distraction during that turbulent time when she shared her house and her daughter with Verlaine; she lavished attention on her promising young protégé, Achille. It was said that she looked after him like a grandmother. With his father in prison, Achille and his mother lived in a tiny apartment not far from the Mautés; most likely, the boy spent much of his time at his teacher's house, as there was no piano at home to practice on. He might have witnessed some of the shocking behavior of the rabid poets. Ten years later he would be writing beautiful songs on Verlaine's verses.

Without doubt, Mme Mauté was a superb teacher. After only one year of lessons, Achille took the highly competitive entrance examination for the Paris Conservatoire National Supérieur de Musique, the finest music school in France, and was one of the eight boys out of thirty-eight applicants who were admitted as piano students that year. It was October 1872. He was barely ten years old.

Manuel de Bussy's prison sentence was commuted to a four-year suspension of his civil and familial rights, and he was released in early January 1873. Victorine had moved her household in the interim, and Manuel came home to a tiny two-room garret in the rue Pigalle, five flights up. His son Achille was already a student at the Conservatory.

At the Conservatory: 1872–1879

He was not a prodigy, just an ordinary child, Debussy told an interviewer in 1910, "very disobedient and very confident that my ideas were the right ones."[4]

Gabriel Pierné described his new classmate as a short, chubby boy, extraordinarily clumsy, awkward, shy, and unsociable. Camille Bellaigue, another student, remembered him as small and sickly-looking, wearing unfashionable clothes: "Nothing about the young Debussy, neither his looks, nor his comments, nor his playing, suggested an artist, present or future."[5]

In Marmontel's piano class, wrote Pierné, he astounded the students with his "bizarre playing." Shyness or clumsiness might have been the cause, but he'd "charge at the piano" and force it to yield. "He seemed to be in a rage with the instrument, rushing up and down it with impulsive gestures and breathing noisily during the difficult bits."[6] Bellaigue remarked on his singular way of exaggerating the rhythms by "emphasizing the strong beats in the bar with a sort of hiccup or raucous gasp."[7] Later, according to Pierné, Achille's faults diminished, but all his life his playing was unique.

Achille's career at the Conservatory started well enough, and his parents nourished hope for his prospects. No longer was he to be a sailor. Rather, his father thought, Achille would have a brilliant career as a pianist, earning riches that would lift the family out of their perpetual poverty.

His teachers found qualities in Achille that young Pierné failed to notice. Albert Lavignac taught him music dictation and solfège (an ear-training and sight-singing method in which the student learns to identify each note with a name: do, re, mi, etc.) and said he was intelligent, industrious, and well organized—"a very excellent pupil." Lavignac befriended the boy, and together they studied the sort of new music that was stubbornly ignored at the Conservatory, including the operas of Wagner. Antoine Marmontel, Achille's piano teacher, wrote that his new student was "a charming child" with "a true artistic temperament," and he foresaw a great future for the boy.[8] This formidable gentleman had taught Bizet, Albéniz, and d'Indy, and surely he did his best with Achille. Before he was twelve, Achille won a Conservatory medal, but only a second honorable mention, for his performance of Chopin's Second Piano Concerto. A year later, he advanced, ever so slightly, to a first honorable mention with the Chopin Ballade No. 1, Op. 23. The top prize eluded him.

In January 1876, in a small town, Achille made his first concert appearance, accompanying a singer and playing chamber music. A local critic wrote an astounding review, calling him a budding Mozart. "What verve! What enthusiasm!" he wrote. "What real spirit! Never again can it be said that the piano is a cold instrument, that the finger which strikes the key is such a long way from the string that vibrates. . . . When he takes over the piano, he imbues the strings with his whole soul. . . . [And] he is still not fourteen years old!"⁹ Interestingly, the pianistic qualities the critic described—the warmth, the spirit, the distinctive way his fingers on the keys summoned an intimate, live sound from the strings— were the very qualities that thrilled Debussy's listeners all his adult life. Nevertheless, it was soon apparent to Marmontel that young Achille found no joy in the tedious hours of practice required of a young virtuoso, and he was uncomfortable performing for an audience. In an about-face, the teacher declared that his playing was "irresponsible and muddle-headed. . . . He doesn't much care for the piano, but he does love music."¹⁰ Marmontel knew, and convinced his disillusioned parents, that Achille would have little hope of a concert career.

In a school famous for its musical conservatism, Achille was, almost from the start, disdainful and dismissive of many of the rules of tonal harmony as codified in the seventeenth and eighteenth centuries. Obeyed more or less strictly by Haydn and Mozart at the end of the eighteenth century, the rules of harmony determine how chords may be formed of certain notes (and not of others), prescribe how a chord may (or may not) be followed by another chord, and limit the way certain dissonant chords (very mild and very few) may be used and then politely tamed by consonant chords. These notions of harmonic propriety were determined, in part, by ancient mathematical principles and the physical properties of sound—ideas that went back as far as Pythagoras, the ancient Greek philosopher—as well as Western cultural notions of beauty. The rules of harmony were numerous enough, and complex enough, to fill a large book. Students also learned the rules determining the structure of musical forms (sonata, symphony, scherzo, rondo) and the complicated rules of counterpoint.

These strict guidelines encouraged composers, essentially, to write in the manner of their contemporaries, because all of them followed the same rules. Their creativity was limited within the boundaries of tradition, and their ambition was confined by the suppression of their originality. It's a wonder that all those rules resulted in so much very great music.

In the days when music was commissioned and paid for by wealthy aristocrats or the wealthier church, composers were usually required to write quickly and prolifically, even brilliantly. At Leipzig, Bach didn't need to waste time thinking about whether to write a sacred cantata this week—his job at the church depended on it. But how could he turn out, almost every week, a new cantata, typically scored for four solo singers, a four-part chorus, and a small orchestra, and lasting twenty minutes or more? Simple, if you're a genius: once you know the rules, your fourth cantata will be easier to write than your first. Your two hundredth cantata will practically write itself. You don't try to reinvent the wheel every time you sit down to work. No one did. With his profound knowledge of the fundamentals of tonal harmony and the musical templates they spawned, Mozart was able to write his hundreds of concertos, symphonies, chamber works, and operas, and still have time for dinner.

In the course of the nineteenth century, composing became more difficult, more complex, and therefore composing each piece required more time. Beethoven, in his last symphonies and string quartets, set new goalposts for composers. These are not pieces you can turn out in a week. The rules of harmony were gradually bent, some were broken, in Liszt's adventurous chromaticism and in Wagner's daring dissonance and tonal shifting. Composers were challenged to think beyond the old rules, and eventually originality came to be highly valued. The number of symphonies that a composer might write in his lifetime declined from 106 (for Haydn) to nine (for Beethoven and Schubert) to four (for Schumann and Brahms). Only one for Debussy, when he was still a teenager.

Though the music was changing, the study of harmony, as it was taught everywhere in Europe and America, had not advanced at all since the days of Haydn. Achille de Bussy won no awards and little encouragement from his harmony teacher, Émile Durand; but despite the boy's instinctive disdain for academic conventions, he learned the rules assiduously enough, and Durand at one point found him to be "extremely gifted in harmony, but desperately careless."[11]

From the very beginning of his time at the Conservatory, he later told an interviewer, he was dissatisfied.

> I was taught that this chord must be like *this* and another like *that*. *This* is a case of perfect harmony, I was told, and *this* is not. Then, as now, I believed there was no such thing as a perfect chord. For a long time I did not want to study what I considered foolishness. Then I realized that I must at least pretend to study in order to get through the Conservatory. So I studied, but all the time I worked out my own little schemes, and whenever we were taught anything I made a note in my mind as to whether I considered it right or

wrong. Don't imagine for a moment that I told anyone of this. I kept it all to myself. Until I could give a proof of my ideas I did not care to talk of them.[12]

Achille's interests were expanding in other directions, however. He avidly read French poetry, immersing himself in Théodore de Banville, Alfred de Musset, Leconte de Lisle, and many others. He began to compose songs when he was about twelve. French art songs, known as *mélodies*, were usually short, lyrical, and often witty settings of poems, whose subjects and subtexts influenced the character of the music. They were perfect vehicles for a very young man to test his mettle in composition. And Achille found that he was talented indeed.

The Education of a Young Sophisticate: 1879–1884

Achille knew little of the world beyond Paris, for which his insufficient home schooling and reclusive childhood had poorly prepared him. He was shy and awkward, blunt and opinionated. And although the rough edges were somewhat smoothed before he was sixteen, we can only imagine the shock to his senses on entering the unimaginable world of the *nouveaux riches*—the preposterously rich families of the industrial age.

Achille's parents had become impatient with their son, who contributed little to the family's household expenses and who, in the throes of adolescence, showed troubling signs of independence. In 1879, Marmontel recommended him to Marguerite Pelouze-Wilson to serve as resident pianist in her household orchestra during his summer break from school.

Mme Pelouze-Wilson was the daughter of an entrepreneurial Scottish engineer who made a fortune setting Paris's streets aglow with gas lamps. In May 1864, married to a physician, Mme Pelouze-Wilson acquired the sixteenth-century Château de Chenonceau. One of the most sumptuous palaces of the Loire valley, the château is built on piles across the waters of the river Cher, as if it had just dropped anchor there. In the sixteenth century, Chenonceau was the residence of King Henri II and his wife, Catherine de Medici, as well as Henri's mistress, Diane de Poitiers.

Mme Pelouze-Wilson was a music lover, one of Wagner's advocates in France and a founder of the *Revue Wagnérienne*, published by the United Richard Wagner Society. She was a woman of lavish tastes and breathtaking beauty, hostess to the most important French social and political figures. But in the summer of 1879, she suffered badly from insomnia, and Achille was asked to play the piano, "to fill out her sleepless nights in an agreeable manner . . . until the good lady's eyelids began to drop."[13]

The following summer, Marmontel again found employment for Debussy, this time with Nadezhda von Meck, a wealthy Russian whose late husband had profited hugely from Russia's great railroad-building boom. She was intelligent, worldly, eccentric, and passionate about music and musicians. History remembers her as Tchaikovsky's generous patroness and closest confidante. Over a period of thirteen years, she and her Russian protégé exchanged over a thousand letters, though by agreement the two never met.

Her letters and other accounts reveal a warmth and fondness for young Achille, an enthusiastic appreciation for his charm and humor, and respect for his talent. In an 1880 letter to Tchaikovsky, she told him about her new pianist. He'll give her children piano lessons, she said. He'll be Julia's accompanist (her adult daughter was an amateur singer), and he'll play piano duets with the Madame herself. "The young man plays well, his technique is brilliant, but he's lacking in sensibility. He's still too young. He says he's twenty, but looks sixteen."[14] In fact, he was not quite eighteen. During that first summer, Debussy caught up with the von Meck entourage in Switzerland and accompanied them to Rome, Naples, and Genoa. In Florence, they lived in an extravagant mansion with mosaic floors and frescoed ceilings—a former home of Napoleon III and the Empress Eugénie.

The young student did what he could to sate his employer's appetite for the music of Tchaikovsky. He was given welcome opportunities to attend concerts and to perform a variety of previously unfamiliar music as a member of her household trio. He found time to write a *Danse bohémienne* for piano and a Trio in G, a youthful, melodic, conventional work that pleased Mme von Meck but gathered dust for more than a century before its first public performance in 1985. Mme von Meck sent both pieces to Tchaikovsky for his opinions, eliciting a curt comment from her beloved friend that the *Danse* was a nice piece, but too short, with themes that lack development and an incoherent structure. When Achille left her employ at the end of October, he "wept bitter tears," she wrote to Tchaikovsky. "Naturally I was very moved, he has a heart capable of strong attachment." He wanted to stay longer, but his teachers at the Conservatory vetoed the idea.[15] A few weeks later she wrote again that she missed Achille terribly: "He played me so much of your music!"[16]

No wonder Achille wept. After acclimating himself to the charmed life of a young prince in royal palaces, he returned to the prosaic realities of a hard-working student and his parents' small, unremarkable apartment.

In early 1881, Mme von Meck received from her young Parisian a Symphony in B Minor, scored for piano duet, which the boy clearly hoped he'd have a chance to play with Madame.[17] Delighted by his attentiveness and talent, she invited Achille to join her family again in July. They stayed in Moscow for over two months and spent the autumn in Rome and Florence; he didn't return to the Conservatory until early December.

His third and final stay with the family was celebrated in a letter from Mme von Meck to Tchaikovsky dated August 28, 1882: "Yesterday, to my great joy, Achille de Bussy arrived. Now I shall gorge myself with music, and he'll bring the whole house to life. He's Parisian to his fingertips, as witty as they come, and a brilliant mimic. He has a good nature, everything pleases him, and he affords us infinite amusement. In short, he's a charming boy."[18] For four or five weeks, Achille taught the children at the family's country estate at Plechtchevo, fifty kilometers from Moscow, then traveled with them to Vienna, where he relished the fine pastries and exceptional concerts.

Years later, Nicholas von Meck, one of Nadezhda's sons, wrote that young Claude was "very pleasant, lively, and even-tempered. . . . We were always sorry when he left us."[19]

No longer a boy, Achille, with his "charming nature," had clearly put behind him the shy, unsociable, maladroit youngster that Gabriel Pierné had known ten years earlier. The von Meck children affectionately called him Petrushka, after the beloved character of the Russian puppet stage. He flirted with thirteen-year-old Sonia. He even proposed marriage—in jest, we assume.

"He is thrilled by your music," Mme von Meck assured her favorite correspondent.[20] Despite Achille's apparent delight in playing Tchaikovsky while in her employ, he wasn't overly fond of the music of Madame's protégé. He simply knew where his bread was buttered, and sometimes he spread some jam as well. His own work was influenced not by Tchaikovsky, but by other Russian composers—Borodin, Balakirev, and especially Mussorgsky—whose works were steeped in the characteristic oriental flavors of Russian folk music. Madame can, however, be credited with taking Achille to hear his first performance of a Wagner opera—*Tristan und Isolde*, in Vienna, probably in a concert performance. This first experience of Wagner (apart from reading scores) was a major event in the young composer's productive engagement with Wagner's music.

His summer at Chenonceau and three seasons with the von Mecks were marvelous opportunities for Achille to learn the politesse of cultured society and to develop a useful patina of social grace. Living in some of the grandest dwellings in Europe, performing for sophisticated, extremely wealthy patrons and their friends, attending concerts in the great halls of Austria and Italy—these also gave him an unhealthy appetite for good food, choice wines, fine porcelains, paintings, and Japanese prints. It was an appetite that would contribute to the perennial indebtedness that hounded him for most of his life.

The Mentor

Just before Christmas of 1880, Achille began his formal study of composition in the class of Ernest Guiraud. A Frenchman born and raised in New Orleans, Guiraud wrote a large number of operas, ballets, and other works, none of which proved sturdy enough to remain in the repertoire. Rather, his renown was achieved primarily by his contributions to the work of other composers.

In 1875, Guiraud's friend Georges Bizet died at thirty-six of a heart attack only three months after his greatest opera, *Carmen*, was first performed. Despite its seductive arias and lively Andalusian rhythms, *Carmen* proved too dark and tragic to appeal to an audience expecting an *opéra comique*. To make it more like a "grand opera" fit for the Viennese premiere, Guiraud was commissioned to write recitatives, replacing the spoken dialogues of the original version. The revised *Carmen* has been, ever since, one of the most popular of all operas.

A few years later Jacques Offenbach died, and Guiraud was asked to complete the orchestrations and compose recitatives for Offenbach's masterpiece, *Tales of Hoffmann*. It was Guiraud's idea to enhance the score with a song that Offenbach had written for an earlier, failed opera—the sweetly swaying "Barcarolle," whose independent celebrity helped win *Hoffmann* the enduring affection of audiences.

At first, Guiraud didn't think much of his new student. Though he found Achille intelligent, he saw something odd in his character and thought he needed to be kept in check, presumably because of his stubborn tendency to ignore musical orthodoxies. Even two years later, Guiraud noted that Achille composed badly. But over time, the good-natured teacher and the wayward student began to spend sociable afternoons together, playing billiards and talking about music; and Guiraud came to understand and even tolerate some of Achille's evolving ideas about harmony, rhythm, and the irrelevance of musty conventions and constraints.

Under Guiraud's tutoring, Debussy gained assurance and self-discipline as a composer. He resigned himself, finally, to the need to master the essential skills that the Conservatory was meant to provide him. He diligently wrote fugues on themes by Massenet and Gounod and vocal music on texts that probably held little interest for him. Yet he also enjoyed improvising bold passages at the piano, to the delight of his fellow students, with harmonies and arabesques that, without recordings, we can only imagine with great curiosity.

The Songbird

As the years passed, Achille felt uncomfortably pressured to help alleviate his family's financial difficulties. In the early 1880s, he reluctantly gave piano lessons, and he played occasionally at Le Chat Noir, a Montmartre nightclub that had recently opened on the boulevard Rochechouart.

At the Conservatory in June 1880, he took first prize in the art of accompaniment—a valuable achievement, as a well-prepared young accompanist is far more likely to find employment than a second-rate concert soloist or a novice composer. His newly acquired skill was exercised almost immediately during his first summer in the employ of Mme von Meck, where he accompanied her children's singing. When he returned to Paris, his friend Paul Vidal recommended him as accompanist for the twice-weekly singing classes of Marie Moreau-Sainti, a former opera singer.

Among the students was a woman named Marie-Blanche Vasnier, who would be Achille's first love. She was a pretty woman with reddish hair and provocative green eyes. She was an accomplished coloratura soprano, an amateur with an exceptionally limber upper range—"the voice of a songbird," said her young admirer. It was reported that she sang with a perfection that is not often encountered even among professionals. Marie Vasnier was thirty-two years old and had two young children. She had a husband, too, a civil servant named Eugène-Henri Vasnier, a devotee of the arts eleven years her senior. And now she had an adoring schoolboy called Achille, fourteen years her junior.

Soon Achille was a frequent dinner guest at the Vasnier home in Paris. In her memoir, Mme Vasnier's daughter Marguerite gives an incisive account of the young composer.[21] "At eighteen Debussy was a large, beardless boy, with clearly defined features and thick, black, curly hair which he wore plastered down over his forehead." When his hair was mussed, Marguerite's parents said, he looked like "a Florentine from the Middle Ages." He had an interesting face; his eyes, especially, drew your attention. "His hands were strong and bony, with square fingers; his touch on the piano was sonorous, rather percussive but also sometimes very gentle."

Marguerite believed that Achille was unhappy in his family life, that his father was stupid and his mother mean and narrow-minded. They gave him little encouragement or support for his musical endeavors. To avoid the disagreeable atmosphere at home and the distractions at the Conservatory, Achille asked the Vasniers if he could come and work at their home, "and from that moment he was welcome to use the house as if he were a member of the family."

The Vasniers gave him a room of his own, with a piano and a desk. It was here that he wrote most of what he produced in the next few years, Marguerite said. He'd arrive at the Vasniers' apartment nearly every evening, and sometimes in the afternoons as well. He'd improvise at the piano for a while, "then walk up and down the room singing to himself," with a cigarette in his mouth or tobacco and rolling papers in his hand. "He never crossed out a great deal, but he searched a long time in his head before writing anything down and was highly critical of his own work."

During the following summers, when he wasn't with Mme von Meck's family, Achille visited the Vasniers every day at their country villa not far from Paris. He'd work long hours but sometimes went for walks in the park or played croquet with Marguerite. These moments of freedom in the countryside made him "carefree and cheerful as a child, [with] moments of extreme gaiety, but these would be followed by hours of gloom and discouragement."

"He was called Achille then," wrote Marguerite, "a name which he found utterly ridiculous. . . . He was moody, touchy, and sensitive in the highest degree," and the slightest thing could send him into a rage. When he read a book of poetry, he and his hosts had long debates about which poems he might set to music. Eugène Vasnier was especially helpful to Achille in literary matters, and they enjoyed talking about art. Achille tried to teach Marguerite piano and harmony, to please her parents, but he proved to be "an appalling teacher" with little patience, unable to explain musical ideas in a way that a young girl would understand. "He was an original and slightly unpolished individual, but utterly charming with those he liked."

Achille gave his first public performance as a composer in Paris on May 12, 1882. He accompanied Mme Vasnier in an aria by Auber and two songs of his own: "Fête galante" and "Les Roses," on poems by Banville. At the same concert, he also accompanied a violinist named Maurice Thieberg in works by Beethoven and several other composers including Debussy himself, the *Nocturne et scherzo* for violin and piano.[22] At a fancy-dress ball, Achille and Mme Vasnier sang his duet "Chanson espagnole."

Until he left for Rome, Achille maintained a sincere friendship with Monsieur Vasnier while enjoying the intimacy of Madame. We can only speculate how this was possible, or, more precisely, what role the husband played in the affair, and why. (The *boulevardier* might reply, "But, *mon dieu*, this is Paris!")

From 1880 to 1884, Achille wrote about forty songs, of which twenty-seven were dedicated to his beloved songbird. One song, from 1881, was inscribed to "the only muse who has ever inspired in me anything resembling a musical feeling (not to mention anything else)." Thirteen of the songs were presented to her before he went to Rome, in what is now known as the Vasnier Songbook. "To Mme Vasnier," the inscription reads, "these songs which have come to life through her alone, and which will lose their enchanting gracefulness if they nevermore pass her melodious fairy lips."[23]

For one song in the Vasnier Songbook, Achille chose a tender poem by Bourget, called "Regret." In the poet's words, the young composer seems to be looking ahead to his long, lonely days in Rome, bereft of his beloved:

> *Under the summer sky, warm and still,*
> *I remember you as in a dream,*
> *And my constant regret savors and prolongs*
> *the hours when I was loved . . .*
> *And my soul, betrayed and forsaken,*
> *remains entirely yours.*[24]

CHAPTER 2

DARLING OF THE GODS (1884–1887)

Among the institutions on which France prides herself, do you know any more ridiculous than . . . the Prix de Rome? . . . The academic detachment of the gentlemen of the Institute, who decide which among a number of young persons shall be an artist [is] astonishing in its ingenuousness. What do they know about it? Are they so sure of being artists themselves? . . . Would it not, indeed, be better for them to have recourse to the simple method of drawing lots? Who knows? Chance is sometimes so inspired!

—Debussy[1]

Established in 1663, the Prix de Rome, France's highest academic honor, was a state scholarship awarded to the winners of rigorous competitions among students of the arts. At first, the prize was limited to painters and sculptors; later, prizes were given also to architects and engravers. In 1803, a prize in music composition was established. In the same year, Napoleon Bonaparte ordered the renovation of a magnificent Roman villa, owned for centuries by the Medici family, where the Académie de France à Rome (French Academy in Rome) would house and host all the prizewinners. Only French-born males under thirty need apply.

Hector Berlioz in Rome

The Prix de Rome winners, in Hector Berlioz's time, were awarded two years of study in Rome, then one year in Germany and two years in Paris. They were provided subsidies of 3,000 francs a year, in return for which they would devote themselves exclusively to the study of composition.

In his entertaining memoir, Berlioz wrote that candidates were required to show they had mastered "melody, dramatic force, instrumentation, and other knowledge"[2] necessary for writing a cantata. After a preliminary round requiring them to write a choral fugue, they were given three weeks to create a large-scale work for voices and orchestra. The young men were then locked up in separate rooms with pens, paper, and a piano until their scores were completed. At eleven o'clock in the morning and six o'clock in the evening, the doors were unlocked, and they gathered to take their meals together. They were not allowed to leave the Institute building.

The rules were strictly applied but capriciously conceived. For example, letters, books, clothes, and everything else sent to the students were scrupulously searched to prevent outside coaching. But every evening, friends were allowed to dine with them, and "any amount of assistance—verbal or written—might be given."[3]

The final stage of the competition was judged by a panel of thirty to thirty-five members of the Académie des Beaux-Arts. Six musicians were among them. The rest were painters, sculptors, architects, and engravers distinguished in their fields but bereft of any qualification to form credible opinions about the music they heard. Furthermore, the vocalists performing the cantatas were accompanied only by a piano, yet an important element in the judging was orchestration. Thus, the music prize was decided by men who were not musicians and who had not even heard a competent performance of the competing works. On the jubilant day when the prizes were bestowed on the winners, the chosen composition was performed with an orchestra. "It seems just a little late," Berlioz observed. "It might have been more serviceable to set the orchestra *before* judgment, seeing that after this there is no repeal."[4]

Berlioz won second prize on his second try for the Prix de Rome. A year later, in 1829, he was an overwhelming favorite to win the coveted first; he was the only student who had already had some success in the real world of the concert hall, after all. And "since they have decided to give me the prize," he reasoned, "I need not bother to write exactly in the style that suits them; I will compose a really artistic cantata." But the jury decided not to award any first prize that year rather than give it to Berlioz, an eccentric composer with "revolutionary tendencies" and a fondness for a man called Beethoven. His teacher, the eminent opera composer François-Adrien Boieldieu, told him afterward, "The prize was in your hand and you simply threw it away."

"But, monsieur, I really did my best," Berlioz replied.

"That's just it!" Boieldieu exclaimed. "Your best is the opposite of your good. How could I possibly approve? I, who like nice, gentle music."[5] In fact, nice, gentle music is what Parisians craved in those days of economic hardship, turbulent politics, and civil unrest threatening the unpopular King Charles X. Daniel Auber, another popular composer, told Berlioz, "The best advice I can give you is to write as insipidly as you can," and if it sounds "horribly flat, *you will have just what [the judges] want!*"[6]

In 1830, Berlioz competed for the fourth time, writing his cantata (based on Lord Byron's play *Sardanapalus*) while a violent revolution erupted in the streets of Paris. This time the judges recognized that he had recanted his "heresies," and their vote was unanimous.[7] When told he had received the Prix de Rome at last, he couldn't take much pride in it, he admitted, since he had deliberately suppressed a thrilling climactic finale, convinced that the Academy would have rejected the cantata if they had heard it.

Of course, Berlioz was among the several Prix de Rome laureates who went on to illustrious careers as composers; many others found their métier as music teachers, conductors, or in fields other than music. Charles Gounod won first prize in 1839, Georges Bizet in 1857, Ernest Guiraud (Debussy's teacher) in 1859, Jules Massenet in 1863. Maurice Ravel competed and inexplicably failed five times. Lili Boulanger, in 1913, was the first woman ever to win the Prix de Rome.

Each year the most promising young composition students at the Paris Conservatory were expected to compete. A Prix de Rome brought with it not just the opportunity to study and work in the Eternal City; it also focused the attention of the musical establishment on the winners, with a consequent expectation of great contributions to the cultural glory of France.

Debussy was nearing his time.

Winning Isn't Everything

"The Prix de Rome is a kind of game," Debussy wrote, later in life, "or rather, it is a national sport. One learns the rules in particular places, the Conservatory or the École des Beaux-Arts, etc."[8] Debussy's friend Erik Satie, with his wit in high gear and his tongue partially in cheek, remarked that, among many honorable people, "the Prix de Rome for Music carries a prestige which is not accorded to recipients of the same diploma for other artistic categories. . . . I have even seen people in fits of laughter at the sight of a Prix de Rome for Sculpture."[9]

In Debussy's era, as in Berlioz's, the finalists for the music prize were required to write a cantata on the same assigned text. On his first try, in 1882,

Debussy didn't get past the preliminaries. Later, with only Guiraud as judge and mentor, he geared up for the next year's contest by working on a cantata based on Banville's comedy in verse *Diane au bois* (Diana of the Woods), the story of the seduction of Diana, the chaste goddess of the hunt, by Eros, the young god of love. Guiraud found the work-in-progress "interesting" but the music too unconventional. Put it away for later, he advised, or you'll never win the Prix de Rome.

In the spring of 1883, Debussy survived the first rounds, then got cold feet. His Conservatory friend Paul Vidal, also a candidate, tried to defeat Achille's multiple objections to going forward. Debussy finally agreed, which meant he, like the other finalists, would endure being cloistered for twenty-five days, a virtual prisoner with only a piano for company. After this monastic incubation period, in an atmosphere of extreme tension, the cantatas were performed for the judges and an expectant audience. Some years, deliberations would go on for days, as a majority of votes was needed to declare a winner; and the winner, Satie quipped, was inevitably "a superior being, in a special category, of the first quality, specially manufactured, out of print and extremely rare."[10]

The assigned cantata in 1883 was *Le Gladiateur*, on a text by Émile Moreau, for which Achille won a disappointing second to Paul Vidal's first prize. The judges noted that Debussy had "a generous musical nature but ardent sometimes to the point of excess," though the music has "some convincing dramatic accents."[11] Not a strong endorsement. *Les Annales du théâtre et de la musique* gave a more prescient judgment: Debussy "has certainly less skill, though perhaps more personality than Monsieur Vidal. The jury has done wisely to oblige him to remain a student for another year; already greatly endowed, he will thus gain the solid instruction which he still lacks."[12]

In 1884, Debussy was again reluctant to compete. He knew Rome—he'd been there with the von Mecks not so long ago. Why would he part with his beautiful songbird only to face years of loneliness in a city he knew he'd loathe? Then, too, did he want to be saddled with the kind of success that such a prize confers—to be expected always to write the same kind of prescriptive, stale, bourgeois music that the judges reward? On the other hand, the annual stipend of 4,000 francs, for four years, was tempting. In the end, Achille did compete, along with several young men of more assured ambition. But he confided to Vidal that even if he won the prize he'd refuse to go to Rome; he would not sever his bond with Mme Vasnier.[13]

If Debussy was conflicted about Rome, at least he hadn't lost his sense of humor, of which too few examples have been recorded from this period. It was shortly before the preliminary exams for the Prix de Rome, and Léo Delibes was unable to teach his composition class. While his students were waiting in their dingy classroom for Delibes's assistant, Achille mischievously poked his head through the door and said, "My dear orphans, in the absence of your parents, I shall provide nourishment for you."[14] Then he sat down at the piano. This remarkable scene was described by Maurice Emmanuel, a student who witnessed it.

"I can assure you that it was no longer the youthful Achille-Claude who mystified us that day," wrote Emmanuel, "but Debussy from head to toe, Debussy unalloyed. He delivered himself of a torrent of chords which, for all their wildness, we could only admire with open mouths. These were followed by a rustling of misshapen arpeggios, a gurgling of trills on three notes simultaneously, in both hands, and chains of harmonic progressions which defied conventional analysis, and which left us bemused." For more than an hour the students stood around the piano and listened, until the janitor, hearing the strange musical ruckus, charged into the room and, bellowing that Debussy was possessed by evil spirits, chased them all out.

Emmanuel and his friends were aghast and yet thrilled at the possibility that Achille's "outrageous harmonies" might be a foretaste of the cantata he would soon be required to write. If that's what it's going to be like, said one of them, "he's heading for a fall!" Schadenfreude was in the air.

When judgment day arrived, Emmanuel and his friends sat in the audience, exchanging excited glances when the opening chords of Debussy's cantata, *L'Enfant prodigue* (The Prodigal Son), filled the air. But as the music continued, they saw on the judges' faces no signs of disdain or outrage. The students listened in disbelief at the surprising tameness of the score, feeling "seriously let down that the expected brouhaha had not materialized."[15]

To the contrary, with *L'Enfant prodigue* Debussy won resoundingly on the first ballot, garnering twenty-two of the twenty-eight votes. The *Annales* for 1884 reported, "The contest was remarkable, and Monsieur Debussy's score is one of the most interesting heard at the Institute for several years."[16] Heeding Guiraud's advice, he was able to suppress his originality sufficiently to produce a cantata traditional enough to satisfy the judges, who found in the music a marked poetic sense and brilliant, warm colors. The biblical story allowed Debussy to indulge himself, moderately, in medieval modes and other exoticisms, as well as Wagnerian leitmotifs, but on the whole the work was, Emmanuel confessed, rather "debonair."[17] Arthur Wenk uses such terms as "cloyingly sentimental," "banal," and "undistinguished," yet Wenk also sees in *L'Enfant prodigue* "the roots for a new way of thinking about music. . . . The harmonic organization of the work suggests the direction that Debussy's new language would take."[18] Charles Gounod voted enthusiastically for him, but most of the other votes came not from the jury's musicians but from its painters, sculptors, and architects.

Meanwhile, Achille's friendship with Vidal, his Conservatory comrade, had become strained. For several years Vidal had been a frequent guest at the dining table of the de Bussy family, a family which he considered dysfunctional. Vidal resented being used repeatedly as an alibi while Achille sneaked out to spend time with Mme Vasnier. He admired Achille, perhaps worshipped him, certainly loved him. But now he felt betrayed by his friend, who seemed ready to refuse the prize—to choose Paris with Mme Vasnier rather than Rome with Vidal.

Weeks after the competition, Vidal found it necessary to write a long letter of apology to Henrietta Fuchs, director of a choral society, La Concordia. Vidal had been the group's accompanist before he won the previous year's Prix de Rome. To replace him, Vidal nominated Debussy, and Gounod, honorary president of the chorus, lent his support. Now Vidal was angry at himself and embarrassed that he had backed his friend. In his letter to Mme Fuchs, he refers to Debussy's "wild passion" and "this sinister tale of adultery. . . . I'm powerless to make him see sense," Vidal wrote. "His present behavior fills me with remorse. . . . His moral sense is undeveloped; he's nothing but a sensualist. But, with all that, he has such talent and such a personality!"[19] Mme Vasnier is pretty, Vidal wrote, and she inspires everything he writes. Who could blame him for wanting to be in Paris and not in Rome, a city he already dislikes?

Earlier, Vidal had struggled to convince Debussy that a Prix de Rome could establish his career, that being in Rome would give him unfettered time to compose. Now that Debussy had won, Vidal ran out of arguments.

Years later, Debussy wrote about his "happiest memory" of the Prix de Rome. He was standing idly on the Pont des Arts, watching the *bateaux-mouches* come and go on the Seine. "I was quite relaxed," he wrote, "and wasn't thinking about anything to do with Rome, for the pleasant sunlight was playing upon the rippling water with that special charm which keeps idlers on the bridges for hours on end, making them the envy of all Europe. All at once someone tapped me on the shoulder and breathlessly said, 'You have won the prize.' . . . My heart sank. I had a sudden vision of boredom, and of all the worries that inevitably accompany any form of official recognition. I felt I was no longer free."[20]

The Etruscan Tomb

The Villa Medici was built in the sixteenth century and, not long after, sold to Cardinal Ferdinand de Medici, the Grand Duke of Tuscany. The villa sits at the edge of a hill, the Pincio, only a hundred meters or so from the top of the Spanish Steps. In his *Memoirs*, Berlioz described the view of Rome, seen from the villa, as one of the most splendid in the world.

The villa overlooks Lenôtre's magnificent gardens, Berlioz wrote, and on the other side, "in the midst of the waste fields of the Villa Borghese, stands Raphael's house."[21] The surroundings and the Villa Medici itself are "the royal quarters that France has munificently provided for her children. Yet the rooms of the pupils are mostly small, uncomfortable, and very badly furnished"—no better than a soldier's barracks.[22]

Debussy delayed his departure for Italy as long as the Academy's rules permitted. First, he claimed, he needed to compose something for the music prize of the City of Paris, but he didn't finish in time to compete. On January 28, his excuses exhausted, Debussy took the train to Rome—a forty-eight-hour journey during which one of the few consolations was a berth in the sleeping car, thanks to the travel allowance granted by the Academy.

"That halo of future glory, of which the Prix de Rome gives one an intimation, is irresistible," he admitted. "So when I arrived at the Villa Medici in 1885, I pretty well thought myself the darling of the gods."[23]

Debussy found the Villa Medici grim and loathsome, especially his room. It was one of the larger rooms mentioned by Berlioz, enormous and forbidding, Debussy said, and he had to walk miles from one piece of furniture to the next; his fellow students called it the "Etruscan Tomb." He complained to the director, Ernest Hébert, who suggested that if the brash young composer didn't like his room, he might rather "sleep in the ruins of the Coliseum."[24]

Judging from the evidence, Achille spent more time in Rome writing letters than writing music. His letters were most frequently addressed to Eugène Vasnier, and if any were written to Mme Vasnier, none has survived. The weather in Rome was terrible, he wrote; his former Conservatory friends were now unfriendly, stiff, egotistical, and competitive; and the highly touted artistic environment was much overrated.

To Debussy, the Villa Medici was a dormitory in the guise of a palace, run with the discipline of an army camp. The walls of the dining room were covered almost to the ceiling with portraits of past Prix de Rome winners, sadness and uneasiness visible on every face. Conversations around the dinner table were uninteresting, he said. Contact with the Romans was rare, even for a young Frenchman traveling in the smaller towns. "Their society is closed, not very welcoming," so the traveler spends his time shopping for postcards and enjoys the pretty smiles of the young ladies who sell them.[25]

Overall, his sojourn in Rome was as unproductive as it was unhappy. Much of the time he was unable to work, and frustrated. The Villa Medici lifestyle didn't suit him; he didn't think he had "the right sort of personality or the intellectual energy" to adapt to it. To Vasnier he lamented, "I've been so lonely I've cried."[26] Pierné, one of those unfriendly old friends, said that although Achille "lived side by side with his fellow students, there was no real intimacy between them."[27] He went out often to scour antique shops for little Japanese *objets* and was rarely seen except at the dining hall. Debussy at twenty-two was as out of place among the young men of the villa as he had been at ten with the Conservatory boys. But though he sometimes complained about his comrades, he enjoyed the soirées given by Hébert and his wife, playing piano duets with Vidal, and singing his songs.

With the hindsight of nearly twenty years, Debussy wrote about the quandary of young prizewinners, of whom so much was expected but to whom so little guidance was given: "We heartlessly abandon very nice young people, giving them a complete freedom that they do not know how to use." When they get to Rome, they are "exempt from all further responsibility." They had no obligations except to send an example of their new work, an *envoi*, to the Institute every year. They know hardly anything about what they're supposed to do there, and no one tells them "how much hard work is necessary for the artistic spirit to develop," Debussy said.[28]

With warmth and sincerity that seem quite genuine, he wrote to Vasnier, "I can't help thinking of those splendidly silly conversations we used to have— they taught me such a lot and opened my mind in so many ways, yes, I miss them. . . . I'll never forget all you have done for me, or how welcome you made me inside your family circle."[29]

In late April Debussy returned to Paris for a few days, and he visited the Vasniers. In May he became ill with a fever. He read Shakespeare and a great deal of French and English poetry, and he studied Wagner's *Tristan*.

By early June he was complaining of fever again and wanted to escape from his "wretched barracks, where life is so miserable," but Vasnier, as sensible as ever, convinced him to stay.[30] In early July he was granted a two-month leave of absence. He spent part of that time in Dieppe with the Vasniers, and then he luxuriated in the warmer winds and waters of the Mediterranean.

An Indescribable Malaise

Among Debussy's closest friends at the villa was Gustave Popelin, winner of an 1882 prize in painting. Gustave's father, Claudius Popelin, a wealthy poet and accomplished painter of enamels, was well connected in society and a former paramour of Princess Mathilde Bonaparte, Napoleon's niece. (Let us for a moment marvel at the fortuitous frequency with which Debussy, even as a near-impoverished youth, found himself befriended, employed, financially supported, or professionally assisted by men and women of great wealth, noble birth, and influence.) Claudius Popelin was a friend of Count Giuseppe Primoli, a scholar and highly regarded amateur photographer who was himself descended from Napoleon's brother. The count, sympathetic to Debussy's unhappy state, offered him the use of his seaside villa, not far from Rome. For several weeks during his summer sabbatical, he again enjoyed the kind of pampered life he had known with Mme von Meck. He rejoiced in his solitude—a blessing after living communally for five months. "I could satisfy my savage instincts as much as I wanted," he wrote to Vasnier. "Not knowing anyone there, I didn't have to talk to anyone except to ask for food."[31] Primoli owned the largest private collection of paintings by Jean-Antoine Watteau, of the kind that inspired Verlaine's *Fêtes galantes*. The paintings were housed at the villa, and Debussy had ample time to enjoy them. He returned to work on *Diane au bois*, took long walks, and imprinted on his mind the ever-changing formations of the clouds and the steady throb of the sea. He loved being there.

Returning to Rome, he was as unhappy as ever, and again he contemplated forfeiting his Prix de Rome and leaving the Villa Medici. He complained to Vasnier that the Roman summer was so hot that his piano "began to sweat like a living person," and hordes of little insects kept him awake at night.[32] He placed several orders with a Parisian bookseller, read Tolstoy and Flaubert, and discovered Mallarmé's symbolist poem *L'Après-midi d'un faune*. He found Rome "positively ugly—a town of marble, fleas, and boredom."[33] He despised ornate Italian churches and disparaged Italian opera. He complained so incessantly and fiercely that he alienated some of his companions. He was bored, he said, weighed down by too much tranquility. His work was suffering badly, and he felt he was sinking into mediocrity. Good ideas abandoned him. His first year in Rome had been a wasted experience, he thought, and staying for another year could only make things worse. His wise friend Eugène Vasnier convinced him to stay. But he continued to complain of "a misery that most people find incomprehensible . . . a malaise which I can't describe" but which comes from homesickness.[34]

The venerated composer Franz Liszt, though afflicted with multiple ailments, sometimes visited the Villa Medici to play his music for the residents, to listen to theirs, and to bestow on them his wisdom and encouragement. Debussy met Liszt at the villa on at least two occasions. In his exhaustive biography of Debussy, Edward Lockspeiser surmises, with scant evidence, that the maestro visited in November 1885, and that it was he who advised the young students to visit the church of Santa Maria dell'Anima, the only place in Rome where Renaissance liturgical music could be heard. This great body of work had virtually disappeared from the European musical canon, and Liszt was among those who were passionately promoting its revival.

For Debussy, Santa Maria dell'Anima was a revelation even more noteworthy than his meetings with Liszt. On one visit he heard masses by Palestrina and by Orlandus Lassus. On November 24, he wrote Vasnier of the "tremendous feats" they produced from their great knowledge of counterpoint, which, he said, "is the most forbidding thing in music. In their work, however, it is wonderful, for it underlines and deepens the significance of the words. And sometimes there are winding melodic lines that recall illuminated manuscripts and ancient missals."[35]

Twice in January 1886, Debussy and his colleagues entertained Liszt at the Villa Medici. On these occasions, Debussy and Vidal played a two-piano duet by Emmanuel Chabrier, which was unfamiliar to Liszt, and a two-piano version of their guest's own *Faust Symphony*, during which the old maestro fell asleep. His death was only six months away.

Early in his second year in Rome, Debussy applied for and was granted another two-month leave of absence. He went to Paris, of course, leaving few traces of his visit for historians to chew over, then requested yet another leave. Several anguished letters from Debussy (in Rome) to Gustave Popelin and Claudius Popelin (in Paris), written in late June and early July 1886, reveal Debussy's frustration, confusion, and despair. His affair with Marie Vasnier was unraveling.

He tells Gustave, who had recently ended his term at the Villa Medici, that a long-awaited letter from Mme Vasnier contained disturbing things that he can't repeat in writing.[36] Two days later, in a letter to Claudius, he reveals the intensity of his attachment and the reason for his despair: His recent visit to Paris has only increased his powerful feelings for her, and when deprived of the source of these feelings he doesn't feel alive. His imagination "ceases to obey" him. Claudius had long ago urged Debussy to break off his adulterous relationship and turn his "insane love into a lasting friendship," but he can't. "Its very madness keeps me from being rational." Thinking about her induces "even greater insanity," and he's haunted by the possibility that he hasn't done enough to nourish her love.

Had it not been for Gustave, he writes, "whom I love so much and whose friendship I now miss sorely, I would very probably have tendered my resignation. I went through periods of such despair that, thank God, [Gustave] was here to cheer me up and help me regain my courage."[37]

His request for another leave of absence was granted, and he planned to return to Paris in early July, but to Gustave he writes, heartbroken, that a letter from Mme Vasnier "barely concealed the pain my presence there would cause her." She said "it would be very unwise for us to see each other." But to go to Paris and not see her would be unbearable, and to force her to see him "would mean losing her." In fact, he had already responded to her letter, saying that he wants her "to be mine completely," and now he admits to Gustave that he's convinced that seeing her would "lead to something irreparable. . . . How silly my former sufferings seem compared to what I'm suffering now."[38]

With his wounded heart at war with his common sense, Debussy left Rome on July 3. In Paris, he found himself unable to pay for his room. He visited his parents, who were "extremely hard up," and asked Claudius Popelin to help him financially, "truly ashamed to have to appeal to your kind feelings toward me."[39]

Diane au bois and the First *Envoi*

Debussy stayed in Paris until the end of August and returned to Rome. Apparently, he did not see Mme Vasnier in Paris, and although both were in Dieppe at the same time there is no indication that they met there. In the fall and winter he thought of little but "the moment of deliverance" when he could put the Villa Medici behind him. He longed to be in the city of the Seine, if only "to see the pictures of Manet and hear Offenbach."[40]

The only important responsibility attached to the Prix de Rome was the requirement to send an *envoi* each year to the Academy—an orchestral or choral composition that demonstrates the composer's attention to serious work. For his first *envoi*, Debussy began writing a "symphonic ode" called *Zuléima*, inspired by Heinrich Heine's 1822 play *Almansor*. But he quickly lost interest in the project. He found that "*Zuléima* is not the right sort of thing at all. It's too old and stuffy. Those great stupid lines bore me to death . . . and my music would be in danger of sinking under the weight," he wrote to Vasnier in June 1885.[41]

Almansor was indeed plot-heavy and plodding, as were many nineteenth-century dramas. The story is set in the early years of the Spanish Inquisition, when the defeated Moors, like the Jews, were persecuted and forced to choose between conversion to Christianity or permanent exile. Heine's play, a lament for the cruel destruction of a magnificent culture, had been a failure and is hardly remembered today except for one prescient line: "Wherever they burn books, in the end they will burn people." In the context of the play, Heine was referring to the burning of the holy Qur'an in the marketplace of Cordoba. His cautionary words gained new currency after the Nazis' infamous 1933 book burnings in Berlin and other German cities.

When Debussy abandoned *Zuléima*, he resumed work on *Diane au bois*. When he first worked on *Diane*, several years earlier, it was at least partly an exercise meant to sharpen his skills for the cantatas he'd be asked to write for the Prix de Rome. But there's evidence that he quickly came to consider *Diane* not as a cantata but an opera. He first wrote an overture, dated November 27, 1881, which contains some of the music he would use later in various scenes.

Debussy's work on *Diane* can be seen as an early step on the long path that led to his success with *Pelléas et Mélisande*. He thought—prematurely, as it turned out—that now he was in command of his music. He knew what he was capable of writing, and he knew how he wanted his music to sound; he also knew what his limitations were. "The nub of the matter is that my sort of music is the only sort I can write," he said. He understood that, as an *envoi*, *Diane* might be renounced by the Academy's judges, as it bore no resemblance to the poems other prizewinners employed for their librettos. And good heavens, he thought, he'd certainly had enough of cantatas, having written at least two in pursuit of the Prix de Rome. But he felt that the liberty afforded by the Villa Medici was, in effect, permission "to produce something original and not keep falling back into old habits."[42] On the other hand, he knew that the judges appraising his work would not agree with him, because they believed their old ways were the only acceptable ones.

He worked on *Diane*, off and on, during his summer weeks at Count Primoli's villa, and continued during the next year and a half. By October 1885, he had finished one scene, but he wasn't happy with it. He thought maybe he had aimed too high. "There's no precedent to go on and I find myself compelled to invent new forms," he told Vasnier.[43] The problem every innovator contends with, whether the goal is a horseless carriage or a new kind of opera, is the absence of precedents. This may seem obvious, but it's crucial. Finding a solution to a creative problem generally takes a great deal of time; it also requires tenacity, a nimble mind, and a talent for obsession. In 1885, Debussy didn't know if he was capable of the sort of innovation he dreamed of, and he couldn't have known where his efforts would lead him. But he knew that he didn't want to walk in the footsteps of the masters. "I could always turn to Wagner, but I don't need to tell you how ridiculous it would be even to try." The only Wagnerism he would want to borrow "is the running of one scene into another."[44]

It would be several more years before he would no longer feel ridiculous in the shadow of Richard Wagner.

In November, *Diane* was still causing anxiety, because he couldn't produce music for the goddess Diana that had the requisite coolness: coolness without passion. Two months later, he wrote, "One day I think I'm on the right track, the next I'm afraid I've made a mistake."[45] He worried that his music would cause an audience to yawn in boredom, and he felt an uneasiness about the work that he'd never felt before.

"I'm after music that is supple and concentrated enough to adapt itself to the lyrical movements of the soul and the whims of reverie," he wrote Vasnier.[46] And thus we know that in 1885 Debussy was reading Baudelaire. A letter from the poet to Arsène Houssaye was published in Baudelaire's book *Le Spleen de Paris*.

In the *Spleen* poems, Baudelaire reflects on modern city life with disapproval and mockery. He wrote Houssaye that being in crowded cities like Paris makes him dream of "the miracle of a poetic prose, musical without rhythms or rhyme, supple enough and striking enough to suit lyrical movements of the soul, undulations of reverie, the flip-flops of consciousness."[47] Living in crowded Rome, Debussy perhaps found a correspondence with Baudelaire and heard in the "lyrical movements of the soul" the music he sought to write. Baudelaire too was an innovator—he brought something entirely new to French poetry. Soon after he left Rome, Debussy began writing music for five of Baudelaire's poems.

Diane au bois was abandoned, but his struggles with the score were not in vain. *Diane* helped him focus on the kind of libretto he needed for an opera and how he would shape the music. In the end he went back to *Zuléima*, which was submitted as his first *envoi* and sternly rejected by the Academy. In the official opinion, dated December 1886, Debussy's music was called "bizarre, incomprehensible, and unperformable," although some passages "are not without a certain character."[48] In the composer's own opinion, *Zuléima* was "too much like Verdi and Meyerbeer."[49]

Printemps

After the rejection of *Zuléima*, Debussy threw himself into *Printemps* (Springtime), a symphonic suite for orchestra and wordless chorus, working quickly in order to send it to the Academy before leaving the infernal Eternal City.

"I've decided to write a work of a special color, recreating as many sensations as possible," he wrote to the bookseller Émile Baron. "I'm calling it *Printemps*, not 'spring' from the descriptive point of view but from that of living things. I wanted to express the slow, laborious birth of beings and things in nature, then the mounting florescence and finally a burst of joy at being reborn to a new life." Debussy added that, despite his description, the piece is not program music, "as I have nothing but contempt for music organized according to one of those leaflets" they give you at the concert hall. Rather, *Printemps* will have to powerfully evoke the emotion we feel when spring comes, "and I'm not sure I shall be wholly successful in this."[50]

Printemps proved almost as difficult as *Diane* had been, especially as he was pushing himself toward a self-imposed deadline. Debussy complained to

Baron, with typical hyperbole, "Compared with mine, a convict's life is one of irresponsible ease and luxury."[51] *Printemps* was performed at the Villa Medici, in a reduction for piano duet, before he left Rome, and the orchestral score was sent to the Academy as his second *envoi*.

The judges were only a bit more impressed with *Printemps* than they'd been with *Zuléima*. Debussy can't be accused of platitude or banality, the report said, but he has a pronounced tendency "toward an exploration of the strange."[52] The wordless chorus bothered some. Saint-Saëns was shocked and offended that Debussy had written in the difficult, rarely used key of F-sharp.

In the end, *Printemps* was rejected particularly because Debussy's exaggerated "feeling for musical color . . . causes the composer to forget the importance of precise construction and form."[53] In their mission to deflect young musicians from excessive originality, the judges condemned Debussy's "vague impressionism, one of the most dangerous enemies of truth in works of art."[54] This hilarious comment, in 1887, was probably the first time the word "impressionism" was applied to a musical work—certainly the first time it was thrown at Debussy. The word had been coined by an art critic, twelve years earlier, as a derisive epithet for a painting by Claude Monet—a sunrise over a river. It was a warning to Debussy, with the force of the French Academy itself, that he had strayed too far from the Conservatory. But "impressionist" was a label that stuck to Debussy like "genius" stuck to Mozart, and he rejected the designation all his life.

Interpreting the truth or applicability of the Academy's judgments is especially difficult, as the orchestral score of *Printemps* has been lost. Debussy published a version for piano duet in 1904. What is occasionally heard in concerts or recordings today is a reconstruction orchestrated in 1912, without the chorus, by Henri Büsser under the composer's supervision.

Some critics see in *Printemps* the first glimmerings of Debussy's mature style, especially his tendency to steer clear of any convention that gets in the way of his artistic vision. Stefan Jarocinski hears in *Printemps* a composer defiantly breaking all the rules the Academy holds dear, writing "melodic themes whose tonality [is neither] major or minor; sequences involving four or five different keys; whole-tone scales; plagal cadences; common chords sometimes combined with chords of the seventh; sequences of ninths and major thirds."[55] If impressionism is at least in part defined by the painter's effort to capture the spontaneous impressions of a visual moment, then Debussy's letter to Baron

shows him in a different artistic zone, in which the genesis of Spring is a duration of eventful time rather than a snapshot of a fleeting instant. Debussy's
Printemps was more allied to the symbolists than the impressionists, as he uses
music the way symbolist poets use words to convey the ineffable, the essence,
the universality of things. In 1887, Debussy was already on the path to symbolism. He would, over the coming years, use music to convey the essence of
the sea, of children's games, moonlight, and myths; and through his mastery
he would evoke pictorial as well as sensual responses in the listener.

"It was the novelty of [*Printemps*] . . . which, in the eyes of the members of
the Academy, constituted a phenomenon totally unlike anything they had
experienced in contemporary music at the end of the Romantic epoch," wrote
Jarocinski. Debussy's art was "contrary to all the laws of common sense."[56]
How dare this young upstart give us a symphonic work in F-sharp major!

Perhaps Debussy's "joy at being reborn into a new life," portrayed in *Printemps*, was his anticipation of a rapturous return to Paris. Debussy left Rome
on March 5, 1887, having completed the mandatory two years (the option of a
third year was never in his thoughts), but without providing the Academy with
even one acceptable *envoi*. Before leaving, he sent Vasnier a letter: "I've tried
everything, but I cannot stay here. I've followed the advice you've given me,
and I swear that I've put the greatest possible goodwill into my efforts. . . . Ever
since I've been here I feel dead inside. I really want to work, and go on until I
produce something solid and original. . . . Please don't be too hard on me. Your
friendship's the only thing I'll have left, so allow me to keep a little of it in my
need."[57]

All in all, Debussy produced less music in Rome than might have been
expected. Besides *Zuléima* and *Printemps*, he completed a few songs ("Barcarolle," "Green," and the two "Romances"). He started and quickly abandoned
an opera based on Gustave Flaubert's novel *Salammbô*, set in ancient Carthage.
He made sketches for a musical setting of Dante Gabriel Rossetti's poem *The
Blessed Damozel*, which he would complete later. Nevertheless, Debussy had
advanced in maturity and begun to find his musical voice. Explaining his
reluctance to finish *Zuléima*, he had written to Vasnier, "I shall always prefer a
subject where, in some way, dramatic action is sacrificed to a wide range of
inner feelings. It seems to me that in this way music becomes more human,
more true to life, and its expressive power becomes deeper and more subtle."[58]
It was as if he were conjuring a libretto like *Pelléas et Mélisande*.

CHAPTER 3
DEBUSSY AND THE FRENCH POETS (1880–1891)

Debussy is a composer of nuance, of half-hinted murmurings, of music overheard, and of mirrored dreams. Little wonder he sought to interpret in his weaving tones Baudelaire and Verlaine, Mallarmé and Maeterlinck. . . . His musical palette proclaims Debussy a symbolist. He knew that the core of music is poetry. . . . A poet himself, Claude-Achille Debussy, even if he had never written a bar of music.

—James Huneker[1]

Debussy's affinity for the arts was essential to his achievements as a composer. Most of his compositions have a direct or indirect connection to French literature; and many of his innovations reflect his interest in the literature, paintings, and music of other cultures and earlier times. Debussy and his generation were "part of a culture that still valued broad learning and connectedness within the arts," Jack Sullivan tells us. "They considered themselves part of a stream of sensibility flowing through all the arts, connecting nationalities, periods, and disciplines."[2]

Debussy was the most literary of all composers—a startling thought, considering his meager formal education in matters other than musical. From his time at the Conservatory, he read voraciously—broadly among translations from English and other languages, and deeply in the literature of nineteenth-century France. It is impossible not to suspect that, in much of his reading, he was searching for a narrative, a character, a mood, or a thrilling bit of verse that he could wrap his music around. Over the years, he set to music poems or plays by Baudelaire, Musset, Gautier, Bourget, Lamartine, Leconte de Lisle, Banville, Verlaine, Mallarmé, and Mendès. He reached back to the fifteenth century for the poets François Villon and Charles, Duke of Orleans, and to the seventeenth century for Tristan L'Hermite. His sources included Dante Gabriel

Rossetti, the British Pre-Raphaelite artist and poet, for the text of *La Damoiselle élue*; the Italian writer Gabriele D'Annunzio for *Le Martyre de Saint-Sébastien*; and his close friend Pierre Louÿs for *Chansons de Bilitis*. At the core of his career stands his only completed opera, *Pelléas et Mélisande*, which he adapted himself from the play by Maurice Maeterlinck. His signature work, the one that established him as a musical visionary, was from a Mallarmé poem, *L'Après-midi d'un faune*.

Debussy's literary interests also inform his piano pieces. Among the twenty-four piano Préludes are "La Fille aux cheveux de lin," inspired by poems of Leconte de Lisle; "Ce qu'a vu le vent d'Ouest," from a Hans Christian Andersen tale; and others evoking Baudelaire, Shakespeare, and Dickens.

The population of literary men and women in Paris, especially in the Belle Époque, was far larger than in other cities at any time in history, or so it seemed, and Debussy knew an impressive number of them personally. He preferred the company of writers; his inner circle included few musicians.

Debussy's literary acuity is seen even in the eclecticism of the projects he planned to write (but didn't) or left unfinished at his death: incidental music for *King Lear*; a ballet based on Pierre Louÿs's erotic novel *Aphrodite*; and operas on Edgar Allan Poe's stories "The Fall of the House of Usher" and "The Devil in the Belfry." "Usher" held deep personal resonance for him, especially in the suffering of his last years. Other projected stage works ranged from a variant of the Tristan story to a rewriting of Cinderella, from Dionysus to Don Juan.

Debussy's difficulty in seeing his literary interests and musical aspirations merge on the operatic stage was a source of frustration and despair. But his extensive reading served him well as a composer of art songs (*mélodies*, as they are known in France). It was easy to find texts for songs, because the poets of Debussy's time were among the finest that France ever produced.

The Flavors of French Poetry

"Every new progressive stage of art corresponds exactly to senile degeneration at the . . . end of the immediately previous school," Jean Moréas wrote. "What was full of sap and freshness becomes dried out and shriveled," and what was new becomes commonplace.[3] In the nineteenth century this regeneration occurred in painting, in music, and in poetry, and the cultural progress of each European country was different.

The Romantic movement in French literature was nurtured by the ashes of revolution and the winds of freedom that ruffled the banners of the new republic. It was at its zenith in the second quarter of the nineteenth century, with poets such as Victor Hugo, Alfred de Musset, and Alphonse de Lamartine. The Romantics wanted freedom from older literary models and Enlightenment philosophies, freedom to explore the human senses and emotions. They used language differently, invented new forms, and expanded the range of what could be expressed in verse.

At mid-century, the Romantics bumped up against the singularity and power of Charles Baudelaire, a Romantic himself, surely; and French poetry became tangled in a muddle of factions and debate. Some poets identified themselves as Parnassians, others as naturalists or decadents or symbolists. By the 1880s the lines were blurred: Parnassians were publishing in symbolist journals.

Baudelaire was the spiritual father of all these factions. He was an urban poet disturbed by the apathy and social injustices of modern French life. His thoughts and themes were focused on humanity and spirituality writ large: God and Satan, life and death, art and the human condition. In his sonnet "Correspondences," he "establishes the aesthetic basis" for his art, "namely that the poet can perceive the subtle analogies in nature which bind the whole universe together," writes Robert T. Nealy. "By a blend of images, sounds, and rhythms [Baudelaire] sought to establish symbols which represent the absolute itself."[4]

The Parnassian movement—led by Théophile Gautier, Banville, Charles Leconte de Lisle, and José Maria de Heredia—was a reaction to the excesses of the Romantics' newly found freedoms and their perceived lack of discipline. Under the banner of *l'art pour l'art* (art for art's sake), they undertook to preserve the classical poetic virtues through objectivity, clarity, and impeccable form. The name they chose for their movement refers to Mount Parnassus, home of Apollo and the Muses, which towers over the sacred Greek temples of Delphi: the classical ideal sheltered by the gods. Teodor de Wyzewa noted that the Parnassians "disencumbered poetry of superfluous functions, so that it could better fulfill its true role of evoking in the souls of readers emotions akin to music."[5] From Baudelaire to Mallarmé, many poets thought music was the ideal language to which all poems aspire. Walter Pater took it one step further: all art constantly aspires towards the condition of music, he said.

In the 1880s and '90s, symbolist writers were preeminent, and of all the French symbolists the best-known are Mallarmé and Verlaine. In the transition to symbolism, these poets took from the Parnassians their devotion to language and the deliberate musicality of their verse. But symbolists cast off the objective, neoclassical mode in favor of an emphasis on the subjective, the personal, and the imaginative. They aimed to express universal experience, sensations, and the inner life by means of finely wrought metaphorical language. Their verses were designed to evoke a sensation, an atmosphere, or an object, rather than to describe it. They emphasized a "turning inward of artistic consciousness."[6] In their poetry the symbol was the essential.

The symbolist poets were "part of the larger pattern of diverse protests mounted by artists and intellectuals against European society in the last quarter of the nineteenth century," writes James L. Connelly.[7] Romanticism lingered in a few brightly lit corners of the culture (as it does even today). Optimism and joie de vivre could still be found in Renoir's paintings and Chabrier's music. Modernism took baby steps to join the party. But the overcrowded, undernourished, polluted, godless, corrupt urban societies of the industrial age that so troubled Baudelaire and the symbolists also spawned the dark moral dilemmas of Ibsen's plays and Dostoyevsky's novels, and the existential angst of Mahler's symphonies and Munch's screaming paintings.

Mélodies: A Marriage of Poetry and Music

The tradition of French mélodies arose in the nineteenth century out of an earlier genre called romances. (Mélodies are what the Germans call *lieder* and we, clumsily, call art songs. Popular songs and cabaret songs are generally known in France as *chansons*.) The six songs of Berlioz's 1841 *Les Nuits d'été* (Summer Nights) were among the first that music historians regard as mélodies. Charles Gounod and Jules Massenet were prolific writers of mélodies, and Gabriel Fauré and Henri Duparc brought the genre to its greatest distinction. Debussy, Ravel, and Reynaldo Hahn each applied his own musical rhetoric to the genre, and Francis Poulenc added dozens of beautiful songs to the repertoire before the mélodie's luster faded in the cataclysm of the twentieth century.

The poem or libretto sets the conditions and limitations for the composer's musical approach. Each of the world's languages has its characteristic rhythms, vowel sounds, phrase structures, and inflections; French mélodies can rarely be mistaken for lieder, which must accommodate the more muscular, assertive German tongue.

A poem resists adaptation to another art form (music) as vigorously as it resists translation to another language. But the composer can tame the poem, and often enhance it, by putting musical emphasis on certain words, or by raising or lowering the pitch, or by slowing the tempo to drive home an important idea. Every mélodie has a complex relationship with the original text; there may be similarities of tone and color, but differences in expression or rhythm. A musical setting "subdues the richness of the multiple suggestions contained in a poem, while highlighting certain of the poem's images, connections, and structural relationships," writes Arthur Wenk. "A composer may create a glorious piece of music with only the most general comprehension of his text."[8]

To make one's own musical voice meld with another person's poetic expression in order to produce an artful and appealing song is no easy task. But "a skillful composer will be able to satisfy both poetic and musical obligations with a minimum of conflict between the two," Wenk assures us.[9] If the composer is talented, persistent, and clever enough, the music and words can combine as naturally as berries and cream, or Rodgers and Hammerstein, to make a delicious new treat for the senses.

Debussy's Early Songs

Vocal music constitutes a large portion of Debussy's oeuvre. He was supremely devoted to the French language and French poetry, and he chose with great care the texts he wanted. Many of his favored poets were known for the exceptional musicality of their verses, a great advantage to the composer.

It's not surprising that young Debussy was strongly attracted to the mélodie. Art songs demand an immersion in creative challenges, a strategic adaptation to imposed limitations, which make them an ideal medium for a young composer to hone his craft. And for this budding composer, still called Achille, there was a marvelous voice to sing them: More than two dozen early songs were written for the expressive coloratura soprano of Marie Vasnier. Eventually there would be an audience for them in the salons of the rich and the parlors of the middle class.

For the thirteen mélodies of the Vasnier Songbook, he chose five poems from Verlaine's *Fêtes galantes*, six poems by Paul Bourget, and one each by Gautier and Musset.

These early songs are characterized by charm and youthfulness, and they follow the examples of Massenet and other mainstream French composers. The piano accompaniments unobtrusively support the voice, and the conventional harmonies are safe from the censure of his Conservatory teachers. Debussy's focus was on the melody. He often took liberties with the text, omitting stanzas, repeating lines, in order to create musical symmetry, intensify an emotion, or help him through a difficult structural problem. Sometimes he added an ornamental phrase, called a melisma, in which a single syllable or vowel is held across many notes, giving the singer an opportunity to show off her agile voice. Melismas were frequent in nineteenth-century operas and are common even today in pop music, but they almost disappeared from Debussy's songs as he evolved, in one decade, to a more austere, less ornamental style.

One of the most lyrical mélodies in the Vasnier collection employs Bourget's poem "La Romance d'Ariel." The sprite Ariel (from Shakespeare's play *The Tempest*) conjures the beautiful Miranda and sings of all the lovely things he wants for her ("just enough breeze . . . to curl the golden tips of your hair"). In the middle of the song, a brief, glowing melisma brings the singer to the very top of her vocal range; and to end the song, a long melismatic vocalise wraps singer and listener in a ribbon of wistful romance. The technical difficulties of melismas, the perilous upward and downward vocal leaps, attest to Debussy's appreciation of Mme Vasnier's skills.

"When I sing Debussy," says the French soprano Sandrine Piau, "I can feel the relationship he had with the women in his life, especially [Marie Vasnier]. . . . She was 'the only lady whose voice is light enough,' Debussy declared, 'to sing songs dealing with butterflies.' Each of his mélodies presents a separate, strange, and fragile world unto itself, something you have to enter into each time. For me, it is like putting on a well-fitting costume."[10]

Banville was the first poet to exert a significant influence on Debussy's music. Banville's verses are fresh and beautifully crafted, though some critics found them lightweight and insubstantial. Like other Parnassians, Banville was attracted to classical themes of love and jealousy among the gods, and he was most admired for his mastery of "musical speech." "Poetry is rhythmic human speech fashioned to be sung," Banville declared, "and, strictly speaking, there is no poem or poetry except the Song."[11]

For young Debussy, the art song became a training ground for the greater goal of writing operas, and when he was only nineteen and not yet master of the mélodie, he looked to Banville for librettos. Banville's play *Hymnis* was meant to be Debussy's first opera, but he didn't work on it for long and left only fragments. His adaptation of another Banville play, *Diane au bois*, was one of his favorite projects, but troublesome and intransigent. The two plays have much in common, as they dramatize love's triumph over indifference in the context of ancient myths.

Debussy's Early Verlaine Songs

The poetry of Verlaine influenced Debussy's music profoundly. In all, Debussy set music to about twenty of Verlaine's poems, more than those of any other poet. Verlaine's often casual, conversational verses—their imagery, the unforced rhymes, abundant musical references, and pervasive lyricism—were easily matched to Debussy's natural manner. Verlaine's poem "L'Art poetique" (Poetic Art), written in 1874, relates the principles that informed the poet's creative process. "Music above all," he begins. And for the music in your verses, Verlaine suggests a preference for odd, vague words and phrases, dissolving in the air, without weight or attitude; nuance rather than color; shadowy verse where precision is joined to indecision. Later in the poem he exclaims, "Music again and forever!"

Even in many Debussy songs and instrumental works unrelated to Verlaine, there is often a tonal quality that echoes the poet—it's one of the characteristics that makes Debussy sound so Debussy-ish. The vagueness of the whole-tone scale so often employed in his middle period; the delicacy and buoyancy of his *Prélude à "L'Après-midi d'un faune"*; the diaphanous phrases of "Nuages"—it's what many listeners find so seductive in his music. What Debussy took from Verlaine's poetry brought him closer to finding his own authentic voice.

There is no record, no letter, no memoir, affirming that Debussy and Verlaine ever met or even corresponded. But it's hard to believe a meeting never occurred, at least casually or briefly, because their paths could have crossed so many times—at Mme Mauté's, at Le Chat Noir, at Mallarmé's, at Bailly's bookstore—before Verlaine's wretched life ended in 1896. Would Debussy not have sought Verlaine's approval to write songs on his poems, or to publish them? We don't know.

Regardless, Verlaine's poems were a rich trove for Debussy. The Vasnier Songbook includes "Pantomime," "Mandoline," "En Sourdine" (Muted), "Clair de lune," and "Fantoches" (Puppets). The last three were revised years later, rededicated to other women, and published in a set called *Fêtes galantes* in 1903.

In January 1885, weeks before he left for Rome, Debussy began the first of his *Ariettes*, based on poems from Verlaine's *Ariettes oubliées* (Forgotten Songs). The word *ariette* signifies a short aria or mélodie, and these songs are indeed brief—two or three minutes each—with direct and plain language and emotions laid bare. Debussy's *Ariettes* were published individually in 1887–1888 but had limited circulation. They were revised and reissued as *Ariettes oubliées* in 1903, dedicated to Mary Garden after her triumph in the role of Mélisande.

The *Ariettes* came only a few years after the earliest Vasnier songs, yet Debussy's musical progress is unmistakable, not least in the depth and darkness of the passions he reveals in the music. We hear less of the clear tonal harmonies and more of his trademark chromaticism and sequences of chords, both simple and complex, that blur the tonality. In the earlier Vasnier songs he took some liberties with the text, but now, in the *Ariettes* and in the Baudelaire songs that followed, he respects the poem's integrity, generally leaving the words and stanzas intact.

The six *Ariettes* reveal themselves slowly and express the various colors of loneliness, sadness, and dashed hopes. Unlike the others, "Chevaux de bois" (Carousel Horses), is upbeat and swirling with the excitement of young lovers pursuing each other, round and round, on the wooden horses. But trouble lurks even here: The riders are drunk and dizzy; a pickpocket lurks nearby; the wooden horses, always at the gallop, have no hope of stopping to eat. The music slows. Night falls, and the velvet sky and golden stars send the lovers away.

One of Debussy's saddest songs is the delicate *Ariette* "Il pleure dans mon coeur" (It's Raining in My Heart). It's raining in the town, too. The beautiful theme heard in the opening measures suggests the sadness, languor, and questioning that we hear in the lyrics. To underscore the singer's loneliness and ennui, Debussy intensifies the unrelenting rain with the drip-drip-drip of sixteenth notes in the piano's upper register. In the third stanza the music almost comes to a halt when the singer realizes that her terrible sorrow has no cause. The song ends on a heartbreaking note: The voice plummets almost an octave on the word "pain."

The Other "Clair de lune," and Yet Another

The majority of Debussy's mélodies—he wrote more than eighty—were written before he was thirty. Because he wrote so many songs in this early period, you can listen to four or five of them in chronological order and clearly hear his music gain in assurance, sophistication, and harmonic complexity. Or you can take a shortcut and examine the differences in two versions of the song "Clair de lune." (Neither resembles the piano piece of the same name.) The first version, written in 1882, is a pretty little song, dedicated to Mme Vasnier. The second, far more nuanced and in a completely different mood, was written in 1891.

"Clair de lune" (Moonlight)

Your soul is a landscape chosen
By charming masqueraders and dancers,
Playing the lute and prancing, somewhat
Sad in their fantastic disguises.

While singing in a minor key
Of triumphant love and a life well lived,
They seem not to believe in their happiness,
And their song mingles with the moonlight.

The tranquil moonlight, sad and beautiful,
Causes birds to dream in the trees,
And the fountains to weep in ecstasy,
Tall, slender water jets among the marble.[12]

Verlaine plants in the reader's soul a scene derived from Watteau's paintings. Bewigged men and richly gowned women of the French aristocracy frolic, flirt, and frivolously while away their abundant time in the decades after the reign of Louis XIV. Some dress up as masqueraders and dancers or as characters of the commedia dell'arte. In Watteau's paintings, the colors of the moonlit scene are soft grays and greens, muted blues and rose. Haze-shrouded trees surround the well-staged people and a rococo marble fountain. Verlaine even suggests the kind of music you hear in your soul: music in a minor key, with a little of the sadness attributed to the revelers. How could a composer like Debussy resist the urge to put this atmospheric scene into music?

Debussy, in the 1882 version, repeats the last line of the second and third stanzas, to complete a musical thought as much as to emphasize the text. The accompaniment features a motif that drifts downward and occasionally sparkles, like the spray of the fountain. The chords in the piano establish a quiet harmony that remains simple and conventional; and strangely, the song is written almost entirely in a major key, ignoring Verlaine's stipulation for the minor. The composer glosses over the sadness and keeps it at a distance.

The second version of "Clair de lune," written nine years later, is far more harmonically adventurous and emotionally intense. Whereas the first version is charming and moderate in tempo, the second is dark and proceeds slowly, like a troubling reverie, and complexity is present in nearly every aspect of the musical architecture. In the opening measures, a flurry of sixteenth notes in a pentatonic scale (played entirely on the piano's black keys) suggests moonlight on a plashing fountain. Just as the voice enters, the piano settles unexpectedly into the forlorn and little-used key of G-sharp minor. The harmonies range over several discordant foreign territories, returning to G-sharp minor at the start of each stanza before ending definitively in that key. Our sense of time is disoriented by the unhurried tension in the vocal melody and by the frequent harmonic shifts. What anchors the song is the persistent repetition of the rippling sixteenth-note patterns.

Unlike the earlier "Clair de lune," in which the singer is an impersonal chronicler of a moonlit scene, the second version suggests that the singer is *living* the scene, or that her soul is infused with it; the emotions that creep through the music forebode an unknown destiny, an existential dread. What did Verlaine intend to convey—the nostalgia and romance of Debussy's first "Clair de lune" or the dark uneasiness of the second? Each of us brings our unique emotional responses to all works of art. In Verlaine's fantastic disguises, the older Debussy found, perhaps, the troubled world of Edgar Allan Poe, who had already begun to haunt Debussy's soul.

CHAPTER 4

THE TYRANNY
OF RICHARD WAGNER

Wagner's art can never completely die. It will suffer that inevitable decay, the cruel brand of time on all beautiful things; yet noble ruins must remain, in the shadow of which our grandchildren will brood over the past splendor of this man who, had he been a little more human, would have been altogether great.

—Debussy[1]

On the highest hill in Paris, there were gypsum mines dating back to the 1300s. Five centuries later, the mines long gone, the land was turned over to agriculture. In 1887, when Debussy returned to Paris after his unhappy time in Rome, there were still some farms and vineyards on the hill, dotted with windmills and surrounded by new apartment buildings. The hill was called Montmartre, the mountain of martyrs, in honor of the bishop of Paris who was beheaded there in the third century.

We know there were farms and windmills on Montmartre in 1887 because that's when Vincent van Gogh painted them. But with an expanding population in the lower regions of the city, the last farms gave way to a maze of little streets that were soon littered with artists, writers, musicians, and other lowlifes looking for a cheaper place to live and congregate. Some well-off bourgeois families lived there, too, including the Mauté de Fleurvilles. In time, all but three of the windmills disappeared, but a vineyard tended long ago by nuns was allowed to remain on a small parcel of land. The vines succumbed to *Phylloxera*, the vineyard gave way to development; but in the early 1930s a disused piece of Montmartre was reclaimed for the growing of grapes.

On the summit, in 1887, construction was well under way on the white travertine stone facades of the Basilica of the Sacred Heart—Sacré-Coeur. Across the river Seine, hundreds of workers began assembling the 15,000 iron parts of Gustave Eiffel's mammoth tower, despite petitions of protest from many distinguished citizens.

The year Debussy returned to Paris, the French premiere of Wagner's *Lohengrin* was to be presented at the Eden-Théâtre, which had earlier presented many concerts featuring Wagner's music. This would be Debussy's first experience of a fully staged Wagner opera. The performances would be conducted by Charles Lamoureux, a devoted Wagnerian who had cultivated a sizable group of dedicated followers. Wagner's very grand operas aroused enormous interest in Paris, as elsewhere. For a while, the prism of Wagner's genius colored and distorted all intellectual studies and discussions of music and, to a lesser degree, of literature and art.

Scheduled to open on April 23, 1887, the mere announcement of *Lohengrin* was greeted with anti-Wagner indignation almost as intense as the furor that had arrived with *Tannhäuser* twenty-six years earlier. The premiere was postponed to allow for additional rehearsals—the official reason—or, more likely, because a diplomatic incident with Germany threatened to escalate to dangerous conflict. The recklessly ambitious French war minister, Georges Ernest Boulanger, had sponsored a series of provocations against Germany; Otto von Bismarck, on the other side, was rumored to be gearing up for war. Then an unimportant French police inspector named Schnaebelé was arrested on the German border by Bismarck's secret police on disputed charges of spying. Boulanger, determined to avenge France's defeat in 1871 and to retake Alsace and Lorraine from the Germans, asked the French Parliament to mobilize the army. But a week after Schnaebelé's arrest, when war seemed unavoidable, Bismarck released his prisoner, military action was averted, and *Lohengrin* was rescheduled. The premiere, on May 3, triggered vehement anti-German riots in the streets of Paris. The opera was allowed to continue to the final curtain, but the French authorities canceled the nine remaining performances and banned *Lohengrin* until it could be mounted without threat of demonstrations.[2]

Two weeks later, Debussy went to another premiere.[3] Chabrier's new opera *Le Roi malgré lui,* based on a play by Molière, opened at the Salle Favart, home of the Opéra-Comique, and was performed twice more before disaster struck. On May 25, during a performance of Ambroise Thomas's *Mignon,* a fire broke out in the offices and workrooms high above the stage. Dozens of craftsmen, stagehands, and singers, and nearly all the dancers, lost their lives, though most of the audience escaped unharmed. Days later, the public was shocked to learn that only thirteen days before the blaze, a member of the Chamber of Deputies was ridiculed when he reported that the Salle Favart was in terrible condition;

that the warren of rooms above the stage, built of old, dry wood and lit with gas lamps, was a tinderbox; and that the building was sure to burn, as several other old theaters recently had done.[4]

Over the next six years Debussy attended eight other performances of Wagner's operas. As a young composer, he was obsessed with the German master; many intellectuals and artists were, in those days. Debussy had served his apprenticeship by writing more than two dozen mélodies and several cantatas. Now he was about to resume work on *La Damoiselle élue*, an ambitious piece that would be as close as he had come to writing an actual opera. Nearly everyone who studied composition at the Paris Conservatory left the institution with a mission to write opera. Debussy was no exception.

The Perplexing Paucity of French Operas

Opera was born in Italy around the year 1600, at the beginning of the Baroque era. Jean-Baptiste Lully, a native of Florence, was a royal composer in the court of Louis XIV, where he established a style of opera adapted to the French language and temperament, distinct from the Italian style. It was no small accomplishment. Lully's brilliant successor, Jean-Philippe Rameau, a harmonic innovator and a master of choral writing, established ballet as an important element of French opera. In his day, Rameau's operas were admired and popular within the precincts of the Royal Academy and the royal court, but they, like Lully's operas, were nearly forgotten before the end of the eighteenth century.

Through much of the nineteenth century, opera was the dominant form of entertainment in Western Europe, attracting the well-born elite and the emerging middle class to the new, gilded opera houses that were the cultural heart of nearly all cities of substance. And for most of the century, European stages were home to the operas of Germans, Austrians, and Italians—Gluck, Mozart, Rossini, Meyerbeer, Verdi, Wagner, and others, in their turn—but not French composers.

The directors of the Paris Conservatory not-so-secretly hoped that each of their young composers would master this difficult art form, but few made the grade, and the French squandered the eminence achieved by Lully and Rameau. France was so barren of native opera composers that they had to import them. In 1773 they enticed Christoph Willibald Gluck from Vienna to write French operas. Florence-born Luigi Cherubini settled in Paris, wrote his greatest operas in French, and became director of the Paris Conservatoire. Gioachino Rossini, Italy's most popular opera composer during the first quarter of the nineteenth century, was for five years at the helm of one of Paris's three great opera companies. Giacomo Meyerbeer was the consummate master of a new genre known as "grand opera." He briefly revived Paris's status as one of the great European capitals of opera, but he was German born, he had studied and achieved his first successes in Italy, and he was soon old hat.

At the moment when the Classical era began to morph into the Romantic, Berlioz appeared on the scene, as if summoned by some cosmic casting director. Berlioz wrote highly original, powerful music and was hailed as the greatest French composer since Rameau. His startling early work *Symphonie fantastique* (1830) summed up the entire genre of Romanticism just as the era was getting started. But his operas were not in the disciplined mainstream of Romanticism; his stream was more turbulent and tended to overflow its banks. Many musical societies found his work too difficult, his ensembles too large, to be performed often. Few composers continued in Berlioz's path. His influence is heard more in the works of Schumann, Liszt, and Wagner than in those of his own countrymen.

From around 1840 and especially during the reign of Napoleon III, the Parisian enthusiasm for music declined gradually into apathy. Even prominent literary Frenchmen belittled the importance of music in French life. Edmond de Goncourt claimed to be deaf to all music except the military kind. His friend Gautier preferred silence to music, and "Balzac hated music," Gautier said. "Hugo could not stand it. Even Lamartine holds it in horror!"[5]

Then along came Richard Wagner.

Wagner in Paris

French musicians of the last third of the nineteenth century suffered severe, lingering post-traumatic stress resulting from the infamous 1861 Paris premiere of *Tannhäuser*. Leon Botstein calls this "the most significant event in the modern history of French music."[6] Several accounts of the *Tannhäuser* premiere in Paris, including Wagner's own, agree on the particulars: the jeering and catcalls; the cruelty of the critics; the withdrawal of the opera after its third performance; and the crushing blow to the composer's hopes. He had come to Paris at the age of forty-six, determined to revive a career that was mired in failure and antagonism in his native Germany.

Born in Leipzig in 1813, Wagner began composing at seventeen. At twenty he was chorus master at a Würzburg theater and completed his first opera, which, like the several that followed, was firmly in the German tradition of its time—a style forged by Meyerbeer and Carl Maria von Weber. Wagner's early operas, like the later ones, were long and complex, expensive to produce, and difficult to sing. For years he couldn't find an opera company that would risk a production.

In 1836, Wagner married a successful actress, Christine Wilhelmine Planer, known as Minna. The long marriage was fraught with unhappiness (his), illness (hers), and infidelities (his and hers). Unsuccessful as a composer and always in debt, Wagner took conducting posts where he could find them. Fleeing creditors in Riga in 1839, he and Minna endured a horrific twenty-four-day sea voyage; traveling without passports or money, they arrived in London and soon found their way to Paris. Wagner hoped to settle there after securing a good conducting post (he wasn't offered one) and a first production of *Rienzi* at the Paris Opéra (the Opéra didn't want it). For several years they were impoverished, and only the generosity of friends made it possible for him to remain in Paris long enough to write *Der fliegende Holländer* (The Flying Dutchman); this too was rejected by the Opéra.

Introduced in Dresden in 1842, *Rienzi* was his first success, despite its six-hour running time, and led to his appointment as music director at the Dresden opera house. There he completed *Tannhäuser* and *Lohengrin* and began writing the libretto for *Der Ring des Nibelungen*. He also became dangerously aligned with liberal political causes.

In the spring of 1848, the spirit of revolution spread from France, where the king was forced to abdicate, to the sovereign states of the German confederation. Hordes of middle-class liberals and working-class poor took to the streets to demand civil liberties, a unified German state, and a constitutional government. Wagner actively supported the Dresden uprising, but the revolution failed. The composer, expecting arrest, fled to Zurich and spent most of the next decade in exile. He put aside the *Ring* and wrote *Die Meistersinger* and *Tristan und Isolde*.

Disappointed again when a promised performance of *Tristan* in Karlsruhe failed to materialize, Wagner returned to Paris in 1859, determined to win over the Parisians. To that end, he presented three concerts of excerpts from his operas. The public and critical reception was decidedly mixed, but Wagner chose to see the venture as a success, and he persevered in the delusion that Parisians wanted nothing more than to hear *Tristan*, in German.

For better or worse, fate intervened—and gave Paris not *Tristan* but *Tannhäuser*.

The particulars of the imminent debacle were recorded in a colorful first-person account written by a well-connected young Bostonian named Edward H. House, who attended all three open rehearsals and the official premiere of *Tannhäuser*.[7] As a youth with an intense interest in music, House had come under the "powerful, irresistible" influence of Wagner and had closely studied the score of the *Tannhäuser* overture to learn "how its extraordinary and unprecedented effects were produced." Born into a prosperous family, House dropped out of school and, at eighteen, began reviewing concerts and drama for the *Boston Courier*, then joined the first-rate reporting staff of Horace Greeley's *New York Herald*. When sober, he was one of the *Herald*'s best journalists, known for his hard work, the thoroughness of his reporting, and the quality of his writing. He aggressively pursued major stories: the abolitionist movement, John Brown's trial and hanging, and Japan's first diplomatic mission to the United States. On holiday in Paris in 1861, House was astonished to find that *Tannhäuser* was soon to be performed by the Paris Opéra. "It was not altogether clear why Wagner should desire to subject himself," House wrote, "to the ordeal that would inevitably await him."

"This is Paris, and that is Wagner"

In House's telling, the reception the composer received at the three 1859 orchestral concerts "was so extremely unflattering as to foreshadow the danger" of presenting an entire opera to the Parisian public "for which he had openly and loudly proclaimed the profoundest contempt." Wagner's earlier residence in Paris had inflicted "experiences so bitter and humiliating" that he could think of Parisians only with acrimony. Wagner had written that the French were burdened with "permanent aesthetic disabilities." He had repeatedly written, House tells us, "in scornful mockery or fiery denunciation" of French audiences, critics, and composers. How could there be any areas of sympathy where volatile, hedonistic Parisians could coexist with the "arrogant, unbending, and sternly conscientious" composer. (It should be noted that the young journalist had great respect and admiration for Wagner's music, and even a little for the man himself.)

It became evident, House wrote, that "Wagner was possessed by an unaccountable yearning to conquer this vivacious populace." But formidable obstacles awaited him in Paris. Well before 1861, Wagner's name was "already a byword of derision.... What was he to expect, even if through some superlative graciousness of fortune, the opportunity of carrying out the most daring of enterprises should be afforded him?"

Alas, fortune provided Wagner with an admirer at the Imperial Court. The Viennese princess Pauline von Metternich persuaded the wife of Napoleon III to prevail upon the emperor to command a presentation of *Tannhäuser* at the Paris Opéra.

Despite Napoleon's support, the decks were stacked against Wagner. French operatic tastes of the time ran to Rossini and Meyerbeer; and concerning these older (but still living) masters, Wagner had written damning critiques, including a despicable anti-Semitic screed against Meyerbeer, which were well known in France.

When rehearsals began, rumors circulated about backstage conflicts involving the composer and conductor. The press reported that the singers and musicians were ill equipped for the challenges of Wagner's music. Opening night was postponed several times to accommodate recasting and additional rehearsals— the work required an astounding 164 rehearsals in all.

Then there was the Jockey Club to be reckoned with. In the nineteenth century, this club, dedicated to the gentlemen's sport of thoroughbred racing, was one of the most exclusive gathering places of the Paris elite. Its members occupied many choice boxes at the opera house and were famous for their insistence that a ballet sequence, by now a common feature of French operas, must be danced in the *second* act, never the first. Many members were reputed to have mistresses among the dancers, and a second-act ballet gave the Jockeys ample time to finish their dinners at leisure *and* see their paramours onstage. Wagner, who had agreed to a French translation and other concessions to Parisian taste and custom, stubbornly refused to have a ballet in the second act. It may have been his biggest mistake.

In Wagner's own report of the *Tannhäuser* affair,[8] he says he "could not possibly disturb the course of the second act by a ballet, which must be senseless from every point of view; while on the other hand I thought the first act, at the voluptuous court of Venus, would afford the most apposite occasion" for a ballet. But the director emphatically rejected his proposal, and the decision was backed by a cabinet minister. Wagner "began to believe I should have to renounce the whole undertaking."

However, when Wagner considered the improbability of a production of *Tannhäuser* in Germany, he "discovered the full value of the Emperor's command; for he placed the whole institute of the Opéra at my disposal, without conditions or reserve." With so much cash and talent available and Napoleon's backing, he could do whatever he pleased. He continued the rehearsals, "persuaded of the possibility of . . . an ideal performance." Such a possibility had "nowhere and never stood within my power, and it was unexpectedly to greet me here in Paris. . . . I said to myself, what care I for the Jockey Club and its ballet?" He revised the first-act Venusburg scene to incorporate the choreography.

His elation was short-lived. When rehearsals moved onto the actual stage, he began to lose confidence in the conductor and the musicians, among others. He felt "compelled to mournfully resign myself to a dull and spiritless rendering of my work."

Meanwhile, House found himself unable to buy a ticket to the first of three open rehearsals; he didn't know tickets were free, but only to invited guests. He brashly sent an imploring note to the composer, and, to his surprise, received a ticket accompanied by Wagner's card. Later, Wagner sent him tickets for the second and third rehearsals as well.

The first audience listened with respect, House reported, and the performance "could not have been rivaled in any German theater." The orchestra was superb, and the principal vocalists "seemed to defy the most censorious scrutiny." However, during the long intermissions, House heard nothing in the foyers and lobbies except a "curious unanimity of disrespect . . . a general sentiment of hostility . . . sweeping abuse. The condemnation was applied with a liberality as comprehensive as it was indiscriminate." A journalist in attendance explained, simply: "This is Paris, and that, on the stage, is Wagner."

Speaking with Parisian friends, House was assured that the disdainful conversations he had overheard did not reveal an organized conspiracy, "but everybody seemed to understand, intuitively . . . about the course to be pursued." Did Wagner know what to expect on opening night? House tried to warn him, but Wagner replied, "I have had more plots confided to me than would go to the making of a revolution," and he refused to believe that a small number of the disaffected could disrupt the performance.

Opening night arrived on March 13, and House recorded his impressions. The audience, slow in arriving, was largely silent during the overture. But before the end of the first scene "the uproar had reached such a height" that the singers and orchestra were inaudible except to those who sat nearest the stage. "There was not even a pretense of waiting to form an opinion. *Tannhäuser* was not to be condemned; it was simply not to be endured.

"And thus the performance proceeded . . . revealing nothing but a succession of fine scenery and a mass of picturesque costume. The public ear received only a continuous cacophony of shrieks, howls, shouts, and groans, diversified by imitations of wild beasts . . . and stimulated incessantly by aristocratic ruffians in the conspicuous boxes, whose favorite instruments of offense were huge keys, by means of which they filled the air with hissing shrillness, like so many whistling devils." It was later alleged that Berlioz was in the opening-night audience and "rejoiced at the German composer's humiliation."[9]

In the aftermath, some journalists claimed that the outcries were occasioned by poor performances, or by members of the Jockey Club in retaliation for the misplaced ballet. "The truth is," House wrote, "that the work was foredoomed—condemned to ignominy and outrage—because the composer was hated. The rancor was so pronounced that I believe the victim would have suffered bodily injury, as well as vicarious insult, if the wildest of the mob could have laid hands on him."

Then There Was *Tristan*

Leon Botstein contends that from the *Tannhäuser* premiere in 1861 to the death of Claude Debussy in 1918, "the debate over whether one ought to succumb to or resist Wagner's ideas defined the character of French music and aesthetics."[10]

What created the problem for French composers wasn't the premiere itself or the nasty, noisy riot that dragged Wagner's dreams through the Paris sewers. It was the audacious German himself. It was the bullying of his influential French admirers. Most of all, it was the music. Composers were confronted with a new music that threatened to leave them behind. Ernest Chausson admitted that Wagner made him feel like "an ant that comes up against a big slippery rock in his path."[11]

The *Tannhäuser* premiere was just the beginning. As the decades passed, the problem came into focus. The authority and dignity of the French were under attack, and their national pride was seriously wounded. First there was the incessant parade of Austro-German composers, a Teutonic conspiracy of music makers—Bach, Haydn, Mozart, Beethoven, Weber, Mendelssohn, Schubert, Schumann, Brahms, Bruckner, and so many others. Then the ignoble debacle of the Franco-Prussian war. Now Wagner.

The French musicians' love-hate relationship with Wagner was intense. After he saw *Rienzi* in 1869, Georges Bizet related his dazed reaction to a friend: "Wretched numbers! Admirable numbers! All in all, an astounding work, terrifically *alive*; a grandeur, an Olympian breath! Genius, immoderate, disorderly, but genius! . . . It is sublime! It's frightful! . . . The audience is perplexed!" But "few people have the courage to persist in their hatred of Wagner," Bizet believed.[12]

Granted, *Rienzi* was one of Wagner's early operas, not one of his best. But then there was *Tristan und Isolde*.

Tristan is based on a medieval legend of passion, adultery, and inevitable tragedy, whose historical antecedents recede into the mists of pre-Arthurian time, in regions from Persia to Ireland. Wagner's interest was kindled by his thwarted love affair with a married woman, Mathilde Wesendonck. Minna discovered Wagner's infidelity, and his domestic life reached new depths of misery. The participants in the love triangle were dispersed; Wagner went to Venice, then Lucerne. *Tristan* was completed in 1859. The Vienna Court Opera agreed to stage the premiere, but the work proved so difficult for the singers that the project was abandoned after more than seventy frustrating rehearsals.

Wagner's exile from Germany ended in 1861, after Paris. Three years later, Bavaria's newly crowned adolescent King Ludwig II brought Wagner to Munich, paid his debts, produced several of his operas, and promised to finance everything he would ever write. It was the fulfillment of Wagner's wildest dreams. And probably Ludwig's.

When *Tristan und Isolde* was first seen (in Munich in 1865), the critics were not happy. One found it "titillating" and "indecent." Clara Schumann said *Tristan* was "the most repugnant thing I have ever seen." But gradually support for *Tristan* grew, especially among musicians, including Verdi. Richard Strauss, after conducting *Tristan* for the first time, said, "It was the most wonderful day of my life!"

Tristan shocks and captivates the senses from the first chord—an unusual, dissonant combination of notes that Wagner repeats at key points in the opera. In Wagner's portrayal of the passionate, doomed lovers, his use of harmony, even more than melody and orchestration, generates a sexual tension that has rarely been equaled in music. He controls the intensity of the emotional pitch with daringly inventive chromaticism, dissonances that build on one another without reaching the restful cadence that our ears are conditioned to expect.

Broadly speaking, Wagner transformed nearly every aspect of opera. Before Wagner, characters sang lively or passionate arias and recitatives (dialogue set to music) interspersed with choruses, duets, dance, and orchestral interludes. But in Wagner's late operas, characters sing mostly in long, loosely structured monologues, rather than formulaic scenes, creating a musical flow that the composer liked to call "endless melody." Choruses, dancers, and ensembles are used sparingly, if at all.

Woven through the vocal melodies and orchestrations are many leitmotifs, which are brief recurring themes. Each theme is associated with a particular character, object, place, idea, or emotion, and is heard each time the character is onstage or the emotion is implied. It's more complicated than that, of course. A leitmotif may be altered or transformed in the course of the opera, or may merge with another leitmotif, or may appear fleetingly or buried deeply in the texture of the music. Leitmotifs help jog the memory and intensify the drama, contributing richly to the listener's understanding of the characters' emotions. They also help give structure to the sumptuous symphonic development that is one of Wagner's hallmarks.

For Hans von Bülow's herculean efforts in conducting the *Tristan* premiere, Wagner thanked him by stealing his wife, Cosima, and fathering several children with her. After Minna's death and Cosima's divorce, Richard and Cosima were married in 1870.

The Wagner family moved to Bayreuth, a quiet city north of Nuremberg, where the cultural life centered on a magnificent eighteenth-century Baroque opera house, one of the finest Baroque theaters in the world and, for a time, the largest opera house in Europe.

But it wasn't big enough for Wagner, so in 1876 the composer inaugurated the Bayreuth Festspielhaus, with Ludwig's financing, for the authentic production of his operas. When the composer died, seven years later, Ludwig ordered all the pianos in all his castles to be draped in black.

The Wagner Dilemma

Ultimately, Wagner's influence on the music world of the late nineteenth century was tyrannical. The overwhelming success of his operas, when they were introduced in the major European capitals, drowned out less obstreperous voices. Musicians and critics agreed that Wagner's music dramas were uniquely powerful and important, and they were persuaded by the composer and his supporters that his musical ideas would sweep away all others and lead Europe into the future.

Composers of opera were not the only ones stymied by Wagner. The tyranny affected all serious musicians who wrote so-called classical music. The greatest challenge, which cut across all genres, was to come to terms with Wagner's harmonic innovations. While Liszt was pushing at the chromatic boundaries of traditional tonal harmony, Wagner brought Lisztian tonality to precarious extremes that risked musical anarchy. Wagner's harmonic language was incongruent not only with the formal training but also the very temperament of most composers. It was a repudiation of their musical values, exile from the musical ground they had lived on all their lives.

Exacerbating the problem was Wagner's grandiose and disagreeable persona. Being known as a Wagnerite was a blot on one's own character. Jeffrey Wasson writes that Wagner's reputation stemmed from "his political and revolutionary views, his disreputable personal morality, his public condemnation of people whose behavior or religious beliefs he disdained, his self-centered, sometimes ruthless professional practices, and his egomania."[13] For the French, especially, a separate problem arose from Wagner's megalomaniacal belief in himself as the heart, soul, and voice of the German people—a superior race, he asserted. Said one critic, "Never perhaps has an artist felt himself so distinctly and persistently as the representative of a whole nation as he."[14]

It was said as early as 1905 that many operas had followed Wagner's principles, and "the failure of all would seem to indicate . . . that Wagner's art-form is one suited to his own gigantic genius, but hopeless for lesser masters."[15] Béla Bartók wrote, "Wagner solved his whole problem, and every detail of it, so perfectly that only a servile imitation of him was possible for his successors; it was almost impossible to derive from him any impulse for further development, and any kind of imitation was barren, dead from the outset."[16] Debussy had earlier come to the same conclusion.

Most late nineteenth-century composers tried to find their way to a non-Wagnerian or even an anti-Wagnerian style of music. This meant a rejection of Wagner's harmonic inventions and his large, overwrought orchestra. It meant renewing one's faith in melody, rhythm, and formal structure; restoring an earlier aesthetic of beauty; and reconnecting with the broader musical audience.

One way out of the dilemma was a return to the music of home. Music, like language itself, was a way to express national pride, solidarity, and aspirations. As the century progressed, composers who had studied music in Germany, as so many did, sought to rejuvenate their compositions with the folk music of their homelands. Anti-Wagnerian exigencies merged with the tide of nationalism and anti-imperialism that swept across much of Europe. Smetana and Dvořák mined the verdant hills and valleys of Bohemia for nuggets of authentic melody and dance rhythms. Grieg in Norway, Sibelius in Finland, Mussorgsky in Russia, Falla in Spain—all established the individuality of their music and built their international reputations, in part, on their use of native idioms. Iberian and Eastern European folk music had particular appeal, as their authentic melodies and harmonies deviate from the European standard, and their dance rhythms offer brighter colors.

If not the music of home, the music of distant lands or ancient peoples could lend a flavor that was not Wagnerian, not remotely German. The culture of the Middle East and Asia generated great interest during this period among European poets, designers, and musicians. The barest acquaintance with the exotic melodies, modal scales, and complex rhythms of the Orient was enough to inspire music that was different. But the differences were superficial: All these works of nationalism and exoticism were built on the increasingly unstable platform of Romanticism, dependent on pre-Wagnerian principles of structure and harmony. For many European composers, it seemed, whatever they wrote was held up to the standard of Wagner, and fell short. The artistic and philosophic ferment of the late nineteenth century was passing them by.

Who was clever enough to lead music out of this fetid haze? Tchaikovsky? Think again. Dvořák? Not likely. Brahms? You're kidding.

Hardly anyone would have expected the French to be resourceful enough to find a winning solution. Certainly no one would have thought that melancholy young Claude Debussy would, before the turn of the century, create a new French music. A non-Wagnerian music. Modern music.

The Sunset and the Dawn

In June 1879, a columnist for *Le Figaro*, offering encouragement to the Prix de Rome contestants then gathering, wrote: "Who knows? Perhaps you are the new musical genius that our time and our country awaits. Perhaps it will be you who will rid our ears forever of Richard Wagner, that German nightmare."[17]

Wagner exerted a strong hold on Debussy's mind from his time as a student. In 1888, with Étienne Dupin, a banker and loyal friend who paid his way, he made his first pilgrimage to Bayreuth. They saw *Die Meistersinger* and *Parsifal*. On a return visit the next year with Robert Godet, Ernest Chausson, Paul Dukas, and Dupin, he saw the same two operas, as well as *Tristan*.

Like other composers of his generation, Debussy was constantly reassessing Wagner in terms of his own music and hearing his own music through the prism of Wagner. So tangled was he in Wagner's web that when he completed *La Damoiselle élue* after his return from Bayreuth, he boasted that he had managed to keep *Parsifal* out of it. His biographer Marcel Dietschy believed it was after his second Bayreuth visit that Debussy's Wagnerphilia peaked and began to turn.[18]

Visiting his teacher Guiraud, Debussy tried to explain that Wagner's music, despite its chromaticism, was written in the classical language of Mozart, in the sense that "classical" signified music written in the major and minor keys, for example. When Guiraud protested that the "insipid, continuous music" of Wagner is nothing like Mozart, Debussy insisted that Wagner is not the opposite of Mozart, but just a "later development." Debussy went on to argue that Wagner's leitmotifs are stated and spun and developed in the time-honored symphonic manner. Debussy's point was that Wagner was part of a Classical–Romantic continuum that had come to a dead end and needed to be replaced by something new. It was a reasonable argument, but Guiraud couldn't quite buy the premise.[19]

In 1890, a friend asked Debussy what he thought of Wagner. He replied, simply, "*Tristan*." And the rest of Wagner? "The rest . . . yes, yes and no . . . It is *Tristan* that gets in the way of our work. I don't see what can be done beyond *Tristan*."[20]

"The time will shortly come when this gentleman [Wagner] gets a merry revenge on Paris," he wrote to Chausson in 1893, "and the two of us will be the sufferers, because he'll become one of those fortresses the public likes to use to block all new artistic ideas. And as, in all honesty, we can't pretend his music's bad, we shall have no option but to keep quiet."[21]

Debussy found it hard to keep quiet about Wagner. The Bayreuth genius was his obsession. He frequently wrote about Wagner in his correspondence and, beginning in 1901, in concert reviews and journal articles. He seemed to enjoy finding positive things to say and, on the other hand, decrying Wagner's influence on French music. He was a lifelong admirer of *Tristan*, and though he loathed the "false moral and religious ideals" of *Parsifal*, he said the beauty of its music was "supreme," and the opera was "incomparable and bewildering, splendid and strong... one of the loveliest monuments of sound ever raised to the serene glory of music."[22]

But "Wagner is not a good mentor for the French," he said.[23]

Debussy's most interesting argument against Wagner's influence was made in a 1908 article for *Le Figaro*.[24] He begins with comments about Rameau and laments the loss of a French tradition that Rameau's music served with charm and wit. Then he carries the argument forward. "The reason why French music forgot about Rameau for half a century... can, perhaps, be explained only by a fortuitous series of historical events." He places the blame upon the tired shoulders of "the queen, Marie Antoinette, an Austrian through and through, [who] imposed Gluck upon the French taste. As a result, our traditions were led astray, our desire for clarity drowned, and having gone through Meyerbeer, we ended up, naturally enough, with Richard Wagner. But why? Wagner was necessary for a blossoming of the art in Germany," Debussy concedes, "but who would have thought he'd ever have any success in France, and influence our way of thinking so much? If only the future can put these things into perspective, we must at least be certain of one hard fact: that there is no longer a French tradition." Reestablishing a French tradition, starting where Rameau ended, was a preoccupation that surfaced several times in Debussy's life, most urgently in the war years.

When *Pelléas et Mélisande* opened in 1902, the composer expressed the personal dilemma of his youth: "After some years of passionate pilgrimages to Bayreuth, I began to have doubts about the Wagnerian formula, or rather, it seemed to me that it was of use only in the particular case of Wagner's own genius.... One could say that he had put the final period after the music of his time, rather as Victor Hugo summed up all the poetry that had gone before. One should therefore try to be 'post-Wagner' rather than 'after Wagner.'"[25]

He often seemed to hear echoes of Wagner—even *wanted* to hear echoes of Wagner—in his own music and in the works of others. He wanted his ballet *Jeux* to have an "orchestral color illuminated as from behind, of which there are such wonderful effects in *Parsifal*." He told Stravinsky, who was not an admirer of Wagner, that *Petrushka* had a "sonorous magic . . . an orchestral infallibility that I have found only in *Parsifal*."[26]

By 1910, Debussy could say to a journalist, "I am neither revolutionizing nor demolishing anything. I am quietly forging my own way ahead, without any trace of propaganda for my ideas—as is proper for a revolutionary. I am no longer an adversary of Wagner. Wagner is a genius, but geniuses can make mistakes. Wagner pronounced himself in favor of the laws of harmony. I am for freedom. But freedom must essentially be free."[27]

"Wagner, if one may be permitted a little of the grandiloquence that suits the man, was a beautiful sunset that has been mistaken for the dawn," Debussy wrote. "There will always be periods of imitation and influence, but one can never foresee how long they will last, still less their nationality."[28]

PART II

WHAT CAN BE DONE BEYOND *TRISTAN?*

CHAPTER 5

TRANSITIONS (1887–1890)

If perchance a man of genius tries to shake off the hard yoke of tradition, he is drowned in ridicule; so the poor genius chooses to die very young, as it's the only thing he can do for which he'll receive much encouragement.

—Debussy[1]

Biographical time is different from your time and my time. Biographical time may stand still for a long while, or jump forward and backward, or it may drift through many days, years, or decades in one dizzying paragraph. While considering Debussy in the years between his leaving Rome in March 1887 and the premiere of *Prélude à "L'Après-midi d'un faune"* in December 1894, all these variants of biographical time are in play. The elements that influence his mature music may coalesce or, instead, collide and split like atoms in a particle accelerator. Each new experience merges with others in unexpected ways, then is put aside and taken up again in some new context to generate a musical molecule that Debussy can consider, or cast away, or build a career on.

During this seven-year period, Debussy was exploring, learning, listening, writing, reading. He absorbed everything that mattered to his art and filtered out most of the rest. His creative engine ran at full speed. He tried unfamiliar genres (piano concerto, string quartet, opera) while mastering more familiar forms (mélodie, cantata). He strove, as most of us do, to reconcile what he wanted to achieve with what was possible. And by 1894, he proved capable of an achievement no one could have predicted: He answered his own question— "What can be done beyond *Tristan*?"—with seductive, pastoral music from the flute of a faun. It took Debussy seven years to reach that milestone, and it will take us seven chapters to do the same.

Debussy's Early Piano Music

The first enduring works of Debussy's rich piano oeuvre emerged in the years 1887 to 1891. The four short compositions of the *Petite Suite* were the first to be published, in February 1889. Written for piano four-hands, we find little of the adventurous, mature Debussy, but nothing that sounds juvenile or inferior. The moods range from calm ("En Bateau"), to festive, happy, and giddy—adjectives that apply more or less to the other three pieces: "Cortège," "Menuet," and "Ballet."

In general, Debussy's early piano works are charming and very French, but not radically new or virtuosic. With their light textures and pastel tones, they are as welcome today in supper clubs as in concerts, and they often turn up on movie soundtracks. The best known are "Rêverie," tender as a lullaby; the two "Arabesques," the first merry and shimmering, the second flighty and impetuous; "Valse romantique," a sour waltz for a love affair that's gone on too long; and floating above them all, the ethereal, eternal "Clair de lune."

Already Debussy had developed a facility for this kind of writing that other composers might gladly have made a career of. But Debussy was never satisfied with the facile. He was striving for something that would define his work, that would help him advance toward an idiosyncratic music that didn't owe its soul to Wagner. One wonders why he waited so long to apply his boundless creativity, in a disciplined way, to the piano repertoire; after all, it was an instrument he had mastered despite the lack of support from Marmontel.

The four graceful compositions of the *Suite bergamasque* were written around 1890 but not published until 1905, when pianists were clamoring for more Debussy. Of the four, "Passepied" is Debussy's revival of a dance form that was often part of a Baroque suite. In Debussy's version, it's less a dance than a jaunty walk on a lovely day, slowing down now and then to say hello to a neighbor. "Prélude" and "Menuet" are perfect partners in the *Suite* that, like many of Debussy's piano works, recall the era of François Couperin, the great early-eighteenth-century master of the keyboard. Of course, "Clair de lune" (Moonlight) is the star of the *Suite*, an exquisite landscape bathed in glistening silver. It has no musical relationship to Debussy's two songs of the same name, except that you might hear Verlaine's spirit in it. Played by a sensitive pianist, "Clair de lune" sounds spontaneous, almost improvised. The composer's instruction to the pianist is *Andante très expressif*—play it slowly, very expressively. This and the later *Tempo rubato* give the performer license for a very personal interpretation: Play it at your own pace, slow it down here and there if it seems right, pause where you want to, reveal the whole scene with the same wonderment that Debussy might have felt.

Paradoxically, Debussy could be persnickety about the way "Clair de lune" (and everything else he wrote) had to be played—at least, if you played it in his presence. He wanted all his music performed precisely the way he indicates in his scores; and his scores were published with very specific and numerous marks for phrasing, emphasis, volume, tempo, and so on. A young concert pianist, Maurice Dumesnil, asked Debussy to coach him on how to perform his music. When the young visitor began playing "Clair de lune," Debussy found Dumesnil's triplets "too strictly in time"; the crescendos and rubato overdramatized; the arpeggios not fluid enough; the harmonic patterns not pure enough; and "in the recapitulation, the C-flat in the left hand was to be brought out, thus emphasizing the change of color."[2] So much for personal interpretations.

"Rêverie" seems to be a simple romantic bauble that the composer could have written in a few minutes before breakfast. Only when you look at the score or try to play it does it unfold its cleverness and surprises, such as this peculiar quirk: The right hand, when it introduces the melody in the third measure, begins one beat too late. (In the seventh measure the two hands find each other, and the rest of the piece is in sync.) While "Rêverie" is played today almost as often as "Clair de lune," Debussy had no fondness for it. It was sold to a publisher in 1891 but wasn't printed and released until fifteen years later. Debussy was angry. "It was a mistake to bring out the 'Rêverie,'" he told the publisher. "It is an unimportant work which was written in a great hurry . . . In other words, *it is bad*."[3] Few people would agree.

Cinq Poèmes de Charles Baudelaire

Altogether different from the *Ariettes* and other songs of the 1880s are the sumptuous *Five Songs of Charles Baudelaire*. Written at the end of the decade, they mark a turning point for Debussy and the beginning of his mature work.

The texts are from Baudelaire's 1857 collection, *Les Fleurs du mal* (The Flowers of Evil): "Le Balcon" (The Balcony), "Harmonie du soir" (Evening Harmony), "Le Jet d'eau" (The Fountain), "Recueillement" (Meditation), and "La Mort des amants" (The Death of the Lovers). These are, for lack of a better category, love songs—unhurried, made of memories and tinged with melancholy, recalling unending kisses, sighing violins, and extinguished flames. Debussy's melodies trace the inflections of French speech, as he was to do in nearly all his subsequent vocal works. The voice is entwined and integrated, far more than in his previous songs, with the piano, which provides emotional context and rich sonic textures.

William Austin suggests that the Baudelaire songs were "the most Wagnerian of all his music, unusually dense with chromatic complexities."[4] Not only was Debussy preoccupied with Wagner at the time he wrote them, but he might also have wanted to illustrate the correspondences in the works of Baudelaire and Wagner, since the French poet was a great admirer of the German composer.

Debussy was "plainly a stylist of the first water," wrote Ernest Newman, and continued:

> He had the two sure marks of style, infallibility of touch combined with simplicity of means. . . . [But] how far can this economy of material and soft transparency of substance be made to go in the expression of profounder feelings? That is the question that Debussy seems to have put to himself in the five Baudelaire songs. . . . He seems to have had an instinct that both his thought and his style were in need of expansion; and he made a brave attempt to achieve that expansion by assimilating what could be of service to him in German music. Not only do the Baudelaire songs touch depths of expression beyond anything that Debussy had reached before; not only is their harmony of a new richness and variety; they have a melodic freedom . . . and above all they reveal a rather remarkable faculty for continuous, spacious design.[5]

At the end of the 1880s, when the Baudelaire songs were written, Debussy's music was still little known to the public. There was no likelihood that the new songs would be commercially published or heard in a public concert, because, according to Vallas, "the words were of a nature to alarm the timorous, the music was calculated to frighten the average amateur, and the writing of the vocal part to dismay the singers."[6] Nevertheless, a private performance was given at the home of Ernest Chausson for a small group of friends. In 1890, thanks to Chausson and Étienne Dupin, the songs were printed in a private edition of 150 copies. Fauré called them "a work of genius," but only after

Pelléas et Mélisande created a demand for Debussy's earlier works were they commercially published.

After the Baudelaire songs, Debussy faced a difficult decision: whether to continue on the narrow path of musical growth and humiliating poverty, or try something new, a crowd-pleaser that might bring him the commercial success enjoyed by Grieg and Saint-Saëns. The result was the *Fantaisie pour piano et orchestre*—a rare failure. But he also completed the Rossetti project he'd begun in Rome, "The Blessed Damozel"—now *La Damoiselle élue*—which proved to be a stepping-stone to his greatest achievements. It was also his first period of immersion in the world of Edgar Allan Poe.

The Grim Tale of Edgar Allan Poe

"The all-enveloping sound and texture of Poe's literary surface come closer to the state of music than the work of virtually any other writer," Jack Sullivan writes. Poe's aesthetic creed was "particularly attractive to European composers: the notion that artifice and music are the way into and out of the mortal struggle he so relentlessly documents. The elaborate depiction of life's fragility through a verbal texture alive with musical sounds and images was, for Poe, the very definition of beauty in art—and art itself became the only antidote to that fragility."[7]

Debussy was the first composer to absorb Poe's literary philosophy and aesthetics and to reconceive them in musical practice. He said that Poe had a greater influence on him than any composer ever did. Ravel, who often followed Debussy into new enthusiasms, claimed that all his own music reflected Poe's literary theories. Sergei Rachmaninoff too was a disciple; among his finest compositions was a choral symphony based on a Russian translation of "The Bells." All three composers identified strongly with Poe's aesthetic theories and his tragic life.

Poe was as accursed in life as any of his characters in fiction. Born in Boston in 1809, he was orphaned at the age of two and raised by a genteel Richmond couple who added their surname, Allan, to the middle of the boy's name. They gave him a solid education but never legally adopted him. Poe's gambling debts forced him to leave the University of Virginia after a year. He won admission to West Point, but after years of quarrels, Allan, who had inherited a large fortune, disinherited his foster son. Wanting freedom to write, Poe deliberately caused trouble, was court-martialed, and was dismissed from the academy.

He published poems, but few people noticed. He wrote and published short stories, worked for a Richmond literary magazine, and gained a reputation as a relentlessly candid literary critic. At twenty-seven he married his cousin Virginia; they were a happy, devoted couple, and very poor. It was an era when few writers were paid well; for Poe's first book of collected stories, the publisher gave him no money, but twenty-five copies of his book. In 1845, the *New-York Mirror* paid Poe nine dollars for "The Raven." With its publication he was suddenly famous, and his well-attended lectures provided a new source of income.

In 1847, Virginia Poe died, adding inconsolable grief to her husband's burden of emotional pain. In 1849, stopping in Baltimore on his way to Philadelphia, he was found in a tavern, delirious and severely ill. He was hospitalized and soon died of undetermined causes that may have included alcoholism, terminal unhappiness, and a lethal dose of rotten luck. He was forty years old.

Even in death he suffered. A scurrilous obituary was written by Rufus Griswold, a rival whose works Poe had attacked in his columns. With lies and forgeries, Griswold portrayed him as an evil, depraved man, a libidinous woman-izer, a drunk. For many years Griswold's accounts were all the public knew about Poe. But Poe's legend and popularity grew on the strength of his stories and poems and, ironically, on the bad-boy mystique manufactured by Griswold.

Poe and the French Literati

Long before Poe's countrymen appreciated him, Europeans loved him, idolized him, for creating beauty from the terrors and mysteries of the psyche—"the rising to the surface of unconscious fantasies," Lockspeiser said.[8]

French writers and intellectuals became familiar with Poe's short stories after Baudelaire's translations were published in several volumes, between 1852 and 1865, with far-reaching effects on the symbolists and other writers. Mallarmé published his translation of "The Raven" in 1874 and some of Poe's other poems in 1888, and he disseminated his thoughts on Poe to the young intellectuals who gathered at his table on Tuesday evenings. Gabriel Mourey's translations of all of Poe's poems appeared in 1889, about the time he and Debussy became friends.

"Europeans were attracted to [Poe's] adolescent New World naiveté," writes Jack Sullivan. "His predilection for the unknown and the fantastic fit nicely with stereotypical European notions about America as a dangerous, mysterious place; his innovations in Gothic horror were admired and imitated" by Baudelaire and many other writers. Sullivan also notes the European fascination with "the exotic atmosphere and verbal music, the childlike fantasy so innocent of adult concerns, [and] the struggle between life and death, converting humanity's terror of mortality into an unflinching poetry of disintegration and resuscitation."[9] The supernatural, the hyperemotional, and the psychological elements in Poe were widely influential. Unlike English and American writers, the French symbolists found in Poe a consonance with their own particular aesthetics and obsessions and interpreted his work through their own perceptions. T. S. Eliot quipped that Poe was largely a creation of the French.

The symbolists considered Poe and Baudelaire progenitors of their tribe. Maeterlinck attributed to Poe "the birth in my work of a sense of mystery and the passion for the beyond."[10] Among the attractions for these writers were the supreme musicality in Poe's verse, the marvelous alliterations, internal rhymes, and flowing rhythms. Poe's essays "The Poetic Principle" and "The Philosophy of Composition" advocated concision, brevity, and the well-constructed unity of mood, atmosphere, and emotional tension that gives his poems and stories their fascination and power.

Eliot sought to explain why Poe's influence in France was so "immense," while in America and England it was "almost negligible."[11] Eliot believed that Poe's early French translators, including Baudelaire and Mallarmé, were not entirely competent in the English language and therefore were blind to the imperfections in Poe's work—his "slipshod writing" and "puerile thinking." Their translations, intentionally or not, minimize Poe's stylistic flaws and occasional incoherence, and since the translators were themselves great poets, the French reverence for Poe is, in part, thanks to the superior writing of his translators. Europeans were also attracted to Poe *because* he was American— and "American" signified a freshness of spirit, adventure, and a sublime terror of the unknown.

La Damoiselle élue

It cannot be surprising that Debussy, the most literary of composers, was drawn to Poe, the most musical poet. Debussy immersed himself in Poe's stories, gripped not only by the American's artistic vision, but also by the man himself, revealed through his writings. His lifelong fascination took a circuitous route that passed through other poets, including Baudelaire (whose translations he read), Maeterlinck, Mallarmé, and Rossetti.

There is a strong link to "The Raven" in Rossetti's poem "The Blessed Damozel." Rossetti was undoubtedly indebted to Poe's assertion, in "The Philosophy of Composition," that "the death . . . of a beautiful woman is un-questionably the most poetical topic in the world."[12] After Debussy completed *La Damoiselle élue*, his mind was churning not with Rossetti but with Poe. He told André Suarès in 1889 that he was contemplating a symphony reflecting the psychological aspects of "The Fall of the House of Usher."

Rossetti was famous as a Pre-Raphaelite artist as well as a poet. As a painter, he is best known for his stylized, sensual portraits of young women, often idealized with flaming hair and milk-white skin, their shoulders draped in lustrous velvets, their eyes focused on the unknown. One of his paintings represents the blessed damsel herself, adorned with white lilies and a halo of stars, gazing down from heaven at her lover. (This is the Romantic era, for better and worse.)

In "The Raven" Poe expresses a lover's grief on the death of his beloved, and asks a mysterious raven to tell him whether he will ever again "clasp a rare and radiant maiden whom the angels name Lenore / Quoth the Raven, 'Nevermore.'"[13]

Rossetti's "Blessed Damozel," published in 1850, is a kind of sequel. The "radiant maiden" is in heaven now, standing on "the rampart of God's house," yearning, in the cadences of Victorian adolescence, for her earthly lover to come to her:

> When round his head the aureole clings,
> And he is cloth'd in white,
> I'll take his hand and go with him
> To the deep wells of light;
> As unto a stream we will step down,
> And bathe there in God's sight.[14]

In his Debussy biography, Marcel Dietschy sees the chaste damsel as "the younger sister of Mélisande, a boarding-school Mélisande . . . an ecstatic Mélisande,"[15] and indeed the music of *La Damoiselle élue* sounds here and there like a precursor of *Pelléas et Mélisande*, especially in the quiet chordal theme that opens the piece and in the way the orchestra is used. Though some critics saw shades of *Tristan* or *Parsifal* in the score, Ernest Newman said *Damoiselle* was "the first [composition] in which we get a hint of the Debussy we were to know later—the lover of vague outlines, of half-lights, of mysterious consonances and dissonances of color."[16] There is also a blurring of tonality by avoiding traditional harmonic progressions and cadences, by using chromatic harmonies, and other means.[17] Twice there are hints of the whole-tone scale, but he hasn't yet unwound all its possibilities. Nevertheless, John R. Clevenger has said that *Damoiselle* "exudes all the warmth, refinement, and evocative splendor of which he was capable toward the end of his formative period."[18]

Gabriel Sarrazin's translation omitted several stanzas, and Debussy trimmed even more from Rossetti's poem to achieve the length and cohesion he wanted. Debussy called his work a "lyric poem," but he later referred to it in a letter to André Poniatowski as "a little oratorio which strikes a mystic and slightly pagan note."[19] It was completed late in 1888, months after Debussy's first trip to Bayreuth, where he was stunned by the beauty of *Parsifal*.

La Damoiselle élue, scored for soprano, contralto, women's chorus, and orchestra, was submitted to the Academy as an *envoi* and was accepted. It was given its first performance on April 8, 1893, by the National Society, with the solo roles sung by Julie Robert and Thérèse Roger. Two important reviews agreed that Debussy's work was original, extremely modern, and exquisite. Julien Tiersot wrote, "The music is artistically wrought, in concise and delicate forms, with a rare and subtle skill."[20] Soon after the first performance, the score was published in an edition of 160 copies. In 1902 the composer reorchestrated the work and, in the wake of his *Pelléas* triumph, it was performed in December of that year with Mary Garden as the Damoiselle. Garden repeated the performance at the Opéra-Comique two years later. In 1908, Gabriel Mourey tried to drum up support for a staged production of *Damoiselle*, presumably with mime and dance, but found little enthusiasm for the project.

Fantaisie pour piano et orchestre

Debussy's visit to Bayreuth was not his only exhilarating experience in 1889. Earlier in the summer he visited the International Exposition in Paris, where he heard the Indonesian gamelan for the first time, as well as concerts of

Russian music. Later that year, with his mind filled with Wagnerian grandiosity, Indonesian gongs, and Russian orientalism, he began writing the *Fantaisie pour piano et orchestre*. The wonder of it is that this ambitious new work was so little influenced by what he had so recently heard.

As always, Debussy was weighed down by poverty and debt, and despite his growing coterie of appreciative friends, no one of consequence, no one with influence—no one at all, it seemed to him—was interested in performing his music. Since returning from Rome he had finished and published the six *Ariettes*, but only two of the songs had been performed. *La Damoiselle élue*, the Baudelaire songs, and the *Petite Suite* were awaiting their first public performances. These were hard times. To earn a few francs he accepted commissions to make piano transcriptions of several orchestral works by Saint-Saëns.[21]

In late 1888 one of his Conservatory friends, René Chansarel, performed the Grieg Piano Concerto at the Concerts Lamoureux. Not long after, Chansarel joined Debussy at home to run through a piano four-hands version of Borodin's Symphony No. 2, with its fresh and exotic Russian flavors. Why couldn't Debussy compose a crowd-pleaser like the Grieg and Saint-Saëns concertos, with the colors of France as radiant as Borodin's Russia? Besides, he needed another large-scale work to send to the French Academy as his final *envoi*.

The *Piano Fantaisie* took him only a few months to write. Soon after completion, it was scheduled for its first concert performance on April 21, 1890, with Vincent d'Indy conducting the orchestra of the National Society. Late in the rehearsal period, d'Indy concluded that the program was too long—besides the *Fantaisie*, it was to include works by Fauré and five lesser-known composers. The conductor asked Debussy if he'd mind if only the first of the three movements was played. Yes, he minded very much. After the penultimate scheduled rehearsal, the peeved composer gathered up his scores from the music stands and walked away. The next day, in a conciliatory letter, Debussy told d'Indy, plausibly, that playing only the first movement would give listeners a "false impression" of the piece as a whole. He said that his decision to withdraw the piece was not made impulsively or in anger, and he apologized for not fulfilling his obligations toward the conductor, to whom he affirmed his gratitude and friendship.

Days after the canceled performance, Choudens bought the publication rights for 200 francs. The engravings were finished and ready for the press, thanks to the financial backing of Catulle Mendès. But Choudens didn't have enough confidence in Debussy or his score to publish it.

Debussy waited in vain for the *Fantaisie* to be reconsidered for a later National Society concert. In deciding not to submit this or any other work to the Academy to fulfill his obligation for a final *envoi*, Debussy was, in effect, saying farewell to Claude the student and good riddance to the unappreciative old men of the Academy. If the *Piano Fantaisie* was a dead end, his willingness to bury it was a new beginning, a step toward musical independence.

The *Fantaisie* can be described, in part, by what it is not. It is not, for example, a typical fantasy or "fantasia," as it was known in the days of Chopin and Liszt—usually a loosely structured piece in one movement. Debussy's *Fantaisie* is more like a late-Romantic piano concerto, in three thematically related movements. But if it has little of the improvisational feeling of a fantasy, there's also little of the virtuosic dazzle audiences expect in a concerto. Some listeners will hear in it an occasional hint of *Pelléas*, a splash or two of *La Mer*, a smidgen of Franck, and a trace of Saint-Saëns.

The first movement is structured in sonata form, like most concertos. The second movement is slow and dreamlike. In the third movement Debussy reintroduces themes from the first two movements and takes them through multiple variations, suggesting the "cyclic" symphonic form of Franck. After some noodling around, Debussy works his way toward a flashy finale. His trademark whole-tone scales and his fondness for certain dissonant chords surface now and then, but the thematic material is unremarkable, and it conjures the labor of a young composer struggling with an unfamiliar genre.

Debussy wasn't particularly proud of the *Piano Fantaisie*, yet he never quite gave up on it. He tinkered with the work from time to time, and even as late as 1909 he mentioned to Edgard Varèse that he might make major revisions to it. In fact, Debussy prohibited its performance or publication during his lifetime. He claimed he'd destroyed the score, but the marked-up proofs of the full score from Choudens's engravings were later discovered, and the *Fantaisie* received its first public hearing more than a year after Debussy's death. It was published by Fromont in 1920, and a revised version, reflecting Debussy's years of tinkering, was issued in 1968.

CHAPTER 6

IN THE SHADOW OF EIFFEL'S TOWER

There used to be—indeed, . . . there still are—some wonderful peoples who learn music as easily as one learns to breathe. Their school consists of the eternal rhythm of the sea, the wind in the leaves, and a thousand other tiny noises, which they listen to with great care. . . . And if one listens to [gamelan music] without being prejudiced by one's European ears, one will find a percussive charm that forces one to admit that our own music is not much more than a barbarous kind of noise more fit for a traveling circus.

—Debussy[1]

With memories of the Villa Medici fading quickly, Debussy eagerly consumed the diverse cultural influences flowing through Paris. His interest in the fine arts and literature were already stoked by his native curiosity and nourished by his travels abroad with Mme von Meck. His widening circle of friends in the late 1880s and early '90s brought him together with painters, sculptors, poets, and musicians who were themselves at the center of the Parisian avant-garde. Paris's International Exposition, which opened its gates on May 6, 1889, was the source of one of Debussy's most important musical discoveries.

The monumental focus of the fair was Gustave Eiffel's tower, not yet fully built but already at its full 300-meter height, revealed to all the world as a magnificent testament to the strength of iron and the power of French industry. It attracted thirty-two million visitors to the enormous Exposition fairgrounds, spreading out from the tower on the Champs de Mars. Many came just for the panoramic views of the beautiful city, never seen before from such a height. You'd pay two francs to climb to the first platform, another franc to climb to the second. Elevators weren't yet working when the fair opened.

Much more awaited fairgoers. The Exposition celebrated the centenary of the French Revolution; a replica of the Bastille, that despised prison, stood as a solemn reminder. Not to be outdone, Russia erected a copy of the Kremlin's facade and exhibited their industrial might in railroads and oil drilling. The Gallery of Machines showcased the triumphs of industry in a structure longer than four American football fields. Thomas Edison demonstrated his new phonograph machines there. And on Alexander Graham Bell's newfangled telephones you could listen to operas being performed clear across Paris. But for the first few weeks, the highly touted ventilation system wasn't yet working, and on a sunny day in May the huge glass roof of the Gallery caused sweat to pour off the thousands of brows below.[2]

Music was inescapable. A large costumed chorus sang Russian folk songs. An a cappella choir from Finland (still part of the Russian empire) sang "mysterious melodies from the North," and a group from Norway (a kingdom united with the Swedish kingdom) sang the "strange and poetic" music of their homeland. Spanish dancers and singers performed Iberian folk music centuries old.

Many of the best European orchestras and soloists played at the fair. Nikolai Rimsky-Korsakov came from Russia to conduct works by Glazunov, Borodin, and Balakirev, as well as his own music and Mussorgsky's bone-rattling *Night on Bald Mountain*. This was more Russian music, other than Tchaikovsky's, than Paris had ever heard.

The United States of America displayed 336 American paintings, including several by Thomas Eakins and John Singer Sargent, and presented a concert of American music. Many in the audience, expecting to hear music imbued, like the Russian music, with lively, native folk idioms, were disappointed that MacDowell's Second Piano Concerto sounded European in style. Those looking for an American experience would find a caricature of it elsewhere on the fairgrounds, at the Wild West Show starring Buffalo Bill and Annie Oakley.[3]

Another big attraction was the "human zoo," an awful moniker for a kind of exhibit that was popular in Europe in the last quarter of the nineteenth century. This exhibit, officially called the Village Nègre, brought crowds of Europeans into contact with non-Europeans (i.e., people of color) in a simulation of their native villages. People who had never traveled beyond their national borders could see unfamiliar faces and cultural traditions from all over the world. The particular intent of the Village Nègre was to flaunt the power and reach of French colonialism. Covering a huge area of what is now Paris's 7th arrondissement, dozens of individual "villages" were occupied by 400 men and women from several continents. There was an Egyptian bazaar and habitations of African tribes. Algerian men were furnished with weapons and dressed as native soldiers, a reminder that they had been defeated in battle by the French. Among the most fascinating displays were those from a newly consolidated colony: French Indochina. In their little ersatz villages they lived as they did in their native lands, or so a visitor might suppose. In view of all, they cooked their foods, prayed in their own ways, and performed their indigenous music.

The Annamite theater, from the Vietnamese part of French Indochina, made a strong impression on Debussy, among many others. Years later he described the performance as an "embryonic music drama" and joked that it was the forerunner of Wagner's *Ring*, but with "more gods and less scenery. . . . A frenetic little clarinet is in charge of the emotional effects, a tam-tam invokes terror, and that's all there is to it. No special theater is required, and no hidden orchestra. All that's needed is an instinctive desire for the artistic, a desire that is satisfied in the most ingenious ways and without the slightest hint of 'bad taste.'" He added, characteristically, that the Indochinese musicians never had to go to Germany for musical instruction.[4]

A dissenting critic called it "music for torturers, made to accompany the agony of prisoners."[5]

The Gamelan

What most delighted Debussy was an exhibition of Javanese village life where a gamelan troupe performed.

The gamelan is an ensemble of many instruments including bowed strings, drums, bamboo flute, wooden xylophone, zither, and the human voice. Most unusual are the metal instruments with bell-like sounds, in several tonal registers, and gongs large and small. (From the gamelan we get our word "gong.") No one instrument is more important than others in the musical hierarchy, and all are believed to be sacred. The gamelan "embraces a diversity of religious, social, political, and ceremonial functions not usually associated with Western orchestras," Arthur Wenk tells us.[6]

It's possible that Debussy had at least a passing acquaintance with the gamelan before the 1889 Exposition. The Dutch government provided the Paris Conservatory with a complete set of gamelan instruments in 1887, and Debussy might have heard what they sounded like, how they were tuned, and what timbres were produced by different combinations of instruments. But nothing could have prepared him for the multiplicity of tonalities and sonorities produced by a large group of skilled instrumentalists performing together. Nor could he have perceived some of the intricacies of gamelan music, which have since been unraveled by Western scholars.

The gamelan helped Debussy think more clearly about the distinctions between Asian and European music. For example, the gamelan does not embrace the European concept of tonal harmony, and for a young man who had spent half his years belligerently rejecting the myriad rules of harmony, this must have seemed like the door to a new world. In a letter to Pierre Louÿs, Debussy recalled how the Javanese music "contained every nuance, even the ones we no longer have names for."[7]

A gamelan performance is built around a fixed melody, which is modified and transformed in the course of the piece by slowing down or speeding up the melody, playing it upside down (inverted) or backward (retrograde), altering the rhythms, moving the melody among different instrumental groups, and so on. It may not have been apparent to Debussy and his friends that the gamelan uses two different scale types and variants of each. There are several five-note scales, including the pentatonic scale we know and identify with Asian music. There are also seven-note scales. Therefore, a gamelan orchestra requires two sets of instruments, each set tuned to a different scale.[8]

The musical structure is complex and various, its rhythmic and metric patterns divided and subdivided into sections of varying lengths in multiples of four. A single beat of a high-pitched gong marks the end of a short section; the largest section ends with the lowest-pitched gong. Thus the gong has a function that corresponds, in a way, with the cadence in Western music. The complexities are multiplied by the elaborate, fundamental use of counterpoint woven by the several instrumental groups.

The distinctive tonal quality of the gamelan provoked Debussy to reconsider the conventions of orchestral writing. For example, in his seminal *Prélude à "L'Après-midi d'un faune,"* he breaks the unity of his orchestra into several solo instruments and small groups that combine and recombine in a fascinating stream of sonorities, textures, and timbres. By doing so, he keeps the music fresh and bright while using only limited thematic material. Even in his piano works, we hear sonorities borrowed from the gamelan; "The Snow Is Dancing" imitates the sound of bells in several registers.

After his exposure to the gamelan, Debussy used exotic scales—pentatonic, whole-tone, modal—more frequently. These scales share a tendency to destabilize the listener's sense of a tonal center and are characteristic of much of Debussy's music after 1890. Coupled with the new timbres suggested by the gamelan, the lax rhythms, the rejection of established structures, and the evocative orchestrations, the untraditional scales helped Debussy differentiate his own music from that of his European predecessors and from his French contemporaries. In truth, he might well have come upon these effects in the course of his quest for fresh sonorities and techniques, without ever having heard the gamelan. But taken as a whole, as a transposition of Asian ideas into Western music, it helps explain why Pierre Boulez and many others consider Debussy to be the first composer of the Modern era.

A Whiff of This and That

The gamelan aside, it's hard to find in Debussy's mature work the influence of specific composers, even if Wagner seems occasionally to be hiding somewhere among the sharps and flats. Virtually all the composers who are said to have influenced Debussy's work had done their job and gone home in the years before he wrote *Faune*. After *Faune*, Debussy rarely sounds like anyone else, although Ravel and a few others occasionally sound like Debussy. After Debussy's death in 1918, a writer at *Le Figaro* noted that the composer succumbed to various influences "only within the limits which even the greatest musician cannot escape. Between what he has received and what he has left us there is an enormous difference, and it marks the extent of his genius."[9]

There is no question that Wagner was Debussy's preoccupation, his conundrum, even his lodestar throughout the 1880s. Lawrence Gilman wrote that Wagner taught Debussy "the potency of dissonance, of structural freedom and elasticity, of harmonic daring."[10] But these provided Debussy with a goal to strive for, rather than the means to reach the goal.

The compositions of Debussy's youth—the mélodies and the early piano music—reflect what he was taught at the Conservatory. According to Paul Vidal, Debussy's earliest affections were for the composers he studied in Marmontel's piano class, including Chopin and Schumann. At various times he admitted admiring the music of Berlioz and Édouard Lalo, and some of Delibes's theater music. He was "fond of Franck," and although he disliked Saint-Saëns's music for its sentimentality, he had praise for *Samson et Dalila*. Debussy "pretended to loathe Beethoven," Vidal writes, but in Rome "I twice saw him display enthusiasm for the German master," specifically for the Fifth Piano Concerto and the Symphony No. 2 in D Major.[11] Despite his immersion in Tchaikovsky's music during his time with Mme von Meck, he was indifferent to it.

In 1889 he noted that his favorite composers were Palestrina, Bach, and Wagner. (He once wrote that Bach was "a benevolent God to whom all musicians should offer a prayer before commencing work, to defend themselves from mediocrity.")[12] A few years later, his list included Chabrier, who came closest to achieving the sort of new French style that Debussy himself sought. At another time he told an inquirer that he liked "the whole of Wagner and Schumann, and certain pieces by Bach and Offenbach."[13]

Debussy admired Chopin's brilliant approach to pianistic technique and harmony, and he felt a vicarious personal connection to the Polish composer, who was (or wasn't) Mme Mauté's piano teacher. Near the end of his life, when illness and war curtailed his income from concertizing and publishing, Debussy happily agreed to prepare a new edition of Chopin's works for Jacques Durand, his publisher and friend. Afterward he wrote his Études, twelve little gems that challenge pianists with Chopinesque technical difficulties.

In Debussy's mature work, Gilman found traces of Liszt, Berlioz, and Brahms, and "a whiff of César Franck or Jules Massenet here and there" (but you could probably find a whiff of Franck or Massenet almost anywhere in those days). In sum, Gilman insisted, properly, on Debussy's near-absolute originality and independence.[14]

Debussy was nothing if not unpredictable in his day-to-day enthusiasms. He admired even Bizet. After reading Nietzsche's *Der Fall Wagner*, Debussy discussed it with René Peter, who recorded this exchange in a memoir.

Debussy told his young friend that Nietzsche claimed it's impossible to find in all Wagner's operas "a passage in which the human heart beats so intensely as in the final phrase of *Carmen*, in the sobbing cry of Don José, . . . facing her whom he has just stabbed." Peter, curious, asked Debussy to play the passage for him on the piano. "In a voice made more beautiful and more bitterly sad by emotion," Peter recalled, "he sang Don José's heartbroken lament," and Debussy was weeping as he sang—"Weeping, with his voice as well as his eyes." "You see, said Debussy, "I sometimes feel there is a little of that emotion, of that color, in my music. Just between us, [*Carmen*] may only be French music, but your little Bayreuth friend has got some way to go before he can twist our hearts like that!"[15]

Among all the musicians who were to stamp their ideas on Debussy's musical mind, there was one above all for whom he felt rare amazement and awe. Debussy's admiration for Mussorgsky was unbounded, and he is rightly credited with helping establish the Russian's reputation in Paris. In 1889, Robert Godet acquired a rare copy of the score of *Boris Godunov*, Mussorgsky's only completed opera, which was first performed in St Petersburg in 1874. Many musicians had been curious about the opera, but few outside of Russia had seen or heard it. Godet placed Mussorgsky's score on Debussy's piano, and for weeks after, when Godet visited he saw the score in the same place. Several years later, Debussy encountered the score again at the summer home of Ernest Chausson and performed it for his friends.

For many years Mussorgsky's music was considered a novelty—that is to say, not to be ranked with the enduring masterpieces—for its explicit use of Russian folk melodies and harmonies, and unexpected phrasing and rhythms. When Debussy was searching for a path to a non-Germanic music, he saw that Mussorgsky was miles ahead of him. In 1901, he wrote an article in praise of Mussorgsky's song cycle *The Nursery*, which portrays a young child's transactions with her nurse, her doll, her stick horse, and her cat. "It's a masterpiece," he said. "Nobody has spoken to that which is best in us with such tenderness and depth [as Mussorgsky]. Never before has such a refined sensibility expressed itself with such simple means [without] stultifying rules or artificialities."[16] We find a refined sensibility and simplicity in Debussy, too, but we can't say he owes those qualities to the Russian master. He observed in Mussorgsky's scores an unusual way of combining words and music, a naturalistic, declamatory manner which permits a wide range of expression and emotion with a minimum of fuss. He clearly had *Boris* in mind when writing *Pelléas et Mélisande*.

While considering composers who exerted an influence on Debussy and his music, we can't ignore Erik Satie. But that's a story for another chapter.

The Church Modes

In Rome, Debussy's exposure to the masses of Palestrina and Orlandus Lassus—apparently the first time he had heard Renaissance polyphony—struck a mighty chord in his musical temperament. He had studied counterpoint at the Conservatory, of course, but strict counterpoint was a dry and brittle thing for which the young student had no use. As a body of work, Debussy's music is not rich in counterpoint, as the music of Brahms or Mahler is. But in 1898, depressed and bogged down in the late stages of writing the *Nocturnes*, Debussy wrote two of the three *Chansons de Charles d'Orléans*, songs that seduce the listener with an unexpected display of counterpoint in four-part harmony.

Debussy found more sustenance in the traditions of plainsong (Gregorian chant), which suddenly became new again. The manuscripts on which the liturgical chants were notated had been lost for centuries in the dusty corners of monasteries scattered all over Europe. The Benedictine monks of the abbey of Solesmes, southwest of Paris, collected thousands of these manuscripts during the nineteenth century. After decades of study and discussion about proper interpretations and performance, the monks published the first collection of chants in 1889, the year Debussy discovered the gamelan and Mussorgsky. The chants were widely circulated in France, and Debussy must have had a special interest in them. What musicians learned from the plainsong was its exhaustive use of the medieval church modes, which dated back, some thought, to the ancient Greeks. Each of the church modes is a scale with seven tones, like major and minor scales. What differentiates one mode from another is the positioning of the half-tone and whole-tone intervals within the scale sequence, and the tone, or pitch, of the final. (The final corresponds to what we call the tonic in major and minor scales; it's usually the pitch that the melody ends on.)

Debussy employed the church modes, emancipated from the melodies and mannerisms of plainsong, in many of his compositions. The use of the old modes helped him escape the predictable sounds of major and minor; and from there he was just a step away from the Asian pentatonic scale and the whole-tone scale, which became hallmarks of the vague "Debussy sound." Other composers of his time made use of church modes; fewer used the whole-tone scale. But "Debussy was the first to adopt them deliberately as the basis of a settled manner of utterance," wrote Gilman, and he used them "with increasing consistency and devotion."[17] The piano Prélude "La Cathédrale engloutie" uses the Mixolydian mode. His early song "Il pleure dans mon coeur" employs the Lydian mode. "Fêtes," from the orchestral *Nocturnes*, blends the Dorian, Lydian, Mixolydian, and Phrygian modes seamlessly in its tonal picture of a street festival. *Pelléas et Mélisande*, too, is a veritable compendium of modes.

Of all the church modes, the Phrygian was of particular interest to Debussy. Spanish music derives its unique character from the Phrygian mode and from a variant of Phrygian introduced by gypsy tribes who migrated to Spain from

South Asia during the Middle Ages. And Debussy had a unique affinity for Spanish music. It wasn't that Spain provided a new flavor for Debussy's tonal spice box; Spanish music was an entire meal in itself, like gamelan music, that Debussy swallowed whole.

Spain is explicitly evoked in several of Debussy's works—*Ibéria*, "La Soirée dans Grenade," "La Puerta del vino," "La Sérénade interrompu"—with such richness of expression that one wonders how he learned so much about it. He was only in Spain once, for just a few hours, to see a bullfight in San Sebastian. But he knew the music of the Spanish composer Isaac Albéniz, who lived in Paris at times, around the turn of the century, and he knew Felipe Pedrell's important collections of authentic Spanish folk music. Besides, Spanish music was often heard in Paris at the time, in all its popular forms, and Debussy could have imbibed it one evening with a nice Spanish wine.

Debussy and the Visual Arts

During his two years in Rome, Debussy was immersed in one of the great art repositories of the world. At home again in Paris, his thirst for knowledge and understanding of art intensified. It was an exciting period, the beginning of the Modern era in painting, when Manet, Renoir, and the other impressionists reinvented the surface of the canvas, breaking free of hundreds of years of artistic convention.

The impressionists found new ways to paint the essence of color, light, form, and movement in the moment of sensual experience, and this became essential to their aims and methods. Rapid development of science and industry provided them with portable easels and ready-to-use oil paints in handy tubes. With these tucked under their arms, many left their stuffy studios to paint *en plein air* (outdoors), where the ever-changing characteristics of light were so much more interesting and challenging to capture on canvas. Typically, their brushstrokes were less exacting but broader, freer, more spontaneous. Colors were brighter and shattered traditional expectations.

"Debussy had a profound visual sense," Jack Sullivan writes, "and his musical impressionism (a term he deplored) owed a great deal to the shifting colors and shapes of Monet, Rodin, and especially Manet."[18] He was never especially enthusiastic about impressionist art as a genre, except for the work of Degas, who rejected the impressionist label and developed a style of his own. Debussy also admired the work of Toulouse-Lautrec, whose paintings and posters captured the eccentricities of the popular entertainers of Montmartre.

But three artists interested Debussy above all: Gustave Moreau, J. M. W. Turner, and James McNeil Whistler. He found artistic resonance in Moreau, who, in hundreds of paintings, overlaid a modern aesthetic on Renaissance themes (historical, mythological, biblical), fashioning a magical realism that presaged twentieth-century surrealism. Turner, an Englishman who preceded and influenced the impressionists, was, in Debussy's view, the greatest creator of mystery in art. His pioneering explorations of sunlight, his depictions of rivers and seas, and the deliberate vagueness of many of his images are echoed in the shimmering tonalities of the composer's *La Mer*.

But if Moreau and Turner were stimulants for Debussy's creative juices, Whistler was an intoxicant. An American in Paris, a devotee of oriental art, Whistler often gave musical titles to his portraits and landscapes: *Symphony in White, Harmony in Green and Rose*, and so on. Debussy was intrigued by Whistler's minimalist approach to color, line, and volume, most remarkably in the many atmospheric *Nocturnes*, in which Whistler turned Turner inside out with landscapes and waterscapes that explored the blues and grays of misty dusk and moonless night. Debussy explored a corresponding musical spareness in many of his works, including the piano Prélude called "Des Pas sur la neige" (Footsteps on the Snow) and in the atmospheric "Nuages" (Clouds) from *Nocturnes*.

The English book illustrator Arthur Rackham drew Debussy's admiration later in life. His daughter's playthings including Barrie's *Peter Pan in Kensington Gardens* and one or two other books illustrated by Rackham. Debussy drew inspiration from the colorful drawings when he wrote *Children's Corner* for piano, the piano Préludes, and the children's ballet, *La Boîte à joujoux*.

Asian art also fascinated Debussy. Europe was importing Chinese porcelains as early as the sixteenth century, but East–West trade increased exponentially in the nineteenth century, and frequent international expositions in the European capitals gave wide exposure to Asian cultures. By the 1880s, stylistic elements from Japanese woodblock prints, such as large areas of flat color, began to show up in the posters of Toulouse-Lautrec and the paintings of Whistler.

Debussy's interest in Asian art and artifacts seems to have derived not from serious study but more casually, from the pottery and art he saw in the homes of his wealthy friends and employers, and from visits to galleries and shops.

Several friends testified to Debussy's love of oriental knickknacks and art. Gabriel Pierné said Debussy liked to visit antiques dealers in Rome and "made a clean sweep of tiny Japanese objects which entranced him."[19] Jacques Durand remembered that in Debussy's study, circa 1906, his worktable was adorned with Japanese objets d'art. In his study was also a Hokusai woodblock print, *The Great Wave off Kanagawa*, reproduced on the cover of the published score of *La Mer* at the composer's request.

In the arts, fundamental change is often a response to a condition of stasis which occurs when long-standing rules are accepted as the only option. Philip H. Goepp, in 1913, argued that accepted rules "are never wholly true." Rules are formulas created to guide students toward an understanding of the best in art, Goepp said, represented by the masterworks that have come down to the students' generation from the past. Rules (at the Paris Conservatory, for example) are meant to guard artistic truth from misguided attacks of vulgarity and distortion. But the *essence* of an art can never be reduced to formulas. Truth in art is an organism that changes gradually, in tiny steps, sometimes in great leaps. Yesterday's truth is enshrined in a museum or a library for all to admire, to understand how things used to be, to be inspired by great craft, to learn how something has been done so as to create something new. "For the highest reaches of an art, the poet must first have grasped all that has gone before. He will not rebel before he knows the spirit of the law, nor spend himself on novelty for its own sake," wrote Goepp.[20] So it was with Debussy. He learned from Bach, Wagner, Whistler, Verlaine, and musicians from French Indonesia, edging ever nearer to something original. But he wasn't yet finished with his transformative education.

CHAPTER 7

NEW FRIENDS, NEW DIRECTIONS (1890–1893)

[Debussy's] room on the rue de Londres was a sort of a paneled garret, untidily filled with a rickety table, three cane chairs, a sort of bed and a splendid Pleyel [piano], on loan naturally. . . . In this room, where everything had to be done, Achille wrote masterpieces.

—Narcisse Lebeau[1]

Welcome now to the fin de siècle, the best years of the Belle Époque, the 1890s, the end of a turbulent, transformative century. For Debussy it would be his most productive period. He became the composer he'd always wanted to be.

He continued to meet people, to make friends, to enjoy the company of those who understood his habitual reticence and sudden raptures and who forgave his occasional irritability. Among these special people were the composer Ernest Chausson and his brother-in-law, Henri Lerolle; the painter Alfred Stevens and his family; René Peter and his brother Michel; Eugène Ysaÿe, the eminent Belgian violinist; Camille Mauclair, a young writer; and several friends from his Conservatory days, including Paul Dukas and Raymond Bonheur.

Gabriel Mourey, who first encountered Debussy around 1889, remembered his "extraordinary charm . . . which few men failed to feel." He could be disagreeable, unpleasant, or dismissive with people of artistic convictions opposed to his own, but he was "delicately kind and cordial with his friends." He was generally uncommunicative, Mourey said, "always reserved, silent, and rather mysterious, then suddenly, with a short, incisive phrase, or a precise but comprehensive word, summing up his thought in a striking perspective."[2] Mourey, a young poet who would go on to become an art historian and influential critic, had recently translated and published the first French edition of the complete poems of Edgar Allan Poe. Debussy's interest in Poe was already profound and might have been the initial spark that ignited their friendship.

They had many friends in common and shared an enthusiasm for *Parsifal* and for the paintings of Whistler and Turner.

A year earlier, Debussy was introduced to Catulle Mendès, a wealthy, influential man of letters—novelist, playwright, critic, and a leader of the Parnassian poets. Mendès had written librettos for two moderately successful operas: *Gwendoline*, with music by Chabrier, and *Isoline*, with André Messager. He had been among the small group who heard Debussy's Baudelaire songs at Chausson's house.

Rodrigue et Chimène

In April 1890, Mendès invited Debussy to compose the score for an opera called *Rodrigue et Chimène*. Mendès's libretto concerns two lovers, Rodrigo Díaz de Vivar, the eleventh-century Castilian warrior-hero known to history as El Cid, and Chimène, his betrothed. Their happiness is crushed by the tragic outcome of a fierce quarrel between their respective fathers, and in the end Rodrigue is sent off to fight the Moors.

Mendès, twenty years older than Debussy, had long been influential in the cultural life of Paris and was well connected to people who mattered. As a young man he was married briefly to Judith Gautier, herself a talented writer and the daughter of Théophile Gautier. After the dissolution of his marriage, Mendès had a long-term relationship with the composer Augusta Holmès, with whom he had five children. A tangential contribution to Mendès's enduring, if modest, renown: in 1888, Renoir painted a portrait of the three young daughters of Mendès and Holmès, with flaming golden hair, clustered around a piano. *The Daughters of Catulle Mendès* is still one of Renoir's most famous canvases.

Why Debussy accepted Mendès's proposal has been something of a mystery, but two plausible reasons surface. First, the poet had earned Debussy's gratitude when he financed the engraving of the *Fantaisie pour piano et orchestre*; and, probably more decisive, the composer supposed that he could ride to public recognition and success on the back of Mendès's celebrity. On the other hand, Mendès, like Judith Gautier and Augusta Holmès, was an outspoken champion of Wagner's music at the very time that Debussy was struggling to find a way out of the Wagner miasma. The *Rodrigue* libretto, written ten years earlier, had already been rejected by several A-list composers before it was offered to Debussy. And, yes, the Paris Opéra had only five years earlier mounted Massenet's opera *Le Cid*, based on the same characters and events, with considerable success.

Regardless, Debussy set to work on the score. While writing *Rodrigue*, which he came to despise, he also worked on projects that held much more interest for him, including his String Quartet; some songs in the new style that arose from the Baudelaire songs; an ambitious work for violin and orchestra; and an orchestral piece based on a symbolist poem by Stéphane Mallarmé.

In January 1892, Debussy wrote Robert Godet, "My life is hardship and misery thanks to this opera. Everything about it is wrong for me," and he lamented "this intolerable feeling" of being an exile in his own city, seeing only a sad, dull routine in his future.[3] Even his pens were sad and exhausted, he said. But despite all his extracurricular writing, he completed the first two acts of *Rodrigue* by August 1892. After that, his commitment to the opera deteriorated further, for he found something far more interesting: a new play by a little-known Belgian named Maurice Maeterlinck. When he saw it staged in Paris, in May 1893, he was convinced that *Pelléas et Mélisande*, not *Rodrigue*, was the opera he was meant to write.

In August 1893, Debussy played the score of *Rodrigue* for Dukas, who reported that the third and final act was nearly finished. Debussy's music wasn't at all what he was expecting, but he was impressed by the "harmonic finesse which recalls his early songs." He was doubtful about the ultimate success of the venture because he found the libretto uninteresting: "a mishmash of Parnassian bric-a-brac and Spanish barbarism."[4] But by then Debussy had already abandoned *Rodrigue* and was making sketches for the music of *Pelléas*. Mendès could not have been pleased. Years later the composer claimed he had burned the *Rodrigue* manuscript, but in fact the piano-vocal score and sketches for the orchestrations survived. Nearly a hundred years later the opera was reconstructed by the musicologist Richard Langham Smith, orchestrated by Edison Denisov, and recorded by Erata.

Living with Gaby Dupont

Before he had written a single note of *Rodrigue et Chimène*, Debussy dedicated the score to his new lover, Gabrielle Dupont, on the first page of his fresh and expectant music paper. It was April 1890. Fourteen months later, he leased an apartment—a "dank attic" costing 150 francs a year—for himself and Gaby.[5] It was the first place he could call his home. He was nearly twenty-nine years old, and he was now signing his name Claude Achille Debussy.

Gaby was born in Lisieux, a small city in Normandy, in 1866. She came from a middle-class family; her father was a factory foreman. As an adolescent, she was called "beautiful, a coquette" who loved pretty clothes, worked as a seamstress, and wished to escape the provincialism of her hometown.[6] At twenty-one she was among the multitudes migrating to Paris in search of a better life. Soon she became the mistress of the Count of Villeneuve—a black-sheep aristocrat, Dietschy calls him. The affair lasted a year, and then she found Debussy.

Gaby was then "in the prime of her beauty," wrote Victor Seroff. She had bleached-blonde hair and "a strongly pronounced personality, accented by the way she carried herself—holding herself straight and often tossing her head back, which gave her a rather haughty appearance. But it was her eyes that caught everyone's attention—blue-green 'eyes of steel,' as Debussy said, and 'deep as the sea.'" Gaby was "remarkably intelligent and well read, with a keen appreciation and taste for music and painting," wrote Victor Seroff.[7] To René Peter she was "the least frivolous blonde . . . with catlike eyes, a powerful chin, and firm opinions."[8] François Lesure adds to her list of charms "an excellent figure" and "a brilliant complexion."[9] Later in life she was said to look like a woman who might have emerged from a canvas by Toulouse-Lautrec.

She wasn't a bit like Mélisande, Peter wrote. She ran the household, such as it was—not an easy task when Debussy was earning very little and "Claude, being a large, spoilt child, . . . emptied his purse without stopping to think where the next day's dinner would come from."[10]

Gaby loved Paris, but she missed her mother and her sister Blanche and often visited them at their home in Orbec, near Lisieux. Blanche's husband disapproved of Gaby's Parisian immorality and refused to allow her lover into his house. As a result, Blanche and Gaby sometimes "met secretly while Debussy strolled along the streets of Orbec," Seroff tells us, or waited in a public garden.[11]

Though Debussy was usually in debt, often despondent, and worn down by the intense joys and agonies of composing, Gaby was completely devoted to him. She found work, when necessary, as a laundress or seamstress. He earned what he could by teaching, performing at fashionable salons, and, for his publisher, writing piano transcriptions of orchestral works by other composers. And while Debussy was absorbed with his music or his friends, Gaby would be out raising money on his treasured knickknacks at pawnshops.

For nearly eight years, with Gaby as his muse, Claude did some of his best work—the String Quartet, *Faune*, *Pelléas*, *Chansons de Bilitis*, and much of the *Nocturnes* for orchestra.

Robert Godet, the Swiss Intellectual

Robert Godet, despite his frequent sojourns abroad, was among Debussy's closest friends. The two were acquainted at least as early as 1889, when they journeyed to Bayreuth together, and they remained friends until Debussy's death. At first their meetings were casual and sometimes coincidental. Godet recalled how, during intermission at a concert, he encountered Debussy leaning against a wall, observing an older man who was scribbling in a notebook. Debussy and Godet exchanged glances, acknowledging that they both wanted to know what was in that notebook. The scribbler was Stéphane Mallarmé, and the incident seemed to have brought Godet and Debussy closer in their friendship, linked by their interest in the poet.

A musician himself, Godet was a fervent Wagnerian, like so many of their friends. He was one of the first in France to appreciate the genius of Mussorgsky and, with Jules de Brayer, sparked Debussy's lifelong enthusiasm for the Russian's idiosyncratic music.

Godet was born in 1866 in Neuchâtel, Switzerland, to a distinguished family of intellectuals and theologians. He settled in Paris and was for many years a foreign correspondent and editor for the daily newspaper *Le Temps*. Lockspeiser described Godet as "a remarkable linguist and a figure of wide culture with an encyclopedic knowledge of philosophy and the arts . . . a shy, erudite scholar, buried in his books."[12] Dietschy tells us he was a solitary person with "a proud but melancholy mind."[13]

In May 1892, Godet came to Debussy's flat, prepared to accompany him to the funeral of Ernest Guiraud, Debussy's teacher, mentor, and friend. Claude was feverish with the flu but determined to go. While he dressed, he babbled something like: "Ah, well, my dear Guiraud . . . now where's the other boot? . . . As it's you, it has to be done . . . Detachable collars really are the worst things I know . . . My dear Guiraud, there'll never be anyone like you . . . Brrr, it's cold!" Claude said there was no way he would miss his friend's funeral. He put one arm in his overcoat, then removed it, and went back to his warm bed.[14]

Godet was supremely important to Debussy as a friend, perhaps the most brilliant of his friends. Today he is almost forgotten, best known for his relationships with Debussy and the Swiss composer Ernest Bloch, and for his French translations of *Boris Godunov* and Houston Stewart Chamberlain's notorious 1899 treatise, *Foundations of the Nineteenth Century.*

André Poniatowski, the Polish Prince

One of Debussy's most interesting companions—one of the few who were not directly involved in the creation or commerce of music, literature, or art—was Prince André Poniatowski. He was about Debussy's age, a wealthy, French-born aristocrat, descended from Prince Kazimierz Poniatowski, the older brother of Stanislaus August Poniatowski (1732–1798), the last king of Poland.

During the brief time Debussy and Poniatowski were friends, in the early 1890s, the prince was well known in Paris's financial and social circles. In the decades before the First World War, he crossed the Atlantic so often that he occasionally drew the attention of the American press. According to the *New York Times*, in 1894 he was one of dozens of European noblemen, depleted of property and power after the political upheavals of the century, on the hunt for a wife—specifically, a rich American heiress who'd give up part of her fortune in return for a slightly tarnished title.[15] The *San Francisco Examiner* was indignant about the dozens of American women who had emigrated to Europe, thanks to their fathers' hard-earned dollars, on the arms of a noble husband. The newspaper listed some titles that had recently been "purchased," including the Countess of Essex, the Duchess of Manchester, and the Duchess of Rochefoucauld.[16]

The *New York Times* described the prince as "tall and unusually fine looking [with] light brown hair and a long mustache, which he twirls proudly. He dresses faultlessly and has very polished manners. He is of a somewhat literary turn of mind."[17] After at least one broken engagement, to Maud Burke (soon to be Lady Cunard), the prince married Elizabeth Sperry, daughter of a millionaire whose Sperry Flour Company was one of the largest in the west. Elizabeth's sister was wedded to the banker William Henry Crocker, one of the wealthiest men in San Francisco. Poniatowski could not have made a more propitious alliance.

In New York during the summer of 1892, the prince met with Anton Seidl, conductor of the New York Philharmonic; and with Walter Damrosch, conductor of the New York Symphony Society, for whom Andrew Carnegie built his great concert hall on Fifty-seventh Street. Poniatowski spoke to them about Debussy and his extraordinary abilities, and Seidl was interested in presenting the *Piano Fantaisie*. But of course the conductor needed to see the manuscript before scheduling the work for a fall concert, and Debussy was asked to send it.

Poniatowski hoped that if the *Fantaisie* had success in New York, he might be able to persuade Carnegie or another philanthropist to take an interest in his friend's career and support him for two or three years. Not knowing Debussy's current address, he sent his letters to Bailly's bookshop, where Debussy often stopped.

On September 9, Debussy sat down to answer his noble friend. "I thank you from the bottom of my heart, a part of me which has suffered under the Barbarians of our time. . . . Your letters reached me on September 2! Bailly didn't know my address and honestly admitted he didn't think the letters contained anything of interest—(truly, Fate can sometimes play cruel tricks!)."

Debussy was worried about the question of his "commercial value on the American market." He was totally unknown and, more problematically, his music was "on the abstruse side." He suggested the compositions he'd want New Yorkers to hear: *Trois Scènes au crépuscule* was almost complete, he said (in fact, he'd barely started on it and would ultimately abandon it); *La Damoiselle élue*, his "mystic, slightly pagan" oratorio; and the *Piano Fantaisie*.[18] He gave Godet his new address, 42 rue de Londres, where he and Gaby had taken up residence earlier in the year.

In the twenty-first century, it's hard to fathom how slowly intercontinental mail moved in those days. No airmail, no email, no text messaging—just very slow, nineteenth-century oceangoing vessels, subject to the whims of storms and currents.

Weeks passed before Debussy received a reply from his friend. Poniatowski had not received Debussy's letter of September 9, and it was too late to fit the *Fantaisie* into the orchestra's fall schedule. On October 5, Debussy answered the prince in the bleak tones that would pervade so many other letters in the course of his life:

> You can imagine the extent of the hopes aroused in me by your letters, both from the material point of view, and for the chance to give substance to my dreams. . . . I can't begin to describe the state my nerves are in. If you had in fact received my letter, then there was no possible reason for us to

lose so much time and see jeopardized the splendid plans you had laid on my behalf.

Whatever happens I shall always be grateful to you for keeping me in mind, an act of imagination in an otherwise utilitarian world, and for helping me escape from the black hole which my life has become. I shall have the courage now to keep going in spite of everything, the failures that crush even the strongest, and the enemies ranged against me. It's strange, but even though my name is almost unknown there are innumerable people who detest me.... So you can understand easily enough how much I look forward to being rid of them, once and for all, and to satisfying my great ambition— to run my own show in my own way and root out the imbecility in musical understanding that these last few years have fostered in the gentle listeners of our time.[19]

Poniatowski was exceptionally fond of Debussy. Being of a literary disposition, he asked Debussy to introduce him to Mallarmé's charmed circle, the Tuesday night Mardis, where Debussy was already a regular visitor. Their arrival at Mallarmé's apartment, Poniatowski recalled, "was greeted by a silence in which there was some element of ill humor.... How had Debussy come to make the acquaintance of this 'clubman'? And having done so, why bring him to such a gathering as this?" But Mallarmé, "the soul of urbanity, set the situation to rights. He tilted his head back and took stock of me ... then, with half-closed eyes, as though summoning up memories, he said, 'Yes, that's it!'"[20] The great poet revealed that he recognized the prince's face from a pastel drawn by their mutual friend, Edgar Degas.

Erik Satie, the Precursor

Erik Satie is frequently if dubiously called a precursor of Debussy, in the sense that the harmonies he discovered in 1887 became an integral element, a few years later, of Debussy's musical language. Satie is often credited with having brought Debussy back on track after Mendès had so thoroughly derailed his career. Satie is also often recognized as the one who tore Debussy from the altar of Wagner and turned him toward the invention of a new French music. The source of these attributions was, for the most part, Satie himself, aided later by Ravel and Jean Cocteau, though there are several grains of truth in his claims.

Debussy admired Satie's early piano pieces, which had few if any precedents in French music: the *Gymnopédies*, with their stately tempos and timeless modalities; the *Gnossiennes*, less repetitive and somewhat oriental in feeling; and especially the *Sarabandes*, in which Satie crowded his pages with ninths.[21] Unquestionably, however, during their many years of friendship Satie learned a great deal more about music from his highly trained colleague than Debussy learned from him.

It was a friendship of mutual dependence. Satie often borrowed money and sought companionship from Debussy; and Debussy gladly received Satie's admiration, affection, and steadfast loyalty, three commodities that would have sometimes been scarce in Debussy's life were it not for his odd and funny friend. Satie was a frequent dinner guest at Debussy's home in the years when Gaby Dupont, Lilly Texier, and Emma Bardac, successively, sat at the table. He enjoyed the well-prepared food and warm camaraderie of these friends, who were as near as Satie had to family. He was more or less estranged from his own family, except for his brother Conrad, by the time he and Debussy established their friendship around 1891.

"The origin of the Saties may reach back into the mists of time," Satie quipped, adding that this is something he "cannot either prove or disprove."[22] He was born in 1866 in Honfleur, a pleasant fishing town on the Normandy coast, where the Seine meets the English Channel. His mother was a London-born Scotswoman from a pious Anglican family; his father, Alfred Satie, came from a French family of Catholic Anglophobes. This uncomfortable marriage ended when Eric's mother died in 1872, after the family had moved to Paris. Young Eric had little formal education because his father didn't believe in it, though he often took his son to lectures and operettas and hired tutors to teach him music, Greek, and Latin. Eric (he adopted the Norse spelling "Erik" when he was eighteen) took piano lessons for several years, and in 1879, encouraged by his father's second wife, he entered the Paris Conservatory as a piano student. After his first exams, his teacher noted that he was "gifted but indolent."[23] The following year he was described as the laziest student in the school." In 1881 he was expelled.

Around that time, Alfred Satie, unlucky in his business ventures, set up a publishing company, primarily to sell the salon music and cabaret songs written by his new wife and himself. Eric too had begun writing music. Certainly the elder Satie hoped he could help his son catch the attention of the public, which ignored the young man with near-perfect unanimity. Before long, Alfred's publishing venture went belly-up.

In 1887, the young man (now Erik) left home and took an apartment in Montmartre, living on 1,600 francs his father had given him. His first published piece was a waltz which appeared in a music periodical. It was dubbed "Opus 62"; clearly he had already learned to use his wit to compensate for the musical experience he lacked. He wrote songs on poems by his Spanish-born friend Patrice Contamine de Latour. He studied harmony and was readmitted to the Conservatory to resume his piano studies but was again expelled; his piano teacher called him "worthless," noting that it took him three months to learn one piece, and that he had no talent for sight-reading. He enlisted in the military but was discharged a few months later with bronchitis.

Soon his father's money was spent or squandered, and he moved into a smaller Montmartre apartment, leaving his furniture behind. "There was just room for the bed," wrote Contamine, "jammed up against a piano which Satie religiously preserved through all his comings and goings, and which he never used.... He was happy there."[24]

Satie at Le Chat Noir

The three *Gymnopédies* were among Satie's earliest compositions. They remain his most famous works and are heard today on radio and television, in piano recitals, nightclubs, and films—the music is almost ubiquitous. Contamine recalled the origin: In the late 1880s he and Satie were brought to Le Chat Noir, a pioneering cabaret, by the humorist and singer Vital Hocquet (also known as Narcisse Lebeau). "Satie was already thinking of his 'Gymnopedies,'" wrote Contamine. "Truth to tell, he had so far found nothing beyond the title, but the strangeness of the word already gave it a kind of halo. The first evening that we went to the cabaret, . . . Vital Hocquet announced imposingly: 'Erik Satie, gymnopedist!' To which Rodolphe Salis, bowing as low as he could, replied, 'That's a very fine profession!'"[25]

Salis, the cabaret's owner-impresario, had recently moved his club to larger, more elaborate quarters on rue Victor-Masse to accommodate the city's writers, artists, and intellectuals who came at night to drink and talk and argue, or just to be entertained. Visitors approaching the building were met by the image of a fierce black cat, the iconic logo on the sign over the door. Up a flight of stairs was a big, crowded room where paintings, some still reeking of turpentine and varnish, hung haphazardly on the walls. Famous singers sang, piano players played, fledgling poets recited their verses. The highlight of the evening was unquestionably the performance of the shadow play, a theatrical concept derived from the ancient *ombre chinoise*. Salis recruited talented people to write the plays; to fashion the little two-dimensional characters out of tin and other scraps; and to design the intricate choreography that moved the characters around, behind a white screen, to tell the story in a naturalistic way. Clever lighting effects threw the shadow story onto the screen, and an evocative musical score established the mood and the locale. Charles de Sivry, son of Mme Mauté and friend of Verlaine, was the composer-pianist for the shadow plays, an accompanist for the singers, and an excellent improviser.

At Le Chat Noir, for a five-franc admission fee, you'd find all sorts of vice and frivolity, if that's what you came for; or music and poetry, if that was your pleasure. The randomness of the crowd provided its own excitement. A ragged student might argue with a foreign diplomat about the failures of the Third Republic. A writer and an entrepreneur, strangers until this evening, might cook up a promising stage play. A young coquette might brush off her lover, a minor marquis, with license to cause a scene if necessary. A sailor, sloshed and sweaty, might start a fight and curse outrageously, and he'd be tolerated by the management. But if a proper Englishwoman, curious, well behaved, and accompanied by a gentleman, lit a cigarette, as women were now permitted to do publicly in London, she'd be politely shown the door by Monsieur Salis.[26]

At Le Chat Noir, "Satie, who had until then been timid and reserved, gave free rein to the treasure-house of mad gaiety which lay within; the contrast between this free, unbuttoned life and the bourgeois correctness of his own showed him the silliness of certain prejudices and the hypocrisy of certain conventions, and awoke in him a distrust of platitudes and received ideas, of superficial boasting and bloated reputations," wrote Contamine de Latour. "He stopped trimming his beard and let his hair grow. . . . He forged a personal artistic style for himself. His musical education was decidedly incomplete, but he put together the things he knew and out of them manufactured a formula of his own."[27]

In 1888 Salis hired Satie as a part-time, second-string accompanist, at five francs per evening, as a stand-in for Charles de Sivry, who was sometimes too drunk to find his fingers, let alone the piano keys. Debussy, recently returned from Rome, was occasionally seen at Le Chat Noir, playing his own music without fanfare or apology.

Satie's Good Fortune

Just how and when did Satie and Debussy first meet? It's not clear. They might have crossed paths in the late 1880s, at Chat Noir or elsewhere, but they didn't get to know each other until several years later. According to Satie, writing sentimentally after Debussy's death, he and Debussy became friends after finding each other, around 1891, at a bookshop. "From the moment I saw him the first time," wrote Satie, wistfully, with a rare absence of irony or cheek, "I was drawn to him and wished to live constantly at his side. . . . We understood one another implicitly, without complicated explanations, for we had known each other— forever, it seemed. I knew him through his whole creative development . . . and I still cannot forget the emotion this music caused me; for I savored with delight its 'cloudiness', precious and new at that time."[28]

Their conversations often turned to Wagner. "I explained to Debussy the need for us French to [pry] ourselves away from the Wagnerian adventure, which did not correspond to our national aspirations, and I explained to him that I was by no means anti-Wagnerian, but that we needed to have our own music—with no sauerkraut if possible." If Satie thought he deserved credit for turning Debussy away from Wagner, he didn't know that Debussy had already been looking for a solution to the sauerkraut problem for several years before they met. "Why not use the means of representation exhibited to us by Claude Monet, Cézanne, Toulouse-Lautrec, etc.?" Satie asked.[29] And so, Satie's advice to Debussy was to learn from the great contemporary French artists. Whether or not Satie planted the idea, Debussy did indeed learn from artists—not the impressionists as much as Turner, Whistler, and the Japanese woodcut masters, none of them French.

When they met, Satie was under the spell of the charismatic Sâr Joséphin Péladan, and he became "official composer" for Péladan's Ordre de la Rose-Croix Catholique, du Temple et du Graal. For a time Debussy shared his friend's interest in the mystical and occult, though any sort of dogma or organized religion was abhorrent to him.

In 1892, Satie and Contamine wrote a bizarre three-act ballet called *Uspud*— a "Christian ballet" dedicated to the "Three Persons of the Holy Trinity." For this project, Satie composed "half a dozen musical phrases, which he called grandly 'his score,'" said Contamine.[30] One of the very few who took the work seriously was Debussy. Listening to Satie play the music at the Auberge du Clou, Debussy immediately understood the seriousness and sensitivity, the restlessness and self-mockery that hid behind "Satie's outrageous clowning," Contamine recalled, and Debussy rose to defend his friend. Later, with his penchant for mischievous provocation, Satie demanded that the director of the Paris Opéra give *Uspud* a hearing, if not a full-scale production at the Palais Garnier. When he was ignored, he challenged the director to a duel. Of course, his challenge was also ignored.

In 1893, Satie broke from Péladan and founded his own "church"—the Église Métropolitaine d'Art de Jésus Conducteur. He was its only member, and he used his exalted platform to issue screeds against those who had in some way hurt him, such as the music critic Willy (the pen name of Henry Gauthier-Villars), whom he accused of "smearing by unfair criticism and indescribable trivialities the efforts of anyone who seeks to fulfill a more useful function than his own." In another missive directed to Willy, he wrote, "Your breath stinks of lies, your mouth spreads audacity and indecency. Your depravity has caused your own downfall," and worse.[31] In return, Willy, more or less good-naturedly, poked fun at his tormentor in his newspaper columns. Satie lost interest in his church a few years after inventing it.

Collaborating with friends, Satie tried to write an opera and a Catholic mass. For a play by Péladan, *Le Fils des étoiles* (The Son of the Stars), he wrote three Préludes, the first of which is remarkable for its parade of six-note, weirdly dissonant chords consisting of intervals of fourths stacked one atop another in parallel motion; and for its staves unbroken by bar lines.[32] Debussy introduced Satie to a publisher, who issued the Préludes and many of Satie's later cabaret songs. Satie met a teenager named Maurice Ravel, who admired him and was impressed by his music. Satie twice applied for membership in the Académie Française, insisting that he deserved the honor; twice he was rejected. He fell passionately in love with an accomplished artist named Suzanne Valadon; when the affair ended six months later, he was left with a broken heart and a shattered spirit.

In 1892, Debussy cemented his friendship with this strange young man when he inscribed a copy of his songs, *Cinq Poèmes de Charles Baudelaire*: "For Erik Satie, gentle medieval composer, [who] strayed into this century to the joy of his good friend, Claude-A. Debussy."[33]

CHAPTER 8

MAETERLINCK (1891–1893)

Well, finally, as I left the Conservatoire I won the Prix de Rome.
So I went to Rome. In the beginning I was bored to death, then
gradually I began to work, and finally got along quite well. Then
I returned to France and didn't know exactly what to do with
myself, until I came across Pelléas et Mélisande.

—Debussy[1]

In August 1893, Debussy wrote a letter to Poniatowski in which he rails against composers who hijack a great work of literature only to generate an inferior opera. As an example he offers Massenet's *Werther*, from a beloved novel by Goethe. This opera, he says, satisfies the dilettante's craving for "all that is poetically empty and lyrically cheap." It's mediocre, and he deplores Massenet's "appalling habit" of subverting that which is good with trivial sentimentalities. Debussy goes on to include in his list of operatic atrocities Charles Gounod's *Faust* and Ambroise Thomas's *Hamlet*. We punish people who forge banknotes, Debussy says, yet we forgive composers who steal and degrade the literary works of others, though forgers and composers alike are doing it for their own profit. He concludes, "I should have every sympathy with an author who printed a notice on his works saying: 'It is forbidden to park your music anywhere on this book.'"[2]

There's irony as well as humor in Debussy's remarks. After all, a decade earlier he had attempted to "park his music" on Banville's *Diane au bois*. Admittedly, Banville ranks well below Goethe or Shakespeare in literary majesty. But Debussy had also taken *La Damoiselle élue* from Rossetti, had begun tinkering with a symphonic rendering of Poe's "Fall of the House of Usher," and was working on a tone poem inspired by Mallarmé's masterpiece, *L'Après-midi d'un faune*. Two years before his letter to Poniatowski, he had been told *not* to park his music on Maurice Maeterlinck's *La Princesse Maleine*. In fact, Debussy wrote very little that did not have reference to literary works; but, to his credit, he is rarely accused of subverting their spirit.

Besides reporting on musical events, there was another reason for the letter to Poniatowski. In a postscript, he adds: "I think I owe you a debt of gratitude for your generosity, which gave me at least some peace of mind."[3] The Polish prince, unable to enlist American support for Debussy, had felt a moral obligation to provide financial assistance to his impoverished friend, enough to enable him to "work in peace for a year or two."[4]

La Princesse Maleine

Just as Debussy believed literature is often "eviscerated" when transformed to opera, Maeterlinck believed a dramatic poem loses its artistic merit and becomes a mere spectacle when staged in a theater. Maeterlinck had no use for actors. Inevitably, he thought, they misinterpret the poet's words; and stagecraft cloaks the poet's ideas in a context different from the one intended. Maeterlinck preferred puppet theater, where the poet-playwright could figuratively, even literally, pull the strings of the characters, thus communicating directly with the audience. When he expressed these ideas in 1890, with his uniquely sublime hauteur, Maeterlinck had never actually had the experience he describes. He had never had anything of his own on a stage, even a small one for puppets. He had only recently completed his first play, *La Princesse Maleine*.

French audiences of the time were well attuned to the tragedies of Shakespeare, Corneille, and Racine; the comedies of Molière; the sturdy dramas of Hugo; the "well-made plays" of Sardou and Scribe; and the melodramas of Dumas *fils*. André Antoine and his Théâtre Libre would introduce Ibsen's radical realism to Paris in 1890. Maeterlinck wanted to bring something new to the theater. He was, if anything, a symbolist, and, like Debussy, he was well acquainted with the strange atmospherics of Poe's stories. His idea (perhaps borrowed from Poe) was that one single disquieting mood should permeate each of his plays from beginning to end. Another idea was silence—the strategic use of silence to enhance the drama of the moment. Samuel Beckett and Harold Pinter surely owed something to Maeterlinck.

La Princesse Maleine was published in Belgium in serial form, then as a book in December 1889. Only 185 copies were printed. Like a dark fairy tale, the play is populated by an old and feeble king, his ineffectual son (Prince Hjalmar), and a beautiful princess (Maleine), who loves the young prince but is torn from him by a fateful misunderstanding. The play is a tangle of love, jealousy, cowardice, ambition, and destiny that ends in murder and suicide.

Maeterlinck sent a copy to Mallarmé, who passed it on to a young man named Octave Mirbeau, an avant-garde novelist and literary critic whose fame eventually rivaled Maeterlinck's. In the influential pages of *Le Figaro*, on August 24, 1890, Mirbeau praised the play with such sincere but preposterous hyperbole that the literary world was shocked into an immediate recognition of a new voice in its midst. He wrote:

> I know nothing whatever of Maurice Maeterlinck. . . . I only know that no man is more unknown than he; and I know that he has produced a master-piece . . . a masterpiece, such as all honest and struggling artists, sometimes, in their moments of enthusiasm, have dreamed of writing and such as no one of them has written until now. In short, Monsieur Maeterlinck has given us a work more richly charged with genius than any of our time, and also the most extraordinary and the most simple, comparable—shall I dare to say?—superior in beauty, to what is most beautiful in Shakespeare.[5]

Maeterlinck was born in August 1862 in Ghent, a medieval Flemish city dominated by formidable guild houses and a gloomy castle. That he was born seven days after Debussy is a coincidence much remarked on, especially as they couldn't have been further apart in temperament. To please his family he studied law, but he was far more interested in literature. In 1889, he published a book of melancholy verses, *Serres chaudes*, as well as *Maleine*. He characterized the latter work as "a play in the spirit of Shakespeare for a puppet theater."[6] *Maleine*, then, was to have been a puppet play.

By the time he read the play, Debussy was at work on *Rodrigue et Chimène*, which held no artistic resonance for him and was a waste of his time. *La Princesse Maleine* caught his attention and must have set his heart racing. It was just the sort of play he was looking for, with "characters at the mercy of destiny," as he described to Guiraud in conversations two years earlier. Maeterlinck was his poet "who only hints at what is to be said."

Maeterlinck's chief contribution to modern drama was "his insistence upon depicting man's attitude in the presence of eternity and mystery—to attempt to unveil the eternal character hidden under the accidental characteristics of the lover, the father, and the husband," wrote Montrose Moses, an American author and scholar.[7] Behind the story performed on the stage lurks the real drama; behind the words lies the true meaning of life. Maeterlinck represented the spiritual restlessness of his age, fully conscious of an unseen force but not quite sure of its direction or its expression.

Maeterlinck invented a new language, a language of "short, childlike sentences, exclamations, frequent questions, endless repetitions, implications between the lines, silences, *non sequiturs*—in short, a language resembling poetry more than prose which transformed dialogue into incantation and drama into ritual," Arthur Wenk wrote.[8] Richard Hovey remarked that Maeterlinck was different from other symbolist writers of his day by "the peculiarity of his technique and the limitation of his emotional range." His vocabulary, Hovey said, "is hardly more copious than that of a peasant," and his rhetorical repetition, while not unusual in normal conversation, is pushed to extreme limits. With respect to Maeterlinck's limited emotional range, his only use of humor is "the hysterical mirth of tragic crises, the grin on the everlasting skull."[9] In a climactic scene near the end of *Maleine*, when the nurse and the prince enter a room where Maleine lies dead, the repetitions seem comical (at least, on the page):

PRINCE: What now? What now? What is the matter?

NURSE: She is dead! I tell you, she is dead! She is dead! She is dead!

PRINCE: She is dead? Maleine dead!

NURSE: Yes! yes! yes! yes! yes! Come in! Come in! Come in!

PRINCE: Dead? Is she dead?

NURSE: Maleine! Maleine! Maleine! She is cold! I believe she is cold!

PRINCE: She is cold.

NURSE: Oh! Oh! Oh![10]

Could the redundancies, tiresome to read and perhaps difficult to perform, be turned to high drama by a savvy composer? All those interwoven repetitions had a certain correspondence with familiar musical tropes and rhythms. For a reader like Debussy, the words sang.

In June 1891, Debussy wrote to Maeterlinck through an intermediary asking permission to use *Maleine* for an opera, but he was refused—the poet had promised it to Vincent d'Indy. Regardless, Debussy remained hooked on Maeterlinck. Two years later, he was in attendance for the first Paris performance of the author's new play, *Pelléas et Mélisande*.

Pelléas et Mélisande: The Play

Even before he saw *Pelléas et Mélisande*, Debussy bought a copy of the script and began having "secret thoughts" of appropriate music. Various events intruded on his thoughts. *La Damoiselle élue* was finally given its first performance by the National Society on April 8, 1893. One of the solo vocalists was Thérèse Roger, for whom he developed a strong attraction. Two weeks later Debussy was elected to membership in the National Society, a mark of honor and prestige, giving him some assurance that his future works would be heard at the Society's prestigious concerts. Catulle Mendès recruited him to perform, with six singers and another pianist, music from *Das Rheingold* and *Die Walküre* to illustrate Mendès's Wagner lectures. Debussy found it distasteful to perform in public, but he was paid enough to overcome his reluctance. On May 12, Debussy attended the French premiere of *Die Walküre* with Mallarmé.

Five days later he took his seat at the small Théâtre des Bouffes-Parisièns, where *Pelléas* was given its one and, for the time being, only performance. According to the play's young director, Aurélien Lugné-Poë, Camille Mauclair had already suggested to Debussy that *Pelléas* would make a fine opera. Maeterlinck was little known in Paris except in symbolist circles, but the play was given enough advance publicity to attract many of the city's cultural vanguard, including Henri de Régnier, who helped fund the production. Critics were not invited, but some came anyway.

Lugné-Poë, who championed the plays of symbolists, staged *Pelléas* as "experimental theater," with theatrical eccentricities that flummoxed many in the audience. The scenery was stylized, and the characters moved slowly, as in a dream play. The actors spoke their lines in uninflected monotones. The stage was kept quite dark and was further obscured by a thin gauze curtain that distanced the audience from the players. Lugné-Poë understood Maeterlinck's deliberate use of silence and emphasized it.

At Maeterlinck's suggestion, the actors were dressed in faux-medieval costumes, though no time or place is indicated in the script. He even specified the shop where the right fabric could be found. Yet he arrived in Paris only five days before the performance and went to only two rehearsals. The director said that Maeterlinck was extremely nervous and acted "like a dog being whipped, at rehearsals of which he understood nothing."[11] How much simpler it is when the actors are puppets!

"Rather childish and often banal," wrote one critic, who said *Pelléas* might have been delightful if seen on a puppet stage.[12] Though the reviews were mostly savage, the play was by some measures a success. It helped establish the bona fides of the author and director among their peers, and it convinced Debussy that his instinct was sound: *Pelléas* would be his first opera. Almost immediately he began sketching musical themes and soon was working on whole scenes.

In August 1893, Maeterlinck received a letter from Régnier:

> My friend Claude Debussy, who is a most sensitive and ingenious musician, has begun to compose some charming music for *Pelléas et Mélisande*, delicately adorning the text while scrupulously respecting it. He would like your authorization to proceed before continuing further with this considerable task.[13]

"A tiny footpath, abandoned"

In 1893, Debussy became a close friend of Ernest Chausson, a fellow composer about seven years older and well settled into a comfortable life of family, work, art, and a social position that Debussy may have envied. They had known each other at least since August 1889, when they traveled together with other friends to Bayreuth. The following February, Debussy's Baudelaire songs were given a private performance at Chausson's house. It was often Chausson who helped pay Debussy's bills when Poniatowski's generosity was not enough.

In his frequent letters to Chausson we learn much of what we know about Debussy's thoughts and activities in 1893–1894. "I'm very fond of you," Debussy wrote in May 1893, not long after their friendship began. "I feel sad at being separated from you." Debussy enjoyed sharing confidences with Chausson, he wrote, while his other friends keep their true thoughts hidden, like people who surround their beautiful gardens with fences. "Long live those who open their gates wide!"[14] Two weeks later he writes that he's "extremely bored" without Chausson there. "I feel like a tiny footpath, abandoned by everyone for the main road."[15]

In early July, Chausson and his brother-in-law Henri Lerolle, a painter, arranged for Debussy and Gaby to move into a more congenial apartment at

10 rue Gustave-Doré. They paid the rent and other expenses and gave Debussy enough money to allow him to continue writing. Yet Debussy tells Chausson that he is depressed. He can't "overcome this black melancholy which makes me dissatisfied with everything I write. . . . What makes it worse is that it means fighting against myself, and that's a battle I don't always win."[16] Debussy suffered from depression numerous times—while he was in Rome, for example, and after Gaby left him in 1898, and when he was suffering from cancer in his last years—and there's no reason to think that his depressions were trivial, despite his dramatic mélange of metaphors. In letters written during those melancholy phases, he described many of its symptoms—a pervasive sadness, extreme boredom, corrosive self-doubt, an inability to work, anhedonia, feelings of abandonment and alienation—long before depression was widely recognized and treated as a medical condition.

Early in the summer of 1893, he was juggling several important unfinished works, including *Faune*, the String Quartet, the *Proses lyriques* (four songs for which he wrote lyrics as well as music), and now sketches for an opera on *Pelléas et Mélisande*. There was also an evolving idea, an orchestral piece called *Trois Scènes au crépuscule* (Three Twilight Scenes), inspired by poems of Henri de Régnier. Nevertheless, twice he found time to visit Chausson at his rented country chateau on the Marne. With him were Raymond Bonheur, an old friend from the Conservatory, and Lerolle.

Chausson had managed to get hold of the score of Mussorgsky's *Boris Godunov*, which was still unknown in France. It was an important event for Debussy, who had seen the score four years earlier, thanks to Robert Godet, and was delighted to see it again. "We were burning to get to know *Boris*," Bonheur wrote. "For hours at a time, over entire evenings, Debussy would be at the piano, initiating us into this amazing work."[17] *Boris* did not reach a French stage until 1908, but Mussorgsky's opera was to have a profound effect on the way Debussy used the voice and orchestra in *Pelléas*.

In his memoir, Bonheur gives us an extensive, valuable impression of his friend at various stages of his life. In the years before the Prix de Rome, he seemed to be "withdrawn and rather distant, with a marked predilection for everything that was rare and precious, but a singularly attractive person none the less, despite a certain brusqueness on first acquaintance." When Debussy returned from Rome, Bonheur drew a more detailed portrait. "One noticed his forehead, that powerful forehead with the strange faun-like cast, which he thrust ahead of him like the prow of a ship; his brown eyes, hidden away beneath the frowning eyebrows and obstinately fixed on a point far away directly in front of him, while his index finger in a characteristic gesture tapped the ash from his cigarette. As often happens with people who are not satisfied with clichés and think for themselves, his speech was hesitant and he generally expressed himself in a voice that lisped slightly, in short, incomplete phrases, in monosyllables sometimes, trying his hardest to find a word supple enough to get across the nuance of an impression or a point of view.

"With his dark hair, sensual nose, and pale face surrounded by a light fringe of beard . . . you could easily imagine him in the lavish surroundings of some Venetian palace," wrote Bonheur. "Born poor, he entered life with the tastes, needs and carefree attitudes of a great lord. Nothing upset him more than to be taken for a professional man, and the very phrase filled him with a secret horror." At the wedding of a friend, Bonheur saw Debussy signing the register, and to designate his profession he wrote not "musician," but "gardener."[18]

The Road to Allemonde

In response to Régnier's letter introducing Debussy as "a most sensitive and ingenious musician," Maeterlinck's approval came swiftly and "wholeheartedly" in early August.[19]

But a month later Debussy was still complaining to Chausson about "the sadness of my existence . . . Sometimes my days are dull, dark, and soundless like those of a hero from Edgar Allan Poe. . . . The bell has tolled now to mark my thirty-first year," he wrote, and he still has no confidence in his musical instincts; he still doesn't know how to write a masterpiece.[20]

He then mentions that Régnier had visited; Debussy played him the unfinished *Prélude à "L'Après-midi d'un faune,"* and Régnier thought the music was "hot as a furnace." The poet spoke to him about certain words in the French language that had become degraded by overuse, "and I thought to myself it was much the same with certain chords whose sound has been cheapened by use in mass-produced music." Music should have been a "hermetical science" so hard to penetrate that it would discourage "the herd of people" who treat it as casually as a handkerchief. He wryly proposes a "Society of Musical Esotericism" that would exclude those whose musical tastes were unacceptable. He has just finished the last of the four *Proses lyriques* and dedicated it to his new friend,

Henri Lerolle. He has been "working furiously" and notes, in a postscript, that he is finishing a scene from *Pelléas et Mélisande*—Act 4, Scene 4.[21]

An important new link in his professional life was forged when André Messager, a composer of light operas and operettas, "in some inexplicable surge of friendship" invited him to dinner.[22] (Five years later, as the new music director of the Opéra-Comique, Messager would express interest in producing *Pelléas*, and in 1902 he would conduct the first performances.)

On October 23, Debussy told Chausson that he'd sold the publishing rights to his String Quartet to Durand for a measly 250 francs.[23] The Quartet was dedicated to Chausson, representing "the beginning of a friendship which, in time, is due to become the best and most profound of my life."[24] Alas, when Chausson later expressed his dislike for the music, Debussy rerouted the dedication to Eugène Ysaÿe's quartet, who played its first performance. The "profound" friendship of Chausson and Debussy would not survive another year.

Early in November, Debussy traveled to Belgium to meet with Maeterlinck at his home in Ghent. With Debussy was a new friend, Pierre Louÿs, who had been born in that city. Debussy's description of the fateful meeting, in a letter to Chausson, takes on an element of farce:

> To begin with, [Maeterlinck] behaved like a girl being introduced to her future husband, but then he thawed out and was charming. When he talked about the theater he was absolutely fascinating. For *Pelléas* he's allowing me to make whatever cuts I like and went as far as to suggest some important ones—*extremely useful ones even!* He claims he doesn't understand anything about music and wanders through a Beethoven symphony like a blind man through a museum. But in fact he's all right and talks in the most entrancing and simple way about his extraordinary discoveries. At one point I thanked him for entrusting *Pelléas* to my care, and he did his best to demonstrate that *he* was the one who ought to be grateful because I was being kind enough to set his words to music![25]

Louÿs had a rather different take on the event, conjuring another kind of comedy. While Debussy describes a lively, if awkward, conversation with Maeterlinck, Louÿs describes a meeting of two extremely shy men. Louÿs was forced to speak for Debussy, he says, because the composer was too timid or anxious to express himself; and because Maeterlinck was so shy that he hardly responded at all, Louÿs spoke for the poet too. With no other reliable witness on record, we can only imagine how the meeting actually went. But Debussy's reticence, especially when he was outside his circle of friends, was well known. And Maeterlinck's exceptional shyness with strangers and horror of confrontation are often mentioned in Georgette Leblanc's memoir, as is his indifference to music. His gratitude with regard to Debussy's interest is plausible since, though his parents were well off, Maeterlinck had little income from his writing before this meeting took place. His *Pelléas* had been given only one performance, and there was no prospect of another. He was less well known in Paris's artistic circles than Debussy, and at least one highly esteemed acquaintance, Régnier, had taken the trouble to encourage his participation in this unexpected and exotic project.

So let Debussy write his opera. What harm could come of it?

CHAPTER 9

THE DEBUSSY FESTIVAL (1893–1894)

Bounding rhythms, violent harmonic jerks, alternating with languid melodies, . . . copious floods of rich, sustained harmonies that evoke the memory of the gamelan. . . . [Debussy's String Quartet] is very distingué, *but one does not know how to take hold of it. It is more like a hallucination than a dream. Is it a work? One hardly knows. Is it music? Perhaps so.*

—Maurice Kufferath (1894)[1]

Dietschy called 1893 "Debussy's decisive year, fertile and fertilizing, a dawning."[2] On the composer's neatly arranged worktable were all the major projects of his next nine years. He was well along on the composition of *Faune*. He worked intermittently on what would eventually emerge as the orchestral *Nocturnes*. He finished the four *Proses lyriques*. He discovered *Pelléas et Mélisande*, secured permission from the playwright, and began to sketch out scenes.

He had never been surrounded with so many supportive people, including Godet and Poniatowski. But Debussy's closest and most constant friend, for most of the next decade, was Pierre Louÿs.

Pierre Louÿs

According to his biographer, H. P. Clive, Louÿs most likely became acquainted with Debussy late in 1892, possibly at Mallarmé's Tuesday salons. When they met, Louÿs was twenty-two years old and had already insinuated himself into the lives of some of the greatest writers of France and England. At the end of the century his writings were more popular than those of his literary friends.

In November of the year he met Debussy, Louÿs was conscripted into the military for a year of compulsory service, but he soon developed bronchitis and was issued a medical discharge in early February 1893. The disease recurred every winter for many years, often prompting long sojourns in the warmth of

Spain and North Africa. Debussy's letters to Louÿs document how much the younger man was missed during those winters.

Pierre-Philippe Louis was born in Ghent, where his family had fled temporarily to escape the Prussian invasion of France. His mother died when he was nine, and five years later he lost an older brother, Paul, to tuberculosis. He had been very close to Paul and grieved profoundly; for many years he believed he too would die young of the same disease. His father, a lawyer, was in his seventies at the time, and was neither attentive to his children nor affectionate. Pierre was afraid of him, so it was natural that the boy turned to his older stepbrother Georges Louis for love, guidance, and encouragement. He grew closer to Georges, and more emotionally and financially dependent, well into his adulthood.

Pierre was educated at the excellent École Alsacienne in Paris, where his rival as star of the French composition class was André Gide. Before long, the two began a friendship that lasted seven formative years. Gide later described Louÿs (he adopted the eccentric spelling in 1890) as a brilliant young man with a certain elegance—in his profile, his charm, his gestures—but with an undercurrent of melancholy. "Endowed with a vast curiosity and, in particular, with a passionate interest in literature, music, and fine art, Louÿs lived almost permanently in a state of feverish intellectual excitement," Clive wrote. "He was himself amused by his propensity to 'catch fire.' . . . His eagerness to share his excitement with his friends made him appear domineering at times, so anxious was he to elicit a response as deeply felt as his own."[3]

In 1889 Louÿs enrolled at the Sorbonne, but he shirked his studies in favor of literary pursuits and soon dropped out. Gide and Louÿs alike longed for artistic fulfillment. For Louÿs, beauty, revealed through literary form, was the supreme artistic ideal, rather than truth, morality, or other intellectual notions. Gide was more concerned with lofty ideas, and he adopted a plain, nonliterary language to express them. Like Banville, Louÿs considered music the perfect vehicle for artistic expression, and in his poetry he emphasized rhythm, rather than rhyme, to make his verses "essentially musical." His ideal poem would be blank verse, almost prose, but with rhythmic structure. He believed that by mastering verse in this way, he would be prepared to write prose, his ultimate goal.

A poem by Louÿs (he pronounced his new name "loo-*ees*") was published in a small journal, and he deliberately set out to widen his circle of literary friends, an enterprise for which he had an impressive talent and ample success. In May 1890, he journeyed to Montpellier to attend a festive celebration of the

600th anniversary of the city's university; there he and Paul Valéry, kindred spirits, began a lifelong friendship. Louÿs soon became acquainted with Mallarmé, Verlaine, and José-Maria de Heredia, a Cuban-born French poet then at the height of his fame.

Heredia had three daughters, and Louÿs found Marie, the ravishingly beautiful middle daughter, especially alluring, as did Régnier, Proust, and several other young men. But someone else had already stolen Louÿs's heart; he was passionately in love with a young woman named Marie Chardon. With his sister as intermediary, he proposed marriage; the offer, while not rejected, was met with a number of onerous conditions set by her father, and Louÿs later withdrew his proposal.

Gide was jealous of Louÿs's new comrades. An ascetic himself, he disapproved of his old school chum's lustful indulgences, and many accusatory letters were exchanged between them. Louÿs was enjoying the life of a Parisian bon vivant, welcomed at the homes and salons of the rich, famous, or merely literary.

For a brief period Louÿs was a friend of Oscar Wilde. When they first met, in Paris in 1891, Wilde had recently made a splash with his controversial novel *The Picture of Dorian Gray*, but had not yet found success as a playwright. A year later Louÿs was visiting London when Wilde invited him to a performance of *Lady Windermere's Fan*, and their friendship was sealed.

Wilde was writing his play *Salome* in French, since he had no chance of getting his blasphemies past the London censors, and needed help. He called on Louÿs to fine-tune the script, sharpen the French idioms, and give the dialogue some of the tone and color, and especially the musicality, of Maeterlinck's *Princesse Maleine*. In February 1893, the French edition of *Salome* was published, dedicated "to my friend Pierre Louÿs." Louÿs's brother Georges gave a dinner party at which Wilde, Debussy, Gide, Régnier, and Heredia were among the guests, as well as Georges's friends from the diplomatic corps.

In April, Louÿs visited London briefly, and he was "bothered a little" by the behavior of Wilde and his friends, he told his brother. Wilde's affair with Lord Alfred Douglas was whispered about in society, even in Paris. Louÿs, who had been unaware of this chapter of Wilde's private life, was afraid he'd be tainted by his association with the brilliant writer. The proof of their friendship was out there in black and white, in the dedication to *Salome*. Georges Louis advised his brother to break off his friendship with Wilde immediately, and he did.

A year or more passed, during which Louÿs's *Chansons de Bilitis* was published and widely praised. In the spring of 1895 his writing career was on the cusp of success when the Wilde-Douglas scandal erupted in the courts and the press, casting a noxious odor over England. The trial of Oscar Wilde versus Lord Queensberry brought to light a poem Louÿs had written in 1893—a versification, in French, of an erotic love letter written by Wilde to Douglas, the son of Lord Queensberry; the poem, "Hyacinthe," was published, with Louÿs's byline, in an Oxford undergraduate magazine edited by Douglas. Whether Louÿs wrote the poem at Wilde's request is not clear, but when the poem was introduced at the trial, Wilde acknowledged the young French poet as "a friend of mine." Louÿs was afraid his reputation would be tarnished by the notoriety; but though Wilde was ultimately sent to jail, and Douglas into exile, Louÿs emerged clean.[4]

Georges Louis, like many of his ancestors, was a civil servant and held important positions in various French ministries. When he took a diplomatic post in Cairo, Pierre, having lived *chez* Georges for years, leased an apartment in the rue Rembrandt. He filled the rooms with fine furnishings and gave lavish parties, funded by a bequest of 300,000 francs from his late father. It was during this time that he and Debussy became friends, bound together by their visit to Maeterlinck; their common interest in symbolist writing, contemporary art, and music; and their appreciation of the excellent cuisine and other pleasures of Paris.

For a couple of months after Ghent, Debussy and Louÿs were nearly insepa-rable. It helped that Louÿs had some pocket money, because Debussy was always poor. Claude, who was eight years older, was for Pierre the sturdy, sensible big brother (a substitute for Georges) who could keep him grounded, safe, and loved. Pierre, for Debussy, was a trusted, loyal, intellectually acute friend who could explain the mysteries of symbolism and, with his greater worldliness, might help interpret the turbulent pulses of a woman's heart. Louÿs's exuberance and enthusiasm were sunlight for the composer's "black melancholy."

Often, when Louÿs was away from Paris, Debussy was "most miserable" and depressed: "I would like to have you by my side, for you are the only one in whom my friendship has confidence."[5] By 1903 both friends were married, and they hadn't seen each other for more than a year. Debussy told Louÿs he'd prefer "one good handshake" to all the letters they occasionally exchanged; and he said that of all his friends, Louÿs was the one he "certainly loved the most."[6]

The String Quartet

It is said that Debussy was inspired to write his Quartet after hearing Grieg's String Quartet in G Minor performed at National Society concerts in 1887 and 1889, or César Franck's String Quartet in 1890. It was an era when French composers wrote few chamber works compared with the Germans, and the National Society encouraged homegrown composers to produce more of them. The String Quartet was his first chamber piece since the Trio written for Mme von Meck.

Debussy was ready for a breakthrough. He was recovering from two major creative failures: the *Piano Fantaisie*, which he suppressed, and the opera *Rodrigue et Chimène*, which he abandoned. These two works had been intended to vault him to greater popular success among audiences who generally preferred Grieg and Massenet to the harmonic complexities that sprang so naturally from Debussy's mind. In the String Quartet, he put aside all considerations of "what the public wanted," and, if he provided instead what the National Society wanted (i.e., chamber music), he was at the same time heading into territory he was happy to visit.

Debussy told Poniatowski in February 1893 that he'd finished the Quartet. In July he was still working on it; the last movement was written over and over again. But by November the Quartet was finally completed. On his way to Ghent to meet with Maeterlinck, he first stopped in Brussels to visit with Ysaÿe, and in one evening he performed for the violinist the Baudelaire songs, *La Damoiselle élue*, and his sketches for *Pelléas*. Ysaÿe liked the new String Quartet and gave it to the other members of his quartet to study.

The piece had its first hearing a few weeks later, performed by the Ysaÿe Quartet. In the National Society audience, as always, were the musical elite and amateur musicians who valued above all else the kind of music Debussy had deliberately turned his back on—the quartets of Haydn, Mozart, and Beethoven. For this audience, even the chamber works of Saint-Saëns and Fauré were contemptible, and indeed most listeners heard Debussy's new Quartet "as a freakish fancy," wrote Léon Vallas. "They were utterly disconcerted by the novelty of the details and bewildered by the harmonic daring of this revolutionary style of writing, by all the effects that seemed to them like a fine powdering of sounds. Consequently, they could not immediately grasp the paradoxical classicisms that were to be found in [Debussy's Quartet], especially in its form and structure." Among these classic elements, Vallas points to the sonata form of the first movement and to the Finale, which bears "an unexpected likeness to Beethoven and Franck."[7] The audience had failed to see that the plan of the entire Quartet is cyclical, in the manner that Franck had famously made his own.

Most of the critics didn't understand the Quartet enough to venture an opinion about it. One critic wrote that the Quartet was "bewildering, full of originality and charm . . . but diabolically difficult, and I must confess I did not greatly relish the middle of the Andante."[8]

The following year, the Guarnieri Quartet played the piece, and Dukas published a glowing review, calling Debussy

> one of the most gifted and original artists of the younger generation of musicians. . . . The melodic essence of the work is concentrated, but of a rich flavor. It impregnates the harmonic tissue with a deep, original poetic quality. The harmony itself, although greatly daring, is never rough or hard. Debussy takes a particular delight in successions of rich chords that are dissonant without being crude, and more harmonious in their complexity than any consonances could be; over them, his melody proceeds as on a sumptuous, skillfully designed carpet of strange coloring that contains no violent or discordant tints. One single theme forms the basis of all the movements of the work. Some of the transformations it undergoes have an unexpected charm that is particularly fascinating.[9]

Taking up Dukas's "one single theme," Vallas wrote, "Thanks to the musicographer's magnifying glass, we can discover the origin of [all] the melodic elements in one insignificant triplet figure of prodigious fecundity."[10]

In the repertoire of string quartets, from Haydn to the present, there's nothing quite like Debussy's. There's an ease about it, a freshness that doesn't diminish with multiple hearings. There's also an early taste of modernism, an originality that probably caught even the composer by surprise. The Quartet was the first major work of Debussy's musical maturity, and his first masterpiece. His incomplete knowledge, at the time, of the technical limitations and aural possibilities of an ensemble of stringed instruments makes his Quartet all the more unexpected and admirable. It would be the last major chamber piece he would write until his dying years.

Dukas, in his review, pinpointed some of the key characteristics of Debussy's emerging style: the harmonies are daring but never grating; the innovative chords are dissonant but never crude or inharmonious. Above all is the notion that, especially in the Quartet, his melodies ride on "a sumptuous, skillfully designed carpet of strange coloring." We would hear these qualities in nearly all his future symphonic and piano works until the piano Préludes of 1909–1913, when a new simplicity, austerity, and emotional edginess brought his music closer to the Modern paradigm then emerging in the works of Stravinsky and Bartók.

Debussy's String Quartet has fascinated music scholars for more than a century. And just as a great painting by Rembrandt shows us something new every time we see it, the Quartet has exposed its intricacies over time. Surprisingly, the work has been linked not only to Beethoven and Franck, principally in its structural design, but also, at its very core, to Wagner. The thematic material and its harmonic underpinnings make extensive and systematic use of the famous "Tristan chord"—the chord that creates the ominous tension at the beginning of Wagner's opera and throughout. It is known to musicians as a half-diminished seventh chord and, for its myriad transitional properties, has since entered the tonal mainstream as a harmonic tool of jazz musicians. For Debussy, in his String Quartet, it was the element that enabled his various excursions into modalities (especially the Phrygian and Lydian modes) and his characteristic whole-tone and pentatonic scales.[11]

Chausson, to whom the String Quartet was to have been dedicated, didn't like it. On February 5, 1894, Debussy wrote to him, "I was really upset for several days by what you said about my Quartet . . . Anyway I'll write another one . . . for you, and I'll try and bring some nobility to my forms."[12] He never did write another.

In the same letter, he asked if Chausson would be in Brussels for the Debussy Festival on March 1.

Thérèse Roger

For a while, in early February, Debussy was in rare form—he seemed happy! "I no longer recognize myself," he wrote Chausson. "I'm to be found in the salons executing smiles, or else conducting choruses at the house of the Countess Zamoiska! . . . Then there's Mme de Saint-Marceaux, who's discovered that I'm a first-rate talent! It's enough to make you die laughing."[13] And Wagner, much to Debussy's surprise, had become a frequent source of revenue for him. As Wagnermania took hold of Paris, there were several well-attended series of lectures on Wagner; those by Mendès at the Opera House and Mme Escudier at her salons featured Debussy at the piano, providing musical examples. Wagner's music was everywhere.

In mid-February, Debussy put the last notes on the first act of *Pelléas et Mélisande.* On February 17, two of his *Proses lyriques* were sung for the first time, at a National Society concert. Thérèse Roger was the soloist, accompanied by the composer. Shortly afterward, he announced to a colleague that he had become engaged to Mlle Roger. Yes, engaged!

It was Marguerite de Saint-Marceaux who brought Claude and Thérèse together and encouraged Debussy to propose. Mme de Saint-Marceaux had only recently married a noted sculptor and opened her house to a salon where Debussy often played. But what was the man thinking? He was apparently prodded by Chausson and Lerolle, who had been on a months-long crusade to domesticate him, to marry him off to someone other than Gaby, whom they didn't like—to see their friend settled into the kind of bourgeois matrimony they themselves enjoyed. But Thérèse was not the mate Chausson would have chosen for him. Her late father was an insurance inspector; her mother was a music teacher; and Thérèse "had the manner of those girls who are chaperoned too much."[14] She was, after all, a "salon singer," and not a very good one at that.

Marcel Dietschy, in his biography, brings to this unstable period of Debussy's life a note of charm and tenderness—mystery, too. Dietschy puts forward a plausible theory: that long before Debussy found Maeterlinck's *Pelléas et Mélisande* he, like many young men, had created a mental image of his ideal woman. The damsel in *La Damoiselle élue* has the touching, innocent, ethereal quality that Debussy dreamed of and had captured in his oratorio. In 1893 she appeared again, as the fictional Mélisande—a young girl, afraid, lost in the woods, hoping someone would write an opera about her.

From time to time, a young woman came into his life who nearly matched his ideal, and he was invariably enthralled by her appearance, her charm, her vulnerability, by the physical reality of his adolescent dream. Such a girl was Yvonne, the daughter of Henri Lerolle and his wife. Yvonne "appeared before Debussy in the grace of her seventeen years," writes Dietschy, "with a reserved and touching beauty."[15] In Debussy's imagination, she was Mélisande, the illusion personified, the ideal made real.

Shortly before he proposed to Thérèse, Claude presented Yvonne with a Japanese fan adorned with birds and flowers and a dedication: "To Mlle Yvonne Lerolle, in memory of her little sister Mélisande."[16] The gift and the inscription suggests that he was bidding adieu to the beautiful young girl, while putting to rest a persistent dream of the ideal woman, perfection itself, in favor of Thérèse, a woman no longer young and less than perfect. (In 1902, his idealized Mélisande would again be made flesh and blood by the singer Mary Garden, who turned Debussy's heart to crêpe batter.)

On February 24, Pierre Louÿs wrote his brother that Mme Saint-Marceaux had committed "a grave imprudence in marrying Debussy to a drawing-room singer. I am convinced that it would be a bad marriage, and I am distressed about it for my friend's sake."[17]

"Debussy's getting married," wrote Lerolle to Chausson, his brother-in-law. "He's in seventh heaven. . . . He has to earn money and not live on Thérèse's. Before he spoke to me, Mme Roger [Thérèse's mother] had come to tell me they were in love with one another and to ask me what I thought about it. . . . I told her what I thought of him as a musician, but explained that as a man I hardly knew him, except that I'm very fond of him." Lerolle went on to tell Chausson that an apartment was rented for them, and they were to move in on April 16, after the wedding. "He's spending all his time with Thérèse and not working much."[18]

"The announcement of Debussy's marriage left me speechless," Chausson replied to Lerolle. "He's deeply in love; and I find lovers so utterly captivating, not to say a rarity in our refined intellectual circle." Chausson was sure the engagement would set tongues wagging but was confident it would be "a very happy marriage. . . . They love each other, that's the important thing."[19]

Debussy's Festival and Its Aftermath

The Debussy Festival, as the honored composer enjoyed calling it, was the first concert program ever entirely devoted to the music of Claude Debussy.

The venue was at the heart of Brussels's flourishing art movement—a salon sponsored by a society of artists, La Libre Esthétique (The Free Esthetic). Housed in the city's museum of modern art, the salon ran for a month and was the

first of an anticipated annual music-and-art event. The exhibition gallery
served as a concert hall, in which four chamber concerts led by Ysaÿe were
performed during the month. The audience was surrounded in the gallery by a
great range of contemporary art, including paintings by Renoir, Pissarro,
Gauguin, Lerolle, and the symbolist artists Redon and Puvis de Chavannes.
There were also cabaret posters by Toulouse-Lautrec, illustrations by Aubrey
Beardsley for Oscar Wilde's *Salome*, and dozens of other works.[20]

Debussy's program was the second. Composers represented at the other
three were Schubert, Bach, Franck, d'Indy, Chausson, and Bréville, with emphasis
on Beethoven. Debussy was singled out for a concert of his own because the
avant-garde artists of La Libre Esthétique considered his music to be in harmony
with their visual aesthetics (or so Ysaÿe, perhaps, informed them). From another
angle, Debussy was seen as a new artist on a musical continuum that began
with Beethoven.

On March 1, 1894, Claude Debussy accompanied his fiancée in a performance
of two of the *Proses lyriques*. Thérèse also sang *La Damoiselle élue* with fifty-one
musicians from the Brussels Conservatory orchestra, with Ysaÿe conducting.
Ysaÿe led his string ensemble in Debussy's Quartet, which was received more
warmly than in Paris. One wonders if Debussy was ever happier than he was
on the day of the Debussy Festival.

A week later, Debussy wrote Chausson that the concert was "a marvelous
occasion for me, chiefly because I owe a large part of its success to Thérèse, who
sang like a fairy," and the sojourn in Brussels "turned out to be an unforgettably
romantic intermezzo." Debussy's engagement and the attention he received in
Brussels brought new, joyous colors to his life, he said, and his emotions were
unsettled. He was so used to "walking in darkness" that when "a sunny road is
open before me I'm afraid at not having deserved such happiness." He asked
Chausson's help in quickly paying off his various debts, with a promise to pay
him back later.[21]

At home in their apartment in rue Gustave Doré, Gaby was unaware of her
lover's betrayal. Elsewhere, the gossip mill was churning. Some of Debussy's
friends felt caught up in the growing scandal, and weren't happy about it. "No
one in Paris is talking about anything else," Lerolle said.[22]

By March 16, Debussy might have felt that his engagement was threatened.
He wrote Chausson asking, almost begging, for more money—1,500 francs to
pay some debts and buy a new dress for his mother to wear at the wedding. He

tells Chausson he has been forthright with Thérèse about his debts but wants to assure her that "a certain friend" (Chausson) has become his only creditor. The overall tone of the letter reveals a man in a tangle of emotions.

Then the bomb exploded: an anonymous person sent a telegram to Thérèse's mother revealing that Debussy had not ended his relationship with his mistress, and that he had considerable debts and not enough income to support a wife. Debussy was portrayed as an irresponsible, reprehensible cad.

On March 19, Chausson suggested to his mother-in-law, Mme Escudier, that in the face of the scandal Debussy's Wagner sessions should be terminated and that half the money should be returned to the attendees, since only five of the ten promised sessions had taken place. "I haven't been able to think of anything else except this sordid affair," he wrote to Lerolle, "and I'm feeling more and more despondent about it."[23]

Thérèse's mother charged "poor Debussy" with lying when she questioned him about his circumstances. Debussy was forced to withdraw his proposal. Chausson was confused and disturbed about the rumors and accusations. He wrote Lerolle: "I can see how he might have told lies, ... but to lie directly to [Thérèse's] face, with indignant protests, about something so serious, that I cannot comprehend."[24] When the dust settled, Chausson broke off his friendship with Debussy, at least partly to preserve his own reputation in society. So did Ysaÿe and several others.

Louÿs tried valiantly to salvage his new friend's reputation. In May he wrote to an acquaintance, "For two months I have supported Debussy against twenty-five people ... so that [my own friendship with Debussy] will not be broken."[25] One of those twenty-five people was Mme de Saint-Marceaux, an instigator of the affair, to whom he sent a long, heartfelt letter. Louÿs said that Debussy's actions had been misunderstood by those who condemned him, but it wasn't surprising that a scandal had resulted.

> Perhaps you will allow me to add that a young man cannot dismiss like a chambermaid a mistress who has lived with him for two years, who has shared his poverty without complaint and against whom he can level no reproaches, other than that he is tired of her and is getting married. Ordinarily, these matters are settled with a few banknotes; it may not be the height of delicacy, but it serves. As you know, this was not a course Debussy had open to him. He felt he had to act with circumspection. It was a question of

kindness, and also of prudence, because if treated more harshly [Gaby] might have sought revenge. So he proceeded slowly. If his engagement had been announced less precipitately, Debussy would have had the time to disengage himself completely. . . . He did not do so, or, if you prefer, he did not know how to do so; and he has been cruelly punished for it.

As for the rumors . . . about his past life, I stand as a witness that they are monstrous calumnies, and I think that the honor of a man . . . cannot be wounded by anonymous letters, which are usually the work of a liar and always of a coward. I know from personal knowledge that Debussy is incapable of having lived as it is claimed.

For confirmation of his assessment of Debussy's character, Louÿs referred Mme de Saint-Marceaux to Bonheur, Lerolle, Chausson, and Dupin. "I write this in a state of profound sadness," Louÿs concluded, "and with an outspokenness which, Madame, I beg you to excuse. I know of nothing more distressing than to see thus dishonored, in a matter of no more than a week, a man who is loved and greatly respected, who has been starved of good fortune for fifteen years and who sees all the doors closed against him *at the moment when it is becoming apparent that he is a genius.*"[26]

CHAPTER 10
MALLARMÉ AND THE PARIS SALONS (1890–1893)

The musician is the soul of the salons. He is almost master of them. Welcomed and well received in aristocratic society, he is courted among the haute bourgeoisie, respected and adulated among the middle classes.

—Aved Poorten[1]

In the heady days of the seventeenth century, a person of consequence, most often a noblewoman, might bring together a diverse group of people, on a more or less regular basis, for the purpose of intelligent conversation. For more than half a century, the Marquise de Rambouillet, one of the most famous of these hosts, entertained her guests and established rules of etiquette for this new social establishment: the salons.

Salons were not exclusively French. The Italians laid claim to their invention a century earlier, and salons were known in other European countries. But the French refined them and gave them a rare importance, as they did with their cuisine, couture, and cabernets.

By the early nineteenth century, salons were among the essential pastimes of intellectuals, artists, writers, aristocrats, and the *haute bourgeoisie*. The news of the day was discussed, philosophical ideas and saucy gossip were exchanged, and guests were introduced to others whose acquaintance might prove useful or merely delightful. Visitors were expected to add a fair measure of wit and charm to the proceedings, which were further enlivened by composers such as Chopin or Liszt, playing their new works.

The salon tradition was interrupted by the Franco-Prussian war. By the time Debussy returned from Rome in 1887, salons were thriving again. Some were established by, and primarily for, writers and intellectuals, and some were perpetuated by the diminished aristocracy and the magnates of the industrial age. But the emphasis had changed. In Debussy's time, music was not merely the entertainment, it was the primary focus.

Salons were "fundamental to the history of French music," wrote James Ross. "These salons connected musicians with the worlds of art and literature, publishing, politics, and patronage."[2] At a time when government subsidies were scanty and the established concert societies rarely presented contemporary works, the salons provided fashionable venues, appreciative audiences, and generous fees for young composers like Debussy. Journalists and critics were often in attendance, and they informed the wider public about the new, often controversial music they heard at these private gatherings. Salons were a forum for discussions about Wagner and fostered the growing acceptance of his operas in France. Without the salon, Fauré might never have achieved the prominence he deserved, because he wrote primarily instrumental music and mélodies in an opera-loving era when such music was largely overlooked. At the salons, they were cherished.

One of the most prestigious salons was that of the Princesse de Polignac, born in Yonkers, New York. Her father, Isaac Singer, was a prolific progenitor of mechanical inventions and children. His tinkering led to the founding of the Singer Sewing Machine company. The twentieth of his children, Winnaretta, became a French princess. With her husband, Prince Edmond de Polignac, she initiated a salon in 1894 and invited composers to come and give first performances of new works. Fauré and Debussy performed there. After her husband's death, the princess used some of her vast fortune to commission new music: Stravinsky's *Renard*, Satie's *Socrate*, and compositions by Kurt Weill, Darius Milhaud, Francis Poulenc, Manuel de Falla, and others. Ravel dedicated his *Pavane pour une infante défunte* (Pavane for a Dead Princess) to Winnaretta, who was still very much alive.

Les Mardis chez Mallarmé

Salons were as important to writers as they were to musicians. The young poets who called themselves Parnassians first gathered at the salon of the Marquis de Ricard, in a setting of rich brocades and rare Gobelin tapestries. But of all the literary salons in Paris, by far the best known were those of Stéphane Mallarmé, the most influential of the symbolist poets.

An English teacher by day, Mallarmé was one of the great masters of the French language. His literary output was slim—a few volumes of poems, prose poems, and essays on various subjects. His French translation of "The Raven," published in 1875 with illustrations by Édouard Manet, helped establish Poe's reputation in France; later he published more of Poe's poems, all rendered in French prose. But Mallarmé is perhaps best known today for his influential salons and, thanks to Debussy, for his poem *L'Après-midi d'un faune*.

Mallarmé's salons, known as *les Mardis* (Tuesdays), began in 1879 and continued almost to the end of his life. Guests were drawn to him by the power of his intellect and by his reputation as one of the best talkers in Paris. At the Mardis you might encounter André Gide, Paul Valéry, Paul Verlaine, Catulle Mendès, Jules Laforgue, Jean Moréas, Octave Mirbeau, Emile Verhaeren, Pierre Louÿs, José-Marie de Heredia, Paul Gauguin, Gustave Kahn, Paul Claudel, and Édouard Dujardin, the editor of *La Revue Wagnérienne*. Over the years, scores of France's great writers, artists, and intellects visited at least once. When they were in Paris, Maeterlinck, Wilde, Whistler, or Stefan George might drop by. The proud professors of the Sorbonne disdained or ridiculed Mallarmé, the outsider; they had no idea of the power and extent of Mallarmé's influence on the young creative minds of his day.

Mallarmé was introduced to Debussy in 1890, after hearing the Baudelaire songs. By the fall of that year the composer was a frequent guest at the Mardis.

The 1890s saw "the swinging together of literature, poetry, painting, decorative arts, and music, the trends of different nations converging toward similar goals," writes Klaus Berger. Mallarmé's importance—particularly to the symbolists—derived, in large part, from his recognition of this convergence and from offering his home as a meeting place for practitioners of the arts. The Mardis "had taken on such significance that everybody who counted in the artistic avant-garde felt ennobled by being admitted."[3]

Mallarmé lived with his wife, Maria, and their daughter, Geneviève, in a small flat on the rue de Rome, up four flights of stairs. The poet, wearing the same rumpled clothes he'd been wearing all day teaching school, "opened the door himself for his guests when they arrived," wrote Francis Grierson, "and went to the door with them when they left."[4] Entering the flat, the guests were greeted by the acrid smell of tobacco smoke emanating from a small reception room where twelve to fifteen men would be seated, crowded around a table. On the walls were paintings by his friends: Manet, Morisot, Whistler, and Redon. Along with ashtrays and an increasing number of elbows, the only other significant object on the large table was a porcelain bowl filled with tobacco for the host and his guests.

Typically, Mallarmé would stand comfortably in front of a white porcelain stove, holding a cigarette in one hand and making graceful little gestures with the other as he spoke. Near the stove was Mallarmé's favorite chair, a wooden rocker. To the left of the rocker was often seated a slender man with a drooping mustache, a monocle in his left eye, and a serene, aristocratic bearing: Henri de Régnier, one of Mallarmé's most devoted disciples. In a diary entry Régnier noted: "Nothing will replace for me those evenings at Mallarmé's house where in addition to the delicious, perfect presence of the master of the house, you have the chance to meet an intelligent company."[5]

"It was like arriving at a cool mountain spring after a long tramp through a burning desert," wrote Grierson. "The visitor came here without fear, hindrance, or hypocrisy. The body rested while the spirit was being refreshed. . . . This little room was the one place in Paris where the soul could manifest itself in freedom."[6]

Mallarmé was "one of the superb conversationalists (or monologuists) of his time, quiet of speech and manner and possessed of a delicate sense of humor," wrote Jules Huret.[7] André Gide wrote of the "almost religious atmosphere" of the Mardis. "Certainly Mallarmé prepared his conversations . . . but he spoke with such art and in a tone that had so little of the doctrinal about it that it seemed as if he had just that instant invented each new proposition, which he didn't affirm so much as seem to submit it for your consideration."[8]

Though known for his monologues, Mallarmé encouraged his guests to comment, to put fresh ideas on the table, and he listened with keen interest. He was uncanny in his ability to embroider on their ideas and perceptions with subtlety and ingenuity, no matter the subject, as if he were merely "brushing the dust off your own ideas, rearranging them a little, before he gave them back to you, your mundane comment now magically majestic and luminous," wrote Arthur Symons. Only later might it occur to you that your part in the creation of the majestic and luminous was small, but you'd cherish the way Mallarmé so nimbly enlightened you without diminishing the value of your contribution. As a friend and fellow writer, he lifted his disciples to the higher altitudes of art.[9]

Those who knew Mallarmé well, knew that his attention to your remarks was not to learn something from you, except to the extent that your thoughts might help him work through the philosophical puzzles and creative issues that were always at the center of his being. But he had a genuine desire to provide a forum where writers and artists could explore their ideas in a congenial atmosphere, far from the ears of unsympathetic critics or bourgeois attitudes, and he did all he could to assist the careers of the young writers he admired. "Here was a man, living very near the borders of want, exercising a power which no millionaire could claim," wrote Grierson.[10]

In discussions at the Mardis, Wagner's name arose often. "The country's growing, if complex, interest in the music of Wagner, . . . together with the urgently felt need to find a French response to his concepts of opera, finds a clear reflection in Mallarmé's writing of the time," Rosemary Lloyd explains, "and it is echoed in accounts of the Mardis."[11]

Mallarmé, Wagner, Debussy

Just as the salons of the Belle Époque were important to the musicians of Paris, so was music important to the evolution of French poetry, and the salons were the vortex of music and poetry. "Any literary history of the end of the nineteenth century that does not speak of music will be of no avail," wrote Valéry. "Nothing can be understood of the poetic movement that developed, if the profound and capital role that music played in that remarkable transformation is not revealed, elucidated, and clarified."[12] Though generations of poets had strived to capture the sounds and rhythms of music in their verses, many, including Mallarmé, felt only disdain for the actual music heard at concerts and salons. But in the latter part of the nineteenth century, a growing number of French writers received their first musical education at the salons, where new music, quite different from the formulaic music of the Classical masters, was heard and enthusiastically discussed. This musical enlightenment "contributed more than all theoretical considerations to orient poetry towards a purer destiny and to eliminate from its works all that prose can render perfectly well," Valéry wrote.[13]

The orchestral societies that sprang up after the Prussian War were impossible for culturally minded people to ignore. Although Baudelaire's musical awakening came with *Tannhäuser* in 1861, the next generation of poets had the Lamoureux Concerts, which presented works of the earlier masters as well as such contemporaries as Saint-Saëns, Chabrier, Chausson, and Debussy. Writers could no longer dismiss music as an art form inferior to poetry.

According to Geneviève Mallarmé, "the magic of music" was revealed to her father around 1885.[14] The poet's interest in music was encouraged by a number of friends, including Chausson and Chabrier, but his most persuasive musical mentor was Augusta Holmès, a native Parisian born to Irish parents, who befriended him about 1870.

As a teenager Holmès was described as a golden-haired beauty, a musician possibly "possessed of genius." In adulthood she was a first-rate celebrity and a second-rate composer. She achieved considerable but fleeting success with her operas, symphonic works, and songs. "Her reputation rested on the sheer exuberance of her dynamic personality and evidently irresistible physical attractions," wrote Rollo Myers. If she is still remembered (in 1967, when Myers wrote) "it is not so much for the quality and intrinsic value of her music as for its quantity and flamboyancy, and for the fact that for some forty years this extraordinary Irishwoman played a prominent part in Parisian musical life and had entrée to all the most exclusive artistic and literary salons."[15] She was one of the few women, and one of the few composers, who was ever seen at the Mardis.

Holmès was an early, outspoken, influential admirer of Wagner at a time when Paris was still closed to him. She knew Wagner personally, visited his home, and was rumored to have had a brief affair with him. "She was so much of a Wagnerian that she almost married the man; the reasons why she didn't are unclear to this day," wrote Debussy in an obituary.[16] She attended the premiere of *Das Rheingold* in Munich, seated next to Franz Liszt. Saint-Saëns said, "We were all in love with her—literary men, painters, musicians—any one of us would have been proud to make her his wife."[17] But after dazzling and rejecting so many men, she became the mistress of Catulle Mendès and bore him three daughters.

Holmès played an important role in Mallarmé's musical education, writes Rosemary Lloyd, "conveying to him, well before the appearance of the *Revue Wagnérienne* [in 1885], the essence of Wagner's image of music" and the composer's ideal of *Gesamtkunstwerk* ("total artwork," a term suggesting a work, such as an opera, that synthesized all the arts).[18] Mallarmé even wrote an essay on Wagner for an early edition of the *Revue*. He wrote about "an ideal theater, ostensibly inspired by Wagner but having little in common with Wagner's music drama," Arthur Wenk explains. "For Mallarmé's ideal theater had no sets, no scenery, and no costumes, but made its stage in the imagination of the reader, who constituted a perfect audience of one." Mallarmé's "music"—that is, the music inherent in his verses, "formed an abstract ideal toward which poetry might aspire."[19] But Mallarmé came to feel that his own writings could never rise to Wagner's high standard. He was torn between aiming for an absolute, which is unobtainable, and disdaining the kind of compromise that is always necessary in creating poetry. Mallarmé thought himself a failure *because he was not Wagner*, Arthur Symons believed. And since Wagner was the most esteemed cultural figure in Europe, it was necessary for Mallarmé "to be something more. . . . Not being able to do that, it was a matter of sincere indifference to him" that he himself had produced only one or two "little, limited masterpieces of formal verse and prose."[20]

So here were two men—a great poet who wished he could have been Wagner and felt himself a failure because he wasn't; and a younger man, Debussy, who spent much of his life wanting *not* to be Wagner, feeling himself a failure because he had not written a masterpiece that was completely *unlike* Wagner, beyond Wagner, not German but French at its core. And these two men, separated by age, education, and their way of understanding the aesthetics of their time, became friends.

It was clear that Debussy "belonged to the inner circle of Mallarmé's friends," wrote Lockspeiser.[21] He was frequently seen at the Mardis. He took Mallarmé to hear Gregorian chant at the Église Saint-Gervais, to the Wagner concerts at the Cirque d'Été, to the first Paris performance of *Die Walküre*, and to the first performance of Maeterlinck's *Pelléas et Mélisande*. He attended the banquet in honor of Mallarmé, in February 1897, when *Divagations* was published. When Mallarmé died the following year, Paul Valéry, the poet's faithful disciple, first gave the news to Louÿs and asked him to tell Debussy. They were that close.

Mallarmé, Debussy, *Faune*

Mallarmé's poems are famous for their difficulty. "How unfortunate," wrote Marcel Proust, "that so gifted a man should become insane every time he takes up the pen."[22] Only those who read and speak French fluently can truly appreciate Mallarmé's work. Even the most proficient translations, in any language, sacrifice the splendor and strangeness of his words, the subtleties of his imagery and ideas. Most daunting to the translator is Mallarmé's wordplay, such as using a phrase that plainly means one thing on the page but sounds exactly like something else when spoken; the trick itself may offer a clue to Mallarmé's underlying meaning or intention, but it can rarely survive translation.

His avant-garde literary theories and practices made his writings famous for their obscurity. According to Arthur Symons, "Mallarmé was obscure not because he *wrote* differently, but because he *thought* differently from other people," and he relied "with undue confidence on the intelligence of his readers."[23] He persistently ignored the differences between himself and other people as well as the similarities that linked them. Even Valéry was stymied by much of what Mallarmé wrote: "There were certain sonnets that reduced me to a state of stupor.... The most surprising contrast was evident between what one might call the *appearance* of these lines, their *physical* presence, and the resistance they offered to immediate understanding."[24] Mallarmé referred to his own writings as "a labyrinth illuminated by flowers," a strange metaphor suggesting, perhaps, that his enigmas can be understood only through the prism of his beautiful language.

His tendency "to place paramount importance on the inner world rather than any aspects of the outer world . . . informs the complexity of his language," Lloyd writes. "He uses it not to convey information but to seek out ways of making language correspond in its beauty and complexity to the convolutions of thought and emotion."[25] And so, we can begin to understand the correlations between Mallarmé's poetry and Debussy's music: if Mallarmé's verses were intended not to convey information but to express thoughts and emotions through the beauty and complexity of language, then Mallarmé was, essentially, writing a kind of music.

Mallarmé, like Baudelaire, Banville, Verlaine, and others, believed music was the artistic ideal that poetry aspired to. "Music revealed itself to Mallarmé and the symbolists," said a founder of the *Revue Wagnérienne*, "not as an art of virtuosity . . . but as the profound voice of things."[26] And Mallarmé wants us to hear his "music," not with our intellect disentangling his meaning, but with our emotions in sympathy with the feelings evoked by the sound of his words. Mallarmé's texts—the meditations, visualizations, narratives—are the media he used to bring about these effects.

Debussy, beginning with his *Prélude à "L'Après-midi d'un faune,"* discovered his own way of conjuring emotions musically. In his music he portrayed meditations, visualized events, fictional characters, poems, and phenomena of nature that evoke the listeners' emotions. It's as if his music were the soundtrack to a silent film—a film projected on the screen of your mind, his music giving the images emotional ballast. These are not simple emotions like the joy or wonderment we feel when hearing Mozart, or the tumultuous passions sparked by Beethoven. Often, the emotions Debussy's music suggests are more specific in the narrative, yet more subtle in the execution: the erotic longing of a mythical creature (in *Faune*), the serenity of slow-moving clouds in the night sky (*Nocturnes*), the restlessness of wind-whipped seas (*La Mer*). Much of his piano music also evokes emotions: romantic nostalgia ("La plus que lente"); the playfulness of children, interrupted by fear ("Jardins sous la pluie"). Although Debussy's titles often refer to a particular scene or event, he wanted his music to stand on its own. Debussy, unlike Mallarmé, didn't seem to care whether we experienced precisely the emotions he hoped to evoke, or the subject suggested by the title, since the goal of nearly all his music was to convey beauty, unalloyed and unconnected to any reality but the listener's pleasure.

When Debussy's *Faune* was first performed, it was considered by many, whether they liked the work or not, to have revealed Debussy in a different light and to have brought something new to the concert hall. Was Mallarmé responsible for this new departure in Debussy's music? Consider that after Debussy's immersion in Wagner, his exposure to the gamelan, his musical experiments with the verses of Banville and Verlaine, and his ill-advised attempts to write for the larger public, he had not yet found his distinctive voice. But Debussy absorbed Mallarmé's symbolist philosophical musings for about two years before he began writing *Faune*, and the result was his musical breakthrough. "It appears that somehow Debussy had made a fundamental choice that released his energy to carry things through to completion," William W. Austin suggests. "We may speculate further that the ideas of Mallarmé contributed something essential to it."[27] How could it have been otherwise? A poem like *Faune* can't be expressed in the language of Beethoven or Massenet. In his earlier compositions, Debussy ignored many rules of harmony, orchestration, and form, but he never found a way to break completely with musical orthodoxy until he passed into the symbolist domain of Stéphane Mallarmé.

CHAPTER 11

THE FAUN

Just as modern poetry surely took root in certain of Baudelaire's poems, so one is justified in saying that modern music was awakened by [Debussy's] L'Après-midi d'un faune.

—Pierre Boulez[1]

Stéphane Mallarmé was twenty-three years old in 1865 when he began his poem *L'Après-midi d'un faune*. It was something entirely new. In a letter written soon after starting it, he said, "I have found an intimate and peculiar manner of depicting and setting down very fugitive impressions. What is frightening is that all these impressions are required to be woven together as in a symphony." He called his poem an eclogue, a pastoral poem in the form of a dialogue or soliloquy. He wondered how he could achieve what he envisioned and what the effect might be. "It demands the theatre," he concluded, and he wrote a draft with staging cues for a narrator and mimes.[2] He showed the manuscript to Banville and Constant Coquelin, a well-known actor. Perhaps naively, young Mallarmé hoped his friends could convince the Comédie-Française to stage *Faune*, but Banville thought it was not sufficiently theatrical.

Mallarmé revised his poem numerous times during the next ten years. In 1875, he submitted a new version for inclusion in a Parnassian anthology. Banville, one of the three editors, wanted to publish it "despite its lack of clarity, because of its rare musical qualities," but his colleagues disagreed and rejected it.[3] The following year, Mallarmé's final version of *Faune* was published as a slim volume, handsomely printed and bound, with an illustration by Manet. It was Mallarmé's first book.

About ten years later, when Debussy read the poem, he must have recognized the similarities between *Faune* and *Diane au bois*. In those days, he was struggling to reshape Banville's verse play as a cantata or opera.

Diane appeared in print only a year or so before Mallarmé's *Faune* was begun, and the coincidences of plot are notable. For example, Mallarmé's faun and his frustrated lust for the two elusive nymphs correspond, in *Diane*, with a satyr and his obsession with two loves named Lyre and Syrinx. But ancient classical themes were common in Parnassian writing; Mallarmé drew also from the well-known tales of Pan, the randy Greek god of wilderness, mountains, and pastures. Pan, like fauns and satyrs, had the hindquarters, hoofs, and horns of a goat, with a man's head and torso. In legend, Pan lustfully pursues the chaste water nymph Syrinx; to save her, the other nymphs transform her, at the water's edge, into hollow reeds. When Pan embraces the reeds, his breath creates sweet music, and he fashions from the reeds a wind instrument, forever known as panpipes.

"Hidden in the myth [of Pan]," Lockspeiser wrote, "is the theory, re-stated by Mallarmé, that a function of the dream is to allow love to be sublimated into music." The poet "attempts to trace the process in which desire first vanishes into the dream and is then transformed into music. . . . [*Faune*] is also an exploration of the borderlands between the conscious and the half-conscious, the waking state and the state of reverie."[4]

Woven through the atmospheric verses of *L'Après-midi d'un faune* is a simple narrative. One afternoon, on a sun-baked slope of Mount Etna, the faun, whose thoughts and reveries constitute the poem, is asleep. He wakes from a dream; lustfully pursues the two reluctant nymphs of his dream, or fantasizes about them; plays a long soliloquy on his flute; attempts to resurrect the dream; and drifts back into sleep. Reading the poem, we're never sure whether the faun is dozing and dreaming or in some stage of wakefulness; and if he's awake, is he "aware of the distinction between primitive desire and the subli-mated artistic vision"?[5] In Mallarmé's eclogue are many mysteries of intent and a corresponding profusion of interpretations, leaving the uninitiated reader free to savor the elusive yet vivid language, submit to the playfulness of the erotic reveries, and pity the frustrated faun.

Valéry considered *L'Après-midi d'un faune* to be the greatest of all French poems.

Prélude à "L'Après-midi d'un faune"

We don't know exactly when Mallarmé and Debussy began discussing a musical interpretation of *L'Après-midi d'un faune*. They first met in 1890, but Debussy encountered the poem earlier, around 1885. By 1891, Mallarmé had revived his original idea for a staged version; a collection of his poems published that year promised a new edition of *Faune* written for the theater. Around this time, Debussy almost certainly read an early unpublished draft of *Faune*—a manuscript was in the collection of his friend Chausson—and saw stage directions in the text. He most likely discussed with Mallarmé the poet's concept of a staged presentation. Would there be incidental music? Poniatowski, a friend of both men at the time, spoke of "long meditations in the course of which the musician received from the poet his conception of the role of music."[6]

And so Debussy's first attempt at *Faune*, in 1892, was to be a suite of incidental music for a staged reading of the poem. When *La Damoiselle élue* was published in the spring of 1893, the cover announced Debussy's forthcoming work: *Prélude, interludes et paraphrase finale pour "L'Après-midi d'un faune,"* and a similar announcement appeared on the program for the Debussy concert in Brussels almost a year later. By late October 1894, the full orchestral score and a two-piano reduction were finished. It was not a suite of incidental music but a sublime ten-minute tone poem—the smoldering desires and rambling meditations of a pagan creature on a steamy afternoon.

The poet was introduced to Debussy's *Prélude à "L'Après-midi d'un faune"* in the fall of 1894, when the composer played it for him on the piano. Debussy later recalled the occasion in a letter to a friend: "Mallarmé came in, with his sibylline look and wearing a Scotch plaid. After having listened, he was silent for a long time, and then said to me: 'I was not expecting anything of this kind! This music prolongs the emotion of my poem, and sets the scene more vividly than color.'"[7] Some observers have written that Mallarmé was not enthusiastic about having Debussy or anyone else set his poems to music, believing there was enough music in his verses already. But judging from his comments on this occasion, Mallarmé seems to have been pleased with what he heard.

On October 24, Debussy sold the score to the publisher Georges Hartmann for a paltry 200 francs. Two months later, the work was introduced to the public at a concert of the National Society.

Debussy invited the poet to the premiere with this florid but good-natured note: "Need I tell you what joy I shall have if you will be so kind as to indulge with your presence the arabesques which I have been led to believe, through a pride perhaps reprehensible, were inspired by the flute of your Faun?"[8]

A few days later Debussy received a reply, accompanied by the sort of quatrain Mallarmé famously liked to write to his friends: "I've just left the concert and am deeply moved: what a marvel! Your illustration of *Afternoon of a Faun* offers no dissonance with my text, except that it goes further, truly, in nostalgia and light, with finesse, uneasiness, and richness."[9]

> O forest god of breathing air,
> If you have made your flute aright,
> Now hear the way that Debussy
> Breathes into it the broad daylight.[10]

For Debussy, Mallarmé's letter was "a first-rate document! In any case, it is my happiest memory from this period, when I was not yet bothered with Debussyism."[11]

Debussy described his music as "a very free illustration of Mallarmé's beautiful poem; it makes no claim to be a synthesis of the poem. It consists rather of a series of backdrops on which the desires and dreams of the faun move in the warmth of that afternoon."[12] Though not a paraphrase, the *Prélude à "L'Après-midi d'un faune"* vividly captures the poet's expressions of mood (languid, seductive), atmosphere (torrid, vibrant), and eroticism. Here Debussy emerged as a mature artist, in full command of his technique, daring to synthesize all his revolutionary musical strategies in one tone poem. Here are the vague, transient rhythms; the ambiguous, unresolved harmonies; the meticulously differentiated orchestral colors; the fragmented melodies, asymmetrical phrases, delicacy, and charm that would mark so much of Debussy's work in the years ahead.

The Triumph of the Tritone

In the world of music, the moment was auspicious. It was even necessary. The music of the Romantic age was overwritten, overwrought, and ridden sidesaddle through the conflagration of Valhalla. Before *Faune*, there was nowhere for young composers to go, nothing to do but imitate Wagner or retreat to Beethoven. Western ideas of tonal harmony were driven as far as the composers' ability, imagination, and cultural morality allowed them to go. *Faune* opened a door to new possibilities, but where were the keys? What language would be spoken on the other side of the door?

Europe was ready for epochal changes in the art of music. Figurative painting had given way to impressionism, which would soon yield to cubism, expressionism, abstraction. Poetry had emerged from the wild dark nights of Baudelaire and Rimbaud to the mysterious dream space of Mallarmé, where syntax gives way to synesthesia, where fantasy and reality blur, where poetry aspires to music. But music was still stuck in the Golden Age of Romanticism, and the precious metal was being chipped away by Wagner.

Debussy took his cue from Mallarmé and found a new musical language for *Faune*. We hear it even in the first measures. It's one of the most astonishing, memorable beginnings in all of symphonic music, ranking with the opening *da-da-da-dum* of Beethoven's Fifth Symphony or the upward flight of the clarinet at the start of Gershwin's *Rhapsody in Blue*. From the first moments, Debussy suggests a distant haze of myth with the pastoral sound of a solo flute—a downward chromatic arc, repeated, rounded off, and answered by the woodwinds, horns, and the harp's broad glissandos. The flute's melody is defined by its upper and lower limits, C-sharp down to G-natural—an augmented fourth (also known as a tritone). In the Middle Ages the tritone was known as the *diabolus in musica* (the devil in music).

That memorable tritone theme generates all the music that follows. Debussy makes it a structural element, giving functional support to all the "vagueness." Never exactly the same, the melody is heard in its original design, attenuated, quickened, fragmented, transposed to different keys, or tossed among various instruments over ever-changing harmonies. At measure 37 the theme is recast in a more melodic, diatonic mode, though it has the same familiar contour—down, up, down, and up again—as the opening measures. Seamlessly it is sublimated in transitional passages until, almost halfway through the piece, Debussy introduces a new theme—simple, spacious, and diatonic, where the first was complex, tight, and chromatic. The music takes on the familiar timbres of the Romantic-era orchestra, with nearly all the instruments involved, full-throated crescendos, and a long decrescendo to the quietest pianissimo. At measure 79, over rhythmic arpeggios in the harps, the solo flute brings back the haunting tune that opened the piece. Although we've been hearing reminders of the theme throughout, this is the first time we've heard it, almost complete, since the first measures. The familiar, languorous theme is interrupted by a lively passage in the winds and horns (a dialogue between the faun and the scampering nymphs?); then we hear several repeated fragments of the melody, nostalgic, as if it were receding in our consciousness. Finally, a quiet, mesmerizing passage (flutes, harps, muted horns, ancient cymbals, whispering violins, double bass) ends the piece as the faun succumbs to sleep.

The musical structure is strengthened, surreptitiously, by the tonal key of E. The E major statement, tentative and inconclusive in the third measure, returns several times at the end of one episode or the beginning of another, and the piece ends, comfortably and definitively, in the key of E major. It's an indication that structural coherence was important to Debussy's scheme, even if we don't hear it the way we do in a Schubert symphony. Pierre Boulez studied *Faune* and concluded, "What was overthrown [was] the very core concept of form itself, here freed from the impersonal constraints of the schema, giving wings to a supple, mobile expressiveness."[13]

Modern Notions

Notwithstanding all the treatises on *Prélude à "L'Après-midi d'un faune,"* subjecting the piece to a full-scale, scholarly musical analysis is a fool's errand. William W. Austin, in his twenty-five-page "Analytical Appreciation" of *Faune*, examines the structural, melodic, harmonic, rhythmic, and other elements exhaustively, sometimes taking issue with the contrary analyses of other musicologists, and comes to the conclusion that analyzing *Faune* is inherently futile: "Wonderment is surely an appropriate response to this music, which analysis should serve not to allay but to intensify."[14]

Debussy himself apparently wanted to throw music analysts off his trail. When the critic Willy (a.k.a. Henri Gauthier-Villars) sought Debussy's comments for an article he was writing in 1896, Debussy replied, with his usual dry humor, "The *Prélude à 'L'Après-midi d'un faune,'* dear sir, might it be what remains of the dream at the tip of the faun's flute? More precisely, it is a general impression of the poem, for if music were to follow more closely it would run out of breath, like a dray horse competing for the Grand Prize with a thoroughbred."[15]

Nevertheless, many characteristics of *Faune* are worth noting, if only to cast light on the ingenuity and freshness of Debussy's work.

Looking at the published score, you can't help but notice the very large number of changes in time signature (meter)—eleven changes in the first thirty-one measures alone, oscillating between 9/8 and 12/8 time, with one measure in 6/8. The sense of meter, or pulse, is eroded not only by the metric freedom but also by the slow pace of the music throughout, by the absence of stresses on the downbeat, and by the inconsistency of stresses within the measures. All this contributes to a rhythmic twilight—you won't find yourself tapping your toes—that reinforces the vagueness of the harmonic structures. The idea that a musical work, whether a Strauss waltz or a Brahms symphony, can succeed without a defined beat, a pulse, to carry you along—this is a modern notion that began with *Faune*.

The orchestration, too, reveals Debussy's originality and independence of thought. The orchestra reached enormous size in the works of Debussy's contemporaries Richard Strauss and Gustav Mahler. The expansions were prompted by the larger size of new concert halls; the invention or improvement of useful instruments (clarinet, valve horn, saxophone, piano); the increased complexity of symphonic music; and the impulse to wow the audience. Debussy, always happy to defy tradition, employs, for *Faune*, a relatively small woodwind section, which takes most of the melodic assignments; a brass section limited to four piquant horns; two harps for lush harmonic support; percussion reduced to tiny antique cymbals; and a string section with much less prominence than in most symphonic music. Debussy's unique textures, timbres, and sonic colors were likely influenced by the gamelan. The delicacy of the instrumentation and its restrained rhetoric helps to recreate Mallarmé's poetic fantasies even as it rebukes post-Wagnerian bombast.

As he was to do on many other occasions, the composer made small revisions to the score during rehearsals up until the last moment. The timbres needed to be just right. Of particular concern were the unusual instrumental combinations, effects that he could hear only in his mind until rehearsals started. His use of timbres in *Faune* "seemed essentially new, of exceptional delicacy and assurance in touch," writes Boulez. "The writing for woodwinds and brasses, incomparably light-handed, performed a miracle of proportion, balance, and transparency."[16]

But what most stunned early listeners and scholars were the colors Debussy achieved with his instrumental choices and his rich harmonic structures. The chords are always layered with "extra" notes that allow the composer to pivot seamlessly to other strange chords and harmonies in ways that never seemed forced, never violate the composer's ideal of beauty, never assail the ears the way Wagner often did. Few composers have been as successful as Debussy in the benign uses of dissonance.

There's No Going Back

Despite the cheers at the first performance, Debussy's *Faune* was not welcomed by the musical establishment. Alfred Bruneau wrote that *Faune* "has its moments of truly exquisite music" and that "Debussy has a rare and original temperament," although the writer preferred "an art more neat, more robust, more masculine."[17] The critic for *Le Figaro* said, "Such pieces are amusing to write but not to listen to."[18] And in the *Guide Musical*: "The Wagnerian influence is so preponderating that it deprives the artist of such style as he might have achieved [!]."[19] Some in the audience, Vallas noted, "wondered anxiously if such music could be approved of, or whether it should not be condemned by respectable people, and whether it was seemly to give themselves up without remorse to the enjoyment of an art so utterly different" from the music they were accustomed to.[20] But many musicians were inspired. Ravel marveled, "On hearing this work I really understood what music was."[21]

Only with the passage of time and the opportunity for several hearings did the artistry and revolutionary aspects of *Faune* reveal themselves. A journalist took issue with Debussy's "absence of tonality," which Debussy uses "beyond all reason," resulting in "fatigue for the ear"; with the modulations "to very remote keys"; and with the use of a "scale with a quite peculiar effect." Yet, he acknowledged, "Debussy has the great merit of having created a style of his own . . . [and] we may get used to it very gladly."[22] Saint-Saëns, writing in 1920 from his lofty position as the éminence grise of French tradition, and with the unremitting disdain he felt for Debussy even after his rival's death, discovered in *Faune* "not the slightest musical idea, properly speaking. It is as much like a piece of music as the palette a painter has worked with is like a painting."[23] A considerable literature on the subject accumulated, "but the annotators never succeeded in conveying the impression of its exquisite charm," wrote Vallas. Debussy's "new expressive mediums" enable him "to create an atmosphere unprecedented in its fluidity and vibration. This work is undoubtedly a masterpiece of musical impressionism. Many years have gone by since its creation, but time has not lessened its originality nor dimmed its tints and colors."[24]

"Something had happened in [*Faune*] from which there was no going back," writes Lockspeiser. "Something had snapped, and something had also disintegrated."[25]

Within a few years after the appearance of his Quartet and *Faune*, many admiring young composers began to borrow Debussy's innovations and mannerisms for their own new works. Willy referred to them, cruelly, as "those nice little young men with long hair and short ideas who pick up the cigarette stumps of Claude Achille Debussy."[26] Soon they were lumped together as "Debussyists," as if they were a cult, and the very fact of their existence bothered Claude Achille for many years.

CHAPTER 12

MÉLISANDE
(1894–1898)

I am working on things that will be understood only by our grandchildren in the twentieth century.

—Debussy[1]

Some biographical sketches of Debussy make the absurd suggestion that it took him nine or ten years to write *Pelléas et Mélisande*. In fact, it took two years—from his first sketches in the summer of 1893 to August 1895, when he celebrated its completion (plus a few months before and during rehearsals for its premiere in 1902). And those two years were not devoted exclusively to *Pelléas*. During this period he also finished his String Quartet and *Proses lyriques*, wrote *Prélude à "L'Après-midi d'un faune,"* and composed several piano works. To help alleviate his poverty he prepared two-piano versions of symphonic music by Schumann and Saint-Saëns for his publisher. He performed Wagner's operas for Mme Escudier and her friends. He and Louÿs began several collaborations, including an opera and a ballet, though none of these ventures with his friend went very far.

His worktable must have been groaning under the weight of all these projects. Nevertheless, for those two years the focus was always on *Pelléas*.

It seems Debussy never doubted that he should write the libretto himself—or, more precisely, extract the libretto from the published text of Maeterlinck's play. Since Maeterlinck had acknowledged during their meeting in Ghent that some scenes were expendable, Debussy felt free to cut those and chip away extraneous material from others. Among the deleted scenes were the first scene of Act 1, which sets the mood but delays the story; a scene at the beginning of Act 3, whose importance to the play was in its symbolism more than its narrative; and a scene preceding Mélisande's death scene, in which the servants chattered about the recent violence. (For a synopsis of the opera, see Appendix C.)

The composer did not seem overly concerned about Maeterlinck's deliberate repetitiveness, as in the opera's opening scene:

GOLAUD: Be not afraid. Has anyone done you a wrong?

MÉLISANDE: Oh! Yes! Yes! Yes!

GOLAUD: Who is it that has done you a wrong?

MÉLISANDE: All! All!

GOLAUD: And what wrong have they done?

MÉLISANDE: No, no, I will not tell you! No, no, I cannot tell you!

GOLAUD: Come, come, you must not weep like this. Whence do you come?

MÉLISANDE: Oh! I ran away, away, away.[2]

Debussy's musical setting of these lines doesn't try to mask the repetitions, but rather uses them to heighten the sense of the girl's anxiety and Golaud's curiosity.

In September 1893, Debussy told Chausson he had finished Act 4, Scene 4, and asked his friend's opinion of it. It is the opera's climactic scene, the most dramatic. Debussy might have wanted to compose it first because it was crucial to the opera's effectiveness. Anguish, passionate love, tenderness, fear, extreme violence—all are expressed in eighteen minutes of dark music. It was unlike anything he had ever written, and his most formidable challenge. Indeed, a few weeks later he admitted to Chausson that his self-assurance was premature: the scene didn't work. "The ghost of old Klingsor, alias R. Wagner, kept appearing in the corner of a bar, so I've torn the whole thing up," and he started again, trying to conjure phrases more suited to his characters.[3] By mid-October, Debussy had rewritten at least part of the climactic scene and played it for Bonheur, who was "quite enamored" with it, and Lerolle, who said "it sent a shiver up my back."[4]

Sorrows to the Moon

At the beginning of 1894, Debussy, despite his poverty, turned down a "dreary accompanist's job in all its horror" that would have kept him at the piano all day and all evening.[5] He wrote Chausson, "My spirits at the moment are leaden, and melancholy bats wheel in the bell-tower of my dreams!" With his musical career at stake, he wonders whether his hopes for an opera on *Pelléas* were "more than just a puff of smoke."[6]

In fact, the puff of smoke arose in a different context: he was courting Thérèse Roger and saw his engagement dishonorably undone. Yet despite the emotional turmoil, he completed the first act of his opera.

In July 1894, Paris is "positively arctic," Debussy wrote to Louÿs, who was then frolicking in sun-baked Algeria. "I'm living with Pelléas and Mélisande for company, and very accomplished young people they are."[7] Weeks later, he's "working like a carthorse."[8] He had finished the vault scene and the scene that follows it (Act 3, Scenes 2 and 3), as well as the difficult scene of the boy and the sheep (Act 4, Scene 3).

By now his characters had come alive in his studio, entangled in "the black foliage of sixteenth notes."[9] Mélisande is beginning to employ her seductive hold on Debussy. He tells Lerolle that Pelléas and Mélisande were sulking. They got jealous and leaned over the composer, "and Mélisande addressed me—you know that frail and gentle voice of hers: 'Leave these silly little thoughts, good only for the great musical public, and let your dreams dwell upon my hair. You know there can be no love like ours.'" He's become so involved in his creation that he knows Mélisande the way Pelléas does, and he can feel the opera the way his audiences will. The vault scene is "full of impalpable terror and mysterious enough to make the most well-balanced listener giddy." Empathy for his characters has erased earlier doubts about his ability to portray them in music, and his music is so powerful that it invades his dreams. Act 3, Scene 4 is terrifying, he tells Lerolle; this is when jealous Golaud forces Yniold, his young son, to spy on Mélisande through her bedroom window, and "there's a 'petit père' that gives me nightmares."[10] ("Petit père" is what the boy calls Golaud. He utters the phrase twenty-eight times during this harrowing scene, with mounting anxiety and fear.)

At summer's end Debussy was having the "darkest misgivings" about Pelléas and "feeling like a stone that's been run over by carriage wheels."[11]

He unveiled a few scenes for Lerolle, who loved the music. Raymond Bonheur was also entranced; he remembered Debussy as an incomparable performer of his own works. His fingers on the piano provided "not only the illusion of an orchestra, but an extraordinary impression of life and movement." His voice was "rich in emphasis and expression," and when he sings "the terrible scene with the hair" he gives it "real tragic power."[12] (Bonheur refers to the scene when Golaud, almost insane with anger and jealousy, forces Mélisande to her knees, grabs her long hair, and drags her across the floor.)

In January 1895, shortly after the premiere of Prélude à "L'Après-midi d'un faune," Debussy could be forgiven for taking some time off, but instead he went right back to his opera. He had ominous thoughts about finishing the work, a tragic finale that seemed to be fast approaching. "Pelléas and Mélisande are my only friends at the moment," he told Louÿs. "Indeed, we're getting to know each other too well perhaps, and every time we talk to each other we know perfectly well how it's going to end. And then, finishing a work of art is rather like the death of someone you love, isn't it?"[13] But the work was far from finished.

Early in August, the composer was reworking Act 2. He had expected these scenes to be easy, but they proved to be "pure hell"—so much conversational dialogue to put to music.[14] The scene between Mélisande and Golaud (Act 2, Scene 2) was especially problematic, he told Lerolle: "That's the point where things begin to move towards the catastrophe, and where Mélisande begins to tell Golaud lies and to realize her own motives." Debussy was pleased with the next scene, when the young lovers find themselves at the mouth of a cave, in the dark of night. "I tried to capture all the mystery of the night and the silence in which a blade of grass roused from its slumber makes an alarming noise. And then there's the sea nearby, telling its sorrows to the moon, and Pelléas and Mélisande a little scared of talking, surrounded by so much mystery."[15]

The opera was almost done, but Mélisande could not rest in peace. Debussy returned to Act 5, trembling as he worked. He was concerned about how French audiences would react to the death scene, and his publisher, Georges Hartmann, affirmed his worst fears. Hartmann was "a fair representative of average intelligence," he told Lerolle, unfairly characterizing a distinguished gentleman who was in no way average. "Well, the death of Mélisande . . . has as much effect on him as on a small bench! For him, it doesn't work! But then whenever a woman dies in the French theater it has to be like the *Lady of the Camellias*." Debussy refers to the play on which Verdi's *La Traviata* was based; here, as in numerous operas, the heroine dies slowly, singing heartrending music. In starkest contrast, Mélisande feels the chill of winter and dies in silence, "discreetly, like somebody who has had enough of planet Earth."[16]

The sea, the moon, the winter chill. Then the work was done.

"Now my anxiety begins in earnest," Debussy said. "How will the world behave towards these two poor creatures?"[17]

"Not an earth-shaking event"

"*Pelléas* was finished August 17," Debussy wrote to Pierre Louÿs. "Nothing in the order of things was disturbed; it was not an earth-shaking event. We only noticed that the barometers had set their minds on rising, but we do not think the incident mentioned above was the reason."[18]

During the next month he reluctantly returned to his *Fantaisie pour piano et orchestre*, abandoned in 1890 but now scheduled for a Colonne concert—and then dropped from the program. He set to work on a libretto for an opera based on Balzac's *La Grande Bretêche* but quickly gave it up. "To tell the truth I haven't done very much," he wrote Lerolle. "Extracting all that music [for *Pelléas*] from a single brain has left me exhausted. I intend now to finish the three *Nocturnes*."[19]

In September 1895, Hartmann began paying Debussy a stipend of 500 francs per month, which went a long way toward paying his debts and promoting his well-being. In return, Debussy agreed to edit manuscripts and prepare piano versions of other composers' music, and he gave Hartmann publishing rights to his future compositions. Hartmann, who published under the Fromont imprimatur after he sold his own company in 1891, was an esteemed participant in Parisian musical life between the Franco-Prussian War and the turn of the century. He was a cofounder of the Concerts Colonne and a patron, friend, and publisher to many of the leading composers of his day, including Saint-Saëns, Lalo, Massenet, and, crucially, Debussy.

In October, a newspaper announced that Debussy's *Pelléas* would be produced by André Antoine's avant-garde Théâtre Libre. The composer was concerned about whether Maeterlinck was still on board and requested a written authorization. The poet asked Camille Mauclair for advice: "You know that I, unfortunately, am not only incompetent to judge, but that music is as unintelligible to me as if I were deaf. You, who are a fervent melomaniac, do me the favor of going to listen to this score, and if you judge it good, I shall authorize it." Mauclair went with Louÿs to Debussy's apartment, where the composer performed the entire score for them. Hours later, his friends were pale with emotion. "What are you going to say to Maeterlinck?" Debussy asked Mauclair. "This," he answered, taking a sheet of paper, on which he wrote: "I have just heard one of the most beautiful masterpieces in all music; be proud and happy to have inspired it; send your authorization immediately."[20]

Maeterlinck replied to Debussy on October 17: "As to *Pelléas*, it goes without saying that the matter rests entirely with you and that it can be performed wherever or whenever you like."[21] This letter later proved to be Debussy's strongest defense against Maeterlinck's unwarranted outrage.

But Antoine's group was in financial trouble, and no more was heard of their plans for *Pelléas*. Debussy, believing with some justification that the establishment venues would reject his opera ("I am badly received everywhere"),[22] harbored the idea that Count Robert de Montesquiou, an eccentric member of the haut monde who liked to think of himself as a symbolist poet, would give *Pelléas* a performance or two at his extravagant mansion. Nothing came of the idea.

Debussy was to endure more than five years of frustration before a production of *Pelléas* came into clear view. Meanwhile, in the fall of 1895 he was asked to provide a symphonic suite from his opera to accompany a London performance of Maeterlinck's play, but he turned down the request. In 1896, Ysaÿe expressed interest in presenting a concert version of excerpts, but Debussy refused, saying that key elements of the work would be lost without the stagecraft.

The increasingly unhappy composer was approached again in 1898 to write incidental music, presumably to be drawn from his opera score, for another London production of the play. It would be performed in a new English translation, with Mrs Patrick Campbell as Mélisande. It was bound to attract enormous attention from the press and public. But again Debussy refused, because he had "understood and envisaged this drama in an entirely musical setting [as an opera], and could not undertake something which would have looked like a degeneration of this."[23] So Mrs Campbell turned instead to Fauré, whose enchanting music accompanied productions of the play for many years. To add to Debussy's discomfort, Fauré's incidental music was stitched into a *Pelléas et Mélisande* Suite, which became a concert favorite before Debussy's opera was ever seen, causing no end of confusion among music lovers and students.

In January 1898, André Messager was appointed music director of the Opéra-Comique. He was the composer of dozens of operettas, operas, and ballets, many of which had great success in Paris and London. By the early 1890s, his successes were fewer and his failures were galling, and he began giving more attention to his nascent career, conducting a wide-ranging opera repertoire. During the same year Albert Carré, an actor and stage director, was appointed director of the Opéra-Comique, and the two set about to reinvigorate this venerable Paris company. In May they visited Debussy, who was already acquainted with Messager, and they listened to him perform *Pelléas*. Debussy was pleased that they expressed interest in producing it, but no dates were mentioned or promises made.

Later in the year, the critic Willy, whose opinions were often acerbic, wrote of "the yet unknown music of *Pelléas* by Debussy, which his intimate friends declare to be exquisite. That does not surprise me, for that [composer] is simply rotten with talent."[24]

CHAPTER 13

SONGS OF BILITIS
(1894–1898)

*The "Chansons de Bilitis" deserve to be numbered among the most
beautiful of French songs.*

—M. D. Calvocoressi[1]

In the spring of 1894, Debussy was spiritually submerged in a cold, dark, northern forest. His emotions were entangled in the seductive golden tresses of Mélisande, drawing around him her web of deceit and passion. The Brussels concert was behind him. Thérèse Roger's affections had vaporized in what now seemed like a bad dream. Fortunately, his deepening friendship with Louÿs was a welcome antidote. Over the next several years they collaborated on several projects, none of them actualized, and wrote dozens of letters to each other, especially when Louÿs was wintering in warmer climes.

In Paris, Louÿs had moved to a new, more affordable apartment, where his Wednesday receptions drew prominent writers, including Régnier, Valéry, and Gustave Kahn. One honored guest was Heredia, whose beautiful daughter Marie had captured Louÿs's heart. Debussy sometimes stopped by to perform for the assembled literati the latest scenes from his new opera.

Louÿs's short story *Léda*, based on the Greek myth of Leda and the swan, was published and won enthusiastic reviews from some prominent critics, reinforcing the author's belief that his writing was finally on the right track. On March 5, he began work on his first masterpiece.

Louÿs's *Chansons de Bilitis*

Her tomb was rediscovered by Herr G. Heim, at Paleo-Limisso, by the side of an ancient road not far from Amathus. These ruins have almost disappeared in the past thirty years, and the stones of the house in which Bilitis may have lived pave the quays of Port-Said today. But the tomb was underground,

according to the Phoenician custom, and it had even escaped the depreda-
tions of treasure-hunters.

Herr Heim penetrated into it through a narrow well filled with earth, at
the bottom of which he found a walled-up door which it was necessary to
demolish. The low and spacious cavern, paved with slabs of limestone, had
four walls, covered with plaques of black amphibolite, upon which were
carved in primitive capitals all the songs which will be read hereafter, with
the exception of the three epitaphs which decorated the sarcophagus. . . .
When the tomb was opened she appeared in the state in which a pious hand
had laid her out twenty-four centuries before. Vials of perfume hung from
earthen pegs, and one of them, after so long a time, was still fragrant. . . .[2]

With these paragraphs and many others, Louÿs scrupulously traced the life
and archaeological rediscovery of Bilitis, a poet of ancient Greece, in his
preface to *Les Chansons de Bilitis*. The book was published on December 12,
1894, "translated from the Greek for the first time" by Louÿs. "Bilitis was born
at the beginning of the sixth century before our era," Louÿs wrote. It was the
time of Sappho, whose verses appear to have been among the models for Bilitis's
own. The first edition included ninety-three of Bilitis's poems, four stanzas
each, rendered by Louÿs in French prose.[3]

Bilitis was a smashing success, and scholars were thrilled to have a new
ancient Greek literary text to argue over. One Greek scholar claimed he had
known for many years that Bilitis and Sappho had been friends. Another
scholar, eager to cash in on Louÿs's effort, published "alternate translations" of
six of the poems.

The poems spring from the memories of the aging Bilitis, looking back to
her idyllic adolescence in Pamphilia, on the southern coast of Turkey; to her
maturity on the island of Lesbos, just off Turkey's Aegean coast; and to her
waning years on Cyprus. "The academy was bewildered or completely fooled,"
wrote H. P. Clive, Louÿs's biographer.[4] But with the publication of Louÿs's
novel *Aphrodite*, in 1896, portraying a courtesan's life in the ancient Greek city
of Alexandria, readers recognized the acute sensibilities of the writer of *Bilitis*.
Louÿs owned up to the hoax: he alone had invented Herr Heim and Bilitis
and her poems. The fame of *Bilitis* spread further; a second edition in 1898,
expanded to 143 poems and three epitaphs, established Louÿs as one of the
most accomplished writers of his generation.

The triumph of *Bilitis* was founded partly on the elegance of Louÿs's flowing prose, which was said to be Parnassian in its meticulous craftsmanship and its classical themes; partly on Louÿs's knowledge of obscure ancient traditions, sacred rites, and poetry; and partly on his ability to imagine and convincingly furnish what he couldn't know. Not least laudable was his uncanny empathy with the heart and mind of a fictional character of an entirely different place, time, gender, and sexuality at several stages of her life. For many readers, of course, the book's main attraction was its eroticism, veiled and subtle when the young, innocent Bilitis is wooed by her handsome shepherd, but more frank when depicting Bilitis's adult life as a courtesan and her carnal preference for women.

André Gide and M. b. A.

By the summer of 1893, Louÿs's boyhood friendship with Gide had reached a stage of diverging pathways, intermittency, and bruised feelings. Louÿs admired Wagner's operas; Gide preferred the purity of chamber music. Gide chastely clung to the vestiges of his Puritan upbringing and was hoping to marry his beautiful cousin Emmanuèle; Louÿs cherished all the pleasures of the flesh. Gide's writing was veering into a new realism, a spare style that favored directness and simplicity; Louÿs was preserving the old Parnassian model, tinged with symbolism now, but elegant, formal, and, above all, sensual.

Louÿs had brought Gide into Mallarmé's circle and encouraged him to send some early writings to Heredia for his astute opinions. "I really think that if it had not been for Pierre Louÿs, I should have continued living in solitude like a savage," Gide wrote, "not that I had no desire to go into literary society, and find friends there, but an invincible shyness held me back, and the fear which still paralyzes me of boring or being in the way of the people I feel most drawn to."[5] Gide acknowledged that Louÿs was "more spontaneous than I, more enterprising, certainly cleverer too and with a more mature talent. . . . [But] there was something aggressive, romantic, and antagonistic about Pierre," so that the terms of their friendship were always unstable.[6] For several years Gide had been trying to gain independence from his overbearing friend, and by 1893 he had created a protective shield for himself, in part by not answering Louÿs's letters soon enough or with the warmth and affection that Louÿs expected.

But then Gide undertook a voyage to Africa that changed the course of his life and spun Louÿs's around as well. For Gide it was an awakening, an understanding that the Puritan morality imposed by his family was nowhere in the teachings of Christ, whom he loved, but was a later construct of Christianity. "In the name of what God or what ideal," he wondered, "do you forbid me to live according to my nature? And where would my nature lead me if I simply followed it?"[7] His friend Paul Laurens was given a traveling scholarship, money enough for a year's journey, and asked Gide to accompany him. They sailed for Algiers in October 1893, and Gide wondered if while there he would "cross the threshold of what is called sin."[8] Gide would be twenty-four years old a month later.

In the town of Biskra, an oasis on the edge of the Saharan desert, Gide was introduced to a prostitute named Meriem bent Atala. She was one of the girls of the Oulad Naïl tribe who were sent out by their families at an early age to acquire the skills of the trade, then sell their services until they'd put by a sufficient dowry to come home and marry a good man. It was an established part of the culture. In his memoir, *If It Die*, Gide described Meriem as amber-skinned, with firm flesh and a somewhat childish figure. She was only sixteen when he met her. She and her cousin danced for Gide and Laurens in the Saharan Arab tradition, shaking their tinkling bracelets, "their heads straight and erect, their busts motionless, their hands agile, their whole bodies shaken by the rhythmic beating of their feet." The music, said Gide, "went to my head, stupefied me like an opiate, drowsily and voluptuously benumbed my thoughts."[9] With Meriem, Gide abandoned his chastity, but he soon discovered he had a disturbing preference for the brown-skinned adolescent boys of Biskra.

In the next months, Gide developed a persistent pulmonary congestion. He returned to Europe to consult with a doctor in Geneva, a family friend who diagnosed "nothing wrong but my nerves." The doctor prescribed a hydrotherapy cure at Champel, near Geneva, followed by a winter in the mountains.[10]

In early July, Louÿs was traveling with his friend Ferdinand Hérold, bound for the Wagner extravaganzas in Bayreuth. He took a detour to Geneva, hoping to rekindle Gide's enthusiasm for their friendship. Captivated by Gide's stories of Biskra and Meriem, Louÿs excitedly set off for Algeria with Hérold in tow. Wagner be damned!

Finding Meriem as delightful as Gide promised but Biskra infernally hot in summer, the two young men settled in Constantine, a picturesque city with a more affable climate. Meriem joined them there in early August. Louÿs had already begun some of the *Bilitis* verses months earlier. In Meriem he found not just a rich lode of inspiration but the very embodiment of his irresistible, libidinous young Bilitis—"a marvel of grace, of delicacy, and of antique poetry."[11] To Debussy he wrote, with his usual enthusiasm, that he'd found a girl "with the most depraved morals!"[12] He stayed in Constantine and wrote feverishly, revising his earlier verses, writing new ones, and finishing his manuscript in September. *Les Chansons de Bilitis* was published in December by the Librairie de l'Art Indépendant in an edition of 500 copies, with funding from Georges Louis. The book bore a mysterious dedication to "André Gide / M. b. A. / Champel / 11 juillet 1894."[13] July 11 was the day, Champel was the place, that Louÿs first learned from Gide about Meriem bent Atala (M. b. A.).

By the time *Bilitis* was in print, Louÿs was in Paris and in extremis. He had barely any income as yet from his writing, and the last of his father's inheritance had been spent. (In April 1895, he claimed that all he had left was a five-franc coin.) He had never thought much about money or cared about thrift. He spent lavishly because he was convinced he would die young, like his mother and his brother Paul, before his funds ran out. He was depressed about facing poverty for the first time, despite Georges's dependable support, yet he was depressed, too, about his financial dependence on his brother. He was annoyed that Georges wouldn't allow him to visit him in Cairo and that Gide hadn't dedicated his recent book to him. He was unhappy in the belief that the Heredia family might not permit him to marry their beautiful Marie, about whom he felt passionate. He was upset about the notorious trial of his friend Oscar Wilde, which was unfolding in London. He was despondent about his frequent bouts of bronchitis, and now a severe intestinal inflammation was causing great discomfort. "I saw myself ruined," he told Debussy later, "without a sou . . . Suddenly I had my hand on a revolver. I would *certainly* have used it on myself, if not for my brother."[14]

Collaborations Abandoned

As *Pelléas* wound down to its final pages in August 1895 and Debussy suffered from an exhausted brain, a question kept surfacing: what's next? Mozart might have been spared this question, as he knew that when one symphony was finished his patrons would want another, if not a concerto or string quartet. Wagner had the adoration of King Ludwig, who would have produced anything that dripped from his protégé's pen. Tchaikovsky had Mme von Meck. Debussy had no patrons, no easy answers. He had no answer at all. In his best-case scenario, he'd have been immersed in rehearsals by this time for an imminent production of *Pelléas*. The scenario he feared was another depression and an inability to work.

Valéry came to Debussy with an interesting idea for a ballet based on the Orpheus legend. It was to be "the clearest ballet in the world, one without a programme," Valéry wrote, "for one should see only what legs and instruments permit." He saw the Orpheus myth as a fable "dealing essentially with movement and order."[15] Nothing came of the project.

Collaborations with Louÿs should have been more successful, because the two men were thoroughly sympathetic with each other's creative temperaments. In the spring of 1895, Louÿs and Debussy were brainstorming a children's play with music—perhaps something like the English pantomimes—based on French folk-tales. It was to be called *Cendrelune*, and it was meant to be staged at the Opéra-Comique at Christmastime. Louÿs wrote several muddled scenarios with other titles, different characters and plots, a mishmash of references to *Parsifal* and ancient myths. Each effort met with Debussy's dissatisfaction until, in a fit of pique, the librettist told the composer to "write it yourself. You are perfectly capable of doing so."[16] Louÿs was not amused by Debussy's suggestion that Gide might be persuaded to help with the libretto. The project stalled, though Debussy made several futile attempts to revive it.[17]

Later in the year, Louÿs, almost as desperate for money as Debussy was, brought his friend a proposal for a ballet. "Would you have the courage to write in twelve days a ballet in three scenes," he asked, "thirty minutes' music on a libretto by myself, the title of which is *Daphnis et Khloé* (with a Beautiful K)?"[18]

Strangely, the idea came from Wilde, who was fond of the story of young lovers by the ancient Greek writer Longus. At first he thought of asking Lord Alfred Douglas to collaborate with him on a libretto. Wilde gave a draft of his notes to Louÿs, and Louÿs, with obvious relish, wrote Debussy that the project was in his hands. Louÿs would write the scenario; Houston Stewart Chamberlain, the producer, would give it two weeks of performances, with payments to the writers in cash—if Debussy could churn out a score in a fortnight. To entice the composer, Louÿs emphasized that Daphnis was a flutist, and the ballet was to open with a flute solo. So couldn't Claude "pinch something from the 'Faun's afternoon'?"[19] After overcoming his initial reluctance, Debussy made an attempt, but soon gave it up. Writing a thirty-minute ballet in two weeks was not in this composer's bag of tricks.

Later, for several months, Louÿs and Debussy collaborated on a musical setting of Rossetti's "Willow-wood," to be called *La Saulaie*. When Debussy brushed off Ysaÿe's request for a suite of excerpts from *Pelléas*, he offered him *La Saulaie* instead, saying the new work was very important and reflected some fresh musical ideas. Like so many other projects Debussy undertook with Louÿs, *La Saulaie* was abandoned.

Finally there was a small project Debussy would take on willingly. In late 1896, he and Satie were among the visitors to Gustave Doret's salon, along with Dukas and several others. At one of these events, Satie played his *Trois Gymnopédies* for Doret; surprisingly, while the pieces are technically simple, the composer's piano technique was even more rudimentary. Debussy offered to play them with a surer hand, whereupon Doret suggested that Debussy orchestrate them, as Satie had no experience writing for an orchestra. Debussy chose the first and third of the *Gymnopédies* to orchestrate. They were first performed, Doret conducting, at a National Society concert in February 1897. The public recognition was an important boost for Satie's languishing musical career, and Debussy's work eventually helped elevate the *Gymnopédies* to a popularity Satie could never have imagined.

If 1896 was an unproductive year for Debussy, 1897 was a disaster. It began with a lackluster banquet he helped organize in honor of Mallarmé and ended with contemplations of suicide.

For Louÿs, however, these were golden years. Late in 1895, his novel, *Aphrodite: Ancient Morals*, was serialized in *Mercure de France*. It was published in March 1896 in book form and was an immediate success. *Le Journal* ran a front-page review in which François Coppée, whose conventional morality might have caused him to reject Louÿs's sizzling tale of a Greek courtesan, effusively praised the beauty of Louÿs's writing. Despite (or because of) the several reviewers who called it scandalous, by the end of the year *Aphrodite* had sold 50,000 copies. It went on to become, according to some estimates, the best-selling French novel of its time and saved Louÿs from the uncomfortable grip of poverty and despair. His fame spread throughout France and beyond, and his pockets were once again engorged with cash.

Louÿs journeyed to North Africa again and again. In February 1897, he was diagnosed with bronchopneumonia and spent four months convalescing in

Algeria, cheered and amused by a young Moorish woman named Zohra ben Brahim, whom he came to love "beyond measure."[20] In May he returned to Paris with Zohra, who lived with him till the end of the year. Zohra was an attractive, intelligent, fun-loving woman, educated by French nuns, and she spoke French like a Parisian. To many of his friends it was a puzzling relationship and a provocation; some people made it clear that Zohra was unwelcome in their society. Zohra's presence and Louÿs's constancy was further compromised when, in October, he resumed his love affair with the intriguing Marie de Heredia, who was now known as Marie de Régnier. She had taken Louÿs's friend Henri as her husband.

Debussy's *Trois Chansons de Bilitis*

It was inevitable that one day Debussy would set some of the *Bilitis* poems to music, but he didn't begin writing them until June 1897. First he asked Louÿs's permission to set "La Flûte de Pan." Louÿs wanted him to use "La Chevelure," which, in a burst of passion for Marie, he had recently written for the second edition of *Bilitis*. Debussy wrote both songs, and early the next year he completed a third, "Le Tombeau des naïades." (For translations of the poems, see Appendix B.)

The three poems come from the first section of *Les Chansons de Bilitis* ("Bucolics in Pamphylia"), in which Bilitis is portrayed as a spirited young girl befriended by the shepherd Lycas, an older youth with seductive strategies. Not by chance, Debussy chose verses that represent the young naïveté of Bilitis, the loss of her innocence, and the troubled end of her childhood in Pamphilia. Listeners familiar with the original text—that is, most Parisians of the fin de siècle—would understand that the composer had chosen the three, of the dozens of poems, that span the entire story of Bilitis's time with Lycas.

This coherent song cycle was a creative departure for Debussy—a giant step from the Verlaine songs and the Baudelaire songs, but recognizably the work of the composer of *Pelléas et Mélisande*. The emotional undertones, present in all Debussy's songs, are here somewhat reticent, as are the young Bilitis's verses. Harmonically, the songs give rein to Debussy's predilection for shifting modalities obscured by unconventional harmonic changes. "[Debussy's] *Chansons de Bilitis* will paint for you . . . the mad, passionate dream of a carnal mysticism designed to shake to the core any being worthy to be called living," wrote Louis Laloy.[21] Vallas writes that the *Bilitis* songs "are amongst the composer's most significant and perfect works."[22]

"La Flûte de Pan" is a charming song, with a lyrical simplicity that befits the chaste young girl. Lycas gives Bilitis a syrinx (panpipes, or flute) made of reeds "held together with white wax that is sweet as honey on my lips." He teaches her to play while she sits on his knees, "trembling a little." Taking turns on the flute, their mouths are united. But it's late; the chirping of the green frogs signifies nighttime. Her mother will never believe she stayed out so long just to search for her waistband.

The song begins in the piano with a flutelike melody that ascends and slowly returns on an archaic Lydian scale suggesting ancient Greece. The simulation of a flute or panpipes in this context is a reference to a pastoral poetic tradition. With this single stroke, Debussy evokes Bilitis's idyllic environment. The vocal melodies are declamatory: They follow the natural intonations, phrasing, and rhythms of speech, and the vocal range is quite narrow. The harmonic character changes completely on "It is late," with chords that suggest trouble. In a brief interlude, the chirping of the frogs is heard in the insistent repetition of a high-pitched, dissonant chord that underlies the thought that her mother won't believe her excuses.

Each of the three songs has its own character. "La Chevelure" (The Tresses) is "agitated and obscure," wrote Vallas, "like the dream of love which constitutes its subject."[23] Lycas says he dreamed that Bilitis's tresses wound around his neck, binding the two youths this way forever, their mouths together, their limbs completely merged. After telling her this, he gently puts his hands on her shoulders and looks at her tenderly, causing a shiver (*frisson*). The dream, if it is that, suggests the possibility that their passion has been consummated.

The piano accompaniment is notable for its obsessive use of chords containing the piquant interval of the second, lending an atmosphere of mystery or unease. In the middle section, the emotional intensity increases. The voice is louder, the vocal range is extended, the tempo quickens; a melodic climax is reached when the lovers' mouths meet and again when they seem to merge into each other. Then the song comes nearly to a halt; the piano's mysterious phrases of the opening bars return, very slowly, when he puts his hands on her shoulders. In the final moments the dissonances unexpectedly dissolve into the most blissfully consonant chord imaginable—perhaps it's what a young woman's *frisson* sounds like.

"Le Tombeau des naïades" (The Tomb of the Naiads) is the last poem of the "Bucolics" section. It represents a culmination. Readers of Louÿs's book know, from the intervening poems, that Lycas has long since satisfied his desire for Bilitis. She has become pregnant, and their relationship will soon end unhappily. The warm springtime of youth has turned now to frost, snow, ice, and disillusionment. It's been a terrible winter; the naiads (river nymphs) and satyrs are dead; Bilitis's sandals are heavy with muddy snow. At the end, Lycas breaks a sheet of ice that covers the naiads' spring; he raises pieces of ice to the sky, looking through them, presumably toward a future without Bilitis.

This is an unabashedly lovely song. The sense of idyllic youth is completely gone, and the music has a more modern feeling. Bilitis, in the first two songs, has the voice of innocent youth, while here in the third she is an older, wiser woman sadly reminiscing. The accompaniment is, in tempo and temperament, more consistent, more flowing, than the others. The presence in the piano's treble range of an abundance of parallel thirds is so uncommon in Debussy's music that you might wonder if this is really someone else's work—Delibes, perhaps, or Saint-Saëns; in his use of parallel thirds Debussy creates a harmonic wash of consonance that sweetens much of the song.[24] In the darker middle section, telling of the death of satyrs and nymphs, Debussy sours the sweet parallel thirds with chromatic dissonance. But he lightens the mood again as Bilitis, nostalgic with love and wonder, describes Lycas's breaking the ice and looking through the pieces.

Vallas describes "Naïades" as "a magnificent fresco . . . festoons of major thirds, fifths, series of sevenths, common chords, clusters of ninths, whole-tone scales, and the rasping dissonances of minor seconds vibrating like cymbals . . . as the voice of Bilitis pours forth a broad, thrilling, irresistible melody. It is a masterpiece of music, of poetry, and one might say, of painting too; in this type of art, neither Debussy nor any other musician has surpassed this supreme standard."[25]

Debussy's *Trois Chansons de Bilitis* was published in 1899 and received its first hearing at a private party organized by one of the composer's young piano students, Michèle Worms de Romilly. After the third and final song, the room reverberated with the outraged voice of an elderly Argentinian—"No, no, that's not music! How do people come to write stuff like that?" He was then introduced by the embarrassed hostess to Debussy, who was merely amused by the passionate gentleman.[26]

The first public performance occurred in March 1900 at a National Society concert, with Blanche Morot singing and the composer at the piano. Though Morot and a few others regularly sang the *Bilitis* songs in recitals, some singers refused to perform them, unwilling to be tainted by Bilitis's loose morals. The songs did not reach a broader public until, in 1909, a great diva at the Paris Opéra, Lucienne Bréval, added *Bilitis* to her concert repertoire. Known for her dramatic roles in Wagner, Gluck, and Massenet, she "gave a passionate, romantic, theatrical interpretation which was not perhaps quite in keeping with Debussy's artistic ideals" but captivated the audience.[27]

In February 1901, a staged version of Louÿs's *Bilitis* poems was given a single private performance at the offices of *Le Journal*. At Louÿs's urging, Debussy wrote some very brief, otherworldly fragments for the production, scored for two harps, two flutes, and a celesta, played during intervals between the poems. Louÿs happily supervised the rehearsals. "This week I spent all my afternoons with naked women," he wrote Georges. At the performance, while a certain Mlle Milton narrated ten of the poems, the women—"sometimes draped with veils, sometimes in Grecian robes, sometimes with nothing at all"—mimed the actions suggested by the verses, or simply posed. [28]

In 1914, when Durand was eager to publish all Debussy could give him, the composer disinterred six of the fragments for a suite of piano pieces, spinning out each morsel to a suitable concert length in a variety of moods and exotic scales. He called them *Six Épigraphes antiques*.

CHAPTER 14

CLAUDE IN LOVE, OR THE HEARTS OF ARTISTS (1890s)

Susceptibility to love is for [Debussy] a tumultuous joy, and is essential. . . . The bewilderment of love is present in all his works, fugitive, cruelly—and happily.

—Marcel Dietschy[1]

To say that Debussy was unlucky in love belies a simple truth: he wasn't very good at it. In fact, Debussy seems to have had little native aptitude for personal relationships. As a youth he was socially clumsy. As a mature adult he could be gruff, dismissive, and disagreeable, especially to strangers and those he believed to be undeserving of his attention; but to close friends and others whom he liked and respected he was genuinely kind and generous. "His passion was tempered by disillusionment and experience," André Suarès said. "There was something catlike and solitary about him, and I think a fundamental melancholy always separated him somewhat from others."[2]

Debussy was a hedonist, and not everyone approved. He certainly loved his pleasures: well-prepared food, pastries, fine wines, fashionable clothing, and beauty in art, music, and all other things. But to imply, as some have done, that Debussy was a libertine is simply wrong.[3] The historical record yields relatively few romantic or sexual relationships (Louÿs said Debussy had only five), and none of these was a casual dalliance. Music was undoubtedly his first and most passionate love, and most women would have found it difficult to play second fiddle.

In his thirties, Debussy seemed eager to be married. It is clear, in hindsight, that his prolonged affair with Gaby Dupont was not entirely satisfactory to him. It is likely he hoped to marry a woman of good family, a woman untainted by a disreputable past; but a woman, like Gaby, who would run his household well and shield him from unnecessary distractions so he could concentrate on his music. It would be helpful if his wife shared his refined tastes, and blissful if she reminded him a little of Marie Vasnier or, better still, had the rare luminosity of Mélisande, but such a woman was hard to find. He proposed marriage to four women. None of the four glowed like Mélisande or sang like Marie, but none doubted the sincerity of Debussy's affections.

There is scant documentation of his affair with Marie Vasnier other than his letters from Rome and the flowery dedications written on the songs he gave her. We have the testimony of a few observers, but Paul Vidal's jealousy colored his opinions, and Marguerite Vasnier was only a child at the time. Did Marie return his love, or was she merely flattered by the attentions of a talented young musician who wrote songs for her? And what was her husband's role in the affair? Of Claude's intense feelings for Marie, the most telling evidence comes from the frantic letters he wrote to Claudius and Gustave Popelin in the summer of 1886, when his paramour was slipping away from him. He wanted her "to be mine completely." He was distraught. He wasn't thinking clearly. To the Popelins he writes of his "insane love . . . its very madness keeps me from being rational." Thinking about her induces "even greater insanity" and "periods of despair."[4]

Not long after Debussy's return from Rome in early 1887, the Vasniers moved from their apartment on rue de Constantinople to another Paris neighborhood, and Debussy never saw them again. Never again would he love a woman with the kind of passion he felt for Mme Vasnier—the passion of first love, rarely repeated in the lives of most adults.

In 1891, his relationship with Gaby was still in flux, and he "desperately needed to unburden" himself about his "sufferings, great and small" in a letter to Robert Godet, his closest confidante at the time. The letter contains almost all we know about a brief romance. He was confused and deeply hurt by an affair that had ended "so miserably and cheaply, with tales being told and unmentionable things said. . . . I loved her so much." He sadly acknowledges "this arrogant weakness of mine, wanting to share my life with someone before making sure she feels the same way."[5]

There has been speculation, for lack of evidence, that the woman in question was Camille Claudel. She was the beautiful older sister of the writer Paul Claudel; the student, model, confidante, and longtime lover of Auguste Rodin; and herself an esteemed, successful sculptor. Lockspeiser mentions Claude's "friendship" with Camille in the early 1890s and attributes to Godet the assertion that "this highly gifted and original artist was an object of rivalry between Debussy and Rodin."[6] Several of Debussy's friends remembered a small sculpture called "La Valse" that Camille gave to Claude in 1893; it was displayed in his home for the rest of his life.

Catherine Stevens

Catherine Stevens was "one of the most radiant and charming figures to whom Debussy ever succumbed," according to René Peter. She was the daughter of Alfred Stevens, a Belgian artist known especially for his portraits of beautiful, fashionably dressed women. Alfred achieved enormous success in Brussels and Paris in the 1860s and '70s, but he suffered financial reversals and illness in subsequent decades.

Claude was welcomed into the Stevens family around 1889. "There can be no doubt of the mutual attraction that soon grew up between the composer and the young girl," wrote Peter.[7] (Actually, Catherine was only three years younger than Claude.) In May 1892, Debussy dedicated the second version of his song "En Sourdine" to her: "In homage and to indicate a little of my joy in being her affectionate and devoted Claude Debussy."[8]

Soon after, Debussy was dining with the Stevens family three times a week. Catherine's memoir tells of her joyous evenings with Debussy in 1893, when Claude and other friends gathered at the Stevens home: "Debussy would go to the piano; we would sing in chorus the operettas of Hervé and Offenbach. . . . When we were alone, we would play [piano] four-hands." He also played bits from *Pelléas et Mélisande*, which was just beginning to coalesce in his mind and on paper. "In spite of the problems of his life, he was usually cheerful, at our house at least. He did not put on airs, he knew how to be agreeable."[9]

In 1895 or '96, flush with the great satisfaction of finishing his opera, Debussy proposed marriage to Catherine. It was a bold move. "He was dealing with a young woman of honor with whom there could be no question of love-making without marriage," wrote Peter. "And why not marry?"[10] He certainly loved her and felt a strong bond with her family. But though the family was fond of him, he was, after all, an impoverished bohemian, and Alfred would consider him an unsuitable match for his daughter. Besides, they knew he had a mistress at home. On the other hand, Debussy thought he could help rescue the family from their declining fortunes—he promised Catherine that after

Pelléas was produced he would be rich. "Once *Pelléas* is performed we'll talk about it," she replied.[11]

Peter quotes from a letter he received from Catherine in the aftermath. "He gave me proof of such disinterested love during the worst moments of a family crisis, he whom people have called 'grasping,'" said Catherine. "I would have married him, despite everything that was being said about him at the time … if I hadn't met Henry," a charming young doctor. "Claude was dismissed gently, to spare his feelings," Peter wrote, "but for some days he was inconsolable. Then he returned to *Pelléas* … and to Gaby, whose triumph was, as always, to be only temporary."[12]

Third-Rate Literature

In early 1897, Louÿs was basking in the critical and public adulation showered on him for *Bilitis* and *Aphrodite*. He was no longer dependent on his brother; and, in the wildly picturesque city of Constantine, he had reached new heights of ecstasy with Zohra.

Meanwhile, Debussy was mired in melodrama. On February 9, he wrote a long letter to his absent friend. He began innocently enough with a proclamation that Louÿs was never far from his thoughts. Then, the terrible surprise:

> I've been mixed up in a tiresome business … Gaby, she of the piercing eye, found a letter in my pocket which left no doubt as to the advanced state of a love affair, and containing enough picturesque material to inflame even the most stolid heart. Whereupon … Scenes … Tears … A real revolver … It would have been nice to have you here, my dear Pierre, to help me recognize myself in all this third-rate literature. It's all senseless, pointless, and it changes absolutely nothing; you can't wipe out a mouth's kisses or a body's caresses by passing an india-rubber [eraser] over them. … However, poor Gaby has just lost her father and this intervention by death has sorted out the whole stupid business for the moment. Even so I've been completely knocked sideways.[13]

"Maybe you'll think it's all my fault," Debussy continued. Of course it was his fault, and he seems to be making light of Gaby's distress, perhaps to hide his embarrassment and shame.[14] Debussy goes on to tell Louÿs about the

Mallarmé banquet, occasioned by the publication of the ailing poet's book *Divagations*. The banquet was by all accounts a failure and left Mallarmé as bored as Debussy was. Debussy asks if Louÿs has done any work on the libretto for *Cendrelune*. The opera would give him something constructive to do, he said, to "sprinkle a little water on this sickly plant which my life resembles at the moment."[15] *Cendrelune*, however, was moldering in the trash bin of abandoned opportunities.

After the sudden death of her father, Gaby worried about her mother's future. She made several trips to Normandy to look after her and rented a small house for her in Orbec. "Debussy believed that these occupations would distract her and make her forget his latest escapade and forgive him once again," Victor Seroff writes, "but Gaby had made up her mind. Although she returned and they continued to live under the same roof, they lived like strangers, and Gaby was only biding her time for an opportunity to leave for good."[16]

Other than the completion of two *Chansons de Bilitis* and the orchestration of Satie's *Gymnopédies*, Debussy accomplished little else that year. On the last day of 1897, he wrote to Georges Hartmann of his "extreme sadness" at the "dreary end" of a year in which he accomplished little and didn't live up to his own expectations.[17] He had been working on the *Nocturnes* again, but they were far from finished.

Meanwhile, according to Seroff, "perhaps just to appease her feminine pride, her wounded ego, [Gaby] had a love affair with a painter"—unknown except by the initials V. M. The affair didn't last long. "Gaby was waiting for someone who could offer her a better life."[18]

On March 27, 1898, Debussy wrote to Louÿs that he was "miserable" since Louÿs's departure for Egypt and had "shed tears copiously," as tears are all he had left in his "wretched condition." He said he had completed the third of the *Bilitis* songs and had resumed work on the *Nocturnes*, which presented many difficulties that he was unable, in his present state of mind, to resolve. "I've never been able to work at anything when my life's going through a crisis." He once again asked Louÿs to complete the libretto for *Cendrelune* so he has something enjoyable to work on. "Otherwise I shall go mad and resort to suicide, which would be even more stupid." Then there's an ominous reference to "the sequence of events which have so cruelly gone against me."[19] Louÿs, his closest friend, must have known what events, what crisis, had put suicidal thoughts in his mind.

In Louÿs's reply we hear his empathy and concern for his friend. He starts by mentioning how moved he was, in Rome recently, to see Debussy's painted portrait "delightfully placed" next to that of Ingres, in the dining hall of the Villa Medici. He reminds Debussy of his own dark moments four years earlier, when he felt his work was worthless, and he was "without a sou," without any hope of being published. Then Louÿs writes:

> Now you, my dear chap, you haven't the shadow of an excuse for nightmares of this kind—because YOU ARE A GREAT MAN. Do you understand the meaning of this? . . . Whatever troubles you may have, this thought must dominate everything. You must continue with your work, and you must get it known. . . . All that you say concerns me deeply. If you think I can be of any use tell me how. I will do everything I can.

Louÿs ends on a note of comfort. Tell me, he says, "if I may bring a little lunch to your place, Monday at one o'clock."[20]

Alice, Gaby, Lilly

The woman who wrote the love letter that Gaby found has never been conclusively identified, but evidence centers on Alice Peter, "a woman of the world."[21] She was married to René Peter's brother Michel but was separated from him. To Alice, Debussy dedicated "La Chevelure" (one of the three *Chansons de Bilitis*), which he completed a few months after the sordid scene with Gaby and the pistol. René Peter wrote of "a certain woman in society who knew how to flirt amusingly, and who, seeing [Debussy] ready to adapt himself to the part of cavalier servant, was happy to draw out the episode as far as it would go, was flattered to become in some people's eyes—and perhaps even to believe herself— 'the muse of the great man of the future.'"[22]

In a letter to Alice Peter written in May or June 1898, Debussy mentions the break that had occurred in their relationship. Near the end of the letter he says, "Don't forget me entirely, and try to let me have some news of you," which suggests that their relationship, if any, would be kept at a distance.[23] There were other troubling circumstances. His continued cohabitation with Gaby was less than congenial. Money was always a problem, and Hartmann was impatiently waiting for the *Nocturnes*. A month later, in another letter to Louÿs, he is still "alone and depressed. . . . I scarcely know where I'm going, perhaps toward suicide, a stupid outcome to something which perhaps deserved better."[24]

The year was not entirely a disaster. For his friend Lucien Fontaine's amateur choir, he wrote two *Chansons de Charles d'Orléans*, on verses by a fifteenth-century duke who wrote hundreds of poems during a twenty-five-year imprisonment in England.[25] The composer himself rehearsed the choir in the new *Chansons*. Michèle Worms de Romilly, a participant, wrote: "He was an excellent chorus-master, with the patience of a saint. . . . He managed to turn a handful of vague and inexperienced amateurs into a musical and disciplined body of singers."[26]

Soon after, young Michèle began taking private singing and piano lessons with Debussy, and she writes of gazing out the window, watching for his arrival. He arrived in a covered carriage "drawn by a nervous pony. He wore a soft hat with a wide brim, his sharp features surrounded by a small, curly black beard. A large cape was drawn around him, a strange sight which made me think of a young Roman in his chariot." Under his cape was the blue serge suit of the kind and color he wore consistently for many years. He looked with disapproval at the scores on the piano, "and put them all aside except those by Wagner and Bach, which were the only ones that found grace in his eyes."[27]

In the spring of 1898, René Peter introduced Debussy to Rosalie Texier, a model for the fashion designers Soeurs Callot. Everyone called her Lilly. She was twenty-five years old and had been living with a man who "dabbled in stocks,"[28] but she was physically afraid of him. At the time, Claude had not yet severed Gaby's hold on him and was still entangled with Alice Peter. Gaby became Lilly's friend well before Claude felt the attraction of her beauty and elegance.

In July, Debussy needed an advance from Hartmann, who was ill, and wrote: "My life is decorated with complications of a sentimental nature, turning it into the most awkward and involved thing I know." He needs a lot of money, he says, in order to overcome the barriers that separate him from someone with whom he wished to find happiness; and since he spends all his time trying not to die of hunger, he risks watching "all my fine, beautiful dreams being smashed to pieces." He tells the publisher he has completed the *Nocturnes*, except for the orchestrations. He urges him to draft a contract with the Opéra-Comique "so they can't keep us on a string indefinitely."[29]

In September, Debussy told Hartmann he would soon deliver the three *Nocturnes*, "which together have given me more trouble than the five acts of

Pelléas."[30] On the first day of 1899, Debussy wrote of a bronchial infection; he has moved to a new apartment (at 52 rue Cardinet); he *won't* yet be able to deliver the *Nocturnes*—and Gaby Dupont "has resigned her position."[31]

Earlier, a wealthy South American banker with a long mustache and a bald head, Count Victor de Balbiani, came to visit Debussy. An amateur poet, he asked the composer to write incidental music for a play he'd written. He offered a large sum of money for Debussy's participation but was rebuffed. "Monsieur, I am offering you half my glory!" the banker shouted. "Keep it all," the composer replied, and showed him to the door.[32] It occurred to Gaby that the stranger was attracted to her, and she wondered how she might cross his path again.

By this time, Debussy and Lilly had established a warmer relationship, and Gaby felt she would be leaving Claude in good hands. As a parting gift, Debussy gave her the original manuscript score of *Prélude à "L'Après-midi d'un faune,"* inscribed "To my dear and very beautiful little Gaby, with the assured affection of her devoted Claude Debussy."[33]

No one can know to what extent Gaby was, if not the inspiration, perhaps the facilitator of Debussy's outpouring of music in the 1890s; how dedicated was her patience and forbearance; or how important was her ability to provide him with the comfort, quiet, and stability required for such an intensity of creativity. These were among the most productive years of his life. During the eight years since meeting Gaby, he wrote *Rodrigue et Chimène*, the String Quartet, *Faune*, *Bilitis*, *Nocturnes*, many mélodies and piano pieces, and *Pelléas*. Why did Gaby leave him? Was it his unremitting poverty, his clumsily concealed affairs, his frequent periods of depression? All these reasons. And a more promising opportunity.

She became the mistress of Count Victor de Balbiani, in all his glory.

"No laughter here with Lilly gone"

By the early months of 1899, Debussy and Lilly Texier were, if not in love, at least inclined toward love. She was bourgeois in her tastes and ignorant about music, but she was beautiful, blonde, and graceful. He was sometimes inconsiderate, but he was a genius.

On May 15, Pierre Louÿs, surprisingly, announced his engagement to Louise de Heredia, the youngest of Heredia's three daughters. Louÿs had known the family for nearly a decade. It was always Marie who most attracted him, and as early as 1894 he was madly in love with her. Marie was perfect—smart, sophisticated, charming, and a talented writer. But in 1894 he was a struggling young writer, unable to provide her with the life she deserved.

According to Claude Farrère, who claimed he was informed by Marie herself, both Louÿs and Régnier were smitten with Marie and made a pact: Neither would formally declare his love for her, unless both did it on the same day, to allow her to choose. Farrère asserted that Régnier unfairly took advantage of Louÿs's temporary absence from Paris to win Marie for himself. Marie took Louÿs's reticence for either a lack of interest or an inability to commit to a relationship, and she married Régnier in 1896. Louÿs was desolate; Marie eventually learned the truth. While married to Régnier, she and Louÿs conducted an illicit affair for years, meeting secretly at a rented apartment. Marie de Régnier's first child, she told Louÿs, was his own. The boy was named Pierre.

By 1899, Marie's sister Louise had insinuated herself into Louÿs's life. She loved him. Her father's gambling debts had rendered the family almost impoverished and left Louise without a dowry to offer a potential suitor. Hoping to earn enough to support herself, she asked Louÿs if he'd hire her as his secretary. She was attractive and had many of the best qualities of the Heredia daughters. He liked her, and he felt sorry about her reduced state. Instead of hiring her, he proposed marriage.

To Debussy he wrote that Louise de Heredia was going to change her name to the more balanced and symmetrical Louise Louÿs. Would his friend write a wedding march for the occasion?—200 measures, "something lascivious and ejaculatory as befits a wedding procession"[34]—the sort of little masterpiece that one might write at a café while drinking beer. After a civil wedding on June 22, the religious ceremony at Saint-Philippe on the 24th attracted the attention of society and the press; in attendance were many literary luminaries and members of the aristocracy wearing the latest Paris fashions. Among the guests was Louÿs's new friend, an aristocrat named Auguste Gilbert de Voisins. Of course, no one suspected that Gilbert, a writer and world traveler, would one day be Louise's husband.

To his friend's request for a wedding march, Debussy responded affirmatively and promised to write one full of "brotherly affection." But it might be the last wedding march he'd write, he added, as he's been so wedded to music for so long that "I don't think there's room for marriage."[35]

Unfortunately, Debussy was ill and couldn't attend the wedding. He had a persistent fever for weeks, giving him ample time to consider his own future. His friendships were dwindling. Mallarmé had died in September 1898. Godet was frequently abroad. Poniatowski was living in California with his new wife, a rich San Francisco heiress. Étienne Dupin was in Mexico (and would be assassinated before the year was over). Chausson, whose relations with Debussy were never quite repaired after the Thérèse Roger scandal, died in June of injuries from a freak bicycling accident. Louÿs, now a married man, would surely be less available. With that in mind, Debussy asked for a memento of their friendship, and Louÿs gave him the inkstand he used for his first books, with a cordial letter: "I am very happy to give [the inkstand] to you and embrace you. Your friendship filled my bachelor life. It still holds long hours for us, does it not? I love you very much."[36]

And there was the admirable Lilly Texier, who loved Claude and wanted to be his wife. Perhaps there was, after all, room in his life for marriage.

On July 3, he wrote to Hartmann, noting that Carré had announced the new season at the Opéra-Comique, which included the premiere of Charpentier's *Louise*. He was worried about the future of his little friends Pelléas and Mélisande. Couldn't Hartmann put some pressure on the Opéra-Comique's directors? Then there was an unexpected revelation: "When I'm not feverish there's a young lady I love with all my heart (a blonde, naturally) with the most beautiful hair in the world and eyes which lend themselves to the most extravagant comparisons. . . . In short, she's good enough to marry!"[37]

With those sweet thoughts in mind, Debussy wrote to Lilly, who had briefly left the city:

The minutes pass heavily and unvaryingly . . . there's no laughter here with Lilly gone. . . . There are things in me which cry out for you like children lost in a forest. . . . Too well my mouth remembers yours, your caresses have left an indelible mark, as hot as fire, as gentle as a flower. . . . And when your eyes are no longer before me I'm rather like a blind man or a poor little boat that has lost its sails—two images of an equal and irreparable sadness. . . .

For me, hours spent without you spell boredom multiplied a hundred times! . . . It's the imperious impatience of a love which is hungry and which will smash windows to steal its bread, it's the need to live for someone else, and it's the most beautiful thing in the world. I promise you, it had to happen like this.

I love you,
Claude[38]

The letter reveals a side of Debussy we haven't seen before—open, passionate, demonstrative, tender. When speaking about love, he was often cynical. Once (probably in the mid-1890s) he advised young René Peter "to tell women that your love for them is on a vast scale, but let them realize intuitively that you feel it only in a pocket format." A woman is happy to be entertained, he said, as long as you don't complicate her life. This way, "love could operate freely with the maximum of embellishments and arabesques, like a melodic work evolving from the sonata to the symphony according to the mood or the whim or the virtuosity of the players, unfettered by any constraints." Peter asked, But what if it's the real thing? Debussy paused for a long moment. "That, my dear fellow, is a point on which so far I have had neither the time nor the opportunity to reflect. . . . Anyway, it's not important."[39]

Sometimes cynicism yielded to sincerity. Sylvain Bonmariage recorded this conversation (undated, but probably around 1903): A woman remarked, "Have you noticed the mysterious way love has of taking over our hearts?" Debussy replied, "And especially the hearts of artists. Burdened as we are by works and worries, we look for an ultimate realization in love. And we give ourselves with our eyes closed, without moderation, without calculation."[40] This was the Debussy who asked Lilly Texier to be his wife. But in 1903, was it another woman he had in mind?

CHAPTER 15

NOCTURNES (1899–1901)

Charles Martin Loeffler once remarked that if the grass could be heard growing, Debussy would have set it to music.

—Olin Downes[1]

On October 19, 1899, Lilly and Claude were married. Michèle Worms de Romilly provided a picture of his wedding day: On that morning Debussy, who always arrived promptly for Michèle's lessons, was very late. Her mother was annoyed. At last, Debussy rushed into the room, out of breath, and asked to be forgiven for his tardiness: "It's not entirely my fault: I've just got married."[2] Mother and daughter told him it was ridiculous for him to think of giving a lesson on such a day, but Debussy refused to leave. He sat down and asked to hear Michèle run through her exercises. He didn't tell them that Lilly was waiting downstairs in the lobby.

He explained that the priest who was to marry them had asked for eighty francs, which neither Debussy nor his witnesses—Louÿs, Satie, and Lucien Fontaine—could scrape together. Instead, they went to the Town Hall for a civil wedding. He couldn't have skipped Michèle's lesson, he said, because he needed money to pay for the wedding supper later in the day. After the lesson, Claude took Lilly for a celebratory ride on the open top of a bus, then they joined his parents and friends at the Taverne Pousset.

In the month of Debussy's marriage he completed, after many creative difficulties, the *Nocturnes*, a symphonic triptych for orchestra and chorus.

"The garden of our instincts"

The *Nocturnes* had a long gestation. In September 1892 Debussy told André Poniatowski he was "almost finished" with a three-movement symphonic piece called *Scènes de crépuscule* (Scenes of Twilight), inspired by poems of Henri de Régnier. "The orchestration is all worked out," he wrote; "it's just a matter of writing it down."[3] The small matter of writing it down proved to be the hard part, and nothing more is known of the *Scènes*. Two years later Debussy began writing *Three Nocturnes* for violin and orchestra, intended for the Belgian virtuoso Eugène Ysaÿe; some scholars have supposed that the nocturnal music was a later iteration of the twilight music.

Debussy described the *Nocturnes* to Ysaÿe as an experiment: each movement would be scored for different groups of instruments, permitting "the different combinations possible inside a single color, as a painter might make a study in gray, for example."[4] Clearly he was taking Whistler's large group of paintings called *Nocturnes* as his stimulus. The paintings are impressionistic scenes at twilight or darkest night, many of them done in London in the 1870s. Each picture is executed in a narrow range of colors: blue and gold, or gray and silver, for example. The reduced color range and dim light allowed Whistler to obscure or blur the objects in his paintings while intensifying the atmosphere. "As light fades and the shadows deepen," Whistler said, "all petty and exacting details vanish, everything trivial disappears, and I see things as they are in great strong masses: The buttons are lost, but the sitter remains; the sitter is lost, but the shadow remains; the shadow is lost, but the picture remains. And that, night cannot efface from the painter's imagination."[5]

Debussy's "experiment," like Whistler's, would be daring and iconoclastic. We must "cultivate the garden of our instincts" and "trample on the flower-beds" of tradition, he told Lerolle.[6] But little work was done on the *Nocturnes* before he finished *Pelléas* in August 1895. In November 1896, he set the *Nocturnes* aside. When he picked them up again a year later the violin solo was lost, along with his friendship with Ysaÿe.

From late 1897 until its completion two years later, Debussy agonized over the *Nocturnes*. His original concepts, bold and ambitious as they were, were formidable in the execution. On the eve of 1898, he wrote Hartmann of his discouragement. The *Nocturnes* were not yet finished. He was finding it difficult "to give orchestral music a little life and freedom."[7]

A few months later, entangled in uneasy relationships with Gaby Dupont and Alice Peter, Debussy told Louÿs he was "most miserable . . . and I have wept a great deal. . . . The *Three Nocturnes* are feeling the effects of my life-style and have been filled with hope, then filled with despair, and finally filled with emptiness!" He adds that people who claim they write masterpieces while weeping in anguish are "incurable fools."[8] In July 1898, he tells Hartmann the

Nocturnes are finished except for the orchestration, and would soon be ready. Two months later, he's bored and depressed, and the *Nocturnes* "have given me more trouble than the five acts of *Pelléas*."[9] In November, he is desperate and begs Hartmann for an advance of 200 francs. On January 1, 1899, bronchitis prevents him from delivering the scores. And on February 16, he says Hartmann will have the complete *Nocturnes* during the next week.

In fact, the score would not be finished until October.

Nocturnes was published by Fromont (Hartmann's firm) in February 1900, scored for three flutes, piccolo, two oboes, English horn, two clarinets, three bassoons, four French horns, three trumpets, three trombones, tuba, timpani, cymbals, snare drum, two harps, the usual string sections, and a wordless women's chorus—a much larger ensemble than Debussy had employed for *Faune*. The first two movements, "Nuages" and "Fêtes," were first performed in December of that year; the first complete performance, including the third movement, "Sirènes," was heard on October 27, 1901. To write the obligatory two-piano transcription, Debussy entrusted three young men: his student Raoul Bardac; a professional transcriber, Lucien Garban; and a little-known Conservatory student, Maurice Ravel.

Trampling on the Flower Beds

The composer himself provided a programmatic description of this, the first large-scale symphonic work of his maturity:

> The title *Nocturnes* is to be interpreted here in a general and, more particularly, in a decorative sense. Therefore, it is not meant to designate the usual form of the Nocturne, but rather all the various impressions and the special effects of light that the word suggests. "Nuages" (Clouds) renders the immutable aspect of the sky and the slow, solemn motion of the clouds, fading away in gray tones lightly tinged with white. "Fêtes" (Festivals) gives us the vibrating, dancing rhythm of the atmosphere with sudden flashes of light. There is also the episode of the procession (a dazzling fantastic vision), which passes through the festive scene and becomes merged in it. But the background remains resistantly the same: the festival with its blending of music and luminous dust participating in the cosmic rhythm. "Sirènes" (Sirens) depicts the sea and its countless rhythms and presently, amongst the waves silvered

by the moonlight, is heard the mysterious song of the Sirens as they laugh and pass on.[10]

Note the deliberate correspondences here with Whistler's paintings: the "special effects of light," the "gray tones lightly tinged with white," the "sudden flashes of light" in the night sky.

From the first quiet chords in the woodwinds, much of "Nuages" is characterized by downward movement, as if the clouds were not passing through the night sky but falling gently, one after another, on our senses. These phrases are repeated many times, with variations, frequently punctuated by a brief, haunting flourish in the English horn. Lockspeiser finds something melancholy and tragic in this tone poem.

A harmonic study of "Nuages" reveals a subtle but stubborn repetition, at pivotal moments, of the pitch B-natural, which must be considered the "key" of the piece even though Debussy avoids employing a B-natural chord or a harmonic progression that might define the key in a conventional way. It's the tonal center not through the usual devices of traditional harmony, but because Debussy weaves it into our consciousness so thoroughly as to prevent another tone from claiming supremacy. He ends the piece on a B-natural so quiet you can barely hear it.

For much of "Nuages," the woodwinds and French horns carry the melodic themes, while the strings remain mostly in the background, often shimmering. A brief contrasting section more than halfway through introduces a solo flute and harp in unison, playing a pentatonic tune that is soon handed off to the strings. Finally, the English horn and flutes bring us back to the themes we heard earlier—but now the pentatonic tune reminds us, strangely, of *Faune*—underscored with rumblings on the timpani just before the music fades into silence.

The silence is abruptly shattered by the string ensemble—fortissimo! This is "Fêtes," one of the most picturesque and evocative compositions ever written for the modern orchestra. In a letter to Dukas, Debussy says he was inspired by "distant memories of a festival in the Bois de Boulogne."[11] Elsewhere, Debussy described "a retreat with torches, evening, in the woods. . . . I have seen from afar, through the trees, lights approaching, and the crowd running towards the path where the procession is going to pass. Then, the horsemen of the Garde Républicaine, resplendent, their arms and helmets lit by the torches, and the bugles sounding their fanfare."[12]

"This is music which makes the listener feel as though his ears had suddenly been opened to a wholly new world of sense and tone and tumultuous joy," Olin Downes wrote. "Here is liberty, ecstasy, the dance of life."[13] From the beginning of "Fêtes" the strings tap out a quick, repetitive rhythmic phrase we'll hear throughout the piece. The winds unravel a jolly tune suggesting an impromptu rustic dance. It's a whirlwind of activity, reaching a raucous climax, then silence, and it starts all over again. New themes emerge. Another climax, then the tempo changes to a brisk march. A choir of muted trumpets announces the approach of a military parade. The winds take the tune, while the strings suggest the precision of marching footsteps. The band grows louder as it comes nearer, reaching an intensity of excitement almost unique in Debussy's music. The soldiers pass by; the revelers resume their frolicking. Echoes of the procession are heard in the distance. The night grows old, the crowds disperse; the music slows and grows quieter. Now we can barely hear the music as it merges with the silence of the empty night.

The third movement, "Sirènes," is an early glimpse of Debussy's next orchestral masterpiece, *La Mer*, written five years later. But "Sirènes" has its own colors, its own way of listening to the moods of the sea. (Sirens, in Greek mythology, were beautiful creatures whose seductive song lured sailors to their death.)

Debussy's innovation here is the use of a wordless women's chorus to carry the main theme. As the voice of the Sirens, the chorus has a musical importance usually given to the violins in symphonic music. Unfortunately, the chorus increases the rehearsal time and expenses of an orchestra wishing to perform *Nocturnes* complete. As a result, some concerts include only the first two movements; some orchestras use an alternative scoring of "Sirènes" without the chorus.

The choral theme at first consists merely of two successive neighboring notes. Hardly ever has a composer done so much with so little. For the second theme, Debussy starts with those two alternating notes and adds a phrase of three rising notes and three falling notes. These can hardly be called melodies— more like musical doodles. But Debussy uses variations of the themes throughout the piece, moving them from the chorus to the strings or winds, transposing to different keys, changing the underlying harmony, turning a theme upside down, slowing it down, or distorting it in a whole-tone scale. There is little else in "Sirènes" that emerges as a theme, but the composer gives us rich tonal colors and timbres, plenty of atmosphere, and here and there the sense of gentle waves or calm winds. The movement ends, like the other two, in an extreme pianissimo, dissolving in nocturnal silence on an almost inaudible B major chord that links the third movement with the first.

Nocturnal Timbres

At the 1901 premiere of the complete *Nocturnes*, some members of the audience tried to drown out the music with whistling to protest its brazen novelty. "Sirènes" drew the most persistent whistling, Debussy told a friend, and the "scandal was provoked, not by the audience, but by a campaign on the part of the all-holy critics."[14] By then, Debussy would have been unsurprised by the hostile reaction. He had been its victim before, more than once. It took the public and the music critics several years, multiple hearings, and the success of *Pelléas* before *Nocturnes* was accepted into the concert repertoire.

Of all Debussy's works, *Nocturnes* is one of the two most often cited for its strong gamelan influence. (The other is the 1903 "Pagodes" from the piano suite *Estampes*.) At least one characteristic gamelan scale has been identified in *Nocturnes*, as well as whole-tone and modal scales. And the piece is strewn with evidence of the gamelan, particularly in the way the composer uses his orchestral forces—for example, the way he uses individual solo players against unique combinations of instruments to produce ever-shifting sonorities, like a painter mixing primary colors for myriad subtle effects on his canvas.

Three characteristics of a musical sound are pitch, volume, and timbre. Timbre is the quality that differentiates the sound of one instrument from another; it's often referred to as tone color. Even within a particular instrumental group, differences in timbre are easily recognized by the casual listener. But attention to this quality was a relatively new idea among composers of the late nineteenth century, and no one was more concerned with it than Debussy, especially in the orchestral works beginning with *Faune*. Whether or not the gamelan was the impetus for his interest in timbre, he certainly noticed in 1889 how the gamelan's timbres differed wildly from those of the European orchestra and how the timbres of the gamelan instruments were so very different from each other.

He might well have wondered why the Western orchestra's timbres were so limited. In their symphonic works, Mozart, Beethoven, and most of the Romantic composers assigned instruments to a particular role on the basis of

their tonal range more often than their timbre, and they treated each instrumental group (strings, winds, brass) as a choir of close relatives rather than a
group of individuals, as Debussy often did. Berlioz was an early exception to
the general apathy toward timbre.

Listen, in "Nuages," to the opening chord sequences, played by clarinets and
bassoons. Where else in nineteenth-century music would you have heard that
strange timbre? Listen to the acerbic, penetrating tone of the English horn, which
has sole possession of the little phrase that grabs our attention at unexpected
moments. What other instrument could the composer have chosen for that
odd, assertive effect? Listen to the pentatonic melody that arrives later on; to
emphasize its oriental sound, Debussy pairs the long, metallic tones of the
flute in unison with the shorter, bell-like tones of the plucked harp strings—it's
perfect. What other composer would have represented the marching footsteps
in "Fêtes" not just with drums, but with a unity of harps, cellos, and double
bass? For that matter, what composers before Debussy would have chosen, for
the song of the sirens in a symphonic work, actual women's voices rather than
violins or winds?

"His esthetic ambition was obliging him to find a new syntax, escaping
from the canons and taboos of the Franckist school," writes Pierre Boulez.
"The freshness and beauty of inspiration that the *Nocturnes* retain give them a
position in the first rank of the contemporary repertoire."[15]

PART III
A TERRACE AT THE SHORE OF A SPECIAL SEA

CHAPTER 16

PELLÉAS (1902)

[On April 30, 1902] the history of music turned a new and surprising page. . . . A new manner of writing music . . . a new way of evolving and combining tones, a new order of harmonic, melodic, and rhythmic structure. . . . The style was absolutely new and absolutely distinctive; the thing had never been done before.

—Lawrence Gilman[1]

In April 1901, a decision had to be made at the Opéra-Comique about the fate of *Pelléas et Mélisande*. André Messager persuaded Alfred Carré to listen to the composer play the score for him, as he had done three years earlier. And then Debussy waited—but not for long.

"My good old Pierre," wrote Debussy to Louÿs on May 5, 1901, "I have the written promise of Monsieur Albert Carré that he will stage *Pelléas et Mélisande* next season."[2] He notified Maeterlinck as well.

For the first time in nearly six years, Debussy gave all his energies to his opera. Primarily, he needed to prepare the orchestrations from the scanty sketches he'd done earlier. After the recent frustrations and anguish of the *Nocturnes*, he knew it would be no easy task. He also made revisions in the score itself, beginning where he began in 1893—the crucial scene in Act 4, the love scene that ends in violence.

At the end of May, Maeterlinck visited Debussy at 58 rue Cardinet to insist that his mistress, Georgette Leblanc, sing the role of Mélisande. According to an official report, the May meeting ended with no clear resolution. To Maeterlinck's demand, Debussy replied, "We shall see," and suggested that the matter of casting be decided later.[3] It was the opening skirmish of a conflict that raged, mostly in the depths of Maeterlinck's ego, for almost a year and threatened to destroy Debussy's dream of seeing his masterwork, at last, on the beckoning stage of the Opéra-Comique.

Georgette Leblanc

The next part of the story comes to us from the pen of the woman at the center of the dispute, Georgette Leblanc.

Near the end of 1901, with rehearsals set to begin in January, Debussy visited Maeterlinck and Georgette at their Paris home; they would hear the entire opera for the first time. "[Debussy's] gestures were rare and he seldom smiled," Georgette wrote in her memoir. "In him one felt a painful sensitivity and even something morbid which was biding its time. . . . What was most noticeable in the musician was his body, built for strength and yet apparently uninhabited by it. His strength had been drained by his genius."

Debussy sang all the roles. "The position of the piano forced him to turn his back to us," Georgette wrote, "and permitted Maeterlinck to make desperate signs to me. Not understanding music in the least, the time seemed long to him. Several times he wanted to escape but I held him back. Resigned, he lit his pipe." Georgette, who had long imagined herself singing Mélisande, gradually perceived the marvels of the score, "but with the prelude for the death of Mélisande I felt that special, that unique emotion that we undergo in the presence of a masterpiece." She noticed that "Maeterlinck was half asleep in his armchair."

Before Debussy's departure, they discussed casting. "I longed to play the role. Maeterlinck urged it." And here is where Georgette's story becomes questionable: "Debussy said he would be delighted."[4]

Georgette Leblanc was well known at the Opéra-Comique; she had made her debut there in 1893. She was a vibrant, strong-willed soprano who loved to wear opulent, flamboyant clothing. Her apartment on rue Victor Hugo was "as busy as a railway station," the singer wrote. "All the homeless rushed in: a pianist without a piano, a painter without canvases, a singer without engagements, a writer without a publisher. With me they found what they lacked—fires, food, and enthusiasm."[5] At times, Sâr Péladan and his Rosicrucians invaded her home, with incense and candles and a lectern with an old Bible. Louÿs visited Leblanc in 1893.

The young writer Camille Mauclair, a frequent guest, fell madly in love with Leblanc, and she became his mistress. Mauclair persuaded her to read the poems and early plays of his friend Maurice Maeterlinck, and he gave her a French edition of Emerson's *Essays*, which had a preface by Maeterlinck.

Mauclaire knew that his friend had given Debussy authorization for an opera based on *Pelléas et Mélisande* and, wanting to further Leblanc's singing career, wrote Maeterlinck: "She has been my mistress for six months. I love her very much. She has the nature of a true artist. . . . I think that if she did anything of yours it would be the Mélisande which Debussy has composed to your play: That would suit her perfectly."[6]

Meanwhile, Leblanc studied the Emerson preface over and over again, enthralled, and was sure that "in all the universe" her preface writer "was the only man I could love."[7] She discovered he lived in Ghent, but knew almost nothing else about him. To be in his proximate orbit, she auditioned for the opera company at the Théâtre de La Monnaie, in Brussels, and was promised roles in the coming season. "I think this winter she will come to play Isolde at La Monnaie," wrote the unsuspecting Mauclair to his Belgian friend.[8]

An art critic told Maeterlinck how eagerly Leblanc wanted to perform Mélisande and arranged for the two to meet at a dinner party. Georgette sat opposite her adored Maurice at dinner, and she was not disappointed, though a little surprised by his youthful appearance (he was about thirty-three), his rustic manner, and his extreme reticence. He had difficulty looking at her when she spoke but couldn't take his eyes off her when he thought she wouldn't notice. Georgette was, by all accounts, immensely attractive.

The narrative in her memoir is the story of a headstrong, romantic young diva and a brilliant, introverted intellectual who lived a solitary life at his parents' home in Ghent. He was still practicing law. She didn't know that his solitude was often interrupted with visits to his several mistresses; she didn't yet know that he often acted like a spoiled little boy. She won him over with her witty, intelligent conversation and ingratiating letters; and, with her persistence and her willingness to endure his need for quiet and solitude, became his mistress. For a long time, she was his only mistress. She moved to Paris where, having returned to the Opéra-Comique, she had great success as Carmen, a character as different from Mélisande as a cat from a mouse. Maeterlinck joined her in Paris but alternated between his Paris house and Ghent, which he strongly preferred. Only later, when they leased and occupied a disused medieval abbey in a quiet corner of Normandy, did their lives unite in a more stable, if not permanent, arrangement.

According to Leblanc, she and Debussy had several rehearsals together in 1901—two or three at Maeterlinck's house and two at the composer's apartment.

Debussy approved of her interpretation, she said. "He told me that after having seen me so violent in Carmen, he had at first doubted me, and that he had not known to what extent I could adapt myself" to play his frightened, sensitive young Mélisande.[9] Yet the singer admits she was unable to judge Debussy's true feelings about her singing the role.

Messager and Carré, who had the ultimate responsibility for casting, discussed Maeterlinck's demand with Debussy over dinner at the Café Weber. According to Marcel Dietschy, they left it to Debussy to audition the singers and make the final decision.

On December 29, Maeterlinck, reading his newspaper, saw that another soprano had been cast as Mélisande. Maeterlinck was furious, Georgette was puzzled. Why didn't she get the role? she wondered. She suspected that Debussy had nothing to do with the decision, that his compliments were sincere. She lost her chance, she believed, because a year or two earlier she rejected the advances of a man who was influential in making decisions about casting at the Opéra-Comique. This could only have been Messager or Carré. Denied the role of Mélisande, she thought, she was paying the price for her defiance. And while the anecdote may be accurate and women's intuitions are said to be infallible, it is much more likely that Mary Garden was simply—in her appearance, her voice, and her temperament—more suited to the role.

The feud was just beginning. Maeterlinck took the matter to the Society of Authors, thinking all rights belonged to him as author of the libretto. He was badly mistaken because, in French law, the rights of composers were given precedence over the rights of authors. There was also the indisputable fact that in his letter he had given Debussy carte blanche to do what he wished with his opera.

Simmering with fury, "Maeterlinck brandished his cane," wrote Georgette, and said he was going to give Debussy "a drubbing to teach him what was what."[10] While Georgette waited anxiously, Maeterlinck ran from his house to Debussy's, his walking stick flying every which way, energized by anger. When he entered Debussy's drawing room, he found the composer sitting peacefully in a chair. Lilly begged the frantic poet to leave and gave her husband a bottle of smelling salts to keep him from fainting. Deflated at last, Maeterlinck had no choice but to withdraw.

Maeterlinck, Leblanc said, didn't like composers any more than he did music. He'd say, "They're all crazy, all off their heads, these musicians!"[11]

Mary Garden

There are many events in history and fiction that scream in bold, black headlines, "A star is born!" Mary Garden had just such a debut at the Opéra-Comique.

Born in Aberdeen in 1874, Mary came to America with her Scottish parents and spent much of her childhood and adolescence in New England and Chicago, where she began singing lessons. Her talent was soon recognized, and at twenty-two she went to Paris to study. There the prominent American soprano Sibyl Sanderson took her under her wing, taught her some of the finer points of the vocal and dramatic arts, and introduced her to important colleagues such as Massenet and Carré. Carré brought her into his opera company in January 1900, despite her abominable French pronunciation. From the start, she watched nearly all the performances and sat in on most of the rehearsals. She studied the scores, observed the staging, and got a sense of company politics.

A few days after she joined the company, Gustave Charpentier's new opera, *Louise*, opened at the theater to good reviews and ecstatic audiences. It was one of the trendy operas that strove for a new realism in their plots and naturalism in their singers. Louise was a Parisian dressmaker who, despite her mother's disapproval and her father's rage, loved and ran off with a handsome bohemian. With its Parisian setting, the opera was both applauded and ridiculed for incorporating the cries of street vendors into the fabric of Act 2. Debussy saw a dress rehearsal of *Louise* and, in a letter to Louÿs, brought his caustic wit to bear on the enterprise. It was necessary to produce this opera, he said, because "it fills to perfection the need for vulgar beauty and imbecile art" beloved by the masses. "It's the sentimentality of a gentleman . . . being moved to tears by the sight of the road-sweepers and the rag-and-bone men—and he thinks he can record the souls of the poor!!!"[12] If scorn was dripping from Debussy's pen, there was a measure of bitterness, too. He was disheartened that *Louise* had taken the stage while poor, doomed Pelléas and Mélisande were left waiting in the cold.

Marthe Rioton was cast as Louise and was perfect for the role. Soon after the premiere, however, she became ill, and her understudy sang several performances. Meanwhile, Mary Garden, who had never sung on any operatic stage, quickly learned the role; and Carré, seeing her as a future Louise, put her through sixteen rehearsals, including at least one with the full cast. On the afternoon of April 10, Carré telephoned Garden at Sibyl Sanderson's house. "He wants to know if you could sing Louise this evening, and I told him that of course you couldn't," Sanderson told her. Garden grabbed the phone and assured Carré she'd be ready.[13]

The understudy was sick, and Rioton agreed to sing that night despite a severe cold. She struggled through the first two acts until there was nothing left of her voice. At intermission, Mary was found at the back of the theater and was rushed to a dressing room to prepare for Act 3. Her coach announced to the restless audience that they were about to hear a new Louise. Garden was a bit nervous, but her first aria, "Depuis le jour"—an outburst of joy at the beginning of a love affair—was a showstopper. The audience went wild. The applause was deafening, and people waved their programs and shouted *Marygardenne!* Messager, who was conducting, brought the entire orchestra to its feet in tribute to Garden. Later, Carré gave his new star a two-year contract with a generous salary.[14]

Almost two years passed, and by the time Mary first sang Mélisande for the composer, she had had a long run in *Louise*, starred in two world premieres at the Opéra-Comique, and elsewhere sung the title roles in Massenet's *Thaïs* and *Manon* and in Messager's *Madame Chrysanthème*.

Privately, Garden had also become Messager's mistress. They carried on a tempestuous affair for two years and maintained an off-and-on relationship for many more.

The First Rehearsals

On the afternoon of January 13, 1902, the cast was summoned to Messager's house to hear *Pelléas* for the first time. (For a synopsis of *Pelléas et Mélisande*, see Appendix C.) No one was present in the drawing room but Carré, Messager and his wife, and the principal cast members: Mary Garden, Jean Périer (Pelléas), Hector-Robert Dufranne (Golaud), Félix Vieuille (Arkel), and Jeanne Gerville-Réache (Geneviève). "We were only there a short while when the door opened and in came Debussy," Garden wrote. "We were all presented to him, and he spoke the usual words of greeting. Without another word, he sat at the piano and played and sang the whole thing from beginning to end."[15] Messager recalled Debussy's "deep, cavernous voice," and his singing "gradually became irresistible."[16]

The cast members followed Debussy's performance in their copies of the score, "heads bowed as if we were all at prayer," wrote Garden. "While Debussy played, I had the most extraordinary emotions I have ever experienced in my life. Listening to that music I seemed to become someone else, someone inside of me whose language and soul were akin to mine. When Debussy got to the fourth act I could no longer look at my score for the tears. It was all very strange and unbearable. I closed my book and just listened to him, and as he played the death of Mélisande, I burst into the most awful sobbing, and Mme Messager began to sob along with me, and both of us fled into the next room. I shall never forget it . . . crying as if nothing would console us again."[17]

"The impression produced by the music on that occasion was, I believe, unique," wrote Messager. At first there was some resistance, owing to the strangeness of the score, the story, the bizarre incongruity of the composer singing soprano as well as bass at the piano. "Then an ever closer attention, with the emotional temperature rising until the last notes of 'Melisande's death,' which fell amid silence and tears."[18]

When he was finished, Debussy turned to the cast and, before anyone else could say anything, announced, "'*Mesdames et Messieurs*, that is my *Pelléas et Mélisande*. Everyone must forget that he is a singer before he can sing the music of Debussy.' Then he murmured a quick 'au revoir' and, without another word, was gone."[19]

"At the end, all of us were carried away with excitement, burning to get down to work as soon as possible," Messenger said.[20] "We all went home and began studying our roles," wrote Mary. She found the first two acts "a little difficult for me . . . that is, difficult getting into Debussy's very individual way of writing. It was all so different from anything else any of us had ever sung." She found the third act easier, and by the time she reached Act 5 and the death of Mélisande, she "discovered I had absolutely nothing to study. I just knew it. How, I haven't the slightest idea."[21]

For the first rehearsals, the cast members were each asked to sing their roles alone with the composer and a piano. Carré instructed the singers, "Remember that when you go into that rehearsal room you are expected to know your parts to perfection." It will rest entirely with Debussy, he warned them, whether or not they would remain in the cast.[22]

"I remember very clearly going up that first afternoon," wrote Garden. "I knew, as everyone knew, that this production had to be perfection itself, and I was fully prepared. . . . I opened my score, and Debussy sat down at the piano. We did the first act, Debussy singing the role of Golaud. His voice was very small and husky . . . I never knew a composer who could sing and few who

could play the piano well. But Debussy was a magnificent pianist. . . . When we
came to Pelléas, he sang that too, and all the other roles as well, except mine.
Then we came to the scene of the tower. I was singing my lines—"

> *Mes longs cheveux descendent jusqu'au seuil de la tour!*
> *Mes cheveux vous attendent tout le long de la tour!*
> *Et tout le long du jour!*
> *Et tout le long du jour!*[23]

"—when, without a word, he got up abruptly and left the room. I had a feeling
I had offended him in some mysterious way, and I began to prepare myself for
the shock of not singing Mélisande. I put on my hat and was about to leave the
rehearsal room when a boy came in and said: 'Miss Garden, Monsieur Carré
would like to see you in the office.' When I walked in, there sat Debussy with
Carré. Rising from his chair, he came right up to me and took both my hands
in his.

"'Where were you born?' he asked.

"'Aberdeen, Scotland.'

"'To think that you had to come from the cold far North to create my
Mélisande—because that's what you're going to do, Mademoiselle.'

"Then he turned to Carré, and I remember he put up his hands, and said: '*Je
n'ai rien à lui dire.* I have nothing to tell her.'"[24]

In her autobiography Mary Garden explained the miracle of her involvement
with the characters she sang. "I never saw where Salomé lived. I never was with
that great dancer of Egypt, Thaïs, but I knew her. I knew them all . . . these
women of opera. I had them all in me, in my very flesh and blood. . . . Was it a
sixth sense? Maybe. I just don't know. . . . I never 'studied' any of these roles. I
never had to rehearse, really. They were always there in me, in my body and
soul, when I sang. It made no difference what country or period it was, it was
always the same, an extraordinary thing that I shall never understand.

"I had nothing to learn about the death of Mélisande. Death was somehow
embedded in the pattern of my living self, and in the last scene I surrendered
completely to it. But what a beautiful death, Mélisande's! It was in childbirth,
you know, and I often think it is a sacrilege to talk about it, it is so tender and
pure a death. Never in the world would I take a curtain call after the death of
Mélisande. I never did."[25]

Beautiful words, poignant thoughts—that's the way Mary Garden told her story. In fact, though, she did rehearse Mélisande. According to Michael Turnbull, that first private rehearsal with Debussy was followed by a week of coaching and rehearsing with an assistant conductor. It was likely at her second session with Debussy, on January 21, that the composer decided definitively to give her the role.[26] In total, Garden had sixty-nine rehearsals before opening night. Such a long rehearsal schedule was necessary, she said, because *Pelléas* "was new in every sense. The harmony... it was almost another language." The words, too, were sometimes a problem for her. "*Je suis si malheureuse.*' [I am so unhappy.] The words alone said nothing to me. But Debussy put music to them, and then they spoke to me and lived. I could not help but be *malheureuse* when I sang it."[27]

Gloomy Days

After the hearing at the Society of Authors, after failing to give Debussy a thrashing, Maeterlinck seemed defeated. Debussy wrote to René Peter, optimistically but prematurely, "The Maeterlinck business is settled, and Carré agrees with me that his attitude is little short of pathological."[28] But the poet was unsatisfied and threatened to take his grievances to court. He was advised to stand down, to reconcile himself to his situation. At some point in this battle of taciturn geniuses, Maeterlinck was said to have challenged Debussy to a duel with swords or guns. But whether truth or rumor, no duel ever took place.

Several friends of Debussy have commented on the vast amount of time and effort he was forced to expend during the three months of rehearsals. Eating up most of his time was the task of orchestration, which was far from finished when rehearsals began in January. Fortunately, said Robert Godet, he not only possessed enormous technical ability but also a mental discipline that allowed him to block out external distractions. He was able "to concentrate all his faculties towards one particular end as soon as he had taken up his pen ... without hesitation or respite, from one act to the next until the last chord was written." For hours on end, he wrote "arabesques of elegant design with equal calm and sureness, untouched by any revision."[29] Scene by scene, he gave the orchestrated score to Messager for study.

The first orchestral read-through was on March 21, and it was followed by a series of difficult and often discouraging rehearsals.

Orchestral scores have to be broken down into individual scores for the string players, for the woodwinds and the brasses, the harps and percussion—another time-consuming job that requires utmost care and attention to accuracy. "Debussy had had the generous but unfortunate idea of getting the orchestral [scores] copied by a friend who was hard up," wrote Messager, "but who was a mediocre copyist and a somewhat rudimentary musician, and it took three or four rehearsals simply to get the corrections sorted out."[30] Godet and the chorus master, Henri Büsser, came to the rescue, helping Debussy with the onerous task of correcting the mistakes, but "more kept cropping up at each rehearsal," and Messager was furious.[31] Besides their exasperation with the copyist's errors, the musicians were "altogether so bewildered by the unusual style of the music that they declared the score to be unplayable, outrageous, and doomed to failure."[32] The composer attended nearly all the orchestral rehearsals, of which there were far more than usual for a new opera, and his nerves were frazzled each day by the tedious process of simply getting the music right. The words that came frequently to his lips were *Quietly! Not so loud, I beg you.*[33]

As for the singers, "rehearsals took place amid growing enthusiasm," Messager remembered. "Each scene was gone over twenty times without any of the singers showing the least sign of temper in the face of the composer's demands—and he was very difficult to satisfy. . . . In the meantime, a new difficulty had arisen."[34]

By the beginning of April, with rehearsals entering their final stages, it became clear that scene changes were taking longer than expected, largely because of the small stage exits and narrow wings. But Debussy had written the musical interludes before the sets were assembled, and the music proved to be too short to fill the gaps. He wrote to a friend on April 2 that on the previous evening Messager had come knocking at his door and asked for seventy-five more bars for the second act. "Naturally he had to have them straight away, so that was the end of the pleasant evening I was looking forward to."[35] "Debussy had to return to work, grumbling and raving," wrote Messager, "and I went to see him every day to snatch away the notes he had written between one rehearsal and another; that is how he wrote the wonderful interludes which provide such a moving commentary on the action."[36]

Finding a child to play Yniold, Golaud's young son, proved difficult. Büsser raided the solfège class at the Conservatory and chose a young fellow named Noël Gallon, but he had the range of a mezzo-soprano, and Debussy wanted a lighter, higher voice. A child named Blondin was plucked out of the children's chorus of *Carmen*; he had the right voice and got the part despite his inexperience. There was some doubt as to his ability to perform his scene in Act 4, when he loses his ball under a rock. The scene was cut from the first performances as a precaution.

Debussy, weighed down by the leaden disappointments of perennial obscurity and tormented by the terrors of an uncertain future so entirely contingent on the success of his opera, promoted himself from composer to micromanager. Should there really be a lighted lamp in Golaud's room in mid-afternoon? Is the theater too dark for the orchestra to see the conductor? Shouldn't Mélisande be sitting in something simpler than that armchair? Then there was the problem of a ridiculous wig, but Mary Garden took care of that. Her hair had to be long, reaching from Mélisande's head leaning out of the tower window to the ground beneath; long enough to wind around Pelléas's face and chest. So Garden sent her coiffeur to Brittany, where "the lovely daughters of the *paysans*" had hair of the color and length she needed. "The whole thing cost me 6,000 francs," she wrote. "I've not worn such beautiful hair since."[37]

Debussy was never permitted a peaceful moment. Georges Hartmann's estate sent daily summonses for debts (disputed by the composer) that he had no means to repay. "It was under such conditions," wrote Godet, "harassed, overworked, betrayed by friends, even by fate, exposed to the worst anxieties, to the worst slanders, that Debussy spent his days on the stage, his nights at his worktable." Though reading was "his habitual recourse against the torments of life," all he had time to read were threats from creditors or telegrams from Messager asking for more music.[38]

And Maeterlinck's anger haunted the proceedings. Though he came to witness only one rehearsal and remained calm, he began writing articles for small journals attacking Debussy and the Opéra-Comique. This campaign culminated in a letter he wrote to the editor of *Le Figaro*, published on April 14—sixteen days before opening night. "The performance will take place in spite of me," Maeterlinck wrote, "for Monsieurs Carré and Debussy have failed to recognize my most legitimate rights.

> In effect, Monsieur Debussy, after having been in agreement with me about the choice of the interpreter whom I thought to be the only one capable of creating the role of Mélisande . . . decided to deny me the right to intervene in

the selection of the artists, by taking advantage of a letter I had written him too confidently nearly six years ago. . . . Thus they were successful in excluding me from my work, and since then it has been dealt with as though it were conquered territory. They have imposed arbitrary and absurd cuts which make it incomprehensible. They retained what I had the intention of deleting or improving. . . . In a word, the *Pelléas* at issue is a piece that has become a stranger to me, almost an enemy. And, deprived of all control over my work, I am reduced to hoping that its failure will be prompt and resounding.[39]

Debussy was dismayed by the letter. Maeterlinck's diatribe was clearly intended to rally the public and critics to his defense and cast the composer, director, and even the opera in the worst possible light. Debussy asked Godet to write a rebuttal for publication, but his friend was against the idea.

The premiere of *Pelléas* was supposed to take place on April 23. On the 18th, the Opéra-Comique announced a postponement to the 29th, and then it was rescheduled for April 30.

The Infamous Dress Rehearsal

For the first dress rehearsal, on April 25, only Opéra-Comique personnel were allowed in the hall. The final dress rehearsal was held on Monday, April 28, at 1:00 p.m. As the audience gathered outside the Salle Favart, a few men were peddling programs. It might have been the first sign, to an astute observer, that something was very wrong: programs were *never* distributed at dress rehearsals.

Tickets, as usual for these occasions, were free, and all seats were reserved for invited guests—prominent musicians and writers, government officials, friends of the producers and cast members—"everybody who is anybody, especially in the arts, is invited," wrote Mary Garden, "but no critics!"[40] Debussy's guests included Godet, Louÿs, René Peter, and Raymond Bonheur; Paul-Jean Toulet, a friend of more recent acquaintance; Léon Blum, a young writer (who in the 1930s would be France's prime minister); the composer Vincent d'Indy; and several others, including Henri de Régnier, who in 1893 had helped bring about the crucial meeting of the little-known composer and the lesser-known poet.

Parisian audiences were often noisy and rowdy during performances they didn't approve of. Think of the shouts and whistles that greeted Wagner's *Tannhäuser* in 1861, or the riot that marred the first performance of Stravinsky's

Rite of Spring in 1913. But such a reception was hardly expected for a symbolist work by the most promising French composer of his generation.

According to Messager, the first act proceeded in "an atmosphere of calm," although the audience was clearly uneasy and "manifestly hostile."[41] But in the second scene of Act 2, "something frightful happened," recalled Garden. "People began to laugh. In moments of the greatest seriousness someone would scream hysterically. We hadn't the faintest idea what was going on, and we were all suddenly paralyzed on the stage. Here was a drama of pure poetry and tragedy, and people were giggling and chuckling as if they were at the Folies Bergère."[42] Some in the audience found Garden's French pronunciation, with its perplexing Scottish-American accent, hilarious. Singing the line "Je n'ai pas de courage" (I don't have courage), she pronounced the last word like *curage*, which means "drain cleaning." Her "Oh! Oh! je ne suis pas heureuse" (I am not happy) was met by loud bursts of laughter.

But the giddiness and restlessness in the audience had more sinister causes than Garden's accent. Copies of the illicit program, with its witty but malicious lampoon of a synopsis, were now circulating through the audience. An orchestra player obtained a copy and brought it backstage during the first intermission. "What language! What illustrations! I have never in my life seen such obscenity," Garden wrote, "clever, perhaps, but in a foul, disgusting way. . . . It explained why the people in the house were in paroxysms of laughter. They had been stealing glimpses at these booklets during the performance, and showing them to one another."[43] It was generally agreed that Maeterlinck was the mastermind behind the travesty; no one has ever suggested a more plausible villain.

Several scenes in the opera continued to inspire hoots and hollers. The romantic tower scene, when Pelléas winds Mélisande's golden tresses around his neck, was punctuated with chuckles and sniggers. In the critical scene where Golaud forces Yniold to spy on Mélisande and Pelléas, the innocent young singer repeated the words "petit père" (little father) so obsessively that it was met by loud and rude outbursts.

In the foyers during intermissions, people argued passionately, but despite Debussy's fervent supporters, the majority held that the opera was doomed. "They condemned the work both from the dramatic and musical standpoint, simply because the utter novelty of the opera reduced them to such a state of stupefaction that they were incapable of understanding it," wrote Vallas.[44] *Le Figaro* reported that musicians in the corridors were divided into two schools:

"Some said it was a musical event of the greatest importance; others said disrespectfully that it was just a practical joke."[45]

After the dress rehearsal, the undersecretary of the Beaux-Arts "pointed out to the author of the new work the inconvenience, in a theater subsidized by the State, of offending the modesty of an [elite] public," Godet reported.[46] The official ordered that Yniold's spying scene be stricken—otherwise he would ban the opera. The official premiere was to take place only two days later! Debussy refused to eliminate the scene, but he agreed to a compromise, cutting fifteen bars from it. The offending dialogue that drew the official's objections (in part):

> GOLAUD: And the bed? Are they near the bed?
> YNIOLD: The bed, petit père? I don't see the bed.
> GOLAUD: Hush, they might hear you.[47]

Debussy, through it all, was "the picture of imperturbability" on the afternoon of the dress rehearsal, wrote Godet. "Were it not for his pallor, one would have sworn he was thinking of other things. He did not even tremble at the hilarious explosions which punctuated—Heaven knows under what petty pretext—the dying agony of Mélisande."[48] Some of the "other things" Debussy might have been thinking about are articulated in an article he wrote in 1908:

> The scenic realization of a work of art, no matter how beautifully done, is nearly always in conflict with the interior dream whence it was born, rising in turn from alternative moods of doubt and enthusiasm. One's characters . . . would sometimes seem to come alive from the silent pages of the manuscript, so that one felt one could almost touch them. . . . One is in some way afraid of them, and one scarcely dare speak to them; they almost seem like ghosts. . . .
>
> From this moment [the staging of a play or opera], one's old dreams seem to be shattered. Some being from without has interposed itself between you and your dream. . . .
>
> In 1902, the year when the Opéra-Comique put on their painstakingly careful performance of *Pelléas et Mélisande*, I experienced some of the feelings described above. . . . The character of Mélisande had always seemed to me difficult to perform. I had tried to convey her fragility and distant charm in the music, but there were still her gestures to be decided. One

false movement during her long silences could have ruined the whole effect, even made her incomprehensible. And above all, Mélisande's voice, which I had dreamed of as being so tender—how was that going to turn out? Even the most beautiful voice in the world could have been quite antipathetic to the special feelings her character requires. I am no longer able—nor would I wish to—describe the various stages we went through while working in rehearsal. Besides, these were my most precious moments in the theater; it was there that I met the boundless devotion of really great artists. Among them, one emerged as quite unique; I hardly had to speak a word to her as the character of Mélisande gradually took shape. . . . I awaited the performance in complete confidence, yet still curious. . . .

At last came the fifth act—Mélisande's death—a breathtaking event whose emotions cannot be rendered in words. There I heard the voice I had secretly imagined—full of a sinking tenderness, and sung with such artistry as I would never have believed possible. Since then, it is this artistry which has caused the public to bow in ever increasing admiration before the name of Mary Garden.[49]

The Horn of Oberon

Often in considering the comings and goings of famous people, we find that their contemporaries have recorded contrary memories that make it impossible to know what's true. So it is in tracing Debussy's steps on the afternoon of the dress rehearsal. According to Büsser, the composer took refuge in Messager's office (Carré's office, says René Peter) during the performance, nervously smoking one cigarette after another. Claude walked home afterward with René Peter, "resolutely changing the subject when *Pelléas* was mentioned" (says Orledge),[50] but it was Robert Godet (says Godet) who accompanied him home. Claude asked Godet to come up for a cup of tea (or he was found "melancholy in front of a beer glass at the Café Riche," says Garden).[51] And, Godet writes, persuasively, "it was then, in a quiet tête-à-tête . . . that he began to praise, with all his heart and all his soul, the 'horn' of Oberon."[52]

It was a reference to the magical horn that makes itself heard at decisive moments in the opera *Oberon*, by Carl Maria von Weber. Weber, whom Debussy called "a prince among musicians," was a key player in the transition from the Classical operas of Mozart and Gluck to the Romantic operas of Meyerbeer and Wagner. Weber's *Der Freischütz*, written about five years before *Oberon*, was a turning point in musical history. *Oberon* was first performed in 1826, a few months before Weber died.

In what reads, in Godet's telling, like a long, discursive monologue by an erudite music professor, Claude told his friend that Oberon's horn kept faithful company with him during the performance of *Pelléas*. Weber was a "refuge," preserving him from his "personal vicissitudes" at a time when he is "parting from his dream and exposing it to reality's challenge." Weber made Debussy think "of the multifarious revelations of music: serious, lively, passionate, mystic, of those which refresh the style, of those which unsettle the expression, and I asked myself, if his music, above all, were not pre-eminently the 'revealer' . . . [of] an undiscovered aesthetic order" or "an unknown type of passion." Debussy speaks of Wagner: "One must go as far as *Parsifal*—to the perfect 'enchantment' which, in its essential being owes nothing but to itself—to find again . . . that simplicity of harmony and especially that pureness of tone with which we associate in our dreams the eternal youth of *Oberon* or *Freischütz*, in contrast to the wear and tear of the too-usual Wagnerian idiom." He speaks of Weber's unmatched palette of orchestral color, and how a sense of it might be explained to a traveler from outer space. "Now, supposing a visitor from Mars were to come this evening to pay us a musical call. . . . I willingly leave to you [Godet] the controversial subjects: theory of sound, scales, chords, form, the whole group. . . . I would take charge of this chapter, 'Orchestra,' and it would hardly give me any trouble." Debussy says that Weber, known for the brilliance of his orchestrations, can teach us the essence, the "timbre," of all the instruments of the orchestra.

Remembering this evening years later, Godet wondered whether Debussy understood, as he drank his tea and mused about Weber, that with *Pelléas* "he had just given a decisive blow to romanticism in music"; that he had brought to a close the illustrious epoch that began with Weber; and that, like Weber, he had revealed to the world an undiscovered aesthetic order.[53]

CHAPTER 17

PELLÉAS AND
THE FRENCH SPIRIT

*For a long time I had been striving to write music for the theater,
but the form in which I wanted it to be was so unusual that after
several attempts I had almost given up the idea. . . . The drama of
Pelléas—which despite its atmosphere of dreams contains much
more humanity than those so-called documents of real life—
seemed to suit my purpose admirably. It has an evocative language
whose sensibility is able to find an extension in the music and in
the orchestral setting. I also tried to obey a law of beauty that
seems notably ignored when it comes to dramatic music: the
characters of this opera try to sing like real people, and not in an
arbitrary language made up of worn-out clichés.*

—Debussy[1]

After days of clouds and rain, April 30 brought sunny skies, and on that evening
in 1902 the official premiere of *Pelléas et Mélisande* took place. But if the weather
outside was calm, the atmosphere in the hall was stormy. The audience was neither
as rowdy as at the dress rehearsal, nor unanimously attentive. One observer
remembered "mocking laughter [and] violent arguments. . . . The tower scene
almost unleashed a tempest . . . people insulted each other." After Mélisande's
death, there was "a storm of shouting" as well as "a thunder of applause."[2]

On this day, said one writer, "the history of music turned a new and surprising page."[3]

The Apaches

The thunderous applause came largely from a group of young men and women
in the upper galleries—musicians, artists, writers, students. Their echoing
cheers gave vital encouragement to the cast and drowned out some of the bad
behavior in the expensive seats down below. Their enthusiasm convinced a

much larger group of friends and strangers that they, too, must come and see this trailblazing new work of art. One of the young enthusiasts later wrote:

> Perhaps one cannot imagine just what *Pelléas* meant to the young people who took it to their hearts at its first appearance, to those who were between sixteen and twenty. A marvelous world, a cherishable paradise where we could escape from our problems.... *Pelléas* was for us a special forest and a special region and a terrace at the shore of a special sea. We escaped there, knowing the secret door, and the world no longer existed for us.[4]

Le Figaro noted that among the audience were "passionate people, some lukewarm ones, some fanatics, some indifferent ones, some who did not give a damn.... Some said that it was a musical event of the highest importance.... Others said disrespectfully that it was a joke."[5] Some critics were downright hostile: The composer displays "an unwholesome craving for novelty"; the singers droned on in "a kind of long-drawn-out, monotonous recitative, unbearable, moribund"; and—perhaps the most cruel—"art of this kind is morbid and pernicious."[6]

Henry Bauër, a friendlier observer, wrote that *Pelléas* "has aroused passionate curiosity, some zealous polemics, some bitter criticisms; it has experienced the fate of contested works, and I imagine that therein lies, for a composer of Debussy's value, the noblest success that he could have desired."[7] Bauër added, "Today or tomorrow, Claude Debussy's music will prevail," and he commended "this intensely artistic work, so youthful, pure, and tender, in which the subject, inspiration, and expression are so full of originality."[8]

The tide of critical negativity didn't change overnight, but the audiences certainly did. At the third performance, there was a large crowd of sympathetic listeners. At the conclusion they shouted for Debussy to take a bow, but he declined, as usual. After the fourth performance, Messager was obliged to leave Paris and begin his seasonal engagement as conductor at the Royal Opera House in Covent Garden. In his place was Henri Büsser, the Opéra-Comique's young chorus master, conducting an orchestra in public for the first time, without benefit of even one complete rehearsal. Büsser was nervous, Debussy wrote, in a letter to Messager, "and didn't seem to know which end of the score to take hold of." At the next day's performance, Büsser looked "like a man heading for a cold bath," but the orchestra played splendidly. "He paid no attention whatever to the singers and threw chords at their feet without the least concern for harmonic propriety." But after Act 4, "three curtain calls rewarded all these excellent people for their efforts."[9]

By then, it was clear that *Pelléas* was destined for a successful run. The seventh performance was completely sold out, and people were turned away. Debussy wrote Messager, "We made 7,400 francs last Friday! You wouldn't believe the respect [the Opéra-Comique's directors] have for me! The fact that I had created *Pelléas* was of purely anecdotal significance, but to have made money, that's what counts!"[10]

Those dozens of thundering young people in the balcony, who cheered vociferously at the first performances, helped give the opera time to find its natural audience. Most of them were soon to congeal as a group, meeting regularly and calling themselves, for reasons lost to history, the Apaches. "Members shared a common belief in Debussy as a musical prophet," wrote Jann Pasler,[11] and they were determined to defend him from his detractors. To that end, they came in large numbers to every performance through the spring and fall seasons until the opera's success was assured.

The Apaches found other common interests besides Debussy, though most of their passions were his as well: the symbolist poetry of Mallarmé, Verlaine, and Rimbaud; the visual arts, especially those of East Asia; and the music of Balakirev and other Russians. They were not all musicians, but it was strictly a men's club; among them were painters, writers, critics, designers, and even some—an engineer, a law student—who had no direct involvement with the arts. They came from aristocratic families and poor ones, from all parts of France. The diversity among the musicians extended to their training, and there was much general antipathy between Conservatory alumni and those who studied at the more conservative Schola Cantorum, but as Apaches they were united. "What began as casual gatherings after concerts evolved into a fascinating microcosm of the French avant-garde, a place 'open to all the changeable winds of fashion, but firmly closed to pedants and spurious aesthetes,'" wrote Pasler. "What made the Apaches distinct" from other groups "was their focus on musical innovation."[12]

The Apaches were a network of friends and acquaintances who shared their ideas and their works in progress, sometimes pitching in with time and effort to help someone out of a jam. Each was dedicated to further the careers of the others. The music critics—Calvocoressi, Vuillermoz—lectured and wrote journal articles about their colleagues and reviewed their concerts. The performers, especially the Spanish pianist Ricardo Viñes, premiered the work of the Apache composers, among whom the most celebrated was Viñes's childhood friend Maurice Ravel. Other composers—Florent Schmitt, Manuel de Falla, Isaac Albeniz, and Igor Stravinsky—joined the group later. Though Debussy never came to their meetings, he knew several of the men and valued the role the Apaches played on his behalf. Viñes was for many years his first choice to introduce his new piano music at concerts.

The French Spirit

Finally the critics, those who were most sensitive to the unprecedented changes that had swept through all the European arts but music, came to appreciate Debussy's efforts as much as the public did. Gustave Bret wrote in the *Presse*: "This music grows on you. You are impressed by the very force of this art, for which I, personally, have more admiration than comprehension. . . . The joy with which it was written illuminates it."[13] Gaston Carraud proclaimed in *La Liberté*: "In order to satisfy the noblest and most courageous of artistic ideals, Debussy has created a music of his own. . . . The music exists for the sake of its own beauty, its own delight. Debussy takes his place, more definitely even than Wagner, amongst the sensualists in music, of whom Mozart was the greatest."[14]

Debussy's triumph was trumpeted all over Europe, but *Pelléas* did not begin to turn up in other music capitals until 1907, when it was performed in Brussels and Frankfurt. From there it spread like wildfire. In 1908 the opera opened in New York, Milan, Cologne, Budapest, Prague, Munich, Berlin, and Lyons; and in 1909 it was performed in Rome, London, Boston, and Philadelphia. Chicago followed in 1910; Vienna in 1911; Nice, Geneva, and Buenos Aires in 1912; St Petersburg in 1915.

In January 1913, the Opéra-Comique reached its one hundredth performance of *Pelléas*.

Surely, wrote Lawrence Gilman, it takes a person with great courage (or foolishness) to write an opera in which the voices, "from beginning to end, [sing] in a kind of recitative which is virtually a chant; an opera in which there is no vocal melody whatsoever, and comparatively little symphonic development of themes in the orchestra; in which an enigmatic and wholly eccentric system of harmony is exploited; in which there are scarcely more than a dozen *fortissimo* passages in the course of five acts; in which, for the most part of the time, the orchestra employed is the orchestra of Mozart." And yet, said Gilman, Debussy's orchestra is

> of indescribable richness, delicacy, and suppleness . . . that melts and shim-mers with opalescent hues . . . that has substance without density, sonority without blatancy, refinement without thinness.
>
> *Pelléas et Mélisande* exhibited not simply a new manner of writing opera, but a new kind of music—a new way of evolving and combining tones, a new order of harmonic, melodic, and rhythmic structure. The style of it was absolutely new and absolutely distinctive: The thing had never been done before. Its beauty is not the beauty that issues from clear and transparent designs, from a lucid and outspoken style; it is a remote and inexplicable beauty, a beauty shot through with mystery and strangeness, baffling, incal-culable. . . . Harmonically it obeys no known law—consonances, disso-nances, are interfused, blended, re-echoed, juxtaposed, without the smallest regard for the rules of tonal relationship established by long tradition. It recognizes no boundaries whatsoever between the different keys; there is constant flux and change. . . . His melodic schemes suggest no known model. . . . [Debussy's] hatred of the obvious is as plainly sincere as it is passionate and uncompromising.[15]

Around 1908, when he was first chair of music history at the Sorbonne, Romain Rolland wrote a persuasive essay on Debussy and his importance to France.[16] "The first performance of *Pelléas et Mélisande* was a very notable event in the history of French music," he wrote, "one of the three or four red-letter days in the calendar of our lyric stage." It owed its success to many factors, he explained: trivial ones, such as fashion, and important ones that "arise from something innate in the spirit of French genius"—moral and aesthetic reasons as well as some that are "purely musical."

Debussy was able to capture in his music the melancholy philosophy of fatalism of many European intellectuals at the turn of the century, a fatalism expressed in Maeterlinck's drama, Rolland wrote. *Pelléas* shows us "we are not master of ourselves, but the servant of unknown and irresistible forces, which direct the whole tragicomedy of our lives." These fatalistic ideas "have been wonderfully translated into music by Debussy; and when you feel the poetic and sensual charm of the music, the ideas become fascinating and intoxicating, and their spirit is very infectious."

But the artistry of *Pelléas* speaks more to the French than to Europeans generally, Rolland believed. The opera represents a natural and inevitable reaction "of French genius against foreign art, and especially against Wagnerian art." The Wagnerian ideal is primarily an ideal of power—the power of passionate and intellectual exaltation and mystic sensualism, which in Wagner's music dramas is "poured out like a fiery torrent." But ideals other than Wagner's do exist, and "another art might be as expressive by its proprieties and niceties as by its richness and force." The French favor naturalness and good taste over "exaggerations and extremes of passion, . . . and anything that oversteps the limits of the imagination."[17]

"As for Debussy's harmonic language," Rolland wrote,

his originality does not consist, as some of his foolish admirers have said, in the invention of new chords, but in the use he makes of them. A man is not a great artist because he makes use of unresolved sevenths and ninths [and whole-tone scales]; one is only an artist when one makes them say something. . . . *Pelléas et Mélisande*, "the land of ninths," has a poetic atmosphere which is like no other musical drama ever written. [The orchestrations are] restrained, light, and divided, for Debussy has a fine disdain for those orgies of sound to which Wagner's art has accustomed us. . . . With Debussy the passions almost whisper. The slightest vibration of his melodic line reveals the love in the hearts of Maeterlinck's unhappy young couple—the timid "Oh, why are you going?" at the end of the first act, and the quiet "I love you, too,"

in their last moments before Golaud shatters their joy. Compare the death of Mélisande, "without cries and without words," to the "wild lamentations" of the dying Isolde.

For Wagner, music is king, drama is prime minister, and poetry is the influential duchess. But as the French conceive it, opera demands a harmonious balance of words and music that are together wedded to the drama. "Debussy's strength," said Rolland, "lies in the methods by which he has approached this ideal of musical temperateness and disinterestedness, and in the way he has placed his genius as a composer at the service of the drama. He has never sought to dominate Maeterlinck's poem, or to swallow it up in a torrent of music; he has made it so much a part of himself that at the present time [circa 1908] no Frenchman is able to think of a passage in the play without Debussy's music singing at the same time within him."[18]

In the Garden of Harmonies

"I tried, with all my strength and sincerity," Debussy said, "to identify my music with the poetical essence of the drama. Before all things, I respected the characters, the lives of my personages; I wished them to express themselves independently of me. I tried to listen to them and to interpret them faithfully. . . . I have never been willing that my music should hinder . . . the changes of sentiment and passion felt by my characters."[19]

Aside from everything that makes *Pelléas* important in the history of opera, wrote Rolland, "there are purely musical reasons for its success, which are of deeper significance still," especially for musicians. "*Pelléas et Mélisande* brought about a reform in the dramatic music of France," and the most important reform is the way Debussy matches his music to the words. France had never had (with a few exceptions) a mode of operatic singing that closely replicated their natural speech. Neither Lully or Rameau, nor anyone until Debussy, had managed it successfully.

The philosopher Jean-Jacques Rousseau, who died in 1778, had perceived the need for reform, Rolland tells us, and had foreseen how Debussy, generations later, would accomplish it. An opera composer himself, Rousseau "showed . . . that there was no connection between the inflections of French speech, 'whose accents are so harmonious and simple,' and 'the shrill and noisy intonations' of recitatives in eighteenth-century French opera."[20] Rousseau even showed the way for Debussy's reforms by calling for melodies that would "wander between little intervals, and neither raise nor lower the voice very much." The vocal melody should have "little sustained sound," Rousseau specified, "and little inequality in the duration or value of the notes, or in their intervals." This is very nearly the declamation that Debussy pioneered in *Chansons de Bilitis* and *Pelléas*. Compare this to the declamation of Wagner, "with its vocal leaps and its resounding and heavy accentuation," tonal acrobatics that were more easily executed by the German tongue. When music lovers and critics complain loudly that there is "no music" in *Pelléas*, they are referring to the austerity of the declamation.[21] But Debussy, working with what Gilman called "the tonal utterance of Maeterlinck's rhymeless, meterless, and broken phrases," put all the melodic writing in the orchestra and used it to inform us of what the characters were feeling.[22]

To no small degree, the orchestral writing, more than the music of the characters themselves, proved to be Debussy's most essential contribution to Maeterlinck's play. "This achievement," wrote Gilman, "—an astonishing tour de force, at the least—is as artistically successful as it is unprecedented in modern music."[23]

Rolland described Debussy's "symphonic fabric" in painterly terms: "a sort of classic impressionism—an impressionism that is refined, harmonious, and calm; that moves along in musical pictures, each of which corresponds to a subtle and fleeting moment of the soul's life; and the painting is done by clever little strokes put in with a soft and delicate touch." Debussy's orchestrations are closer to Mussorgsky's than to Wagner's, Rolland noted. Instead of leitmotifs, Debussy uses "phrases that express changing feelings," and the phrases change with each new emotion. "In the garden of harmonies, [Debussy] selects the most beautiful flowers." Pleasing the ear is of primary importance; sincerity of expression is second. In this, too, Debussy reflects "the aesthetic sensualism of the French race, which seeks pleasure in art and does not willingly admit ugliness, even when it seems to be justified by the needs of the drama and of truth." Rolland invokes Mozart, who said, "Music, even in the most terrible situations, ought never to offend the ear; it should charm it even there; and, in short, always remain music."[24]

Debussy's reforms responded "to an unconscious yet profound need of the French spirit," Rolland insisted. "I would even venture to say that the historical importance of Debussy's work is greater than its artistic value. . . . Among all his gifts he has a quality which I have not found so evident in any other musician—except perhaps Mozart; and this quality is a genius for good taste."

Debussy's musical works are "the perfect flowers of the French spirit," said Rolland. But he pointed out that there is another aspect of that spirit that is *not* represented in *Pelléas*: the aspect that incorporates "heroic action, the intoxication of reason and laughter, the passion for light, the France of Rabelais, Molière, Diderot, and in music, we will say—for want of better names—the France of Berlioz and Bizet. . . . It is the balance between these two Frances that makes French genius. In our contemporary music, *Pelléas et Mélisande* is at one end of the pole of our art and *Carmen* is at the other. And this double ideal is the alternation between the gentle sunlight and the faint mist that veils the soft, luminous sky of the Isle de France."[25]

CHAPTER 18

WOMEN AND THE SEA
(1902–1904)

In France, even more than in any other country except Italy, a
musician wins renown only through the theater. . . . So the name
of Debussy did not become famous until the morning after the
presentation of Pelléas et Mélisande *at the Opéra-Comique,*
April 30, 1902. The composer was then forty years old.

—J. G. Prod'homme[1]

Pelléas et Mélisande was launched. Debussy gave it to the world, and it wasn't
his concern if we didn't know quite what to make of it.

But his great triumph at the Opéra-Comique was for a time clouded by
more transient matters. He was extremely tired from the months of rehearsals,
the last-minute requests for additional music, the inevitable compromises, the
persistent aggravations. His brain, he said, was like a squeezed lemon that has
no more to give. And with the success of *Pelléas*, Hartmann's executor increased his efforts to force the composer to repay the advances paid over several years. Debussy thought his legal troubles would never cease. Some of his
friends saw a radical change in him; René Peter said "he moved into a different
category of being . . . he was no longer a god, but a *maître*. . . . A score of concert societies fought to put on his works, his name leapt out from a hundred
posters."[2]

In July 1902, at Messager's invitation, Debussy visited him in London. Mary
Garden was in London, too, for her debut at Covent Garden, where Messager
was conducting. Garden accompanied Debussy to the theater to see Forbes
Robertson as Hamlet. "At that performance," she said, despite Debussy's limited
knowledge of English "[he] seemed like a child in a trance. . . . I have never
known anyone to lose himself so completely in the spectacle of great art."[3]

When he returned to Paris he found Lilly in severe pain from kidney
stones. To provide her with a serene, comfortable place to recuperate, the
couple traveled to the little Burgundian village of Bichain, about some sixty

miles southeast of Paris, where her father had come to live. Debussy enjoyed a complete rest, took long walks in the countryside, listened to no music at all, and sometimes thought about his next project.

By September he had recovered his creative energies and agreed to work with Paul-Jean Toulet on an operatic version of Shakespeare's romantic comedy *As You Like It*. It was clear that one of the attractions of the play was its atmospheric and literary distance from *Pelléas*. He had once railed at writers and composers who repeat their successes over and over, with diminishing returns.

Another reason for *As You Like It* was his infatuation with its leading lady: Rosalind, the brilliant, beautiful, resourceful daughter of the Duke. Undoubtedly he would bring Rosalind into his life while writing this opera, just as he kept Mélisande at home to reach out from a tapestry, to jealously whisper in his ear when he wrote music for another character. What a luscious idea it was, to spend a couple of years in Rosalind's company! But the fair maiden of Arden grudgingly gave way to a more august figure: King Lear. André Antoine, a pioneer of naturalism in theatrical acting and staging, asked for incidental music for a new Paris production of Shakespeare's tragedy. Debussy wrote some music for him (including a *Fanfare* that has survived) before Antoine decided to give the job to someone else.

In January 1903, Debussy pinned a beribboned medal to his jacket, ran a red sash across his chest, donned an overcoat, and took a cab to the suburban house where his father lived. The elder Debussy was on the lawn of his little garden, polishing his shoes, and he was surprised to see his son. Claude approached his father and, without a word, threw open his overcoat to reveal the gaudy accoutrements of a Chevalier of the Legion of Honor. Manuel stood speechless: this was the boy who chose not to become a sailor, the man who failed to make his father rich, but now—now he's received one of the highest honors given to a French citizen! Tears ran down Manuel's cheeks, and he embraced Claude with torrents of love and astonishment while he absentmindedly pummeled the new chevalier's back with blows from the waxing brush in one hand and his shoe in the other. It was a story that Debussy loved to tell—at last, approval and acceptance from a father who had never seemed to value his rare abilities. "You see," Debussy told René Peter, "in that brief moment I could feel pride at having been good for something."[4]

What Can Be Done Beyond *Pelléas*?

A year after the *Pelléas* premiere, Debussy could feel that he'd put Wagner behind him, along with the sauerkraut. It was a turning point. His goal was achieved, his mission was accomplished. He had introduced France to a new kind of musical experience, and he'd done it on his own terms, without the fusty traditions of the Conservatory.

In the spring and summer of 1903, he revised the four pieces of the *Suite bergamasque,* which were finally going to be published after years of neglect. He finished the three *Estampes* for piano and began work on "L'Isle joyeuse."

A saxophone rhapsody, barely started, sat heavily on his worktable. The woman who had commissioned the work was Elise Boyer Hall, a prominent member of the Orchestral Club of Boston. She learned to play the saxophone when she was forty-seven, and set out on a crusade to develop a repertoire for this new instrument, commissioning music from several composers. Hall paid Debussy his fee in 1901. He quickly spent the money, and by June 1903 he had forgotten about the commission when an unexpected visit from Hall's emissary sent him back to work. The project didn't interest him much. "The saxophone is a reedy animal with whose habits I'm largely unfamiliar," he told Louÿs. On his manuscript pages it was "murmuring melancholy phrases" in which he seemed to have little confidence.[5] He wanted to finish the piece quickly, but musical ideas came and fled like butterflies, he said. He was frustrated by the "ridiculous" instrument, a hybrid of the woodwind and brass families, but he wanted to write something good for Hall to reward her patience. Eventually the butterflies returned, and by early August, he had more or less completed the short score, now called *Rapsodie arabe*; he sold the publishing rights to Durand for 100 francs. Thereupon he put the rhapsody away and started work on some ideas he had for a sea symphony.

Though Hall hounded the composer for many years, he never quite finished her saxophone piece. After his death, the composer Jean Roger-Ducasse revised and orchestrated it from the incomplete score. The *Rapsodie pour orchestre et saxophone* was given its first performance in Paris in 1919. Only ten minutes long, it's not a virtuosic showpiece; Debussy knew too little about playing the sax to attempt virtuosity. The music demonstrates the instrument's mellow, assertive timbre in its solo flights, though it seems uncomfortable in the mid-range of a full symphony orchestra.

Also during the summer of 1903, Debussy signed a contract with Durand for three series of *Images*.[6] Two series would be for piano solo, and one would eventually become the *Images pour orchestre*. He put his mind to work on the scenario for *Le Diable dans le beffroi*. Even at Bichain, new ideas were flooding his brain.

Almost 200 miles from the English Channel, in landlocked Burgundy, Debussy envisioned the three movements of a new symphonic work, to be called *La Mer*. He gleefully reminded friends that his father had steered him toward a sailor's life; and though he devoted himself to music, he'd always had a great love for the sea. Childhood afternoons at Cannes, Arcachon with the von Mecks, Dieppe with the Vasniers, Count Primoli's Fiumancino villa—his vast store of memories were more helpful to him now, he believed, than gazing for hours at the ocean, because reality can stifle the imagination, he said. As for the nasty weather at Bichain, he told Messager of "the wind, which causes the sea to dance"—a mental image he'd give voice to in the third movement of *La Mer*.[7]

Debussy had turned a corner. His creative juices were replenished, his mind freed of *Pelléas* and Wagner. His focus was on building the Debussy repertoire as quickly as he could.

Marcel Dietschy saw in this outburst of activity, including the concentration on *La Mer*, a premonition of the events that would soon turn Debussy's personal life in unexpected directions. Judging from Debussy's stray comments in letters and bored expressions in photographs, Dietschy suggested that by the end of summer 1903, Claude was no longer in love with Lilly. He enjoyed the rural countryside enough to consider buying land at Bichain, wrote Dietschy, but "it was as if Lilly scarcely existed any more."[8]

Emma Invites Him to Dinner

Debussy had, at most, a few pupils at any given time. One of them was a bright young man in his early twenties, Raoul Bardac, who aspired to be a composer. Raoul's father was a wealthy banker named Sigismond Bardac. His mother, Emma, was an amateur singer with a fine voice; she admired and sang Debussy's songs. Always curious, she often pestered Raoul, wanting to know more about his teacher. Emma was prominent in society; she hosted salons from time to time, and she knew a number of musicians. Years earlier, she knew Gabriel

Fauré well enough that when her daughter was born, in 1892, there was well-founded suspicion that Fauré was the father. He took a kindly interest in baby Dolly (her name was Hélène, but everyone called her Dolly), and in her first years he wrote for her, on her birthdays and other occasions, six of his most charming piano works, later collected and published as *Dolly Suite*. To Emma, Fauré dedicated his song cycle *La Bonne Chanson*.

In the months after the *Pelléas* opening, Mary Garden became fast friends with Lilly and Claude. She visited the couple in the rue Cardinet to study his songs with him, and the Debussys came two or three times a week to dine at her apartment. After dinner, "Debussy would sit at the piano," she later remembered, "and for an hour or so he would improvise. . . . Those hours stay like jewels in my mind. I have never heard such music in my life. . . . My God, how beautiful it was, and haunting. . . . [The music was] remote, other-worldly, always saying something on the verge of words."[9]

According to Garden, Emma Bardac invited Claude and Lilly to her home more than once, and he always refused. When Mary asked him why, he had no answer.

It was at this time of his life, or perhaps the following spring, that, according to Garden, Debussy declared his love for *her*. For almost ten years he had lived with a woman named Mélisande, he told her, "and I never thought I would ever find anybody who could make her come to life. . . . And you did that, Mary. I am obsessed with love of you, Mary. . . . I can't live without you, and I must know if you have any feeling for me." She told him she liked him as a friend, she adored his music, but he meant nothing to her in a romantic sense. After some reflection, she said, "Claude, it isn't me you love, much as you believe it. It is Mélisande you love. You've loved her for ten years, and you still do, and it is Mélisande that you love in me, not myself."[10]

Garden's anecdote reads like soap opera, but there may be a grain of truth in it. He was, in a way, in love with Mélisande, his idealized woman; and he did admire and adore Garden. In 1903, he dedicated the *Ariettes oubliées* to her "in affectionate and grateful homage." But the grain of truth appears to be awash in a sauce of romantic fantasy, and it was never corroborated by the man in question. Garden herself wrote that Lilly was the only woman Debussy ever loved, if he ever loved something other than his music.[11]

Debussy did finally go to the Bardacs for dinner, apparently in October 1903. He found Emma gracious and attentive, knowledgeable about music, and always eager to sing his songs. She was clearly *not* Mélisande. Her feet were firmly on the ground, her mind was whirring with ideas and opinions, and she was open and generous in her relationships.

Emma Moyse was born in Bordeaux of Jewish parents. She was seventeen when she married Bardac, and she gave birth to Raoul two years later. Dolly described her as "small and pretty, with auburn hair and topaz-colored eyes." Others remarked on her youthful appearance. She was intelligent, outspoken, and impulsive, with a femininity that attracted many men. Dolly recalled her "incomparable charm, to which nobody could remain insensible."[12] "She could not have been more feminine," wrote Dietschy. "She had turned many heads, but she was fascinated only by uncommon men. One was never bored in her company."[13] In her maturity, her self-reliance, and her musical sophistication, Emma was worlds away from Lilly.

Debussy returned to Emma again and again. When Lilly was suffering from bronchitis she urged Claude to attend Emma's soirées without her; in fact, she advised him to go there more often, since associating with Emma and her influential social circle could further his career.

In the spring of 1904, Debussy dedicated to Emma Bardac his *Trois Chansons de France*. He left Lilly for days at a time (at least once going to Arcachon) and returned each time to find his wife angry and seething. By now she must have known he was involved with Emma, and she was afraid of losing her husband.

On June 6, Emma sent him flowers. In a thank-you note, Claude said he was "profoundly happy" for her gesture: "Forgive me if I have kissed all these flowers as though they formed a human mouth."[14] Though the dates and duration of the trip are not known, Claude and Emma spent more than a few June days together in Pourville, a little resort town near Dieppe, on the northern coast of France.

In late June or early July Debussy completed work on "Masques," perhaps the most agitated and aggressive of his piano pieces. He was planning to run off with his new *amour*; Lilly would be terribly hurt, despite their already strained relationship. In the first part of "Masques" a torrential display of virtuosity ends abruptly in midair. A central section is calmer but disjointed—a discussion between the masculine bass and the feminine treble, without a resolution, and yielding to a return of the tempestuous music that began the piece. If this were a film soundtrack, in the final, quiet measures you would see onscreen a middle-aged, bearded man walking through a door, never to look back.

On July 15, Debussy sent Lilly off to Bichain. The next day he sent her a strange letter that begins with chitchat: "I'm pleased to know you arrived safely. . . . I had dinner out, came home at 10." It's a letter of farewell, but it never says what he needs to say, and must have been a complete puzzle to Lilly. "I've got to find something new," he wrote. "I think I've found a new path. . . . Try to understand me and not be resentful."[15] There's no goodbye, no mention of Emma, no clear sign Lilly has been abandoned. A second letter, in August, was more explicit.

The Island of Joy

On July 16 or soon after, Claude and Emma began their mysterious elopement. Where did the lovers go? To the Isle of Jersey, a quiet little outpost of Britain just off the French coast.

They stayed at the fashionable Grand Hotel at St Helier, the island's capital and largest port. It was a lovely, peaceful place where he was at last relaxed and able to work. "The sea has behaved beautifully toward me and shown me all her guises," he wrote Durand.[16] He's returning the proofs for "Masques" and *Fêtes galantes*, a second set of three mélodies on poems by Verlaine; and for the songs, he reminds his publisher to be sure to include the dedication: "In gratitude for the month of June 1904," followed by the letters "A.l.p.M." The mysterious letters stand for "À la petite mienne," which translates to something like "to my dear little one," a term of endearment he'd continue to use for Emma. He tells Durand he'll soon be in Dieppe but insists that his whereabouts must remain secret. Actually, the couple settled in nearby Pourville.

Besides reviewing the proofs for Durand, Debussy finished a piano piece he'd begun more than a year earlier, aptly called "L'Isle joyeuse." It's been said that Debussy conceived and wrote it while on Jersey, inspired by Emma. That's preposterous on several counts. First, it's known that the composer played an earlier version of it for Viñes in 1903, months before he met Emma. Second, the piece is so structurally and harmonically intricate that it's doubtful he could have created it in his brief time on Jersey, along with checking proofs, pondering *La Mer*, and spending quality time with his lover. If Debussy's newfound happiness on Jersey persuaded him to make some Emma-inspired revisions and complete the work, so much the better for his legend. But its provenance aside, "L'Isle joyeuse" is a marvelous showpiece for concert pianists (at least, for those who have a few extra fingers), and it's thrilling to listen to. It's a characteristically Debussyan romp featuring extended whole-tone passages interspersed with a brief rhythmic tune in Lydian mode and a bold, passionate theme in familiar major mode. There's a pure, muscular energy in "L'Isle joyeuse," as in "Masques," but the joy is uninhibited and builds to an ecstatic finale. In the concluding flourish, the pianist spans seven octaves, from the highest A to the lowest, in a flash.

Apparently, Claude and Emma stayed in Pourville through most of August and September. Increasingly his joy was tempered by sorrows and by a severely damaged conscience. Debussy dreaded returning to Paris, where he would face the condemnation of friends. He wrote to Messager, on September 19: "These past months, my life has been singularly strange. . . . I miss the Claude Debussy who worked so happily upon *Pelléas* for, between ourselves, I cannot find him any more, and that is one cause of my wretchedness, among many others."[17]

The Gunshot

Debussy's friendship with Louÿs diminished after their marriages began and ended when Claude left Lilly. The last known correspondence of the two old friends was in the spring of 1904, before the signs of Claude's passion for Emma were evident to others. Louÿs sent Debussy a note in January, followed by a humorous letter in March on the subject of gramophone recordings. Debussy answered him on June 12, telling Louÿs their relationship had become absurd and untenable, as his friend had already observed. "We're not even dead, which would at least be an excuse. However, I have a chronic need to see you."[18] Debussy invited Louÿs to choose a time when they might get together. Then summer came, and everything changed.

In October, Louÿs wrote to his brother, Georges: "I went yesterday to see poor Mme Debussy, who fired a pistol into her chest on October 13 after being abandoned by her husband. The bullet went through the stomach twice . . . the operation was successful, and the unhappy woman seems out of danger, but she's penniless and without a home. . . . Her husband has run off with a Jewish woman more than forty years old."[19] A subscription was created to help Lilly financially, to which Louÿs contributed anonymously.

Mary Garden, in her memoir, tells us more about Lilly's desperate act. One day in September Lilly came to her door, "wild with sorrow. . . . 'Claude has left me!' And she burst into a frenzy of tears." The distraught, discarded wife wrote a letter to Claude and sent it, for lack of another address, to his father. In it she said she'd be dead before he received the letter. On October 14, Garden was summoned to a Paris hospital. There she found Lilly, "with a bullet in her chest, wanting to die because her Claude had not come back to her."

"You must understand," Mary explains, "that this young girl never knew anything else in her life but her love of Debussy. She took care of him like a child. They had worries and debts and disappointments, but nobody ever got into the little apartment on the rue Cardinet to interrupt Debussy at his music. Lilly kept the world away, so her beloved Claude could work."

"Oh, Mary," Lilly said, from her hospital bed. "I didn't aim right, and I don't know how long I lay on the floor. I never lost consciousness. I heard someone coming into the bedroom. It was Claude." Debussy flew down the stairs and came back with an ambulance. When they arrived at the hospital, Debussy asked a doctor if Lilly's life could be saved. After an hour or two he was told his wife would survive and, wrote Garden bitterly, Debussy "muttered just one word— 'merci.' And he walked out of the hospital and out of the lives of all of us."[20]

CHAPTER 19
EASE, UNEASE, DISEASE (1904–1908)

By a unique stroke of irony, [the] public which demands "something new" is the same one that is bewildered by, and which jeers at, anything new and unusual. . . . This may seem hard to understand, but one must not forget that with a work of art an attempt at beauty is always taken as a personal insult by some people. . . . I have tried to forge a way ahead that others will be able to follow. These are the fruits of my experience, which will perhaps release dramatic music from the heavy yoke under which it has lived for so long.

—Debussy[1]

After the seclusion and quiet of two less-than-idyllic months in Jersey and Pourville, Claude and Emma returned to Paris to face the consequences of their elopement. On September 25, 1904, Debussy leased a small apartment for himself on avenue Alphand. The new lovers lived separately for a while, or at least had separate addresses.

The report of Lilly's attempted suicide was announced to the public in *Le Figaro* on November 4. The identity of the principals was thinly disguised—Lilly was "a very pretty young woman . . . who tried to kill herself . . . because her husband had been unfaithful to her"; Debussy was "a very distinguished composer, acknowledged as the leader of the young school, and whose opera has been much applauded recently"; and Emma was "Mme B., the young divorced wife of a well-known financier."[2] (In fact, Emma's divorce would not be final until May of the following year.)

The gossips whispered that Debussy left his wife in horrible circumstances and ran off with a rich married woman—a Jew, at a time when the Dreyfus affair was still unresolved and anti-Semitism was more pervasive in France than ever. The fact that Emma was believed to be rich made Debussy seem like a craven opportunist. The reproaches escalated when, in early January 1905, *Le Figaro* reported, falsely, that Lilly had again attempted suicide.

Stinging as it was, the black eye he received for leaving Lilly was not all Debussy endured. There was an especially fine-honed edge to the sword of condemnation that greeted his acquisition of gentility. Upward social mobility, in Debussy's day, was a perilous path. The lower classes were not encouraged to pull themselves up by their bootstraps or any other devices. Marrying above their station was unacceptable or, at best, unwise.

When he was young, Debussy's wealthy friends did not judge him harshly for the misfortune of his persistent poverty; they helped him financially and cheered his successes. But the letters he wrote to these friends reveal the humiliation of his dependence. His pleas for monetary relief, sometimes leavened with strained humor, were more often brushed with well-oiled compliments, lavish gratitude, and obsequious apologies: the puppy wagging his tail and begging for a bone.

When *Pelléas* was acclaimed, when Debussy became famous—well, good for you, *mon ami*! When he married Emma Bardac, an educated, accomplished, well-to-do woman of society—well, who do you think you are, *monsieur*? You're not one of us.

Debussy was disconsolate about the loss of many friends—both those who could not forgive his betrayal of Lilly and those who could not tolerate his moving into their high society. Laloy and Durand remained loyal. A few others came back to him before long: Godet, Satie, Dukas, Toulet, Viñes. The remnants of his cherished friendship with Louÿs were beyond repair. Someone proposed reconciliation with Lilly, but Debussy rejected the idea. To ease his tormented soul and help restore his reputation, he concentrated on completing *La Mer*.

The Perpetual Debtor

Debussy's irksome need to lean on his friends and publishers for loans, subsidies, and free meals was understandable in the early years. His poor parents, living hand to mouth, never thought to teach him what little they knew about handling money—its value, uses, and temptations, not to mention rainy-day savings. Well into his adulthood he spent like a foolish, undisciplined child on oriental knickknacks, fancy pastries, and other small luxuries that emptied his pockets. But now he'd had a triumph with *Pelléas*, and even his earliest compositions were in demand. Why was he still so poor and needy? History and speculation provide multiple reasons, including his admitted laziness and the mental indolence caused by periods of depression.

While other students and young musicians fed themselves with earnings from private lessons, Debussy had no patience for teaching children and little aptitude for the job. He was never a virtuoso-composer in the manner of Liszt or Paganini, who wrote flashy showpieces for their concert tours; he played occasionally at the salons of people who paid well for such services, but he did not enjoy performing for strangers and didn't seek opportunities. He was more at ease in supporting roles—playing with small chamber groups or accompanying singers at National Society concerts—for which he was paid little or nothing.

Until *Pelléas*, when he was already forty years old, his composing didn't earn enough to sustain him. Publishing rights for the early piano pieces and songs brought him only 100 francs each—100 francs for "Rêverie," 200 francs for the two "Arabesques," 300 francs for *Trois Chansons de Bilitis*, and the same for the three remarkable *Estampes* of 1903. Not until 1905 did the first set of *Images pour piano* finally earn a 25 percent increase in his fee. Additional royalties from sales of sheet music were negligible.

When inspired, Debussy could write a song or a piano piece in just a few days, but orchestral works took months or years to complete. He worked on *Prélude à "L'Après-midi d'un faune"* for two years, on and off, and was paid a paltry 200 francs for it. Until *La Mer* there was little incentive to devote so much time to a major work for orchestra.

On Sunday, March 5, 1905, at 6:00 p.m., the great sea symphony was finished. He sold the publishing rights to Durand for 2,000 francs, reaching a new peak in his earnings.[3]

A few weeks later, Debussy, who had held onto the rights to *Pelléas et Mélisande* until now, released the opera to Durand (with Maeterlinck's agreement) for 25,000 francs, of which two-thirds went to the composer and one-third to the author. Debussy also received 9,000 francs for the piano-vocal score. Performance royalties for *Pelléas* would be paid at the usual rate of 12 percent of ticket sales, shared equally by composer and librettist. During Debussy's lifetime, *Pelléas* was performed 107 times at the Opéra-Comique, and ticket sales ranged from about 5,500 francs per performance in the early years to over 8,000 francs in the prewar years; between 1903 and 1913, he might have earned, on average, about 4,000 francs a year from the Opéra-Comique. Beginning in 1907, *Pelléas* performances in other countries yielded additional income.

By the summer of 1905, Debussy's financial independence should have been assured. On July 17, Debussy gave his publisher the exclusive rights to all his future compositions in exchange for a guaranteed annual income of 12,000 francs; earnings above that amount would be paid as well. The harried composer was grateful and appreciative. He would now be valued, in a material sense, more or less on a par with most of his successful French contemporaries (though most composers had significant additional income from teaching or conducting).

He needed Durand's money, and much more. He was about to dedicate his life to a woman accustomed to stylish clothes and all the comforts of affluence, a woman who was already pregnant with Debussy's child. When Emma's divorce was granted, in May, she received a pension from her ex-husband, Sigismond Bardac, of 10,000 francs annually. She was also expecting a large portion of her Uncle Osiris's fortune when he died. Osiris was about eighty years old, but surely Emma was not yet picking out a dress for his funeral.

With contracts signed, Claude and Emma went to Eastbourne, across the Channel. It was a favorite summer holiday resort for the English, its streets lined with handsome Victorian homes and flower gardens. Debussy found it charming and enjoyed the way the sea behaved in this particular place. It was a working holiday, and what a fine place to work! In his proximity there was no noise, not even from pianos; there were no musicians wanting to be famous, no artists wanting to be musicians, just happy children chasing each other on the perfect green lawns.

The Turbulent Sea

On August 2, 1905, Debussy received notice that his divorce from Lilly was final. The court ordered him to pay alimony of 400 francs a month. Jacques Durand ensured Debussy's obligation by agreeing to issue the checks to Lilly himself; the payments were deducted from Debussy's earnings or added to his debt to the publisher (which was, in July 1905, a staggering 50,000 francs).

October was an eventful month for Claude and Emma. They leased a house owned by an alcohol-steeped Englishman named Mr Fairbin. It was in one of the most fashionable neighborhoods in Paris, on the elegant avenue du Bois de Boulogne, in the 16th arrondissement. The Place de l'Étoile and the Arc de Triomphe anchor the eastern end of the elegant avenue, the widest street in Paris, lined with chestnut trees. At the western end is Porte Dauphine, site of one of the gates in the fortified wall that once surrounded the city. A few steps beyond Porte Dauphine is the immense green expanse of the Bois de Boulogne; and nearby, just off the busy avenue, is a small cluster of houses built around a circular cul-de-sac. Among this cluster is Debussy's elegant house, 64 avenue du Bois de Boulogne, on a plot just big enough for some hydrangeas and other flowers.[4] The 10,000-franc annual fee was covered neatly by Emma's alimony. She had no other significant income or assets except for the expectation of a bequest from her uncle. As for the household expenses—cook, housemaid, eventually a nanny and a chauffeur, an automobile, food, clothing, furnishings, and summer holidays at seaside hotels—Claude would have to earn enough to pay for them.

On October 30, the new family in the elegant house welcomed a baby girl named Claude-Emma. Her father called her Chouchou, and she was known by that name to everyone. He loved this child, his only child, more than he could ever express in music.

Many visitors to Debussy's house—Satie, Maurice Dumesnil, Robert Schultz, and others—have left descriptions sufficient to create a mental collage of the interiors. The large parlor had tall windows that allowed ample daylight to filter through the curtains. Blue-gray draperies matched the plush wall-to-wall carpeting. The Louis XV furniture, as it was described by one visitor, would suggest elegant tables with carved, curved wooden legs, possibly gilded, and comfortable chairs upholstered in fine needlepoint tapestries. A low marble-topped table displayed an assortment of little objets d'art. Given pride of place near the middle of the room was a Blüthner grand piano.

The composer's studio, on the ground floor near the parlor, was neither large nor cluttered. His workaday piano was a fine Pleyel upright (a gift from the manufacturer). Fewer than a hundred books could be seen in the room, but they represented many authors whose writings were transformed by Debussy's vocal music: Mallarmé, Rossetti, Maeterlinck, François Villon. Many visitors commented on his large worktable, which was kept very neat but always displayed his collection of small ceramic or carved wooden animals from China and Japan. One of them, a porcelain toad, was called Arkel, after the old king in *Pelléas*, and Debussy never traveled without it. On the walls were prints and watercolors that held special meaning for him, including Hokusai's famous engraving *The Great Wave off Kanagawa*, a detail of which was, at the composer's request, reproduced on the printed score of *La Mer*.

Durand, a frequent visitor, remarked that the studio was always filled to over-flowing with fresh flowers, even in winter. On a sunny day the two windows flooded the room with light and gave Claude a view of the garden.

The house was always quiet—even the colors were subdued—and visitors sensed that it was well managed by Emma. The Debussys seldom entertained on a large scale; too many visitors might have disturbed his serenity, thought Robert Schultz, and serenity was essential to Debussy's ability to work. But often a few friends would be invited for lunch or dinner. For years, Satie dined there once a week, and sometimes Debussy himself would make him a perfect omelet. Stravinsky, after his triumphs at the Ballets Russes, was a favored guest. "A simple tea was as lavish as most dinners," Arthur Hartmann recalled, "while a dinner at his house was nothing short of sumptuous."[5]

This was the first home that ever offered Debussy a sense of comfort and pleasure. He took advantage of its proximity to the Bois de Boulogne, where he'd often go for walks. Getting around Paris was easy, as horse-drawn trams and omnibuses covered the city. At Porte Dauphine, a Métro station opened in 1900—a link in the new but fast-growing web of tracks tunneling underground; this station still preserves its elaborate, glass-roofed Art Nouveau entrance, designed by Hector Guimard. Very nearby, in Debussy's day, was a station on the Ligne de Petite Ceinture, a ground-level passenger rail line that encircled the city. Debussy could hear the noise and horns of passing trains while he worked, but he didn't seem to mind.

La Mer, **Never Out of Tune**

On October 15, 1905, the month they moved to their new house, the premiere of *La Mer* was to be performed at the Lamoureux Concerts. Debussy told Durand that his two days of rehearsals with the conductor, Camille Chevillard, were excruciating; the composer's new impressionism and the conductor's Lisztian romanticism seemed irreconcilable. Worse still, the scores for the instrumental parts had been badly proofread, and correcting the mistakes had eaten up valuable time.

La Mer carries the formidable subtitle *Three Symphonic Sketches for Orchestra*. The sketches, or movements, are "De l'Aube à midi sur la mer," "Jeux de vagues," and "Dialogue du vent et de la mer" (Dawn to Midday on the Sea, Play of the Waves, Dialogue of the Wind and Sea).

Debussy was deeply hurt by the many unfavorable reviews. Pierre Lalo's remarks were devastating, especially since he'd been an early supporter of *Pelléas*. "I do not hear, I do not see, I do not smell the sea," he wrote. For the first time, "listening to a descriptive work by Debussy, I have the impression of standing, not in front of nature, but in front of a reproduction of nature," though the reproduction, he admitted, was "wonderfully refined, ingenious, and carefully composed."[6] While the early critical disapproval might have been influenced in part by Chevillard's poor interpretation, the reviews of Debussy's nervously conducted performance in 1908 were only a little kinder.

Laloy, who penned the first authoritative Debussy biography in 1908, wrote admiringly and at length about *La Mer*.[7] After the first performance he declared that Debussy's new work was "among the loveliest, the most harmonious, the most captivating" in the orchestral repertoire. His impression, he admitted, wasn't shared by many of his colleagues, who reproached the composer for not portraying the sea in its universal, eternal aspect. But in each of the three movements, Laloy said, Debussy was "able to create enduringly all the glimmerings and shifting shadows, caresses and murmurs, gentle sweetness and fiery anger, seductive charm and sudden gravity contained in those waves." To the Debussyites who hoped the new work would echo the *Nocturnes*, Laloy said that *La Mer* has a "different character, an almost a resplendent maturity. It is larger and broader, firmer in its foundations and richer in its contours."[8]

La Mer, said Laloy, gave French art, "which has for so long been a prisoner in our houses, our salons, and our concert halls, a dizzying view of the universe."[9] The harmony

> is as fine and rich as ever. Instead of being presented in the primitive form of chords and being entrusted to one instrumental choir, the harmony is distributed across the whole orchestra, passes from one group to another, swells out then falls back, and above all is translated into lively accents, into resolute motifs, even into complete melodies, which bring life to the backgrounds that have hitherto been motionless, dividing them into successive planes and giving them movement....An agile polyphony...awakens the rhythm from the summit to the depths of the orchestra.[10]

What these perceptions suggest is nothing less than an analogue of the sea itself, in music that—with its constant ebb and flow, its interweaving of contrary motions, its unpredictable and complex rhythms—describes the sea with its tides and eddies, its creation and devolution of waves, and its turmoil in the context of immutable, infinite perpetuity. In *La Mer* and other works of the period, Laloy sees a new maturity, balance, "and a reconciliation with life."[11] Debussy's melodies, once evanescent, were now explicit and strong.

Returning to the study of *La Mer* in 1908, Laloy compared Debussy to one of the great French composers of the Baroque: "Since François Couperin, we have never had a composer in France who was more the master of the art, more capable of making the notes say what he wanted, of directing his thoughts in the only order that was appropriate to them."[12]

Debussy once described the sea as an instrument of "strong and beautiful music, yet never out of tune."[13]

Visitors

After *La Mer* and the groundbreaking piano music of this period, many writers and musicians wanted to meet Debussy. A fledgling composer named Edgard Varèse struck up a friendship with him in 1908 that lasted until the young man emigrated to the United States seven years later. Richard Strauss, a more famous composer than Debussy and a celebrated conductor as well, arranged to have lunch with Debussy at Durand's publishing house. Strauss talked at length about copyright law, Debussy gave his full attention to his meal, and neither man enjoyed the meeting. André Caplet, winner of the Prix de Rome in 1901, began an association with Debussy that led to many collaborations.

Arthur Hartmann, a Philadelphia-born violinist on a European concert tour, wrote Debussy with a request: would the composer please send all the violin music he had written, so Hartmann could add it to his concert repertoire? When Debussy replied that he had nothing to send him, Hartmann wrote a violin-piano arrangement of Debussy's mélodie "Il pleure dans mon coeur" and asked for permission to play it in public. Hartmann was invited to the house, and Debussy was delighted with the transcription—with the transcriber, too. The violinist and his wife, Marie, became close friends with the Debussys and moved into a house around the corner.

In 1907, Manuel de Falla made a difficult and risky move from his home in Madrid to a humble apartment in Paris. The need to find friends—people who could help advance his career—among the legions of Parisian musicians was torturous for a man as mild and reticent as Falla. The first composer he called on was Debussy; they had earlier exchanged letters when Falla was preparing a piano reduction of the *Danses sacrée et profane*. Debussy was on vacation, so he sought out Dukas, who received him warmly. Falla had brought with him the score of his opera *La Vida breve* and played it for Dukas, who suggested it was good enough for the Opéra-Comique. Dukas introduced Falla to Isaac Albéniz, who effusively praised the opera, as did Debussy when he finally heard it. Falla was introduced to Viñes, who introduced him to Ravel, and soon the Spanish composer was invited to musical soirées and welcomed to meetings of the Apaches. Durand accepted Falla's *Four Spanish Pieces* for publication.

Debussy, Dukas, and Messager each met with Falla numerous times, coaching him in orchestration and other matters. *La Vida breve* (Life Is Short) made its debut in Nice in April 1913 and at the Opéra-Comique a year later. Falla scurried back to Madrid when the war erupted.

It has been said that the turning point in Falla's creative life was his meeting with Debussy. Up to that time the Spaniard "had been expressing the letter of Andalusian music; he began now to realize how Debussy had managed to convey the spirit," wrote J. B. Trend.[14]

Uncle Osiris

Daniel Iffla is not a person we hear much about, and Debussy never met him, but Iffla had a profound effect on his life. He was born in Bordeaux in 1825, and long before he died he had become the richest man in France. Unlike the Rothschilds of his era, he did not inherit his wealth. Rather, Daniel began his career working in Paris for other people's banks and made some smart investments. In 1861 he took the surname Osiris, after the ancient Egyptian god of the afterlife, for reasons that are unclear. Having made more money than he'd ever need, he began giving away his fortune. He founded and financed seven synagogues in France and as far afield as Tunis. He gave the city of Nancy a bronze statue of Joan of Arc astride her horse, and he gave a monumental statue of William Tell to the people of Lausanne. In 1896 he bought and restored the historic Château de Malmaison, once the home of Napoleon Bonaparte, and gave it to France in 1904. He was a collector of important Napoleonic relics, and when Daniel Iffla Osiris died in February 1907 he bequeathed the collection to the Pasteur Institute along with a considerable portion of his remaining fortune. To his niece, Emma Moyse Debussy, he left nothing.

Emma and Claude had been counting on the Osiris estate to liberate them from the mounting financial obligations of their life of luxury. It was widely assumed that Osiris disinherited his niece after she eloped with Debussy; the scandal brought shame to her family. If Osiris had some other motivation, it lies buried with him at Montmartre Cemetery, where his tomb is brazenly topped with a copy of Michelangelo's large sculpture of a powerful Moses.

Illness

Debussy's illness began, or began to be severe, near the end of 1908. In January 1909, he saw a doctor, who advised a change of diet and plenty of exercise. By February he was hemorrhaging almost daily. He sought relief with morphine for the pain, and with cocaine, known at that time as an anesthetic, a stimulant, and as a treatment for depression and other conditions for which its efficacy was doubtful. We don't know if Debussy's symptoms were sporadic during the next few years, or constant for long periods; neither do we know what his doctors thought was causing his distress. It is likely that the diagnosis of rectal cancer was not confirmed until some years later.

CHAPTER 20

DEBUSSY AND
THE MODERN PIANO

Debussy's greatest piano music belongs to the twentieth century...from Estampes *onward....In the mesmerizing* pianissimo *sonorities of the opening measures of "Pagodes" and "La Soirée dans Grenade," he exploited and extended some of the greatest secrets of nineteenth-century piano writing; and in the scintillating, tactile precision of "Jardins sous la pluie," he reinterpreted the keyboard style of Bach and Chopin.*

—Paul Roberts[1]

Throughout his life Debussy spent an inordinate amount of time and energy finding ways to secure enough money to live on. His financial problems multiplied when the promise of Osiris's fortune vanished and doubled again when illness weakened his strength and broke his spirit. Fishing for francs among the captains of the music business was a humiliating effort in the best of times. What he needed was a rich patron, his own King Ludwig. Where was Poniatowski? Building an industrial empire in California. Chausson? Dead. Louÿs? Estranged. Durand? Generous, but stretched to his limit.

In 1909, Fauré asked Debussy to become a member of the Paris Conservatory's advisory committee, and he served as a judge for the mandatory performance competitions. Durand pressed him for orchestral arrangements of his piano works, as there was a growing demand, but Debussy often preferred to leave the work to Caplet or Henri Büsser. And for years, he was in demand as a music journalist—for *La Revue blanche* in 1901, then for *Gil Blas*, *SIM*, *Comedia*, and others. His articles were admired for the clarity and forthrightness of his ideas about musicians and music, including his own, and for his insights into the cultural life of a great city. Perhaps if he'd lived longer, or later, when recording royalties made orchestral writing more profitable, he'd have made the effort to produce more of it.

But what he *could* do, with great skill and satisfaction, spending less time for greater profit than journalism or teaching—he could write for the pianists (and their audiences) who loved his music.

During the first years of the century Debussy produced the most important body of piano music since Chopin—*Estampes*, "L'Isle joyeuse," *Images pour piano*, *Children's Corner*, the twenty-four Préludes—and no one since his death has equaled his achievements. Pierre Boulez has called Debussy's piano music of this period "one of the monuments of piano literature." This was, Boulez writes, "an extremely brilliant period in the composer's evolution: He would go no farther in the utilization of the piano's resources, in the specific use of its timbre and colors. With that series of collections, he inaugurated a new way of writing for the instrument, one that most of his listeners would call impressionism. Never before had writing for the piano been so fluid, so varied, even so surprising."[2] But Debussy wasn't yet finished. In the last years of his life he wrote the twelve Études, among which are the most difficult and delightful pieces a virtuoso will encounter.

As an adolescent, he wrote mostly art songs, and his piano writing was limited almost exclusively to the vocal accompaniments. His serious attempts for the piano began with an outpouring of compositions, written between 1888 and 1891, that have become mainstays of the repertoire. They include the two "Arabesques," "Rêverie," "Ballade," "Valse romantique," and the four movements of the *Petite Suite* for piano four-hands. The *Suite bergamasque* (including "Clair de lune") also belongs to this brief period but wasn't published until 1905. (These early piano works are discussed in chapter 5.) After 1894, Debussy wrote nothing for solo piano for about six years. His mind was occupied with *Pelléas*, the *Nocturnes* for orchestra, and *Chansons de Bilitis*.

After the turn of the century, he left behind most traces of Chopin, Fauré, and Grieg and wrote music characterized by a simpler mode of expression, lighter textures, and the modern harmonic language he'd been exploring since the Quartet and *Faune*. The piano music written after 1900 owes a great deal to the aesthetics of the symbolist poets and to the spirit of Couperin and other French keyboard masters of the eighteenth century. It was this heritage that he hoped, in the last years of his life, to restore for the people of France.

The Piano

In the early Baroque, before the development of the piano, keyboard instruments were harpsichords or clavecins, whose sounds are produced by plucked strings; or organs, which move air through pipes to produce musical tones. The piano (or pianoforte), a keyboard instrument with strings struck by hammers, was born in the eighteenth century and matured during the nineteenth. The piano had a more expressive tone and greater dynamic range than the harpsichord.

When Mozart was born, the piano keyboard had five octaves, so his piano pieces were limited to a sixty-note span. (The keyboard octave has five black and seven white keys.) Around the time of his death in 1791, the first six-octave pianos were built; Beethoven and Chopin wrote for the expanded instrument. When Chopin died in 1849, the best concert grands had seven octaves, and the keyboard expanded again before the century's end, when eighty-eight keys (seven octaves plus a third) became the accepted standard.

While pianos were sprouting more keys, piano makers dramatically improved the other parts—hammers, dampers, soundboards, and so on. The double-escapement action permitted rapid repetition of notes. Piano wire made from iron was replaced by superior high-carbon steel wire. The modern pianos available to Debussy had one thick, coiled steel string for each of the lowest bass notes; three thin strings for each note in the upper, treble range; and two strings for each note in the middle-to-lower range. In the early 1870s, Julius Blüthner, a Leipzig manufacturer, invented a variant of the instrument adding one additional string, called an aliquot, for each note in the treble range, to improve the character of the sound. The aliquot strings are set in a horizontal plane slightly above the regular strings so the hammers don't strike them, but when a hammer strikes a regular treble string, the corresponding aliquot (tuned an octave higher) vibrates, boosting the overtones, or harmonics, of that note. The result is an upper range with richer, more complex tones and more brilliance, with enhanced dynamics that help tinkly high notes compete with rumbling bass notes.

In 1905, while vacationing in Eastbourne, Debussy played a Blüthner aliquot piano, apparently for the first time. He was enthralled, and there, or possibly a few weeks later in London, he purchased a magnificent Blüthner aliquot grand and had it shipped to Paris. This piano remained in his house for the rest of his life, and he was immensely proud of it.

Debussy, more than most composers of his day, often employed the upper and lower tonal extremes in his music. He had a keen sense of timbre and was careful to give any particular chord or melodic line the characteristics of pitch, emphasis, and volume it needed. The extremes added new timbres to his tonal palette. Listen to "Pagodes," written in 1903, in which Debussy evokes the sound of a gamelan orchestra; the upper notes take on the sonic quality of small bells and little harps.

At Eastbourne in 1905, he tried to complete the three *Images pour piano*, Book 1. One of the three, "Reflets dans l'eau" (Reflections in the Water), displeased him so thoroughly, he told Durand on August 19, that he scrapped it and wrote another one "in accordance with the most recent discoveries of harmonic chemistry." He was very likely referring obliquely to his discovery of the Blüthner. "I'm starting to see things clearly again, and my thinking machine is gradually getting back into gear," he said.[3] When he finished the *Images*, he was quite pleased with them, confident they'd have a place in the piano repertoire.

Debussy's frequent use of the upper and lower tonal extremes is significant— one reason among many that his piano pieces sound so modern, so unlike the well-known works of his great predecessors. Of course, Mozart, Beethoven, Chopin, and Liszt wrote for the pianos of their time, with their narrower range and comparatively primitive technology.

Debussy was always the best performer of his own music. Léon-Paul Fargue, an Apache friend of Ravel, said that Debussy "appeared to be giving birth to the piano. He cradled it, talked to it, like a rider to his horse, a shepherd to his flock."[4] No one, Arthur Hartmann said, could surpass Debussy in the sheer beauty of his tone, in his keyboard technique, or in the nuances of expression. "[Debussy's piano compositions] reveal his profound understanding of the piano and its possibilities, and are as original in their pianism as those by Chopin and Liszt."[5]

The writer André Suarès said that Debussy conceived piano music "as for an original instrument in which, when the keys are pressed, the strings give the blend of melody and harmony that there is in the legato of a string quartet."[6] Marguerite Long follows Suarès's thought with this: "To obtain this legato the pianist, while taking care of his touch, must feel the sound at the end of his fingers and ensure that he maintains gentleness in force, or force in gentleness. . . . No one has made us feel more deeply [than Debussy] the mysterious correlation of sound and thought, [thus evoking] an aspect of nature, with its light and shade, a shimmer of poetry and dream, in one single chord."[7] Taken together, these comments help us understand that the music Debussy wrote for the piano was ideally intended for his own hands, which were, from an early age, well adapted to the kind of music he wrote.

Debussy's piano writing took a turn toward the modern around the time of his elopement with Emma Bardac and his discovery of the Blüthner piano. Debatable, certainly, is the extent to which his keyboard adventurism was fostered by either of those events. A little, perhaps. But Debussy's orchestral works had also taken a radical turn, beginning in 1894 with *Faune*. The *Nocturnes* and *La Mer* had marked a great evolution in his musical thinking, and it was only natural that his piano music should follow a similar path.

Debussy's Piano Music

From the beginning, an essential characteristic of Debussy's writing for piano was its consistent pianistic authenticity. From Beethoven to Brahms, composers wrote their most serious works for the piano—the sonatas, particularly—as if the piano were an orchestra in a box. With its six- or seven-octave range and its great expressive power, the nineteenth-century piano had become "an orchestra of reduced means, the echo of an immense instrumental phalanx," wrote Guido Gatti in 1921, and compositions for the piano often sound like symphonic music compressed for the two hands of the pianist. By contrast, Debussy's piano music is "intrinsically pianistic in its nature. . . . Every dynamic and timbre effect is born of the instrument itself, and . . . generates an ample, novel, and fascinating sonority."[8] One of the few nineteenth-century composers known for his pianistic integrity is Debussy's lodestar, Chopin.

After the turn of the century, Debussy rarely wrote piano music in the keyboard language of the Romantic era. It was a language that he almost single-handedly rendered obsolete.

Pour le piano

The Baroque pervades *Pour le piano*, a set of three pieces published in 1901 in which Debussy returns to old classic forms of the French Baroque suite. The "Prélude" overlays Debussy's supple energy with the delicacy of Couperin. The "Toccata" is a flamboyant *perpetuum mobile* of rapid arpeggios and bright colors. The middle movement, "Sarabande," written earlier than the others, in 1894, is played slowly and with a certain elegance. Here Debussy uses modal scales to establish an archaic tonal picture of great solemnity and beauty; sumptuous harmonic effects arise from his unresolved seventh and ninth chords, often in parallel motion.

"Lindaraja"

Often overlooked in the Debussy inventory is "Lindaraja," written in 1901 for two pianos but not published until 1926. "Lindaraja" is named after a Moorish courtyard in the Alhambra palace in Granada, a tree-shaded little garden with a fountain and a large windowed balcony. Debussy's music captures the delicacy, dignity, and magical aura of the place, even though he had never been there. (Also inspired by the Alhambra is "La Puerta del vino," from the second book of Préludes.)

Estampes

In many of his works, including the *Estampes* (1903), Debussy shows us what the pianist Alfred Cortot calls "the invisible in Nature." Instead of engaging our emotions exclusively through melodies, rhythms, and harmonies, Debussy suggests to us in his tonal pictures (an *estampe* is a print or engraving) "the indefinable that sings and vibrates under the appearance of things and beings"; and it's the vibrating song of those puppets and festivals, clouds and nymphs and Delphic dancers, that intimately pervades our senses and stirs our emotions. It was in *Estampes* that Debussy first achieved this creative miracle that for Cortot is "the poetry of the piano . . . the new essence of his music."[9]

In *Estampes*, Debussy gives us three tone pictures of China, Spain, and France. "Pagodes" (Pagodas) reflects Debussy's fascination with the gamelan; he plays with all the possibilities of the pentatonic scale to sketch a luminous landscape of splashing water, birdsong, and chimes. "La Soirée dans Grenade" (Evening in Grenada) is an atmospheric pastiche of Spanish dance rhythms, brittle percussive interruptions, and chains of ever more weary chords that bring the evening to a sleepy halt. When Debussy finished the piece, he wrote excitedly to Louÿs, "If this isn't exactly the music they play in Granada, so much the worse for Granada."[10] The third of the *Estampes*, "Jardins sous la pluie" (Gardens in the Rain) is a popular favorite, at once virtuosic and delightful. The piece, in the manner of a toccata, suggests children playing happily among summer raindrops. Debussy weaves into his shimmering sketch two tunes of childhood, a *ronde* called "Nous n'irons plus au bois" and a lullaby "Do, do, l'enfant, do." The music turns darker—perhaps the children are lost or frightened—but ends amiably with a flash of radiant sunlight in E major.

"D'un Cahier d'esquisses"

"For Debussy," Guido Gatti wrote, "the piano was a faithful friend and the guardian of his most profound secrets."[11] "D'un Cahier d'esquisses" (From a Sketchbook), written in January 1904, is born of his intimacy with the piano.

The musical ideas in this pensive piece are mostly very quiet, strung loosely together like a literary train of thought. The tempos are unpredictably variable; the rhythms are obscured by syncopations, pauses, and silences. Debussy often said he wanted certain compositions to sound as if they were improvised. He came closest to that effect in his "Sketchbook."

"Masques"; "L'Isle joyeuse"

"Masques" and "L'Isle joyeuse" are virtuosic, exciting, and more muscular than most of Debussy's piano writing, but they lack the kind of fresh, startling musical ideas that began with *Estampes*. (See chapter 18, pages 226–228.)

Suite bergamasque

The four pieces of the *Suite bergamasque*—"Prélude," "Menuet," "Clair de lune," and "Passepied"—were written around 1890, though they were possibly revised before publication in 1905. (See chapter 5, pages 76–77.)

Images pour piano, Books 1 and 2

The two sets of *Images pour piano* (Book 1 written between 1901 and 1905, Book 2 in 1907) offer six more examples of Debussy's musical poetry. "Reflets dans l'eau" (Reflections in the Water) shows us a unique little world that exudes music only Debussy can hear. Instead of an image and its inversion, Debussy focuses on just the rippling reflection; and we can guess, if we like, what appears above the reflection, or what animates the ripples. In arcs of harmonious chords, three notes—A-flat, F, and E-flat—independent of the arcs, "sing with poetic intensity," says Marguerite Long.[12] But at the core of the piece are arpeggios of such beauty and delicacy that they can only be followed by a near silence, allowing only the whisper of those three poetic notes. (Halfway through the piece, listen for a brief, surprising fragment of Gershwin, who was six years old when Debussy wrote "Reflets.")

"Et la lune descend sur le temple qui fut" (And the Moon Descends on the Temple That Was) achieves, says Laloy, "what was believed forbidden in modern times: an entirely melodic music. Here, there is no longer a tune resting on chords, as in the Classical and Romantic periods, or emanating from them, as in symbolist art." Debussy gives us "a vast, sleeping landscape, caressed and consoled by intermittent rays of moonlight, evoked by a melody so sustained that it can do without any external support. . . . It is a three-dimensional figure into which the composer, a sculptor of sounds, has condensed all the dispersed life around him."[13]

"Mouvement" is made of delicate triplets interrupted at times by a harshly contrasting theme. "Hommage à Rameau" is a tribute to the eighteenth-century composer whom Debussy considered his musical ancestor. "Poissons d'or" (Goldfish) is not a mere snapshot but the life of a goldfish as it shimmers, quivers, darts and flashes, jumps and pauses, aware of us, and amusing us in every way it knows how. The piece was inspired by the gilded fish on the black-lacquered panel, inset with gold and mother-of-pearl, that hung on the wall in Debussy's study.

"Music like this has the right to be free," said Laloy, "and to show itself *unfaithful* to the conventions which have been the most highly respected up to now, including those of the diatonic scale, . . . traditional harmony, . . . and Classical development. . . . It has the right, because [music] expresses primordial truths, and our own lives are revealed to us."[14]

Children's Corner

When *Children's Corner* was first performed, Debussy was "scared to death at the thought that his reputation might be compromised because he had written something humorous," said Harold Bauer, the pianist.[15] These six pieces were inspired by Chouchou, an adorable toddler when her father wrote them in 1906–1908. But Chouchou and her toys, says Paul Roberts, "are a pretext, a starting point, for an exploration through music of the psyche of a child." Debussy wants us to see Jimbo and Golliwogg and the doll "with the simple, unaffected faith of a child [for whom] imagination and reality are the same phenomenon, and this is also true of artists such as Debussy."[16] The composer chose English titles for these pieces, in part, because Chouchou was growing up with an English nanny and would soon be learning to speak the language, as her mother did. Nevertheless, the music is as French as the Champs-Elysées.

"Doctor Gradus ad Parnassum" refers to the well-worn book of piano pieces by Muzio Clementi, the bane of many piano students. Debussy seems to be imagining a child, much older than a toddler, learning piano à la Clementi—perhaps bored at first, then finding joy in playing the music.

"Jimbo's Lullaby" expresses the tender relationship of a young child and her stuffed elephant. Jimbo sings a lullaby to the child, but she doesn't want to sleep. She and Jimbo play quietly together. Finally, the child sings the same lullaby to her elephant and falls asleep before she's quite finished.

"Serenade for the Doll" (or "*of* the doll"?—a typographical confusion in the original printed edition) isn't what a child might sing to her doll, or vice versa. To Paul Roberts, it sounds rather like the serenade of one doll to another, a notion that any child could conceive, especially a child with a father like Claude Debussy in the house.

"The Snow Is Dancing" is a seemingly straightforward evocation of a gentle snowfall, with some odd moments. Perhaps the child wants to be outside playing in the snow but is restrained by a parent and isn't happy about it. Listen for all the intrusive dissonances that spoil the child's enjoyment of the dancing snowflakes.

"The Little Shepherd" is a strange, delicate miniature. The shepherd—a wooden doll? an etching?—is playing his pipes, brief improvised tunes that echo in the vast landscape he occupies. Three times he plays, and each time the music comes to a complete stop.

"Golliwogg's Cakewalk" takes its name from a little black doll that appeared in a droll series of children's books published in England at the turn of the century. The dolls themselves became favorite toys of many youngsters, including Chouchou. The highly syncopated cakewalk was an early version of ragtime, introduced to France at about the same time as the Golliwogg books. All who listen to this delightful piece are required to pay attention halfway through, when the composer tosses impolite barbs at Wagner's *Tristan und Isolde*.

"To speak of the stylistic perfection of [*Children's Corner*] is no hyperbole," wrote Guido Gatti. "The beauty of the compositions is revealed in their harmonic entirety, in the balance of their episodes, in the delicacy of their detail." In no other music did Debussy combine "a greater lucidity of expression with a feeling so full of humanity and of tenderness."[17]

"La plus que lente"

"La plus que lente" (More Than Slow) is a gracious waltz, written in 1910, nostalgic for a past that can only be evoked through music. Alfred Cortot, echoing some other critics, said it was "half a parody, half serious, and beyond question totally insignificant," though there's no evidence that the composer was less than earnest about it. Debussy wants tempos and expression that are nuanced and free; but if the performer exaggerates the effects, the music enters the realm of schmaltz, or even kitsch. When Durand had the piece orchestrated,

Debussy rejected it; with its trombones and percussion it smacked of the beer hall, he said; what he wanted was something for the teatime concerts where the beautiful people gather.

Préludes

Debussy's twenty-four Préludes—a single, unified work of art—are among Debussy's most important achievements. Here, he goes beyond the ornamentation of *Estampes* and the spareness of the *Images*, Book 2. "The time has come for Claude Debussy, having made music capable of conveying impressions which had been impossible to express before now, to arrange these elements according to his mind's will," wrote Louis Laloy. He compares Debussy, with his "gift of innocence and clarity," to Mozart, both of whom "have the power to spread a limpid serenity over everything they touch, and their minds rise spontaneously towards peace and joy."[18]

Each of the Préludes muses on something—a landscape, an entertainer, an event—that the composer found worth exploring. That he put his titles at the end of each piece, instead of the beginning, has drawn much comment. It's been said that the titles occurred to him after the music was written; but for most of the Préludes, scholars have found direct links between the titles and books, objects, or newspaper accounts that prompted the music into being. It's also been said that he wanted listeners to guess what the music meant before they saw the title; but most people, listening for the first time, probably enjoy the Préludes more when the titles suggest a way to hear the music.

The twelve Préludes of Book 1 were all written, remarkably, in just one month, "each precisely dated, from December 7, 1909, to January 5, 1910."[19]

I. "Danseuses de Delphes" (Dancers of Delphi). At the Louvre, Debussy was inspired by a Greek sculpture or column, probably taken from the Temple of Apollo at Delphi, carved with the images of three bacchantes. Siglind Bruhn is intrigued by the way "Debussy's tonal language and texture seem to reflect the gradual clouding of the mind, and subsequent entry into trance, of the priestess at Delphi," the voice of the famous oracle.[20]

II. "Voiles" (Sails) conjures a vision of sailboats in the harbor, rocking gently in a calm wind. The whole-tone scale is used through most of the piece. In the bass, Debussy maintains an irregularly repeated pedal tone, a drone, on B-flat that anchors the music (and the boats) in time and place. It's hard to believe Varèse's assertion that the piece was inspired by the veils (also *voiles* in French) employed by the American dancer Loïe Fuller, who performed in burlesque and vaudeville before taking her voluminous silks to Paris.

III. "Le Vent dans la plaine" (The Wind on the Plain). Here the wind is gentle and steady as it crosses the fields, with occasional gusts.

IV. "Les sons et les parfums tournent dans l'air du soir" (Sounds and Perfumes Swirl in the Evening Air) is the third line of "Harmonie du soir," by Baudelaire. In the sounds and scents are memories of the day, muted by the stillness of evening, but it's the swirling air that sets everything in motion.

V. "Les Collines d'Anacapri" (The Hills of Anacapri). A hill town on the island of Capri comes alive with a festive tarantella, pausing briefly for a young Romeo to sing a Neapolitan love song to his sweetheart.

VI. "Des Pas sur la neige" (Footsteps on the Snow) suggests the slow, faltering, aching steps of someone slogging through a heavy accumulation of snow on a cold, lonely day. It's one of the saddest pieces of music ever written, and there's no happy ending.

VII. "Ce qu'a vu le vent d'Ouest" (What the West Wind Has Seen) is from a tale by Hans Christian Andersen, "The Garden of Paradise." Of the several Préludes about wind, this is by far the most violent. In Andersen's story, the West Wind "looks like a wild man . . . smacks of the sea and brings a heavenly chill along with him."[21]

VIII. "La Fille aux cheveux de lin" (The Girl with the Flaxen Hair) is a poem by Leconte de Lisle which Debussy had earlier used as a song lyric. This is one of his best-known piano pieces, as simple and pleasing as a pretty ribbon. Consonant harmonies, used liberally, convey the sweetness of his early piano pieces.

IX. "La Sérénade interrompue" (The Interrupted Serenade) is a very strange work. What's going on here? The singer doesn't enter until measure 32; we hear his sad, tremulous melody several times, in the treble. He is each time interrupted by the guitarist, who ends the piece without remorse. Most of the music is in the Phrygian mode—typical, like the rhythms, of flamenco.

X. "La Cathédrale engloutie" (The Sunken Cathedral) describes an ancient Breton legend about the coastal town of Ys, swallowed up by the sea in retribution for the sins of its people; the cathedral spires are sometimes seen by their descendants at sunrise. Debussy's opening measures are "profoundly calm, in a mist of gentle sound." We hear distant bells and the muffled ancient chants of priests. A long, powerful crescendo expresses the turbulence of the sea as the cathedral rises. Then the climax: in a bright, sunny C major scale, powerful organ chords announce the emergence of the cathedral, but the structure sinks back into the sea. We hear the sad chant of the priests again. We glimpse the sunlit spires as they disappear under the water. We hear the fading bells and the rumbling of the sea.

XI. "La Danse de Puck" is for the sprightly, mischievous character in Shakespeare's *Midsummer Night's Dream*. Debussy gives him an appropriately English musical setting.

XII. "Minstrels" is a humorous piece apparently sparked by an American minstrel show that Debussy saw in Eastbourne in 1905. He took the spirit and rhythms of the Americans and brought them into the music hall, where clowning and tomfoolery mix with vaudeville ballads in a jolly pastiche that brings the first book of Préludes to a close.

The Préludes for Book 2 were composed in 1911 and 1912.

I. "Brouillards" (Mists) is all atmosphere—dark, dense, and drizzly, but now and then mysterious or electric.

II. "Feuilles mortes" (Dead Leaves) is a vision of late autumn, when the leaves fall not in a cascade, but one at a time, as if reluctant to leave the tree. Unlike the densities of "Brouillards," the musical textures here are exceedingly spare, the colors are muted, and the emotions run the gamut from *ppp* to *p*.

III. "La Puerta del vino" (The Wine Gate) is a Moorish gate at the palace of Alhambra. It was a meeting place for the large gypsy population in the city. Debussy asks the pianist for the steady rhythm of a habanera, overlaid with "sudden contrasts of extreme violence and passionate gentleness." The music has nothing to do with wine, but everything to do with Andalusian temperament.

IV. "Les Fées sont d'exquises danseuses" (The Fairies Are Exquisite Dancers) is the title of an illustration by Arthur Rackham for J. M. Barrie's book *Peter Pan in Kensington Gardens*, a Christmas present for Chouchou, sent to her in 1911 by Robert Godet. The pages at the beginning and end of this piece contain delicate, fluttering music of such rapidity as to confound any amateur pianist and amaze anyone listening to a well-rehearsed performance in recital.

V. "Bruyères" (Heathers) is a musical landscape, a French or English heath where cool breezes carry the fragrance of heather. As unpretentious as the shrub itself, the delicate, melodious arabesques in the right hand are grounded by complex harmonies in the left.

VI. "General Lavine—excentric" (Debussy's misspelling) was inspired by a clownish American-born entertainer named Edward Lavine who performed in Paris during the summer of 1910. His performance, Siglind Bruhn tells us, "included impersonations of a wooden puppet, tightrope walking, playing the piano with his toes, fighting a duel with himself, etc."[22] Debussy's music is, start to finish, eccentric in the awkward attempts at melody, the fragmented structure, the juxtaposition of contrasting phrases, the sudden pauses, and even the unwieldy harmonic devices.

VII. "La Terrasse des audiences du clair de lune" (The Terrace for Moonlight Audiences) was suggested by a newspaper article reporting on the coronation of King George V of England as King-Emperor of India at Delhi in 1911. Among the palace halls and gardens mentioned by the reporter was the moonlit terrace that Debussy took as his title. The music describes two mingling cultures: Europe in the long chains of shapely and misshapen triads; exotic India in the delicate, chromatic arabesques and bells. The textures, sonorities, and moods are unlike those found in any other Prélude, and the piece has some of the most enchanting moments in all of Debussy's writing.

VIII. "Ondine" is a water sprite whose parents send her to live among humans. A new French translation of the fairy tale, illustrated by Arthur Rackham, appeared in 1912 and caught Debussy's eye. The music establishes the tension in Ondine's dual temperament as a sensuous, seductive young woman and a mercurial sprite in her watery element.

IX. "Hommage à S. Pickwick Esq. P.P.M.P.C." honors the good-natured Dickens character Samuel Pickwick. It begins with a suitably pompous rendering of "God Save the King" and concisely conveys Pickwick's humor and his disappointments.

By this time we should recognize that, among other things, the two books of Préludes are a compendium of the literature, art, natural elements, and other creative stimulants most dear to the composer—not least, his love for his daughter. Paul Roberts has examined the relationships among these subjects and the relationships in the music itself. He concluded that the order in which Debussy placed the pieces and the correspondences between the first book of Préludes and the second are not random or incidental, but quite deliberate.[23]

X. "Canope" here refers to a kind of Egyptian burial urn with the head of Osiris, the ancient Egyptian god of the dead, pictured on its lid. Debussy had two of these urns on his desk. The opening theme may depict "the slow pace of an ancient funeral procession," says Siglind Bruhn, and there are themes suggesting lamentation.[24] The piece ends quietly but abruptly—Debussy omits the final note that we expect.

XI. "Les Tierces alternées" (Alternating Thirds) is one of Debussy's astonishing *perpetuum mobiles*. There is constant alternation between an interval of a third in the left hand and another in the right hand, ranging all over the keyboard, and played—except for a few contrasting bars at the start, the middle, and the end—at breakneck speed. It's a preview of the Études written a few years later.

XII. "Feux d'artifice" (Fireworks) commemorates Bastille Day, July 14, when fireworks erupt all over France. The music, among the most virtuosic of the Préludes, sounds disjointed, as if pasted together, which makes it all the more exciting when, after a quiet passage, a loud rocket explodes in a burst of color or a comet streaks over the city. A fragment of the "Marseillaise" is faintly heard as the crowd of spectators disperses.

The Politics of Fame

Around the time that Debussy began writing the second book of Préludes, he was drawn into a disagreeable episode involving Erik Satie and Maurice Ravel.

By now, Ravel's talent was widely recognized, and he was a prominent figure in musical circles, but he had not yet had a breakthrough triumph and was, naggingly, always cast in the shadow of the eminent Claude Debussy. He decided it might be better to be seen, instead, in the smaller shadow of Satie, where he would appear to be a giant.

Satie's claim to have been Debussy's precursor was based in large part on a comparison between his "Sarabandes," written in 1887, and Debussy's, written seven years later, by which time the two had been friends for about three years. Satie's pieces, like Debussy's, are characterized by the parallel motion of block chords and by the liberal use of unresolved ninth chords, a particular dissonance that was all but outlawed at the time. Whatever truth there is to the claim of "precursor," it must be said that in every musical era and every culture, artists in all media learn from one another and borrow ideas, within tolerable limits, without a fuss being made about it. It's possible that Satie's reputation rests almost as much on his loudly proclaimed influence on Debussy as on his own very real musical achievements.

Over the years, Satie wrote dozens of silly or clever or lovely pieces for piano, and his music was largely ignored. At the same time, he earned pocket money by writing songs for Montmartre's café-concerts, songs largely patterned after those of music halls and cabarets. The singer Vincent Hyspa was an early collaborator; later Satie wrote chansons and waltzes for the popular chanteuse Paulette Darty. He seemed content to be a composer of music in a popular or satiric vein and he had little expectation to be taken seriously as a musician.[25]

Nevertheless, Satie was shocked by Debussy's success in subverting musical orthodoxy with *Pelléas et Mélisande*, a work in which, he believed, his own original harmonic devices had been repurposed. *Pelléas* was, to Satie, "the perfect final result of an aesthetic which he felt he had played a hand in developing," writes one of his biographers.[26] There was no point continuing along the lines that Debussy had redrawn, so Satie had to find something new. He too could be subversive, but he'd have to learn more about writing music. In 1905, he enrolled in the Schola Cantorum, a conservatory whose curriculum stressed old-fashioned technique and the music of the Baroque. Satie left the Schola three years later with a diploma in counterpoint, and he continued studying composition with d'Indy for at least three years more.

His friend Claude had no more respect for the Schola and its teachings than he did for the Conservatory, and he thought Satie was wasting time learning counterpoint.

Maurice Ravel, born in 1875, enrolled at the Paris Conservatory as a piano student when he was fourteen. Like Debussy, young Ravel failed to win the requisite medals for piano performance and turned instead to composing, studying with Gabriel Fauré. Ravel and Satie struck up a friendship in 1893. Debussy knew Ravel and tapped him in 1901 to collaborate with others on a two-piano transcription of the *Nocturnes*. Ravel was one of the loudest and most fervent supporters of *Pelléas*, cheering at its first performances when the opera struggled for acceptance. Thus, for a number of years, the three composers—Debussy, Ravel, and Satie—were loosely linked in a not-quite-mutual admiration society.

In 1899, Ravel's *Shéhérazade* overture was performed at a National Society concert. It was his first work for orchestra, and his conducting debut. The audience rewarded his effort with a burst of applause, hisses, and boos. Willy, in his review, called *Shéhérazade* "a clumsy plagiarism of the Russian school," referred to Ravel as a "Debussyian" for his generous use of whole-tone passages, and insinuated that Ravel aspired to be another Erik Satie.[27] (Willy despised Satie.)

After competing for the Prix de Rome four times without winning, Ravel was the obvious front-runner on his fifth attempt, in 1905; by now he was admired for some fine piano pieces and chamber works. But when he failed to pass the preliminary round, many supporters cried foul. All the finalists, by no coincidence, were students of the musically conservative teacher Charles Lenepveu, a member of the jury. The resulting scandal, magnified by the press, ended with the resignation of the Conservatory's director, but Ravel couldn't compete again because, at age thirty, he was too old to qualify.

The first sign of discord between Ravel and Debussy was the petulance of the younger composer when he discovered, or supposed, that Debussy, in his "Soirée dans Grenade," had used material from Ravel's 1895 "Habanera" for two pianos. Debussy had seen Ravel's score, and it must have made an impression on him, but there are great differences in what Ravel did and what Debussy did with the material. (Ravel later orchestrated the "Habanera" for the third movement of his 1907 *Rapsodie espagnole*.)

In January 1909, Ravel resigned from the National Society after the organization rejected the works of three of his students. In response, he cofounded a new, competing organization, the Société Musicale Indépendante, with other disaffected composers, including Fauré. The new society, known as S.M.I., gave its first concert in April 1910.

For an S.M.I. concert on January 16, 1911, Ravel scheduled performances of some of Satie's piano music. Except once, when Doret conducted Debussy's arrangements of the *Gymnopédies*, Satie had never before been exposed to a large audience of music lovers on a program of "serious" music. But rather than selecting Satie's more recent work, shaped by the Schola Cantorum, Ravel chose earlier music, written between 1887 and 1891.[28]

A note in the concert program, probably written by Ravel, reminds readers of Debussy's debt to Satie. Since Debussy's "Sarabande," written in 1894 and published in 1901, would have been familiar to many in the audience, the inclusion of a Satie "Sarabande" on the program drove the point home. The program note said:

Erik Satie occupies a truly exceptional place in the history of contemporary art. On the fringe of his age and in isolation he wrote, years ago, a few brief pages that bear the stamp of an inspired pioneer. His works, regrettably few in number, astonish by the way in which they anticipated the modern idiom and by the near-prophetic character of certain harmonic inventions. . . . Claude Debussy paid a brilliant tribute to the "explorer" when he orchestrated two of his "Gymnopedies," which have since been performed at the Société Nationale. Today, Maurice Ravel will play [Satie's] second "Sarabande," which bears the astonishing date of 1887, and will thus indicate what high esteem the most "progressive" composers have for the creator who spoke, a quarter of a century ago, the bold musical "jargon" of tomorrow.[29]

About six weeks later, the editor of the *Revue Musicale de la S.I.M.* organized a soirée in Satie's honor, which the composer politely declined to attend. On March 25, Debussy, at a concert devoted to his own music, conducted his orchestral versions of the *Gymnopédies* Nos. 1 and 3. Satie was delighted. He'd been afraid his music would draw hostility, but his young fans in the audience made themselves heard. Two weeks later, Satie told his brother he was bewildered that Debussy wasn't more pleased with Satie's dramatic burst of success. "Why won't he allow me a very small place in his shadow?" Satie wondered, adding, "I have no use for the sun."[30]

In April 1912, *Symphonic Scenes*, written twenty years earlier by a little-known contemporary named Ernest Fanelli, received a belated but triumphant concert premiere. Listeners heard in Fanelli's *Scenes* the origin of Debussy's impressionism, particularly his use of the whole-tone scale, and stirred up a controversy. Ravel, in a published review of the work, lavished Fanelli with faint praise and pointed out that the whole-tone scale had been used even earlier by Liszt and Dargomijsky, thereby clouding the common belief that Debussy had invented the scale. Then Ravel told his readers that "the discovery of [Debussy's] harmonic system was entirely due to Erik Satie, that his stage works derived from Mussorgsky, and his orchestration from Rimsky-Korsakov. We now know the source of his impressionism," he adds, but "despite this paucity of invention, Debussy only remains the most important and profoundly musical composer living today."[31] It was clear that Ravel was belittling Debussy's very real musical achievements for no other reason than to deflect arguments that Ravel was a Debussyian.[32]

Satie knew that, however sincere Ravel's motives were in giving his music a hearing in the concert hall, his young admirer had caused a rift between Erik and Claude. From then on, the precursor's relations with Ravel were, at best, frosty.

And Debussy, who had once described Ravel as gifted, but a trickster and "a charming fakir,"[33] was now more inclined to be openly hostile.

PART IV
THE LAST YEARS

CHAPTER 21

THE SORRY, STARRY STAGE (1908–1913)

One continuity that we may recognize in Claude Debussy is his un-ceasing evolution—his perpetual reinvention and self-exploration, both personal and creative, throughout his life.

—Jane F. Fulcher[1]

Telling the story of an important, sympathetic public figure is often difficult for the biographer at the inevitable turning point: the ampersand between rise and fall. The greatest successes are in the pages at the left. The pages on the right may be strewn with mishaps, unfinished projects, marital problems, sadness, illness, and endnotes. Even when those pages also offer modest joys and major triumphs, as they did for Debussy, the reader knows how the story ends.

The ampersand for France's greatest modern composer is here.

Debussy on the Concert Stage

Claude Debussy was not a conductor. He never wanted to be a conductor, never studied conducting. Furthermore, he was nervous and uncomfortable when performing for a large audience. On tour, he was embarrassed that he knew only a few words in any languages other than French, and he was lonely without his family. Then why did he burden himself with odious conducting commitments from London to St Petersburg? Major orchestras paid well to attract a famous musician, and especially after Osiris's betrayal, his income was always, *always*, inadequate.

Debussy's first invitation to the podium was unexpected but impossible to refuse: an elderly but distinguished conductor, Édouard Colonne, was drowning in *La Mer*; rehearsals had gone so badly that he postponed the performance and asked the composer to rescue him.

Debussy's heart was beating furiously when he took the baton for his first rehearsal, but he found the experience, surprisingly, profoundly moving. "I really reached the heart of my own music," he wrote to Victor Segalen, his collaborator on a proposed opera based on *Oedipus Rex*. When the orchestra played well, he had the feeling, he said, "of being myself an instrument of many different sonorities, animated, so to speak, by movements of the little stick."[2]

The performance itself took place on Sunday, January 19, 1908. When Debussy turned to the audience after the tumultuous finale, there were "wild yells of joy," wrote Willy in his column.[3] The boisterous applause brought Debussy back to the stage repeatedly to take a bow. "The conquering hero, who had rushed away down a staircase, had to be brought back once again, this time in his overcoat and his bowler hat," Willy reported. The applause continued even after the orchestra, Colonne conducting, began playing the next piece on the program. Debussy told Segalen, "What lunatic screaming! . . . I felt like a freak showman or an acrobat who has carried off some perilous jump."[4]

Debussy was asked to repeat his performance a week later. Furthermore, he was soon to conduct in London. He wrote to a friend about his new vocation, but, oddly, he neglected to mention that he and Emma were married on January 20, at the Town Hall of the 16th arrondissement.

Plans for the London engagement had been hatched months before Debussy's sensational conducting debut. A wealthy music lover, Edgar Speyer, conspired with his conductor, Henry Wood, to bring Debussy to London. Speyer was the financial manager of Queen's Hall, a vast concert venue with the city's best acoustics, and with his own fortune he had saved the resident orchestra from ruin. Eager to bring the greatest foreign composers to his venue, Speyer sent Wood to Paris with a mission. Was Debussy a proficient conductor? Was he a conductor at all? It didn't matter. Bring him to London, Speyer demanded—whatever it takes, whatever the cost.

Wood recalled his first impression of "that dark, bearded Frenchman: his deep, soulful eyes; his quiet and rather grating voice; most of all, his enormous head."[5] When Debussy balked at the offer of 100 guineas, a large sum for even the best conductors, Wood offered 200. Debussy found it hard to believe that London wanted him at all.

Shortly after his second Paris concert, Debussy and Emma left for London. He had agreed to conduct *La Mer*, never heard before in that city, and the *Prélude à "L'Après-midi d'un faune."* Wood rehearsed the orchestra prior to his arrival; Debussy conducted rehearsals for each of the instrumental sections. "To begin with, it was dreadful," wrote Segalen, who watched the rehearsals. "Then, little by little, it began to take shape."[6]

The concert was a triumph. "The ovation he received . . . was like nothing else I can remember," Georges Jean-Aubry said. After the performance, his emotions in turmoil, Debussy could murmur only, "How nice they are, how nice they are." Leaving the hall, he was mobbed by autograph seekers as he climbed into his carriage.[7]

The success prompted Speyer to bring Debussy back a year later. This time, on the afternoon of February 27, 1909, he conducted *Faune* and the *Nocturnes*. Wood said he'd never seen anything like it.

"It" occurred during the playing of "Fêtes," the second of the three *Nocturnes*. In this energetic music, the meter and tempo change frequently, and the orchestration is tricky. At times, each instrumental group and soloists within them play independently of the others, making it difficult for conductors to target cues precisely to the right players at the right instant. Furthermore, "Fêtes" contains some of the noisiest passages Debussy ever wrote, so any mishap is bound to be loud and ugly. The performance was going reasonably well when to everyone's astonishment Debussy "lost his head, and his beat," Wood recalled. When the flustered conductor realized what was happening, he decided to restart the movement from the beginning. He tapped the desk repeatedly to draw the players' attention, wanting desperately to stop the performance. But the orchestra kept playing, and after a rough patch or two "the work (which they liked immensely) was going beautifully, and they meant to give a first-rate performance of it." Most in the audience knew what had happened, and when the movement ended they responded "in truly English fashion" with such an ovation that Debussy and the orchestra were compelled to play it again. This time the performance was brought off without a hitch, and the ovation was greater than before. "Debussy was nonplussed," said Wood, "and certainly did not understand the English mind; but I was proud of my orchestra that afternoon and had the satisfaction of seeing that [Debussy] had been proud to conduct it."[8]

After the concert, Debussy wrote Durand that he'd been ill since arriving in London two days earlier; he canceled his conducting engagements in Edinburgh and Manchester. He told Durand that the concert, only hours earlier, had gone splendidly, and that the audience called for an encore of "Fêtes." They wanted him to repeat *Faune* as well, he said, but he was too tired, too weak, to stay on his feet. He tried to think what excuse might allow him to skip the evening reception.

Apparently he couldn't find a suitable pretext. The rather formal supper-and-concert reception at Aeolian Hall was given by the Music Club.[9] A selection of Debussy's music would be played. Arnold Bax, an English composer who attended, described Debussy at this event as a "thick-set clumsy figure" with "a huge greenish, almost Moorish face beneath the dense thicket of black hair" and a "morbidly sallow complexion."[10]

As the evening progressed, Debussy's torments were excruciating, Bax recalled. The Frenchman, who was generally shy among strangers, was seated on a platform where everyone in the hall could observe his discomfort. The speaker welcoming him had poor French and spoke very quietly; and the honored guest, hearing little and understanding nothing, could only rise and bow awkwardly when his name was mentioned. Afterward he told someone that he "would rather write a symphony on commission" than suffer through another experience like this one.[11]

Years later Bax learned that Debussy, on that day in 1909, was already suffering from the malady that would eventually kill him.

His appearances in London set off a wave of serious discussion about Debussy's music. Filson Young, a critic for the *Saturday Review*, wrote perceptively: "He speaks to us in a new language, which we are obliged to learn before we can form any judgment of his work." Debussy consciously rejected old musical forms that had enabled composers to write great music in the past, Young wrote, but that no modern composer can justify using in the post-Debussyan future. His music "will help us discriminate between what was and what was not inspired in the works of the great, instead of accepting everything as pure gospel" that bears the name of Mozart, Beethoven, or Bach. Debussy's music, "whatever its faults and failures, appeals boldly on the single ground of beauty, and not of erudition, imitation, or conservatism."[12]

Undeterred by his early mishaps, Debussy continued to tour when his debts were unsustainable.

In the fall of 1910, rehearsing the orchestra in Vienna, he found the musicians making a nightmare of the *Nocturnes* and *La Mer*. Consequently, he dropped those from the program and focused instead on *Ibéria*. It took great effort to whip it into shape with only two rehearsals. Since the players didn't understand his French, he could only communicate through an interpreter, who was not a musician but a lawyer, and by gesturing and singing the effects he wanted. He wrote Emma that at one point a violist simply stopped playing and gazed at Debussy as if he were a shop window. It's like being a tamer of wild beasts, he wrote. But the concert went surprisingly well, and *Ibéria* was "stunning," he told his wife the next day. "It's the first time an orchestra has ever thought to thank me for conducting them."[13]

Debussy and the Devil

In 1902, after the successful launch of *Pelléas*, Debussy began work on a short opera based on Edgar Allan Poe's story "The Devil in the Belfry." But "The Fall of the House of Usher" continued to haunt him, and in 1908 he started to focus on the libretto for the opera that would occupy him until the end of his days. He hoped to pair the two operas—*La Chute de la maison Usher* and *Le Diable dans le beffroi*—as a double bill, and he sold the first performance rights to New York's Metropolitan Opera company, in 1908, with the stipulation that the two must always be performed on the same program.

Debussy didn't live long enough to complete either opera. In fact, no completed work in the Debussy repertoire is directly linked to Poe's writings. Yet the composer assimilated the author's dark atmospherics, and perhaps even shared Poe's morbid fascinations, so thoroughly that in some of his music (portions of the *Nocturnes*, some of the later songs, and the Préludes) we sense the spirit of Poe as surely as the ghost of Wagner haunts his early works.

Pelléas et Mélisande reeks of Poe. His spirit suffuses the stifling, rancid air of the vault when the two brothers pass through it; the bottomless well in the park; the dark, mysterious cave of the three blind men; the oppressively dank forest. There are parallels with "Usher" in Pelléas's incestuous love for Mélisande and in the portrayal of the young princess metaphorically buried alive in Arkel's desolate realm. Maeterlinck's characters, like Poe's, live less by their volition than by fate, and it's likely that Debussy's visceral response to Maeterlinck's play was triggered by its pungent vapors of the tragic American writer.

What was it that drew Claude Debussy to the bad boy of American letters?

Poe's curiosity, his delight in the supernatural, cryptograms, puzzles, labyrinths, mechanical chess players, and wild flights of speculation—these are enthusiasms typical of a preadolescent boy, T. S. Eliot said, concluding that Poe's work is what he'd expect of a man with a "very exceptional mind and sensibility, whose emotional development has been in some respect arrested at an early age. His most vivid imaginative realizations are the realization of the dream."[14] Debussy, too, had an exceptional mind and the enthusiasms of a child, and his imaginative music, like Poe's writing, often has a dreamlike ambience.

After *Pelléas*, Debussy did not want his adaptations of "Devil" and "Usher" to suggest the earlier opera in any way. The inspiration of Poe, he said, was completely different from that of Maeterlinck, and he believed his stage works on Poe—he didn't like to call them operas—would be as successful as *Pelléas*. (Success, to Debussy, was a work that found equal numbers of detractors and supporters.) He thought it strange that no American composer had yet adapted Poe's stories. Taking on Poe was a risk, but for Debussy there was "no greater pleasure than going into the depth of oneself, setting one's whole being in motion and seeking for new and hidden treasures. What a joy to find something new within oneself, something that surprises even ourselves, filling us with warmth."[15]

"The Devil in the Belfry" does not seem a likely subject for (for lack of a better word) an opera. In the remote Dutch village of Vondervotteimittis (pronounced "vonder vot time it is"), time has stood still since earliest antiquity. All the houses are alike; each has a mantel clock, and each citizen carries a watch. All day the townsmen watch the clock in the belfry atop the town council house. The belfryman is the most important person in the village. When the bell strikes at noon, all the townspeople check their clocks and watches. But one day, a small man prances into town, dressed in black and carrying a fiddle. Before noon, he scurries up to the belfry, slams the belfryman repeatedly with his fiddle, and rings the bell thirteen times. The townspeople go berserk, as do their clocks and their cabbages, while the little devil sits in the belfry, tormenting them with the screeching sound of his fiddle.

In Debussy's expansive rendering, the devil never speaks or sings, but expresses himself by whistling and by his fiddle playing. There are a few individualized characters, but the singing is entirely choral. Debussy was after something as unique and important to his opera as the choral writing in *Boris Godunov*: "some kind of inspired aural deception . . . a real human crowd in which each voice is free" and the individual voices combine to produce an ensemble.[16] The second scene is set, inexplicably, in Italy. At the end, the belfryman's son, whose love for the mayor's daughter makes him impervious to the devil's power, climbs the steeple, prays to God, and rings the bell twelve times.

The devil disappears in a red flash. The villagers check their watches, and the curtain falls.

Debussy worked on the *Diable* libretto during the summer of 1903. In September he said it was nearly complete. He sold Durand the publishing rights and, accordingly, received monthly payments for several years before it became clear that *Diable* was little more than a pipe dream. In 1911, he was still challenged by the choral writing, and in 1912, he played a few musical fragments for Henri Büsser. After that, *Diable* was no longer on his agenda.

The House of Usher

Debussy had been thinking about adapting "The Fall of the House of Usher" for many years before he actually started working on it in 1908.

In Poe's story, Roderick Usher is sickly, depressed, and ultimately driven mad by the ancestral curse that lives in his mansion's stone walls, and by his repressed love for his twin sister, Madeline, who is gravely ill. He summons a childhood friend (the narrator) to visit, hoping the visitor can lift his spirits. Very little actually happens in the story. The narrator catches a glimpse of the ghostly Madeline. He tries to cheer his friend by reading him stories. Roderick improvises dolefully on his guitar, which emits strange sounds. Sometimes he sings rhymed improvisations in which his friend hears snippets of a poem, "The Haunted Palace." Madeline dies, and Roderick wants to temporarily preserve her body in a vault within the walls of the house so that doctors can examine the corpse in the interest of science. A storm engulfs the house in an unearthly glow. Weird sounds are heard, the wind blows a door open, and Madeline appears in a bloodied white robe. She falls heavily on her brother, killing him. The friend flees from the scene as Usher's house crumbles into the lake that surrounds it.

Poe's story has only two principal characters, Roderick and his friend, who together have only a few lines of dialogue. Debussy had to reinvent the story with an abundance of musical monologues, enough to keep audiences in their seats for at least fifty minutes. He expanded the plot and made Madeline's doctor a villainous character.

His correspondence over many years reveals his increasing obsession with Roderick Usher. The character invaded his life, as Mélisande had done. On June 18, 1908, he tells Durand he's working on the *Usher* libretto and adds: "There are moments when I lose contact with the ordinary things around me: If Roderick Usher's sister came into the room, I should not be particularly surprised."[17] A month later, "the Usher family heir barely left me a moment's peace."[18]

By June 1909 he had finished a long monologue for Roderick Usher that was "sad enough to make the stones weep."[19] He was now writing music as well as the libretto, and for better or worse, he was immersed in the phantasmic horror of Poe's story.

In August 1909, he wrote to Caplet, "Of late, I have lived in the House of Usher. . . . One takes on, in there, the peculiar mania of listening to the dialogue of stones; anticipating the crumbling of houses as a natural phenomenon."[20] A month later, he wrote that Poe "exercises an almost tyrannical influence on me, which is nearly anguishing, and I lock myself like a brute in the House of Usher, lest I be keeping company with the Devil in the Belfry."[21]

"How does a composer who has devoted much of his music to sensory pleasure move into the realm of sensory hell?" asks Julie McQuinn.[22] The question may be the key to Debussy's prolonged difficulty in finding appropriate music for *Usher*. For *Pelléas* he created music of repression, jealousy, and murder. But his credo was to write beautifully even when describing the most hideous human conditions, and his most impassioned music for *Pelléas* was necessarily tempered by Maeterlinck's restrained, austere poetry. It was different now. Poe's language could not help him. He had to invent the libretto in its entirety, to find words and music in the soul of a madman, which meant he had to internalize the story, with all its despair and horror, and to live day after day in "the realm of sensory hell."

Le Martyre de Saint-Sébastien

In February 1911, Debussy spoke to an interviewer about religion:

Who can render us that pure love of the pious musicians of olden times? . . . the magnificent passion of a Palestrina? . . . I myself am far from such a state of grace. I do not worship according to the established rites. I have made the mysteries of nature my religion. I do not think that a man in abbot's attire is necessarily closer to God, nor that one particular place in a town is especially favorable to meditation. . . . The whole expanse of nature is reflected in my own sincere but feeble soul. Around me the branches of the trees reach out toward the firmament, here are the sweet-scented flowers smiling in the meadow, here the soft earth is carpeted with sweet herbs. . . . And unconsciously, my hands are clasped in prayer.[23]

At the time of the interview, Debussy was busily engaged in writing music for, of all things, a miracle play—a kind of medieval dramatic ritual depicting the life of a saint. Gabriele D'Annunzio had asked him to participate in a theatrical project on the martyrdom of St Sebastian. D'Annunzio would write the libretto, Michel Fokine would choreograph, and Diaghilev's stage designer, Léon Bakst, would create the sets and costumes.

Ida Rubinstein, a Russian dancer fresh from her triumph in *Scheherazade*, would portray the martyred saint. With her flat chest, slim torso, and noble face, she would look the part, thought D'Annunzio—androgynous, in keeping with his conception. Rubinstein had little formal training or professional experience. Her acting was more lauded than her dancing, but with her personal fortune she was able to finance projects that showcased her best qualities.

Debussy, for whom deadlines and commissions were loathsome, replied to D'Annunzio's proposal: "The thought of working with you fills me with feverish anticipation."[24] His report to Emma was far less enthusiastic. The compensation—20,000 francs, in three installments—was generous and badly needed. The charismatic D'Annunzio was one of Italy's most famous writers, honored for his dazzling use of the Italian language in poems, novels, and plays, and he was just as adept in French. He was a prototypical self-important, luxury-loving celebrity, inventing outrageous stories about himself to feed the hungry press. He was notorious for his well-publicized affairs with famous women. Italians knew him also as a former member of Parliament and a champion of nationalism, the political precursor of Mussolini's fascism. He had come to France to escape his creditors.

Sebastian was a third-century captain of the Praetorian Guard who secretly performed miracles of healing and converted heathens to Christianity. When his heresy was discovered, the Roman Emperor Diocletian ordered him tied to a tree and killed by the very guards he had commanded; the martyr rejoiced as the arrows pierced his body.

Over the centuries Sebastian was draped by artists and clerics in various personas. For medieval Europe he was the saint of soldiers and the plague stricken; for Renaissance painters he was a heroic figure to be idealized on their canvases. His legend was associated with Jesus, not surprisingly, and with Apollo, the Roman god of many things, including poetry, music, and archers. D'Annunzio's libretto links Sebastian to Christ and Apollo; but when Sebastian is killed, Adonis is the name evoked by the chorus of women: "The beautiful Adonis is dead! Women, weep!"[25]

Le Martyre de Saint-Sébastien is an amalgam of drama, poetry, music, dance, and spectacle. Debussy was asked to write a prelude, interludes, vocal music for soloists and chorus, and three ritual dances for Rubinstein, including a dance on red-hot coals. Discontinuous sections of the libretto were sent to him over many weeks, and he struggled to find the right music. He said he was terrified that the moment was approaching "when I shall positively have to write something."[26] He told Robert Godet that if he had two years instead of two months, he could make some beautiful musical discoveries.

The libretto was not complete until March 2. Opening night was scheduled for May 22, 1911. Faced with an implacable deadline, he asked Caplet to help with the rehearsals and orchestrations. When rehearsals began in early May, Debussy was still working on the score. "According to those who watched him," wrote Marguerite Long, "Debussy worked in a veritable state of exalta-tion . . . taken with the same fever that ravaged D'Annunzio. . . . Debussy himself said that he worked 'like a slave without having time to turn my head. The days fly—it is already tomorrow!'"[27] He had a vague but thrilling notion that this could be his Parsifal, a work he admired as much as any in the musical canon, in which mystery and magic, eroticism and virtue, Christianity and paganism all share the stage.

Six days before the premiere, the archbishop of Paris denounced the work for its demeaning portrayal of a Christian martyr. He advised Catholics to stay home rather than be subjected to this sacrilegious spectacle, in which a Jewish woman would portray a man, a saint. Though gender was a mutable thing onstage, mustn't a line be drawn somewhere?

Ultimately, Sébastien was a spectacular failure. The extravaganza lasted more than five hours at its first performance. Critics found the drama incomprehen-sible. Debussy's delicate music was overwhelmed by D'Annunzio's swollen rhetoric, they said. The stage was poorly lit, the performers underrehearsed, the evening far too long. But if the critics were displeased, Marguerite Long reported, "the attitude of the audience was even more cruel . . . they dribbled out of the theater like water from a cracked vase."[28]

Ida Rubinstein revived *Sébastien* several times in the 1920s, but it has rarely been performed since. The composer and the poet briefly considered a film adaptation. Someone proposed *Sébastien* as an opera. Several versions of Debussy's score, usually much abridged, were prepared for the concert hall, including one by Germaine Inghelbrecht, whose husband was the choral conductor for the original Paris production.

There is a great range of opinion about the score. Some say it's an overblown mishmash; others hear music of power and passion, a reminder of Debussy's earlier work and a foretaste of music yet to come. The composer-conductor Oliver Knussen describes the score as "full of striking orchestral inventions . . . But what is really remarkable . . . is its restraint and, for want of a better word, dignity." Although Debussy's orchestra was the largest he ever used, "the big forces are there to give relatively austere sound panels a wealth of subtle, tender shadings."[29]

Turin, June 1911

One more conducting appearance deserves mention for its poignant portrait of Debussy, exhausted from months of collaboration with D'Annunzio. Debussy went to Turin, Italy, to conduct *Prélude à "L'Après-midi d'un faune"* and *Ibéria*.

In Turin, a few young musicians came to meet Debussy at the railroad station and again at his hotel. They were surprised by his casual, unpretentious friendliness—so different from other visiting celebrities, puffed up with self-importance. Debussy was especially friendly toward Vittorio Gui, the conductor, and Gui soon found himself feeling "real affection" for the composer.[30] The orchestra, composed mostly of musicians not long out of school, was predisposed to be respectful toward this Frenchman who was perhaps the greatest composer alive. So at the rehearsal, they too were startled when Debussy arrived, a cigarette dangling from his lips, so unlike the majestic Gallic god they had expected.

Gui was prepared to rehearse the orchestra that day, but Debussy insisted that "conducting was an old unfulfilled passion of his, and that he would be only too pleased to be left to do everything on his own," Gui wrote.

It was a painful spectacle. On the podium during the rehearsal, Debussy's head was inexplicably buried in the scores he must have known so well, his beat was unsteady, and he turned the pages with the hand that held the baton, causing him, more than once, to lose the beat and confound the musicians. "Things became really desperate during the unraveling of the suite *Ibéria*," Gui wrote. "It was the first time an Italian orchestra had been faced with this difficult score." Debussy was unable to help the musicians comprehend his music and was clearly distressed. Entangled in a cacophony of noise, he called for a brief intermission and abruptly left the hall. It was then agreed that Gui would prepare the orchestra and that Debussy would take the baton (and the acclaim) for the actual performance.

At the next morning's rehearsal, Gui was at the helm, and the musicians began to play with confidence. Debussy arrived and asked to hear how they had progressed. Then "the miracle happened," Gui recalled. "The first movement was played easily, delicately, with the clarity of morning light.... The two clarinets had hardly ceased to sigh the evanescent major third with which the picture dissolves in a luminous cloud, when I felt two arms encircling my neck (I feel them still), and the great musician imprinted a kiss on my burning cheek; around us a burst of clapping enveloped his gesture and my natural emotion."

The concert was postponed a couple of days to allow for additional rehearsals. In their off hours, Debussy and Gui cemented a personal bond of a sort that we rarely find in the history of this composer. Though his friendships with Pierre Louÿs, Robert Godet, and Jacques Durand were warm and companionable, they took much longer to develop. Gui found Debussy to be a "conversationalist full of verve ... seeing always the amusing side and enjoying himself in the play of his subtle but good-humored irony, so that one could never tire of listening to him. "A sense of real aristocracy was innate in his speech as in his whole conduct, a witness of the natural nobility of this prince of good taste," wrote Gui. "Above all an immense, indisputable honesty, a perfect conformity between man and artist, between his way of living and his high ideals— these were the things which fired me with admiration in those halcyon days when I was his constant companion."

The day of the concert arrived. With Debussy conducting, *Faune* was played well and warmly applauded. *Ibéria* was scheduled to end the program, and Debussy mounted the podium again with "childlike trepidation," Gui observed. "He conducted as best he could, woodenly, mechanically, without fire, and without really leading his forces; no calamities, but no poetic feeling. The real significance of that beautiful but elusive music was lost without the poetry which was its real essence." A pouring rain pounded the glass roof during the final minutes, ruining the musical effects and distracting the listeners, who hadn't brought their umbrellas.

Debussy remained a few more days in Turin, and the two friends continued to enjoy their wide-ranging conversations. At the moment of leave-taking, Debussy took from Gui's hands the *Ibéria* score, "already a symbol of precious memories for me, and wrote on it words of affection and gratitude . . . words which fill me with pride, but also with confusion when I think of all that he, perhaps unconsciously, had done for me in these days and yet . . . the one who got the thanks was I!"[31]

Images pour orchestre; "Ibéria"

Images pour orchestre is composed of three symphonic poems with strong folkloric associations. The middle portion, "Ibéria," is often played alone, as it was in Turin, and has since become one of the most performed of Debussy's orchestral works.

Debussy began *Images pour orchestre* in 1905 and worked on it intermittently for several years, interrupted by concert tours, domestic convulsions, and beginning in early 1909, pain. "For two days I never stopped suffering miserably," he told Durand. "Only with the help of a variety of tranquilizers— morphine, cocaine, and other such lovely drugs—was I able to cope, but at the price of total stupor."[32]

He was besieged with pressures from all quarters—his publisher, critics, creditors, devotees, and especially his own ego—all eager to know if he could produce another success to equal *La Mer*. Other difficulties were unique to the musical effects he was trying to achieve. He wanted *Images* to sound as if it had been improvised—it "should seem not to have been written down," he said.[33]

Images pour orchestre is developed from folk-dance music representing three distinct European cultures, and it's among Debussy's most consistently buoyant scores. In 1908 he completed "Ibéria," and the next year "Rondes de printemps" (Rounds of Spring).

"Gigues," the first of the three *Images*, was the last to be finished, in 1913, three years after the other two were first performed. The original title, "Gigues tristes," gives a more accurate description of the music, which can't conceal an underlying melancholy and restlessness heightened by the prominence of the oboe d'amour (an alto oboe), with its plaintive, mellow timbre. The dominant melodic theme in "Gigues" is "The Keel Row," a jaunty Scottish folk tune that Debussy tosses back and forth among the orchestra players like a memory impossible to shake off.

"Rondes de printemps," the third of the *Images*, is a typically Debussyan rhapsody suggesting the colors and pleasures of spring. Prominent among the themes are the same two French folk songs he had used earlier in "Jardins sous la pluie." The "ronde" evoked in the title is the familiar folk dance in which participants form a circle and move together in circular motion, as in the maypole dance of England and the hora of Israel and Eastern Europe.

The longest and most substantial section of *Images*—the pièce de résistance—is the central one, "Ibéria," which is itself divided into three movements and is best known as a twenty-minute stand-alone showpiece. The movements are "Par les Rues et les chemins" (On the Streets and Roads); "Les Parfums de la nuit" (The Perfumes of the Night); and "Le Matin d'un jour de fêtes" (The Morning of a Holiday). "Ibéria" uses characteristic rhythms to present a picture of Spanish life full of spice and salt, the everyday flavors, washed down with a robust Rioja. It has none of the voluptuous romanticism of Ravel's *Rapsodie espagnole*, whose premiere in 1908 coincided with the completion of "Ibéria." Debussy's rhapsody starts off with a bang, literally—a furious fortissimo after the misty, slumbering whispers at the close of "Gigues." It's a shock for anyone who knows Debussy only from the sedate delicacies of "Clair de lune."

For "Ibéria," Debussy didn't intend to write "Spanish music," said Manuel de Falla, Spain's preeminent twentieth-century composer, "but rather to translate into music the associations that Spain had aroused in him." Falla's admiration for "Ibéria" is apparent in his description: In the first part, "a sort of *sevillana*, the generating theme of the work, suggests village songs heard in the bright, scintillating light. The intoxicating magic of the Andalusian nights [in the middle part], the light-hearted holiday crowds dancing to chords struck on guitars and *bandurrías* [in the final part]—all these musical effects whirl in the air while the crowds, as we imagine them, approach or recede. Everything is constantly alive and extremely expressive."[34]

Falla believed that Debussy's innate feeling for Spanish music was tied to his fascination with the medieval church modes. "Since Spanish folk-song is largely based on modal music, . . . even in works which Debussy wrote without any idea of Spanish associations one finds modes, cadences, chord sequences, rhythms, and even turns of phrase which clearly reveal" a relationship with the folk music of Spain. Among these works, Falla mentions the early song "Fantoches," the piano "Masques," and the pizzicato-strewn second movement of the String Quartet, which "might well be one of the most beautiful Andalusian dances ever written." Falla says it was Debussy, in "Soirée dans Grenade," "La Puerta del vino," "Sérénade interrompue," and other piano pieces, who showed Spain's native composers how to incorporate guitar figurations imaginatively in their compositions.

Falla wrote that the self-described *musicien français* had caught the essence of Spain despite his lack of Spanish blood or direct experience. "The character of the Spanish musical language had been assimilated by Debussy," Falla wrote, "and this composer, who really did not know Spain, was thus able to write Spanish music spontaneously, perhaps unconsciously, at any rate in a way which was the envy of many who knew Spain only too well." He added, "If Debussy used Spanish folk music to inspire some of his greatest works, he has generously repaid us, and it is now Spain which is indebted to him."[35]

Khamma—the Egyptian Ballet

Aside from the dances in *Sébastien*, Debussy's first ballet score was *Khamma*, commissioned by the Canadian-born dancer Maud Allan, who gained notoriety in 1907 for her performance of Salome's Dance of the Seven Veils. In September 1910, three months before Debussy signed on to *Sébastien*, he accepted Allan's commission.

Khamma takes place in the temple of Amun-Ra, where a stone statue represents the Egyptian sun god. The city is under siege. A priest summons Khamma to dance in order to persuade the god to save his devotees. Bathed in moonlight, she performs three exotic dances. The statue signals that Amun-Ra will intervene in the conflict. Khamma continues dancing, now in an ecstasy of joy. Suddenly she falls dead. In the brief final scene, citizens celebrate their victory (trumpets, bells, cymbals). The music diminishes to a whisper as the body of Khamma is blessed by the priest.

Debussy called the project a "wretched little Anglo-Egyptian ballet."[36] But the 20,000-franc commission was persuasive. Through the next year he was too occupied with *Saint-Sébastien*, *House of Usher*, a clarinet rhapsody, and "Gigues" to spend much time on *Khamma*. He finished the short score and a small portion of the orchestration in the first months of 1912.

Allan wasn't happy with the music. She demanded that Debussy double the length of the ballet and double the number of her solo dances. He refused. She asked him to reduce the orchestra by more than half, to fit into the typical theater's orchestra pit. He refused and told Durand he had a "profound loathing for the whole business."[37] Allan insisted that Debussy dedicate the score to her, rather than Durand's wife. She finally threatened to have another composer write the score, and the matter went into arbitration, but Debussy prevailed. The orchestration was completed brilliantly by Charles Koechlin, at the composer's request. And there *Khamma* rested, while Allan toured several continents with her ballets.

The project was nearly consigned to the trash bin. *Khamma* received its first concert performance in Paris, in 1924. The ballet itself, without Allan's participation, was first seen at the Opéra-Comique in 1947.

Today *Khamma* is almost, undeservedly, forgotten. It's an exciting score and stands confidently on its own—ominous, mysterious, mercurial, even violent. If *Khamma* borrows a touch of Stravinsky in its trumpet calls and propulsive rhythms, it also presages, in the opening bars, the modernist, mechanistic music that was to arise in Paris after the First World War, and it anticipates the spooky music that issues even now from Hollywood thrillers. Tune in just about anywhere in these twenty minutes, and the last composer you'd think of would be Debussy.

Diaghilev and the Ballets Russes

Serge Diaghilev, born into a wealthy Russian family, was almost unknown in the West when he introduced Russian art to Paris in a 1906 exhibition. He followed this success in 1907 with five concerts of Russian music, treating Paris to large portions of Mussorgsky's *Boris Godunov*, with the legendary bass Feodor Chaliapin in the title role. Rachmaninoff played his Second Piano Concerto, and Joseph Hoffmann played concertos by Scriabin and Lyapunov. A year later Diaghilev brought Chaliapin to the Paris Opéra for the long-awaited French premiere of the complete *Boris Godunov*. Debussy was in the audience, of course.

Having set Parisians agog with Russian art and music, Diaghilev next gave them Russian ballet. From the Imperial Ballet in St Petersburg he enticed the best young dancers, choreographers, and designers—Nijinsky, Pavlova,

Karsavina, Fokine, Benois, Bakst—to come and dazzle the audience. Debussy was in London with *Pelléas* when the company opened its first season in May 1909, but in June he saw their performance of Rimsky-Korsakov's opera *Ivan the Terrible*, which had been wedged into the ballet schedule.[38]

The Ballets Russes was a primal force in European culture for the next twenty years. Diaghilev was the consummate impresario of his time, and in the subsequent dancing, teaching, and choreography of his disciples (including George Balanchine), his artistic presence was felt throughout the twentieth century.

One aspect of Diaghilev's genius was his recognition of great talent. Picasso, Braque, Miró, Dalí, and Matisse were among his stage designers. Nearly all the important composers who lived in or passed through Paris were commissioned to create new ballets: Ravel (*Daphnis et Chloé*), Prokofiev (*Prodigal Son*), Falla (*Three-Cornered Hat*), Satie (*Parade*), and Respighi (*La Boutique fantasque*), among others. But Diaghilev's earliest and greatest discovery was Igor Stravinsky, who, across twenty years, established his reputation with music for the Ballets Russes: the ballets *Firebird*, *Petrushka*, *The Rite of Spring*, *Les Noces*, and *Apollo*; and the operas *Renard*, *The Nightingale*, *Mavra*, and *Pulcinella*.

A year before he first met Stravinsky, Debussy had already been drawn into the Russian orbit when Diaghilev commissioned him to write a ballet with a scenario by Louis Laloy. It was to be called *Masques et bergamasques*, set in the Piazza San Marco in Venice, and populated with characters from the commedia dell'arte. Though the scenario was published, little music was written and none has survived. Diaghilev went on to other projects, including a ballet on Debussy's masterpiece, *Prélude à "L'Après-midi d'un faune."* For the latter project, Vaslav Nijinsky was to make his choreographic debut and would dance the role of the Faun.

Afternoon of a Faun was a project Debussy would soon regret. Nijinsky and his sister, the dancer Bronislava Nijinska, were reportedly inspired by ancient Egyptian paintings and artifacts shown at the Louvre showing figures frozen with heads in profile, torsos facing front, arms raised at stiff angles. Nijinsky, a very young man already considered the world's leading dancer, wanted to experiment. The movements he devised were, for the most part, more mime than dance. His chorus of nymphs walked in tandem or posed stiffly, like the women on the ancient vases. Nijinsky, with knees bent, gestured at times like a lecherous animal, moved stealthily, barely danced at all. Diaghilev, whether horrified, or merely wary of such a radical approach, or hoping Nijinsky would renounce it, postponed the ballet for a year.

What Nijinsky did with Debussy's beloved score has never been forgiven by many aficionados of music and ballet. While the audience at the dress rehearsal managed a smattering of applause, the premiere, on May 29, 1912, brought a chorus of boos, a noise the Ballets Russes had never before encountered. Few observers believed that the choreography had any reference to the music. Many were outraged at the end when, alone on the stage, the Faun picked up a scarf dropped by one of the nymphs and pretended to make love to it; this was, for those worshipping at the temple of Terpsichore, obscenely, unpardonably crude. The scandal was widely promoted by the press, and the remaining performances were sold out. On tour in Berlin, Vienna, and London, *Afternoon of a Faun* was met with varying degrees of hostility and praise, and it was soon dropped from the company's repertoire.

Nijinsky's original staging was recreated a few times during the last century, most successfully in 1981, with Rudolph Nureyev as the Faun. But *Afternoon of a Faun* survives in the ballet repertoire with Jerome Robbins's minimalist choreography and a simple scenario: A man and woman wearing rehearsal clothes dance, sometimes together, in an empty studio. The *New York Times* critic at the 1953 debut was not enthusiastic but reported, "Certainly the choreography does no violence to Debussy's music."[39]

Jeux—the Tennis Ballet

In June 1912, Debussy was fending off Maud Allan, trying to complete "Gigues," and working on the second book of piano Préludes when Diaghilev came to him with a new project: a ballet about tennis, with choreography by Nijinsky.

The composer at first refused to consider it. Only three weeks earlier, Nijinsky had perhaps forever linked Debussy's exquisite *Faune* with his disgraceful dancing. Parisians had read, in a morning-after review in *Le Figaro,* "We are shown a lecherous faun, whose movements are filthy and bestial in their eroticism, and whose gestures are as crude as they are indecent."[40] But Diaghilev offered Debussy 10,000 francs for the new ballet, and the composer agreed. "How did a simple man like me come to be involved in a story with so many repercussions? Because one needs to eat," he wrote, "and because one day I dined with Serge Diaghilev, a terrible but wonderful man who could make even the stones dance."⁴¹ An idea was perpetuated, in the aftermath, that Debussy—who wrote the score in little more than four weeks; who only did it for the money; and who seemingly, for this score, pasted together every little tune that came into his head—had little interest in the music of *Jeux* (Games). But in fact he seemed to enjoy writing it, despite the deadlines and the intrigues of his collaborators. He valued *Jeux* as much as any of his other compositions. And *Jeux* remains, in the opinion of many whose opinions are valued, the composer's most important and influential orchestral score.

The contract signed on June 18 stipulated that Debussy complete the piano score by August 31. The scenario didn't reach him until mid-July. For once he actually finished the piano score a few days *early*, but Diaghilev asked for changes and additional music at the climax of the ballet—"it's hard to get it right," Debussy said, "because the music has to convey a rather *risqué* situation!"— and he worked on it until September 12.⁴² Six weeks later, Diaghilev needed another eight bars of music, and Debussy made additional small changes in December. Nearly all these alterations involved the last few minutes of the seventeen-minute ballet.

For *Jeux*, Debussy was able to "forget the troubles of this world and write music which is almost cheerful," he told Caplet, explaining that he wanted an "orchestral color which seems to be lit from behind," like parts of *Parsifal*.⁴³

After the bizarre ambulating of the Faun, Debussy had reason to be skeptical about Nijinsky's choreography. He knew that the young dancer, whose body was a remarkably efficient instrument but whose mind was immature, had come under the influence of Dalcrozian theory. Émile Jaques-Dalcroze was a Swiss composer and pedagogue who developed a way to teach people to appreciate music by learning to hear it intensely, not just with their ears but with their entire body; and by expressing its rhythmic pulses, accents, and dynamics in spontaneous motions and postures. His method was called eurhythmics. Some observers saw Dalcroze's influence in the odd, angular choreography of *Afternoon of a Faun*, but for most it was difficult to see any connections between the dancing and the music.

Jeux opened at the new Théâtre des Champs-Elysées on May 15, 1913, with Pierre Monteux conducting.

The ballet takes place at dusk on a tennis court in a garden or park. Two young women find the court a congenial place for a quiet chat. Their privacy is disturbed when a stray tennis ball rolls onto the court, followed by a young man in search of it. (Nijinsky made his entrance with a spectacular leap.) He flirts with the women and is irritated when they resist. They try to flee, but he stops them. He dances with one, the other is petulant; he dances with the other, the first is upset. The women fall into each other's arms. The young man persuades them to submit to the beauty of the night and indulge their fantasies. They dance together as a threesome, and the man, in a passionate gesture, brings their heads together in an ecstatic "triple kiss" (the risqué part Debussy had so much trouble with). A stray tennis ball falls at their feet, and they flee into the darkness of the park.[44]

The critic from Le Figaro complained that "composer and choreographer take absolutely no notice of each other in this ballet" and that Nijinsky turns "the insignificant into absurdity."[45] The music critic Adolphe Julien wrote that the dancers moved "with the stiffness of marionettes, and then stop suddenly as if a spring broke, and then settle into some bizarre posture"—until the final scene, when the three characters "finally agree to move, to run, to dance" like normal people.[46]

Debussy had wanted the dancing to be continuous and synchronous with the music, but Nijinsky, "with his cruel and barbarous choreography . . . trampled my poor rhythms underfoot like weeds."[47] Nijinsky's stylized dancing is "ugly," he told Godet. "It is in fact Dalcrozian, and I consider Monsieur Dalcroze one of the worst enemies of music! And you can imagine what havoc his method has caused in the soul of this young savage, Nijinsky!"[48]

After the Games

The failure of the ballet Jeux involved several quite unusual circumstances.

Debussy's ballet was eclipsed two weeks later by one of the most memorable, controversial premieres in history: the Ballets Russes's production of Le Sacre du printemps (The Rite of Spring), choreographed by Nijinsky, remarkably, while working simultaneously on Jeux. Stravinsky's violent, groundbreaking score destabilized prevailing notions of music as nothing had since Pelléas et Mélisande in 1902. The audience rioted and fought among themselves. By the time the earthy dust settled around Sacre, no one cared about Jeux.

Then, after only a few performances, Diaghilev dropped Jeux like a hot potato. He dropped Sacre too, which was a much bigger mistake. In fact, he scrapped everything that represented Nijinsky, who, three months after Sacre, betrayed his supremely possessive boss by getting married.

Jeux was further compromised by the scenario, which stirred up more prudery than many ballet companies could tolerate. Some critics saw intimations of lesbianism in the embraces of the young women; others were offended by the smarmy three-way kiss. The condemnation escalated when the public learned that the original concept involved three mutually attractive men and was changed at the insistence of Diaghilev (or Nijinsky, depending on whom you believe).

Audiences were puzzled to find a trio of ordinary modern people doing such trivial things as flirting on a tennis court. The Ballets Russes had famously populated its stages with an Egyptian queen, a dancing rose, and the sylphs, nymphs, firebirds, marionettes, and Arabian princesses of legend. By contrast, everything about *Jeux* seemed, for all the sexual innuendo, rather tame and colorless, and the denouement left the question of morality unanswered.

Debussy's music seemed destined for obscurity. Shorn of its dancing, *Jeux* had few champions in the rarified world of ballet. But succeeding generations of musicians and critics kept the music alive.

Like many of Debussy's scores, *Jeux* needs more than one hearing before it reveals its beauty, its innovations, and especially its structure. Unlike his earlier works, in which he fashions a musical universe from minimal thematic material, *Jeux* employs a multitude of brief, fragmented themes to create busy music that can seem incoherent and evanescent. Melodies appear and disappear in a flash; some return later, altered or disguised, but it takes an acute listener to recognize unity in the kaleidoscopic effects, even in the last four minutes, when swirling tempos build to an ecstatic climax and a startling kiss. Anthony Tommasini of the *New York Times* finds a "dangerous eroticism [lurking] below the surface" of the music[49]—a characteristic largely missing from Debussy's scores since *Pelléas*.

Debussy's large orchestra seems to breathe like a living creature, with frequent changes of tempo, volume, pitch, and density of the soundscape. (Tommasini calls *Jeux* "a conductor's nightmare.")[50] Undercurrents of rapid thirty-second notes, in the strings or treble winds, keep the music constantly in motion, while the consistency of the 3/8 meter gives the music a propulsive unity. The orchestral groups weave in and out and around each other in an organic tapestry of sound.

When *Jeux* was first performed as a ballet, then as a concert piece, Debussy's detractors—fewer in 1913 than a decade earlier—thought it revealed a composer who was tired and past his prime. Some said he was trying to compete with Stravinsky, who had replaced him as the darling of the avant-garde.

Today the critical mass is overwhelmingly in favor of *Jeux*. Andrew Clements, in *The Guardian*, calls *Jeux*

> arguably Debussy's supreme achievement, and certainly his greatest orches-
> tral work. . . . Perhaps it was the very speed of composition that allowed
> Debussy's musical thoughts freer than usual rein, and gave an intuitive
> shape to the piece that came closer than ever before to the ideal of free
> musical association to which so much of his mature music aspires. . . . But it
> was the fact that the score seems to defy rigorous analysis that raised it into
> a modernist icon for the post-Webern generation of serialists, who pored
> over the subtle interrelations of its themes and the ambiguity of its overall
> form, clothed in ever-changing orchestral colors.[51]

The Children's Ballet and Other Theatricals

Many times in the post-*Pelléas* years Debussy had opportunities to collaborate on other theatrical projects in addition to those discussed above. He briefly worked with Charles Morice on an opera-ballet based on Verlaine's poems; discussed an opera on Euripides' *Orestes*, with Louis Laloy; and considered an opera about the Buddha and another on the Orpheus legend, both with Victor Segalen. He discussed with Paul-Jean Toulet an idea for a Persian ballet. He was asked to write incidental music for several plays. All these disappeared without a trace.

Several ideas from Gabriel Mourey were promising, especially an opera based on the legend of Tristan, whose character Debussy believed had been misinterpreted by Wagner. His new work, to be called *L'Histoire de Tristan*, was heralded in the press in 1907. Wagner's Tristan was not the French Tristan, Debussy told Arthur Hartmann: "Wagner's is a sighing and sentimental hero who does nothing valiant. My Tristan is a doughty warrior, a man, every inch of him; in fact, he is the real Tristan of legend, with less idealism but more mascu-linity."[52] The next year, when the Metropolitan Opera came calling, *Tristan* was one of the operas the composer promised. But Mourey's libretto was based on a novel by Joseph Bédier, who had already given the theatrical rights to his cousin, causing a tangle of literary interests that prevented Debussy from proceeding.

In 1913, Mourey asked for incidental music for a staging of his dramatic poem *Psyché*. Debussy, busy with other projects, wrote only a short cantilena to articulate the imminent death of Pan—a flute solo, appropriately. Debussy called it "La Flûte de Pan"; after his death a publisher renamed it "Syrinx." Like much of Debussy's late music, "Syrinx" sounds improvised; a haunting, mournful theme yields to heart-stirring melodic complexities with each repetition. The writing took the composer only a few days, but "Syrinx" ranks very high on the list of Best Flute Solos Ever Written.

Even before *Jeux* made its debut, Debussy agreed to write a ballet, *La Boîte à joujoux* (The Toybox), with a scenario by André Hellé, a writer and illustrator of children's books. Another ballet project, *Le Palais du silence* (The Palace of Silence), came to Debussy in November 1913—this one from Georges de Feure, an artist and writer, and André Charlot, producer at the Alhambra Theatre in London.

La Boîte à joujoux is a children's ballet involving a toy soldier in love with a beautiful girl doll who prefers a nasty clown doll. A battle ensues between wooden soldiers and clowns. The lovelorn soldier is severely wounded and nursed back to health by the chastened girl doll. Debussy envisioned *La Boîte* performed by marionettes.

Writing during the summer of 1913, Debussy drew inspiration from his darling Chouchou, now seven years old, and her horde of dolls and toys. There was talk of mounting the ballet at the Opéra-Comique, with children dancing the roles, but the outbreak of war quashed any hope for a production. After the armistice, Caplet faithfully orchestrated *Boîte* from Debussy's piano score. The music is mostly light and humorous, with parodies of Mendelssohn and Gounod, excerpts from French folk songs, and echoes of Debussy's own piano pieces. The ballet was first performed on December 10, 1919, in Paris, with adult dancers. In 1962, in the Netherlands, it was performed for the first time with marionettes.

Le Palais du silence (also known as *No-ja-li*) is set in ancient China. It's about an unhappy prince who, because he cannot speak, enforces a decree of silence throughout the land. Debussy began working on the score in early 1914 but was burdened with unfinished projects. Negotiating with the Alhambra producer, Debussy offered as a ballet score, in lieu of *No-ja-li*, his early symphonic work *Printemps*. This was the score the Academy had rejected years earlier for its "dangerous impressionism"; it was now published with a less dangerous orchestration by Henri Büsser. Hurriedly choreographed and rushed into rehearsal, *Printemps* became the unlikely showstopper in the 1914 Alhambra revue *Not Likely!* The revue was a smash hit, Debussy's score was well received, and *Printemps* was heard by 305 London audiences, probably more than half a million theatergoers, before the show closed. Ironically, *Printemps* reached far more people than any of Debussy's other orchestral works during his lifetime.

CHAPTER 22

WAR AND SUFFERING (1913–1916)

I have been relearning music. . . . It is even more beautiful than they deem it in the various Societies. . . . The sum of emotions a harmonic arrangement can provide cannot be found in any other art! Forgive me! I give the impression that I am discovering music, but, very humbly, that is almost how I feel.

—Debussy (September 1915)[1]

A Claude Debussy no longer creating music no longer has a reason to live.

—Debussy (June 1916)[2]

In the years before the First World War, there was great tension, division, and uncertainty in Europe. Among nations and empires, alliances were made or broken; smaller countries were taken and governments overturned like cards in some imperial poker game. Mobilization of troops in one country caused its adversaries in another to mobilize. Small, regional wars proliferated: Italy against Turkey in 1911–1912, the Balkan states against Turkey in 1912–1913. The Ottoman Empire was brought almost to extinction, then the victorious Balkan states fought among themselves. The Austro-Hungarian Empire was teetering. And France sought revenge for the humiliations of 1870–1871.

Russia, December 1913

On Debussy's earlier conducting tours—Brussels, London, Turin—Emma had accompanied him; but lately, traveling alone, he missed her and Chouchou tremendously and, weakened by illness, suffered doubly.

His state of mind was precarious; he was not inclined to be gracious to foreign hosts while feeling ill, lonely, and anxious. From Russia in December 1913, his letters to Emma illuminate his love and despair, passion and apprehension, with a vivid, strange sensuality that is almost Nabokovian. "It is snowing softly, obstinately, possibly never ending," he writes, from his compartment on a train, crossing the "infinite steppe." He thinks about Emma: "How genteel you look with your big glasses . . . How pretty your nape is when your head bows to read those 'damned books.' Will I go and embrace you? . . . Oh! well, of course." At a station stop, Emma's telegram is given to the conductor, who questions all the ladies on the train, looking for a "Claude," because it's a woman's name in Russia. The telegram gives him "a thrust of joy which goes to the heart, and almost at the same moment, a chilled heart, horribly pained! This telegram, I saw you writing it . . . I saw the room, the table . . . I no longer had any recourse against truth: in reality, you were far from me." He arrives in Moscow an hour late, "in the blackest mood," met by a delegation from the Moscow Musical Society whose welcoming speech is gibberish to Debussy.[3]

His return to Russia after so many years, to conduct in Moscow and St Petersburg, was prompted by an invitation from Serge Koussevitzky. Koussevitzky and his wife are gracious, generous hosts, he tells Emma. They house him in a sumptuous apartment—"it is lovely, 'my suite!' . . . I go to bed depressed." He can't sleep. He gets up and paces "like an idiot, . . . ingeniously conjuring up the voluptuous tenderness of our life. . . . And I see your poor, dear face on the platform of the station, your beautiful eyes full of tears and this last kiss your hands send me. (That hurts.)" He falls asleep and is awakened by the cold—"a nasty dawn." He returns to bed and tries to sleep by "counting up to one thousand, back and forth." They come to ask him what he'll take for breakfast. "Oh, if I could only take the train back to Paris!"[4]

At the rehearsal, the musicians greet him with a standing ovation and play "a very precise fanfare in E-flat." The players are well disciplined, young, and "full of good will." Afterward Koussevitzky takes him to a grocery that resembles an Asiatic palace, where "every day they cut up 500 kilos of smoked salmon."[5]

Her first letter arrives. Claude replies, "I found it natural that you should suffer and be lonesome" because that's also what he experiences. "I rehearsed four hours today without stopping for more than five minutes. I am exhausted, my legs are cotton batting, my head feels like a drum at the entrance of a carnival booth. I might perhaps have the strength to embrace you, but you're not there."[6]

He spoke to the director of the opera house, who planned to produce *Pelléas*. He had dinner with Diaghilev, who told him comical stories about the Ballets

Russes's South American tour, while carefully avoiding any mention of Nijinsky. The next night he was to take a midnight train to St Petersburg.

Rome and Holland, February 1914

In February he conducted in Rome. He was away for less than a week but wrote every day to Emma. No telegrams were waiting at train stations, no letters had reached his hotel in Rome, and Claude was distraught. His letters allude to serious marital strife. He was afraid of losing her. "Not knowing anything," he wrote from his hotel, "being here all alone . . . It doesn't seem real . . . I must have been condemned to be exiled for a very great crime, because the chastisement is terrible and, already, I cannot bear it. During this trip where each station, the stations of Calvary, distanced me from you, my heart throbbed in the thought that it was over, that never again would I see you."[7]

After Rome, he had only two days in Paris before he had to leave for Amsterdam. Richard von Rees, the Concertgebouw orchestra's president, had asked Gustave Doret to persuade the reclusive composer to conduct the orchestra. To help Debussy through the ordeal, Doret traveled with him, rehearsed the orchestra for him, and sat by his side while Claude conducted and played piano at the concerts. Claude and Emma apparently had come to an amicable understanding, and Emma's telegrams reached him at Brack's Doelen Hotel. He told Emma he'd arrived in Amsterdam in a "dismal state, but with my nerves on edge."[8]

At The Hague, the program opened with a work by Saint-Saëns, for whom Debussy bore no affection, but, he told Doret, "you have to admit it's damned cleverly put together."[9] Claude took the baton for his *Nocturnes* (the first two movements), *Faune*, and the orchestral version of his early piano duet "Marche écossaise." He also played three of his piano Préludes. The next morning, he sent Emma a brief report (he was "indifferent" that the Queen Mother attended). The Amsterdam concert would begin soon, he said, after which he was to dine at the home of von Rees.

The Concertgebouw audience greeted his appearance with a standing ovation. On the rostrum, von Rees observed, Debussy seemed clumsy and uncomfortable—"his robust physique made an agreeable impression . . . but there was over his whole personality a faint cloud of lassitude and boredom, such as you find with people suffering from homesickness."[10] The orchestra was well trained and responsive, and despite Debussy's inadequacies, the concert was a success.

Debussy was restless at dinner that evening. Von Rees hoped the composer would be impressed with his fine collection of Louis XVI furnishings; but Claude focused on a small clock, seen from his seat at the dinner table, because, he told his hostess, "every minute that passes brings me closer to Paris." When von Rees stood up to speak, Debussy briefly held up a dinner plate to hide his face from the embarrassment of the accolades to come. Afterward, Doret had to kick the composer under the table to prompt him to thank his host for his generous hospitality. He could only muster a few words. But when the guests took their leave, Debussy unexpectedly stayed behind, smoking a Havana cigar, feeling more at ease. He talked casually, at surprising length. He complimented his hostess—"Madame, I didn't know one could dine so well outside Paris." He congratulated her son on the wines—"they were exquisite." He talked for an hour about his family and their small pleasures. He was "as chatty as a magpie," Doret said, "and was the life and soul of the occasion."[11] Finally, his friend urged him to leave, because they had little time to pack their bags for the morning train to Paris.

"I still have so much to say"

In March and April, Debussy accompanied Ninon Vallin, a French soprano, in the first performance of his *Trois Poèmes de Stéphane Mallarmé* and a few weeks later in the *Chansons de Bilitis*. On May 4, the new ballet *Spring*, with Debussy's *Printemps* for its score, opened at the Alhambra in London. Three days later, in Paris, extracts from *Children's Corner*, orchestrated by Caplet, were danced by Loïe Fuller.

In May, Debussy was interviewed by the composer-critic Michel-Dimitri Calvocoressi for the June 1914 edition of a Philadelphia music journal, *The Etude*; it proved to be the last interview he would ever give. Asked to speak about the future of music, he said that it was "almost a crime to judge prematurely." Young artists should be allowed to "ripen in peace" and shouldn't be judged "until their art had fully asserted itself. . . . This feverish haste to dissert, dissect, and classify is the disease of our time." He mentioned in particular "Hungarians like Bartók and Kodály" who are "eagerly seeking their own way . . . [and] are pretty sure to find it." He said Stravinsky has a "keen and vivid curiosity," but "he will sober down in due time." The Spaniards, like the Russians, "have sought and found in national folk songs the foundations of their musical style"; and Albéniz has "drunk at the springs of folk music deeply enough to be absolutely imbued with its style and its very spirit." Italian opera composers of the day are incapable "of rising above mediocrity."[12]

As late as June 1914, it was not clear whether France or England would be able to maintain neutrality in a possible war between Germany and Russia. Belgian and Dutch armies—though both countries were fervently neutral—began to mobilize. Canada prepared to send troops to defend England. On June 28, the Austrian archduke was assassinated at Sarajevo. The engines of diplomacy and militarization began running at warp speed, and the engines of peacemaking broke down in tears.

In mid-July, despite the crisis enveloping Europe, Debussy went to London to conduct a concert at Queen's Hall; it was the last time he would ever leave France.

For eight months he had been more active as a performer than ever before in his life, but he had written little during that period. "I still have so much to say; and there are so many musical ideas which have never been expressed," he told a friend, in late July.[13] But he revealed to Godet the "hours in which one can hardly think of anything but suicide as a way out. . . . For a long time now—I must confess it—I have been losing myself, and I feel frightfully shrunken." He thinks of himself as "an unfortunate charlatan who will soon break his back in a final, unbeautiful pirouette."[14]

What had brought about this despair? The unpleasant journeys that took him away from his family to perform, always nervously and sometimes poorly? His lingering illness and the exhaustion of recent months? His endless financial worries, which, perhaps by now, he attributed to Emma's stubborn need to maintain her life of luxury? The imminent war?

Was he also troubled by the diminishing interest of a public thrilled by *Le Sacre du printemps*, weary of waiting for a Debussy creation as fine as *Pelléas*? If he still has much to say in his music, will anyone listen?

"What are we to do?"

Austro-Hungarians declared war on Serbia. German troops occupied Luxembourg and invaded Poland. On August 2, Russia declared war on Germany and crossed the German frontier. The next day, Germany declared war on France, and the day after, German troops invaded Belgium and moved into northeastern France.

Of course, Debussy had, in his own way, been at war with Germany since the 1880s.

By early September, German troops had fought and marched to within thirty miles of Paris. Preparing for a prolonged siege, the French government was moved to Bordeaux for safety; many priceless masterpieces of the Louvre were taken to Toulouse. But at the First Battle of the Marne, at a great cost in lives on both sides, the Germans were turned back, Paris was saved, for now, and the government returned to its capital.

Satie became a socialist, though he had never been known to have any political interest, let alone affiliation. He roamed the working-class streets of Arcueil with a loose-knit gang of citizen soldiers looking for enemies where there were none, and he took a casual, ironic attitude toward the dangers that France faced.

Debussy, fighting illness, wished he could fight for his country. While Ravel, Caplet, and many other colleagues were sent to the front lines, he was tormented by his inability to contribute to the war effort. All he knew how to do, he said, was write music.

So he wrote for a world at war. In late 1914, he was asked for a musical homage to the Belgian King Albert, who had courageously led his troops into battle. He responded with *Berceuse héroique*, an elegy for the Belgian people savaged by a fierce German invasion. In 1915, he wrote the words and music for an emotionally wrenching song, "Noël des enfants qui n'ont plus de maison" (Christmas of the Children Who Have No Home), full of rage and empathy for the thousands of poor French children, their parents gone, nothing to eat.

> *They burned the school and our teacher, too.*
> *They burned the church and Jesus Christ,*
> *and the old beggar who could not get away!* . . .
> *Of course, papa is at the war. Poor mama died*
> *before seeing all this. What are we to do?*[15]

It was his last song.

On March 26, 1915, Debussy wrote to his friend D. E. Inghelbrecht: "My poor mother died yesterday afternoon at 1:30. For her, it was a release! For me, a great sorrow."[16] Emma's mother died a week later. Debussy never spoke much about his mother and rarely mentioned her in his letters. When he was a child she was a disciplinarian and occasionally struck him, and when he was grown she seemed to take little interest in his musical successes.

"The sun's come out at last"

The spring of 1915 saw a shocking escalation of Germany's prosecution of the war. In April the Germans began using large deployments of poison gas for the first time, in Belgium, in violation of international agreements. Weeks later, a German U-boat torpedoed and sank the mammoth Cunard liner *Lusitania* off the coast of Ireland, killing more than a thousand passengers and crew.

Many orchestra players and other musicians were conscripted or enlisted to fight for their country. Concerts were canceled, and some concert halls and theaters were shuttered. As the war deepened, it was clear that French composers and publishers would be severely affected. Royalties from foreign sales of music published in France, and from performances abroad, would no longer be collected, or wouldn't reach their lawful recipients. It would be impossible to import musical scores published in Germany—the works of virtually all the German masters from Bach to Wagner, and many non-Germans as well. Jacques Durand set out to fill the void with new French editions of the great classics, and he paid composers to edit and annotate the scores, using the available earlier editions for reference. In October he asked Debussy to edit the works of Chopin (the études, waltzes, ballades, impromptus, and rondos) and later the violin sonatas of J. S. Bach. It was a job Debussy relished, not only because his income had been diminished, but because of his reverence for the music of these two composers.

Regardless of the war, or perhaps because of the unspeakable threat of annihilation, Debussy began to write and write, hardly stopping to breathe.

On June 5, 1915, he began *En blanc et noir* (In White and Black), a tonal picture of war's devastation. At first he called it *Caprices en blanc et noir*. He had in mind the *Caprichos* of the Spanish artist Francisco Goya, an album of eighty satirical prints depicting "the innumerable foibles and follies" of an ignorant, immoral, deceitful society. Debussy probably also knew a later Goya series called *The Disasters of War*.

The first movement of *En blanc et noir*, written for two pianos, begins as busily as the "Toccata" from *Pour le piano*. The mood is interrupted by darker themes suggesting the restlessness and anxiety of people living on the cusp of danger. The second movement begins with the raw, somber silence that follows a bombing raid. A little tune evokes a frightened child calling to whoever might be alive to hear her; persistent treble chords repeat like chimes in the distance. A rumble in the deep bass gives way to a frenzy of activity among the survivors—Luther's hymn "A Mighty Fortress Is Our God" struggles to be heard—before sobriety and caution dampen the excitement.[17]

From July to October, the Debussys stayed in Pourville, where Arkel, Claude's totem ceramic toad, "seems to like it."[18] The sea is "blue as a waltz, gray as a useless piece of sheet metal," but mostly green as absinthe. He admits he never goes bathing in the ocean. "It is too big! And then, I don't know how to swim."[19] A shocking admission from the master of *La Mer*! The Debussys stayed at a pleasant villa called Mon Coin, graciously provided by the owner. He wrote Durand, "If I had lots of money I'd buy Mon Coin immediately, out of gratitude at being able to think and work again. When I think back to the void of the last year, I get shivers up my spine, and I'm afraid to go back to Paris and the factory of nothingness my study had become."[20]

This three-month period was perhaps the most productive of his life. At Pourville, he completed *En blanc et noir*, even though he was without a piano during his first week there; and he spent considerable time editing Chopin. His immersion in Chopin inspired him to create a set of twelve Études of his own. And with many new ideas underscored by a crescendo of latent ambition, he revealed to Durand his plan to write six sonatas for various combinations of instruments. In fact, he had already begun writing the first, a Sonata for Cello and Piano, and sent the manuscript to Durand in early August. Before he returned to Paris he completed the second sonata. It was a miraculous recovery of creativity after a nine-month period in which he'd written almost nothing.

At the beginning of a letter to Durand, he mentions the heavy rains that have been drenching Pourville, but, "the sun's come out at last . . . what can it have been doing over the other side, to get here so late?"[21]

The Chamber Sonatas

Debussy was not a prolific composer of chamber music, perhaps because he was less at ease in the formal realm of "pure music" without the stimulus of a visual, mythological, or literary subject. Certainly, for most of his life he was less interested in writing pure music—it was the music of Mozart and Beethoven, the music of the past, and he was intent on forging the music of the future. His String Quartet of 1893, the first Modern quartet, was Debussy's only true chamber music—until the summer of 1915.

His cancer and the kaiser changed everything. Debussy knew his time on earth was coming to an end. He had not yet given French composers all they needed for the future. There was a legacy to shape. He had to claim his rightful place among the emerging modernists of the twentieth century—Stravinsky, Schoenberg, and Bartók—whose music blazed paths they couldn't find until Debussy opened their eyes.

Along one of those paths, later to be known as neoclassicism, Debussy took his first tentative steps with the sonatas. He had touched on the themes of neoclassicism many times in the past—in the Baroque dances, "Cortège" and "Menuet," of the *Petite Suite*; the "Prélude," "Passepied," and "Menuet" from the *Suite bergamasque*; and the "Sarabande" and "Toccata" from *Pour le piano*. Other aspects of neoclassicism are represented by the madrigal-like *Chansons de Charles d'Orléans* and certainly, now, in the three sonatas. As early as 1902, Gaston Carraud understood that Debussy "is really a classical composer." (The term "neoclassical" hadn't yet been imagined.) "After the unbridled romanticism to which music had fallen prey," Carraud wrote, "he has the lucidity, the tact, the restraint, and the sense of proportion that characterize the classical composers. He has the same controlled emotion as they; he has their charm and dignity of expression, their scorn of emphasis, exaggeration, and mere effect."[22]

The sonatas were conceived as a set of six, and they were probably meant to be performed consecutively in a single concert. The Sonata for Cello and Piano and the Sonata for Flute, Viola, and Harp were written at Pourville; the third, a Sonata for Violin and Piano, was finished in April 1917. His creative energy diminished before he could write the others. The fourth would have been a Sonata for Oboe, Horn, and Clavecin. Vallas said that Debussy had wanted to employ an eighteenth-century clavecin with two keyboards—one set of keys behind and a little above the other; and this sonata would have been the first Modern composition to use that antique clavecin. The fifth sonata was to be for trumpet, clarinet, bassoon, and piano. In the sixth, the small orchestra would have included only the instruments used in the other five sonatas. Leaving aside the suppressed *Piano Fantaisie*, the sixth sonata might have been the piano concerto that many music lovers wish Debussy had written.

The three sonatas are works of maturity and wisdom, made from some of the elements that brought neoclassicism to the fore in the years between the world wars: a striving for simplicity, for the smaller ensembles and lighter textures that dominated music before Mozart, for the spirit of classicism without the restraints, and for a tonal language with no affiliation with the Romantic era. Given that the word "neoclassicism" has since been carelessly applied to all manner of music, it's odd that Debussy is almost always overlooked as one of its pioneers. The genre that Debussy evoked in his three sonatas was not the Germanic sonata of Mozart, Beethoven, and Brahms; Debussy's paradigm was the sonata of the Baroque, when successive movements were linked together "in a concertante style which came from Italy" but "acclimatized in France through the tender care of François Couperin [and] took on the quality of the soil."[23]

The sonatas are steeped in melancholy. The livelier movements are halting, distracted, and strange, and they seem to reveal Debussy's anxiety about living in wartime. The Sonata for Flute, Viola and Harp, the longest and most ambitious of the three, is layered with exoticism; when Debussy first heard it played, he found it terribly sad and written by "a Debussy which I no longer know."[24] Falla thought it was "music for paradise."[25]

Boulez sees in the sonatas "the musician's drive toward a more delicate, more austere art, freer of immediate seductions but unequalled in richness of inspiration." Like his score for the ballet *Jeux*, the sonatas "sound an esthetic truth without visible precedent."[26]

To emphasize the sonatas' connection to a lost French tradition, Debussy asked Durand to use on the covers a typeface suggesting Couperin's era. And for the first time, he asked that his name on the covers identify his modest place in the musical pantheon: "Claude Debussy, musicien français."

The Études

On August 28 of the fruitful summer of 1915, Debussy told Durand he's sending six Études to him, but he's run out of manuscript paper. (Shortages of commodities were always a problem in wartime.) "I've invested a lot of passion and faith in the future of the Études," he wrote. He says that although the pieces are highly technical exercises, he didn't want them to be somber. "A little charm never spoilt anything."[27] Elsewhere, he said, "Truly this music is written for the heights of execution!"[28]

The Études (Studies) were directly inspired by Debussy's months of editing and revising Chopin for Durand; in fact, Debussy was still working on the project when he began writing his Études. He delighted in Chopin's "delicate harmonic flavor and the purity of the melodic design," said Cortot. "In Debussy's own circle they liked to say that he played the piano like Chopin. In fact, his touch was delicious, easy, sweet, and mysterious, made for fine nuances and intimacy, without jerks or interruptions; he used the pedals with infinite art and, like Chopin, he preferred pianos with a tone sweet to an extreme."[29]

In the war years Debussy was an unwavering nationalist, especially in musical matters. He was determined to show that the French addiction to German music was not just unwise but unnecessary, just as he was eager to reestablish France's forsaken legacy of classicism. In the dedication of his Études, he was of two minds and asked his publisher for an opinion. A nod to Couperin, "the most poetic of our harpsichordists,"[30] would have been a vote for France's heritage. But after much thought, he dedicated the Études "to the memory of Frédéric Chopin," who had inspired him ever since his piano lessons, more than forty years earlier, with Mme Mauté de Fleurville.

Written at Pourville in only five weeks, the twelve Études are among the most technically challenging pieces ever written for the piano. When he first saw them, Durand complained that they were too difficult to play, which brought from Debussy an admission that some of the rapid passages bring his fingers to a halt and make him feel "as though I'd been climbing a flight of stairs."[31] Debussy made the Études harder to learn than necessary, because he did not provide the student with fingering notations. He said that since every pianist's fingers are different, no suggestions would work equally well for everyone. "These Études will be a useful warning to pianists not to take up the musical profession unless they have remarkable hands," he said.[32] That they have entered the piano repertoire is a testament to the determination of many serious concert pianists to master them.

The Études are divided into two books of six each. Each piece focuses on one particular technique or sonority that pianists must master and puts the fingers through Olympian gymnastic effort, sometimes at perilous speed. But the Études are far from dry and scholarly. In each of the studies, he writes with such originality and musicality that they "give the impression of a free translation of an inspiration which could find no more natural way of expression," wrote

Cortot. Besides the pleasure the pianist finds in the Études, Cortot affirms the work's "exceptional didactic importance."[33]

To persuade us that the hard work of piano study can be enjoyable, Debussy starts his series with a jolly parody of the most famous exercise of all, Czerny's insufferable Five-Finger Exercise. The "Étude for Five Fingers, after Monsieur Czerny" begins as it might be played by a seven-year-old novice; but the fingers rebel and introduce "wrong" notes and figurations that, like butterflies emerging from the chrysalis, flutter excitedly all over the keyboard. While this level of whimsy isn't carried through the rest of the Études, the "Czerny" announces that the remaining eleven will be full of surprises.

The Étude for Eight Fingers, for example, is intended to be played without thumbs, as those digits would just get in the way of the others. The Étude for Fourths ("in which you'll find unheard-of things," Debussy said)[34] is a dazzling display of almost nothing except intervals of a fourth. There are Études for octaves, Études for arpeggios, for chromaticism, for repeated notes, for ornaments, and others. There are virtuosic passages with the delicacy and charm of Debussy's early piano works, and some with the spareness of the Préludes.

The Études are perfectly transparent in their effects and easy to listen to—if they're played as the master intended: with the illusion of effortlessness.

When the family returned to Paris in October, Debussy wrote a long, fascinating letter to Godet. In Pourville, "I rediscovered the possibility of thinking musically, something which had not happened to me for a year. It certainly isn't necessary that I write music, but I don't know how to do anything else reasonably well. . . . I have been writing like an enraged person or better, like one who is to die in the morning."[35]

"Destiny should allow me to finish it"

On December 6, 1915, Debussy wrote to Durand: "My dear Jacques, Tomorrow is definitely the day I am being operated on . . . I didn't have time to send out invitations; next time, I'll make an effort to plan ahead."[36]

At the end of one of the most fertile periods of his life, Debussy had colostomy surgery in an attempt to cure the rectal cancer that had been developing since 1908. The operation initiated the most agonizing year of his life: 1916 was a year that all creativity was crushed by pain, when despair was alleviated only by the mental numbness of morphine. The colostomy procedure wasn't new, but by today's standards the technique was crude and the outcomes often un-satisfactory. A month after the operation, he explained to Godet how it came about: "I was ill for a long time . . . yet I lived with it, paying little attention. Abruptly, everything worsened, and so an operation; nasty moments, painful aftermath, etc. . . . Healing can only be slow and by natural means. . . . Well, all this is no game, and I grumble in vain, Mother Nature being, in general, deaf to the suffering of her children." Before his surgery he was, he said, "putting the finishing touches—or a reasonable facsimile thereof—on *La Chute de la maison Usher*, and illness blew all my hopes away. . . . [I] am ill disposed to accept this turn that my destiny has taken; furthermore, I am suffering like one who has been damned!"[37]

The surgery was followed by radium treatments—a dangerous process at the time, although Paris was a major center of medical experimentation with radium. Marie Curie had discovered the element in 1898 and presented her findings in a doctoral thesis in 1903. In 1916, treatment of internal cancers was still very rare. Doctors would insert pellets or tubes containing radium into a body cavity near the tumor, over a period of days or weeks, in an attempt to destroy it. The treatments were painful and highly problematic because the optimal duration of exposure to radiation was not known. "[The doctors] give me hope of some improvement in a couple of weeks," he wrote to a friend, on February 1. "But I haven't much confidence, and radium rather abuses its right to be mysterious."[38]

A few days later he told Godet, "Not long ago, I inaugurated a new treatment. It is all so shrouded in mystery and yet they ask me to be patient. . . . Lord! where to find it? after sixty days of assorted torture." He was "wallowing in the 'factories of oblivion,'" he says, a reference to the effects of morphine.[39] A month later he told Godet, "So many days have gone by . . . wretched hours of suffering more, suffering less, while all the while being unable to distinguish one from the other," and in his morphine haze, his memory is unreliable. "The operation unleashed other miseries, and all that ever brings on is the same refrain: 'Have patience!'"[40] Three months later, "I am feeling better but not enough to sing a song of victory," and he would soon be renewing his acquaintance with radium, he wrote. "Things do not look very bright, and I ask myself if it is worth struggling so much for so little."[41] During Debussy's convalescence, Satie was a frequent visitor and tried to cheer up his old friend with conversation and backgammon.

By July, Debussy's aggravations included new financial pressures. He had not paid Lilly's alimony since 1910, and the court ordered him to pay 3,600 francs for each year he missed.[42] "People commit suicide for less," he told Durand, "and if I did not feel anxious as much as duty-bound to finish the two little dramas based on E. Poe, this would already have taken place."[43] Then Emma and Chouchou developed whooping cough. It was "one dismal thing after another, and my supply of philosophy ran out a long time ago," he wrote. "So I grumble despairingly. . . . If I don't go mad, it is because a compassionate god is watching over me. . . . But I have had enough, enough, enough!"[44]

A month later he wrote Dukas, "It is possible that *The Fall of the House of Usher* will also be the fall of Claude Debussy. Destiny should allow me to finish it, for I shall not wish to rely entirely on *Pelléas* for the harsh judgment of future generations."[45] He had been working intermittently on the *Usher* libretto for eight years, and on the third version for about a year. In late August 1916, he finally finished it and was able to put what little energy he had into the music itself.

He knew he was dying, though no one would talk about it. His house "has some strange affinities to the house of Usher," he wrote Godet. "Aside from the fact that I do not have the mental disorders of a Roderick Usher, . . . a hyper-sensitivity binds us closely together. . . . On that subject, I could give you details which would make your beard fall off. . . . Ah my poor Godet, to live this way is the worst of nightmares!"[46] Later he apologized to Godet for all his complaining: "You are my only friend (alias Roderick Usher) and naturally I take advantage of that."[47]

In mid-September, the Debussy family left to spend a month at the Grand Hotel in Arcachon. Emma wasn't well, and Debussy wasn't happy to make the journey, despite the "doleful atmosphere" at home. But "I will again see the Atlantic, which is the father of all oceans."[48]

December was more eventful, if not happier. Durand hosted the first performance of the Sonata for Flute, Viola, and Harp. At a charity concert, Walter Rummel introduced the twelve Études. And a few days before Christmas, the composer joined Roger-Ducasse to perform *En blanc et noir* for another war charity.

The score of *Usher* was far from completed when Debussy stopped working on it, early in 1917. Besides the finished libretto, he left numerous piano sketches for the first scene and the beginning of the second, and a few hints about orchestration—enough that, twice in the 1970s, the unfinished opera was presented to audiences, with the unavoidable gaps. In 2002, the intrepid Debussy scholar Robert Orledge began the task of completing and orchestrating the opera as a whole. He filled the gaps by weaving together some of the characteristic chords, harmonies, and themes that Debussy had used repeatedly in his sketches, and, for the rest, did his best to guess what Debussy might have wanted. Orledge's version was presented in 2004 and several times afterward. Andrew Clements, reviewing a 2011 production by the Welsh National Opera, praised Orledge's "seamless" score, which "sounds like late Debussy—there are echoes of the orchestral *Images*, especially 'Gigues,' and even of *Jeux*—and the prevailing mood of a doom-laden house is recognizably similar to that of *Pelléas et Mélisande*."[49]

CHAPTER 23

TOO MANY KEYS (1917–1918)

I watch the days go by, minute by minute, like cows watching trains. I go to bed just about convinced that I shall not sleep, hoping that tomorrow will be somewhat more kindly; and it starts all over again! . . . Sickness, that old servant of death, has chosen me as her guinea pig. God knows why. I work only so that someone will convince me that I shouldn't. When will it all end?

—Debussy[1]

The friendship of Claude and Erik, despite the manipulative interventions of Ravel in 1911, continued almost uninterrupted. They were like brothers, and as different as siblings can be—incompatible, cantankerous, but with unflagging affection for one another. Their common devotion to music bound them together but also created a rivalry. From the time of *Pelléas*, Debussy's rise to fame was correlated to Satie's increasing jealousy and depression. Debussy, when his health problems worsened, became less tolerant of Satie's alcoholism and self-inflicted poverty, more harsh in judging his friend's work, incredulous of his friend's sudden success. And perhaps Debussy felt that his own audience had deserted him. Satie came to resent his old friend's penchant for teasing and belittling as a means of communication. Still, he dined regularly at Debussy's house, then walked home each night to Arcueil, more than ten kilometers, despite rain, cold, darkness, and the availability of a train to take him there. He had moved to his tiny apartment in 1898, desiring a cheaper and quieter community than Montmartre. Friends considered his daily treks between Paris and home to be just one of his eccentricities; that he never let anyone into his apartment was another. But the townspeople of his shabby suburb cherished him; their kind, gentle *bon maître d'Arcueil* was often seen scribbling on music paper at the local bistro. Chouchou called him Kiki.

Satie's *Parade*

In the afterglow of Ravel's spotlight, Satie's career stalled, though more of his music was published and his circle of acquaintances grew rapidly. Satie was always an amusing person to have a drink with, but by 1916 he was a darling of the exclusive soirées given by the Princesse de Polignac, one of Diaghilev's major financial supporters. The Russian dancers had spent long months touring the United States while war raged in Europe. They hadn't presented a Paris season for three years. But despite the unending carnage, Diaghilev brought his troupe home, and he needed a new ballet for the 1917 season.

Diaghilev was sought out by Jean Cocteau, who wanted to be associated with the Ballets Russes's cultural eminence. Cocteau, known to later generations mainly as a dramatist and filmmaker, was first a brilliant young poet who aimed to know everyone of consequence and who helped shape the careers of many writers and artists. Now Satie had become someone of consequence; young musicians were flocking to him and studying his unconventional music.

Cocteau asked Satie to collaborate on a project for the Ballets Russes.

For the music, Cocteau wanted Satie's *Trois Morceaux en forme de poire* (Three Pieces in the Shape of a Pear), but the composer preferred to write a fresh score for the occasion. Cocteau gave Diaghilev a scenario portraying a once-familiar scene on Parisian streets: a sideshow (a *parade*, in French), where circus performers gave passersby a preview of the big show inside. For sets and costumes, Cocteau introduced the impresario to Picasso, who, like Satie, had never worked on a ballet. Léonide Massine was now Diaghilev's choreographer.

Much of Satie's music for *Parade* is drawn from his early days at the café-concerts and cabarets, but the ballet begins with a solemn, instrumental chorale and a brief fugal passage that flaunt his laborious training at the Schola Cantorum. Beyond that, Satie stretched the limits of his talent for witty and entertaining nonsense. There are bits of ragtime, waltzes, marches, and insistently repetitive tropes that suggest a mechanistic industrial age which, in 1917, was not yet perceived as sinister. *Parade* became known for the novel nonmusical sounds in the score—a clackety typewriter, splashing water, a lottery wheel, a foghorn, pistol shots—but they were Cocteau's idea, not Satie's, and most of the noises were vetoed by Diaghilev.

After Satie's subdued chorale, two Managers appear onstage, wearing Picasso's ten-foot-tall papier-mâché costumes; they run the sideshow. The circus performers, who do most of the dancing, miming, and posturing, are a Chinese Conjurer, a Little American Girl, a pair of Acrobats, and a Horse.

Avant-garde is hardly the word to describe *Parade*'s eccentricities. Apollinaire coined the word "surrealism" when he wrote the ballet's program notes. At the premiere on May 18, 1917, the crowd—this was Paris, after all—protested with hooting and booing. Many in the audience were offended by the absurdity and occasional hilarity of the goings-on, so inappropriate, so insensitive to the hundreds of thousands of French soldiers on the battlefields. Even before *Parade*, conservative critics considered Picasso's cubist paintings incendiary; now his stage designs and Satie's music seemed a subversion of the patriotic rhetoric of war, a rude guffaw in the face of national peril. Some said *Parade* was an attack on French culture, and thus a gift to the Germans.[2]

With *Parade*, Cocteau turned Satie's career in a new direction. Whereas Ravel had promoted Satie as the precursor of the recent past, Cocteau established him as the leader of the futurists. A new wave of French composers—Darius Milhaud, Georges Auric, Arthur Honegger, and a few others—gathered around Satie and called themselves the Nouveaux Jeunes. The Princesse de Polignac commissioned him to compose something new, and even before *Parade* opened, he began writing a vocal work for her called *Socrate*. With a libretto drawn from the *Dialogues* of Plato, the music is as serene and serious as *Parade* is raucous and provocative.

But Satie couldn't keep himself out of trouble.

Most reviews of *Parade* were unfavorable or worse, including one by Jean Poueigh, who savaged the music and its composer. Satie retaliated by sending his tormentor several postcards with inflammatory epithets—among them, "lousy asshole" and "Monsieur Fuckface Poueigh"[3]—that prompted a libel suit. Some of Satie's friends testified at the trial on his behalf, but Satie lost the case. He was sentenced to a week in jail and fined 100 francs, plus 1,000 francs awarded to the complainant, leaving the defendant profoundly depressed about the whole affair. He was afraid the judgment would destroy his new celebrity, that the police would throw him in jail on the slightest pretext, that he would be bankrupt. The verdict was appealed, and while waiting for a hearing he was told that his sentence might be reduced if only he'd apologize to the wounded critic. He began writing a repentant letter to Poueigh but put down his pen in mid-sentence.

After *Parade*, Cocteau called Satie a "great, sensitive inventor, hidden behind his spectacles, without whom neither *Pelléas* nor the *Rite* would have been possible."[4] Cocteau drove a public wedge between Debussy, whom he portrayed as obsolete, and Satie, leader of the Nouveaux Jeunes. His sometimes mendacious campaign continued even after Debussy's death and shaped the way future generations viewed the two visionary composers. Cocteau's machinations were self-serving. He dissolved the Nouveaux Jeunes and formed a new faction with some of the same composers, who would be known as Les Six. Satie just walked away.

Parade brought Satie another unexpected consequence. Debussy had undoubtedly seen the *Parade* score, and he attended at least one rehearsal. Satie learned that his old friend had made unkind remarks about the music. It was not the first time Debussy had publicly disparaged him. The friendship had run its course, and it was time to end it. He wrote a brief note to Emma Debussy, declining a dinner invitation:

Thursday, March 8, 1917
Chère Madame—decidedly, it will be preferable if henceforth the "Precursor" stays at home, far away.
Amicably,
ES
Painful teasing—and again and again! Yes. Quite unbearable, anyhow.[5]

The Last Summer

In April 1917, Gabriel Fauré asked Debussy to play the Études at a benefit concert. He declined the request "for the simple reason that I can no longer play the piano well enough to risk a performance of the Études. . . . In public a peculiar phobia takes hold of me: There are too many keys; I haven't enough fingers any more; and suddenly I forget where the pedals are."[6]

But the composer continued working through the spring of 1917. For Durand he finished editing Bach's Six Sonatas for Violin and Piano, and he finished writing his own Sonata for Violin and Piano. For the first performance on May 5, Debussy accompanied the violinist Gaston Poulet, despite the frailty of fingers that might have bungled the Études.

On July 3, the Debussy family left for their summer holiday, this time at Saint-Jean-de-Luz, a seaside resort on the Basque coast of France, far from the battlefields. They leased the Chalet Habas, the residence of an English colonel who was away at war. It was "a place in which you might come across S. Pick-wick on the staircase," he wrote Godet.[7] Debussy regretted that he couldn't view the sea from the house, but there were mountains nearby, and the bay was only a fifteen-minute walk. In these last years of the war, Godet was living in Switzerland; he and Debussy rarely (if ever) saw each other, but they maintained the intimacy of their friendship in correspondence. Debussy was always forlorn and often suffering pain; Godet was always kind and lifted his friend's spirits with tender words: "Let me embrace you on your fine luminous forehead. Let me wish you good work and, as far as possible, good health."[8]

Marguerite Long, one of the foremost French pianists of her time, was summering not far from the Debussys at Saint-Jean-de-Luz. But even after Debussy's popularity had soared, his works did not appear on her programs—not because she didn't admire them, but, as she admitted, she couldn't really understand them. She thought the virtuosos of her day didn't do justice to Debussy's music, and she couldn't imagine herself doing any better. But when Debussy himself played his music, she wrote, "it was marvelous, incomparable. I just did not understand." Her reluctance annoyed Debussy, she knew. One day in 1914, he asked, "You don't want to play my music?"[9]

Of course she wanted to play his music! Debussy helped Long prepare for a charity concert, and for a short while she became a regular visitor to Debussy's house on the avenue du Bois de Boulogne, learning from the master. Then war was declared. Long's husband, a noted musicologist and a captain in the French infantry, was called to rejoin his regiment; twelve days later he was killed in action. In her grief, Long turned her back on the piano and canceled her concert engagements. Not until 1917 did she resume her career at a benefit to raise money for prisoners of war. At Saint-Jean-de-Luz, she resumed studying with Debussy.

"Those summer months of 1917 could be regarded as the gift of Providence in permitting so great a love of life to a man as ill as was Debussy," Long wrote. "His courage in suffering was a continuing, purposeful example. There was alleviation in music for both of us"—the composer so often in pain, the pianist still grieving for her husband. "For three months I did not leave the piano."[10]

There was a day when the heat was so oppressive that Long's muslin blouse was soaked through with perspiration. She and Debussy had been studying "L'Isle joyeuse" and the Études. "Seeing my state of fatigue," she wrote, "the master said: 'You must forgive me for being so exacting, but you understand that when I am no more, there must be someone who will know exactly what my wishes are.'"[11]

He seemed always to be conscious of the fragility of his hold on life and did what he could to ensure the permanence and correct interpretation of his music.

Debussy's last two public performances took place at Biarritz, just up the coast from Saint-Jean, in September. He reprised the Violin Sonata with Gaston Poulet.

The Last Winter

The Debussys returned to Paris in mid-October after a train journey that Claude described to Godet as "a strange and dangerous enterprise." At home, entering his study, he found himself staring at blank sheets of manuscript paper—"empty of music and yellow with boredom. . . . Music's completely abandoned me."[12]

Against all odds, he kept his focus on the future. He wanted Durand to find a producer for *La Boîte à joujoux* and told him the orchestration was almost done. (It wasn't.) Incredibly, for a man so incapacitated, he planned to collaborate with Laloy on an operatic version of *Le Martyre de Saint-Sébastien*. He urged Paul-Jean Toulet to finish his adaptation of *As You Like It*, for which Debussy was to write incidental music—a project conceived years earlier.

In a letter to Toulet's wife, Emma reported on Claude's condition. She mentioned that their house was often unbearably cold, as the scarcity of coal allowed them to heat only Claude's room.[13] Later she tells another friend that Claude "is eating, reading, singing!—but he is often in pain from his illness and still cannot sit up in his bed. Moreover, nothing has been found to relieve this exhausting enteritis."[14]

At the end of January 1918, German planes, thirty of them, began bombing Paris for the first time in two years. On the first night, 144 bombs exploded, and the assault continued day after day. Debussy was by then confined to his bed.

On February 8, Louis Pasteur Vallery-Radot, the grandson of the famous scientist, told Toulet that he'd seen Debussy—"very thin, but not too discouraged. . . . As if this war did not kill enough people, this illness had to strike a man like him. What injustice, what blindness of fate!"[15]

The Last Weeks

Several concerts in March were dedicated to the music of Debussy. Viñes came to see him and played the Études for him; a piano had to be brought into his bedroom for the occasion. Inghelbrecht paid a visit. Laloy came and sat with the invalid for a while; he remarked on Debussy's hollow face and the emptiness of his gaze.

On March 15, the minister of the interior approved a reduction of Satie's sentence in the libel case to five years' probation on condition of good behavior. Days later, Satie wrote a letter to his old friend. Little is known about the letter or Debussy's reaction to it. "Forgive me," the dying man reportedly murmured.

After Debussy died, Satie told a friend, "I wrote to him—fortunately for me—a few days before his death. Knowing that he was doomed, alas, I didn't want to remain on bad terms with him. My poor friend! What a sad end."[16] In his letter, did Satie apologize for abandoning Debussy during the tragic final year of his illness? Did he explain why he felt compelled to end their relationship—the teasing, the lack of support? Perhaps Satie thanked Debussy for his steadfast friendship; for making him feel welcome in his home, with his family; for his mentoring and musical guidance in the early years. Perhaps he reaffirmed the boundless affection he'd felt for his friend, even while Debussy refused to accept the validity of Satie's music. Whatever it was, it's hard to imagine that the dying man wasn't moved to tears.

On March 19, at the instigation of friends, Debussy agreed to apply once more for membership in the Académie des Beaux-Arts, an honor that had twice been blocked by Camille Saint-Saëns. Emma prepared a letter to the Academy, and Debussy signed it. There was no doubt that in the estimation of the Beaux-Arts, of France, and of the world at large, Debussy was preeminent among French composers, the man who had boldly moved the art of music beyond Wagner's Germany, the man who had made Paris the leading center of the musical avant-garde, and who had ushered in the Modern era. But for membership in the Academy, it was too late.

At 7:18 on the morning of March 21, Parisians were shocked by a fierce attack—unlike any other—when a shell exploded on the quai de la Seine with enough force to be heard everywhere in the city. There wasn't the usual warning, no roar of enemy planes approaching, so people thought it had been dropped from an aircraft flying too high to be observed or heard. Twenty more shells exploded that day at fifteen-minute intervals in seemingly random parts of the city. Every day thereafter about twenty shells hit Paris. The Allies soon determined that the shells were fired from a colossal long-range German cannon, a deadly new weapon.[17] The explosives were not powerful enough to level a neighborhood, but they were enough, the enemy hoped, to demoralize the French and force a surrender.

These were the unearthly explosions that Debussy heard for five days, as he lay dying.

Durand visited the house on the avenue du Bois de Boulogne, hoping to see his friend one last time. Debussy said how pleased he was to see him. He described the horror of the night before, when the explosions were so close. Emma and Chouchou wanted to take him down to the relative safety of the cellar, but he hadn't the strength to get out of bed, he told Durand, and his wife and child wouldn't leave him. He was tormented by his pain, by his incapacity, by the deafening sound of the bombs and the cries in the street, by the abysmal despair of so many citizens. Durand tried to reassure him. He told Claude, without evidence or conviction, that his health would improve. Debussy thanked him, then peered at Durand "with eyes which could already see beyond this life." Claude said it was over. He knew it. It was only a matter of hours. The ailing man moved, tried to embrace Durand. Then he asked for a cigarette, "his last consolation."[18]

Debussy died during the evening of March 25, 1918. At his side were his wife and child and three friends: Roger-Ducasse, Caplet, and Vallery-Radot.

Chouchou's Letter

Weeks later, Raoul Bardac, fighting at the front, received a letter from his step-sister, who was then twelve and a half years old. Chouchou had already sent him a telegram informing him of Debussy's death. Now, in her letter, she tells Raoul about that night, when Emma was called to Claude's bedside, "because the nurse thought he was 'very bad.'" Chouchou wrote:

> We sent at once for two doctors and they both said he should have an injec-tion to stop the pain. I understood then—Roger-Ducasse was there and said to me, "Chouchou, come and kiss your Papa." At once I thought it was all over. When I went back into the bedroom, Papa was asleep, breathing regularly but very shallowly. He went on sleeping like that until ten o'clock in the evening and then, gently, like an angel, he went to sleep for ever.
>
> I can't describe what happened afterwards. A flood of tears was building up behind my eyes but I forced them back because of Mama. All that night,

alone in her great bed, I couldn't sleep for a minute. I had a fever, and with dry eyes I gazed at the walls and couldn't bring myself to believe the truth! . . .

I saw him one last time in that horrible box—lying on the ground. He looked happy, so happy, and then I couldn't control my tears. . . . At the cemetery Mama, naturally, couldn't have behaved better and as for me, all I could think of was, "I mustn't cry because of Mama." . . . Tears restrained are worth as much as tears shed, and now it is night for ever. Papa is dead. Those three words, I don't understand them or rather I understand them too well. And to be the only one here struggling with Mama's indescribable grief is truly terrible—for several days it's made me forget my own, but now I feel it more bitterly than ever. You're so far away, Raoul! Think occasionally of your poor little sister who would like to embrace you so much and tell you she loves you. Can you understand all I feel but can't put into words?

A thousand kisses and all my love

Your little sister

Chouchou[19]

"Coming in these days through which we are living," wrote J. G. Prod'homme in an obituary, "[Debussy's] death will arouse emotion in the little world of musicians only, for the general public cares less than ever at the present time for any art but the art of war." He then writes of "the too short career of a composer whom the future will judge more calmly than his contemporaries and who will hold, whether people like it or not, the chief place in our musical history of this quarter of the century."[20]

Farther afield, the great French composer was more unreservedly mourned. The director of the Santa Cecilia Academy in Rome wrote that Italians owed their musical renaissance to Debussy, in whom they found their "spiritual roots and flowers." In Spain, Falla interrupted a concert to declare that Debussy was "a Latin, one of our own people . . . immortal and unconquerable."[21]

The French composer and music critic Gaston Carraud reclaimed Debussy for France. Léon Vallas wrote that Carraud considered Debussy "so essentially national that he was misunderstood in other countries. He . . . was national in the extraordinary subtlety of his most intimate emotions, in his very vision, so to speak, and in his delicate conception of form. . . . [Carraud] described how, between the years 1892 and 1905, roughly speaking, this Frenchman . . . 'overthrew the very foundations of musical art, destroyed its highways, opened up a horizon of almost illimitable discoveries, at the same time renewing the entire material of musical expression.' . . . [Debussy's music] separated the music of the twentieth century from that of the nineteenth, in the same manner as the art of Beethoven . . . separated the nineteenth and eighteenth centuries."[22]

Debussy's funeral was held on March 28, 1918. Among the twenty or so who attended, besides his family, were André Caplet, Paul Dukas, Henri de Régnier, Louis Laloy, Camille Chevillard, and Gabriel Pierné. Many others had fled the city or were too frightened to venture into the streets. Alfred Debussy, Claude's brother, left the trenches of war and arrived in time for the funeral procession. The small group of mourners was led by France's minister of education. Above them was a gray sky from which, at any time, metal cylinders might fall to the ground and explode.

It was Debussy's wish to be buried at the cemetery at Passy, in the 16th arrondissement. He thought it less gloomy than elsewhere and wanted to "lie there," he said, "among the trees and the birds."[23] But the family hadn't bought a plot, so he was interred temporarily at Père-Lachaise Cemetery. A year later his body was moved to Passy.

Epilogue

Eighteen months after Debussy's death, Emma wrote a letter to Arthur Hartmann and his wife:

> My God! How can I tell you—it's so dreadful—and to write it myself, what torture. Chouchou, my sweet and beautiful little girl, my radiant and adored Chouchou—in four days is gone. From diphtheria or meningitis—the doctors don't know—they know nothing. My whole treasure, my whole life, all that remained most precious to me—the living image of her father—gone, as well.
>
> Weep for her—made for life with all her youth, her health, her intelligence.
>
> Weep for her—and have pity on me![24]

APPENDIX A

PEOPLE PASSING THROUGH

Do you ever wonder what happened to certain people who pass through a book you've read and disappear from view? Here are some who played a role in Debussy's story.

Serge Diaghilev (1872–1929). After the war, Diaghilev and the Ballets Russes continued to produce brilliant new modern ballets, though they never again enjoyed the fabulous acclaim of their first Paris seasons. The impresario died in Venice, as he had once predicted. The Ballets Russes disbanded but spawned two competing companies (Ballet Russe de Monte Carlo; Original Ballet Russe) led by members of Diaghilev's company.

Gaby Dupont (1866–1945). After Gaby left Debussy, Count de Balbiani set her up in "a sumptuous apartment on avenue Kiel. . . . She shared her charms with more than one man whose name could be found in the Paris social register," wrote Victor Seroff.[1] In 1910 she bought a house in Orbec, in lower Normandy. In later years, she visited her friends in Paris less and less and lived a quiet life in her small town.

Mary Garden (1874–1967). Garden was the first genuine diva of the twentieth century. After her success in *Pelléas et Mélisande*, she sang many roles at the Opéra-Comique, in Aix-les-Bains, and in London. In 1907, she began dividing her time between the United States and France. By 1910 she was in Chicago, and over the next twenty years she performed for two of the city's opera companies, then served as director of the newly established Chicago Civic Opera. She retired from the stage in 1934, made recordings, gave chatty lectures about her career, and often helped young singers launch their careers. She spent her last decades in Aberdeen, Scotland, where she was born.

Robert Godet (1866–1950). Godet was Debussy's intimate friend for twenty-eight years and was friendly with the Jewish Swiss-American composer Ernest Bloch, who called Godet "the most extraordinary man I ever met" and "the worst anti-Semite that ever existed."[2] Godet's French translation of Houston Stewart Chamberlain's 1899 treatise, *Foundations of the Nineteenth Century*, aligned Godet with the axis of anti-Semitism that reached from Wagner through Chamberlain to Hitler; the book was a facilitator of the Nazi rationale for Aryan supremacy and the extermination of the Jews. When Godet's translation was published in 1913, Bloch found the work highly offensive, and their friendship was dissolved. It is not clear if Debussy, whose second wife was Jewish, knew anything about Godet's anti-Semitism.

Edward H. House (1836–1901). House's reporting on Japan's first diplomatic mission to the United States, in 1860, sparked in him a passionate interest in Meiji-era Japan, a country in transition from medieval feudalism to an industrial, imperial power. After his brush with Wagner in 1861, House developed a strong friendship with Mark Twain, then settled in Japan for many years. He edited an English-language newspaper in Tokyo, introduced Western music to Japan, and became a leading voice in educating the American people about this previously isolated and impenetrable culture.[3]

Georgette Leblanc (1869–1941). Leblanc, when very young, had been married briefly to a Spanish Catholic; unable to obtain a divorce, she was never free to marry Maurice Maeterlinck. Poet and singer lived together for many years, and the public believed they were husband and wife. Leblanc sang Debussy's Mélisande for the first time in Boston in 1912. Her relationship with Maeterlinck ended in 1918. By then, Georgette's star was fading, though she continued to act and sing and wrote several books.

Georges Louis (1847–1917). After a distinguished career in the French foreign office, Pierre Louÿs's brother was named ambassador to Russia in 1908. In 1912, he became embroiled in a diplomatic kerfuffle that brought worldwide attention to a rift between France and Russia and exposed controversial Russian activities in the Middle East. The affair caused a sensation when it was reported in the French press, and in February 1913, under pressure from the Russian foreign ministry, President Raymond Poincaré recalled Louis to Paris. Though Louis's role in the crisis was probably exaggerated, the "Georges Louis affair," and its contribution to international tensions in the run-up to the First World War, was debated by historians for many years after.

Pierre Louÿs (1870–1925). After *Les Aventures du roi Pausole* (1901), Louÿs's writing gained little attention, though several stage plays, operas, and films were based on his novels; Luis Buñuel's 1977 film, *That Obscure Object of Desire*, derives from Louÿs's *La Femme et le Pantin*. The marriage of Pierre and Louise was fraught with difficulties. Louÿs's free-spending habits and sporadic earnings often left them impoverished; his philandering was exasperating and sometimes cruel. By 1913 Louise was suffering from tuberculosis, and she obtained a divorce. Two years later she married Count Gilbert de Voisins. From 1914 to 1920, Louÿs had an affair with a young Montmartre dancer, Claudine Rolland, who died in 1921. In the same year, Claudine's half sister, Aline Steenackers, gave birth to a child fathered by Louÿs. Louÿs became gravely ill, but he rallied and resumed an extravagant and self-destructive, drug-addled life. His physical and mental health deteriorated rapidly. Three days after his funeral, Aline gave birth to their third child.[4]

Maurice Maeterlinck (1862–1949). Maeterlinck wrote more than twenty plays, most of them with prominent roles for Georgette Leblanc, but they are rarely revived today; his earliest plays, including *Pelléas et Mélisande*, remain his most influential. His relationship with Georgette had a long run, from 1895 to 1918, but in 1919 he married a young woman he'd been in love with for years. In 1912, he was awarded the Nobel Prize for literature.

Vaslav Nijinsky (1888–1950). After marrying Romola de Pulszky in September 1913, Nijinsky was fired from the Ballets Russes by Diaghilev, his betrayed and angry lover. The newlyweds settled in Budapest, and when the war began, Nijinsky was placed under house arrest as an enemy alien. Diaghilev, wanting his star to dance with the Ballets Russes on a North American tour, enlisted the king of Spain, President Woodrow Wilson, and others to have Nijinsky released by the Hungarians in 1916. After the war, Nijinksy began showing clear signs of schizophrenia. He never again danced in public. The most famous dancer in the world spent most of the next thirty years in Swiss mental hospitals.

Marguerite Pelouze-Wilson (1836–1928). By 1879, the summer of Debussy's employment, Pelouze-Wilson was not only the mistress of Chenonceau, but also of the French president, Jules Grévy. Grévy's daughter was married to Pelouze-Wilson's brother, Daniel Wilson Jr., a minister in Grévy's government.

The entanglement was made more consequential some years later when Wilson was caught selling unauthorized Legion of Honor awards for up to 25,000 francs each. The scandal precipitated Grévy's resignation in 1887. A year later, Pelouze-Wilson, deeply in debt, was forced to sell her château.

André Poniatowski (1864–1954). After marrying the heiress Elizabeth Sperry in 1894, Poniatowski, with the backing of the Crocker family and European investors, bought several productive California gold mines in the Mother Lode of the Sierra Nevada. He built the Sierra Railroad to haul the ores and supply the miners, then he built the Electra hydroelectric power plant on the Mokelumne River to supply electricity to the mines; service was later extended to Oakland, San Jose, and San Francisco. At 219 miles, it was the longest span of electric power lines then in existence.[5] Poniatowski and Elizabeth moved to Paris in 1904 and raised four sons. The prince, a successful financier when the First World War began, served in the French army as a liaison officer.[6] Curiously, the *New York Times*, on August 7, 1911, breathlessly reported that Princess Elizabeth Poniatowski had died two weeks after she and her sister attended the coronation of King George V in London. The obituary was premature. Elizabeth died in 1943.

Arthur Rimbaud (1854–1891). Before he was twenty-one, Rimbaud gave up writing and spent most of his adult life in exotic outposts far from France—as a soldier in the Dutch Colonial Army in Java, as a stone-quarry foreman in Cyprus, as a coffee exporter in East Africa—before dying of cancer at thirty-seven.

Erik Satie (1866–1925). Satie was saddened by the death of Debussy, perhaps more so as time went on. For the Debussy homage in 1920, he wrote a mournful chanson on a poem by Lamartine: "What to me are these valleys, palaces, cottages, / Useless things whose charm for me has fled? / Rivers, rocks, forests, solitude so precious, / One person is missing and the world is empty."[7] After Satie's raucous *Parade*, the serene *Socrate* showed another side of his creativity, but some admirers thought it was another of his sly jokes. He drank more and more. A few of his last works enhanced his standing as a pioneer, but his reputation suffered as new questions were raised about his essentially musical, as opposed to his visionary, importance. Satie died of cirrhosis of the liver, complicated by pneumonia. He was mourned by many friends, including Milhaud, Picasso, Brancusi, and Cocteau, as well as the townspeople of Arcueil.

Paul Verlaine (1844–1896). While in prison after shooting Rimbaud, he converted to Roman Catholicism but continued to live a life of alcoholism and debauchery, which led to long periods in hospitals. He died a pauper at fifty-two, but by that time his poetry had won a vast following. His funeral was a public event attended by thousands of mourners.

James Whistler (1834–1903). Stéphane Mallarmé, Whistler's close friend, used his cultural influence to persuade French government officials of the artist's genius. Enlisting the support of art critics, gallery owners, Claude Monet, and Georges Clemenceau, Mallarmé prevailed upon the fine arts minister to pay 4,000 francs for Whistler's *Arrangement in Gray and Black, No. 1*, painted in 1871, to be hung in the Musée du Luxembourg, in Paris. It was a great coup for the American artist, though he'd been hoping for the Louvre, not the Luxembourg.[8] The painting, colloquially known as *Whistler's Mother*, is one of the most famous artworks by any American. It now hangs in the Musée d'Orsay, in Paris.

THE SONGS OF BILITIS
Pierre Louÿs

The texts of the three poems Debussy set to music for *Trois Chansons de Bilitis*, translated by the author.

"La Flûte de Pan" (The Panpipes)

For the day of the Hyacinthes, he gave me a syrinx made of well-cut reeds, held together with white wax that is sweet as honey on my lips.

He teaches me to play, seated upon his knees, but I am trembling a little. He plays after me, so softly that I can barely hear him.

We have nothing to say to each other, so near are we to one another; but our songs want to answer each other, and turn by turn our mouths are united on the flute.

It is late; here is the song of the green frogs that begins at nightfall. My mother will never believe that I stayed so long to search for my lost waistband.

"La Chevelure" (The Tresses)

He said to me, "Tonight I dreamed. I had your tresses around my neck. I had your hair like a black necklace around my neck and on my chest.

"I caressed it, and it was mine; and we were bound this way forever, our hair intertwined, our mouths together, like two laurels that have a single root.

"And little by little, it seemed to me, our limbs were so completely merged, that I became you, or that you had entered into me like my dream."

When he had finished, he gently put his hands on my shoulders, and he looked at me so tenderly, that I lowered my eyes, with a shiver.

"Le Tombeau des naïades" (The Tomb of the Naiads)

Through the wood covered with frost, I walked; my hair in front of my mouth bloomed with little icicles, and my sandals were heavy with muddy, packed snow.

He asks me: "What are you seeking?" "I am on the trail of the satyr. His little cloven hoofs alternate like holes in a white mantle."

He says to me: "The satyrs are dead. The satyrs and the nymphs also. For thirty years there has not been a winter so terrible. The trail that you see is that of a goat. But let us remain here, where their tomb is."

And with the iron of his hoe he broke the ice on the spring where the naiads once laughed. He took big, cold pieces of ice and, raising them up to the pale sky, he looked through them.

APPENDIX C

PELLÉAS ET MÉLISANDE: SYNOPSIS

MAURICE MAETERLINCK AND CLAUDE DEBUSSY

This synopsis is based on the libretto published in 1903 and performed by the Opéra-Comique in the early twentieth century.

Act 1, Scene 1—A forest in the remote, mythical land of Allemonde. Prince Golaud has lost his way while hunting a boar. He sees a young woman, Mélisande, beside a fountain, into which her golden crown has fallen. She has run away from people who have harmed her. She is lost, weeping, frightened, ready to throw herself into the well if Golaud touches her. But night is falling, dangers lurk in the forest, and she agrees to go home with the tall, graying, kindly stranger.

Act 1, Scene 2—Months later. A room in Arkel's castle. Arkel, king of Allemonde, is a very old, nearly blind man. Geneviève, daughter-in-law of Arkel and mother of Pelléas, reads a letter Pelléas has received from Golaud, his half brother. Golaud, whose wife has died and left him with a young child, has married Mélisande, and asks Arkel's permission to bring her to the castle. Pelléas wants to make a journey to a friend who is dying; but Arkel asks him to stay because Pelléas's father is also very ill and because Golaud is coming to introduce his young wife.

Act 1, Scene 3—A garden, shrouded by trees that envelop the castle in gloom. Geneviève and Mélisande look out to the sea, where the sky is less gloomy. Pelléas enters. They watch a ship leaving the harbor—the ship that brought Mélisande to Allemonde. Geneviève leaves to look after Golaud's son, Yniold. It's getting dark; a storm is coming and the ship is sailing into dangerous seas. Pelléas tells Mélisande he may be leaving in the morning. She asks, why?

Act 2, Scene 1—A well in the park. It's a very hot day, but the deep well holds icy water. Pelléas tells Mélisande that the well once had miraculous powers to heal the blind. Mélisande leans over to wet her hands, and her long hair tumbles into the water. She tosses her wedding ring up in the air, repeatedly, and catches it, until at the stroke of noon it falls into the bottomless well. What should she tell Golaud? "The truth," Pelléas replies.

Act 2, Scene 2—A room in the castle. Golaud is lying on his bed, having been thrown from his horse at the stroke of noon. He is not badly hurt. Mélisande cries, because living in the dreary castle makes her unhappy. Has someone offended her? Has Pelléas? No, she says, but she thinks Pelléas dislikes her. Golaud asks why her ring is gone from her finger. She lies, telling him it slipped off in a cave by the sea, but the tide was rising so she couldn't look for it. The ring was very important to Golaud, and he orders her to return immediately to find it, even though darkness has fallen. He tells her to ask Pelléas to accompany her.

Act 2, Scene 3—At the mouth of the cave, so dark that Mélisande and Pelléas cannot enter. Soon the moon floods the cave with light. Three white-haired paupers are asleep inside. There is famine in the land. Mélisande is afraid, and they leave.

Act 3, Scene 1—A tower of the castle; evening. Mélisande sits at an open window, combing her long hair and singing a folklike song. Pelléas enters on a path under the window. He asks her to lean out so he can touch her hand; he wants to kiss it. He is leaving in the morning. She says she won't lean unless he promises not to leave. He says he'll stay. She leans as far as she can, and her long hair cascades down from the window and envelops Pelléas. Thrilled, he kisses her hair passionately. Her hair becomes tangled in a tree branch. Mélisande's doves escape from the tower and fly away. She pleads with him to let go of her hair. Golaud enters and laughs at them, playing like children; he takes Pelléas away with him.

Act 3, Scene 2—The dark vaults beneath the castle. Golaud leads Pelléas there, apparently to frighten him, and points to the pools of stagnating water with the stench of death. Pelléas is gasping for air and wants to leave.

Act 3, Scene 3—A terrace at the entrance to the vaults. Pelléas is happy to breathe the fresh sea air. Golaud tells him he overheard Pelléas and Mélisande the previous night and knows there is something between them. She is pregnant, and he instructs Pelléas to stay away from her.

Act 3, Scene 4—Outside the castle. Below the window of Mélisande's room, Golaud questions little Yniold, who has been spending all his time with Mélisande, his stepmother. He wants Yniold to say whether she has often been with Pelléas. Yes. Do they quarrel? Yes, they quarrel about the door, that it must not be kept open. Golaud's insistence makes Yniold cry; he promises the boy a gift if he answers honestly. What do they talk about? Me, always of me, they say I'm very big. Golaud is losing patience. Don't they tell Yniold to go and play? No, *petit-père* [dear little father], they're afraid to have me go away, *petit-père*. A light goes on in the room. Golaud lifts the boy high above him to look through the window, to spy. Yes, Pelléas is with Mélisande in the room; they're not speaking. Golaud is enraged by the boy's answers, and Yniold is frightened: *petit-père*, put me down!

Act 4, Scene 1—A room in the castle. Pelléas's father is feeling better, and the castle seems more cheerful. But his father has seen the look of impending death on his son's face and wants him to embark on a voyage. Pelléas asks Mélisande to meet him that night at the well—a final rendezvous because he's leaving in the morning and won't return. They exit.

Act 4, Scene 2—Arkel tells Mélisande he's sorry that she's been confined to such a gloomy castle for so long, that she seems always waiting for some dreadful doom. Golaud enters, searching for his sword, hinting that he's discovered something about Mélisande. He's on the edge of madness and chastises her for every gesture. He grabs her by the hair, forces her to her knees, and drags her by the hair across the floor. He suddenly grows calm and says he'll leave their fate to chance. Arkel: "If I were God, I'd have pity on the hearts of men."

Act 4, Scene 3—A terrace, twilight. Yniold has lost his ball under a big boulder and can't reach it. He hears the bleating of a flock of sheep and thinks they're crying and frightened; he does not understand they're being led to slaughter.

Act 4, Scene 4—The fountain in the park, late at night. Pelléas, in a soliloquy, says he's been childishly playing with the snares of destiny. But he's awakened, and with both joy and dismay he will flee as if his home were on fire. She's not here yet; maybe he should go. He wants to look into the depths of her heart, to say things he has never told her. Mélisande enters, out of breath. For the first time they acknowledge their love for one another; she has loved him since they first met, but he is leaving her tomorrow. He sees her loveliness as if for the first time. The castle doors clang, locked for the night; it's too late to go back. Thank God! she replies. They kiss. Their hearts are pounding. She hears a noise nearby—it's Golaud, coming their way! They embrace, with wild passion and despair. They kiss again, defiantly. Golaud enters suddenly and kills Pelléas with his sword. Mélisande flees in terror, and Golaud pursues her.

Act 5—A room in the castle. Mélisande lies asleep in her bed, gravely ill. The physician tells her anguished husband that she won't die of the wound he inflicted. Golaud suspects that she and Pelléas were as innocent as children and that his actions were unjustified. She awakes and asks that the window be opened; the sun is setting on the sea. She says she's never felt better, but she's confused. Golaud asks Mélisande's forgiveness, but she doesn't know why. He says all that has happened to her has been his fault, but he loved her so! He says he's going to die but he wants first to know the truth: Did she love Pelléas? She says she did. Did she love him with a forbidden love? Was she ever guilty? No, neither of them was guilty—why does he ask? He doesn't believe her. He tells her they're both going to die but first he wants the truth. She drifts into sleep. Golaud is desperate. She awakens, tells Arkel she's cold, winter is coming. He tells her she has had a child, a daughter. A nurse brings the infant, but Mélisande is too weak to take her. Maidservants file into the room, ominously. Mélisande drifts silently into sleep, into death. She was such a quiet little creature, says Arkel—a lonely, mysterious being, as we all are. The child will now replace her, it's the poor little creature's turn.

NOTES

Prelude: December 22, 1894

1. Arthur Johnstone, *Musical Criticisms* (Manchester: University of Manchester Press, 1905), 28.

2. Joseph Kerman, ed., *Music at the Turn of the Century: A 19th Century Music Reader*, (Oakland: University of California Press, 1990), 162: "The actual *Prélude* was performed at the end of a long and varied program (Glazunov's *La Forêt*, Bordier's *Suite Serbe*, Duparc's *La Vague et la cloche*, Bourgault-Ducoudray's *L'Enterrement d'Ophélie*, Saint-Saëns's Third Violin Concerto, Guy Ropartz's *Prière*, and Franck's *Redemption*)." Another source—Michel Duchesneau, *L'Avant-garde musicale et ses sociétés à Paris de 1871 à 1939* (Sprimont: Mardaga, 1999)—lists the same works in a different sequence. I have found no definitive program sequence for this concert, but Edward Lockspeiser agrees with the Kerman version.

3. Lawrence Gilman, *Century*, May–October 1918, 465–471.

4. Ibid.

5. Léon Vallas, *Claude Debussy: His Life and Works*, trans. Maire O'Brien and Grace O'Brien (New York: Dover, 1973), 11. The quote is from a report by Alfred Bruneau.

6. Marcel Dietschy, *A Portrait of Claude Debussy*, ed. and trans. William Ashbrook and Margaret G. Cobb (Oxford: Clarendon Press, 1990), 93.

7. Claude Debussy, *Debussy on Music*, trans. and ed. Richard Langham Smith (New York: Alfred A. Knopf, 1977), 248. From an interview with Henry Malherbe in *Excelsior*, February 11, 1911.

8. Quoted by Gilman, *Century*, May–October 1918.

9. Ibid.

10. Vallas, *Claude Debussy*, 115.

11. Edward Lockspeiser, *Debussy: His Life and Mind*, vol. 1, Appendix B (Cambridge: Cambridge University Press, 1978), 206–207.

Chapter 1: A Confluence of Circumstance (1862–1884)

1. Debussy, letter to André Caplet, December 22, 1911; in Dietschy, *A Portrait of Claude Debussy*, 1.

2. Ibid., 14–15.

3. Vallas, *Claude Debussy*, 3n.

4. "Debussy Discusses Music and His Work," interview, *New York Times*, June 26, 1910.

5. Roger Nichols, *Debussy Remembered* (Portland, OR: Amadeus Press), 13.

6. Ibid., 4.

7. Ibid., 14.

8. Lockspeiser, *Debussy*, 1:26.

9. Nichols, *Debussy Remembered*, 5.

10. Lockspeiser, *Debussy*, 1:29.

11. Centre de Documentation Claude Debussy, http://www.debussy.fr/encd/bio/bio1_62-82.php.

12. "Debussy Discusses Music and His Work."

13. Memoir by Robert Burnand, quoted in Lockspeiser, *Debussy*, 1:37.

14. Nichols, *Debussy Remembered*, 14.

15. Ibid., 15.

16. Lockspeiser, *Debussy*, 1:46.

17. Debussy's first published work was one of his several piano arrangements of Tchaikovsky's orchestral music. It was published in Russia. The score of Debussy's Symphony in B Minor was discovered many years later and published, also in Russia, in 1933. John Trevitt, "Debussy Inconnu: The Later Vocal and the Instrumental Music," *Musical Times* 114, no. 1568 (October 1973): 881–886.

18. Nichols, *Debussy Remembered*, 15.

19. Ibid., 17.

20. Ibid., 14.

21. Ibid., 17–21. Quotes in this and the following four paragraphs are from this source.

22. Lockspeiser, *Debussy*, 1:69. "The original violin version of the *Nocturne et scherzo* has disappeared, but the music was preserved in an arrangement that Debussy made for cello and piano the following month"; Richard E. Rodda, notes for the Chamber Music Society of Lincoln Center.

23. Roger Nichols, *The Life of Debussy* (Cambridge: Cambridge University Press, 1998), 25.

24. From Debussy's song "Regret," on a poem by Paul Bourget; author's translation.

Chapter 2: Darling of the Gods (1884–1887)

1. Debussy, writing in the voice of his fictional interlocutor, "Monsieur Croche"; Claude Debussy, *Monsieur Croche, the Dilettante Hater*, trans. B. N. Langdon Davies (New York: Lear, 1928), 18–21.

2. Hector Berlioz, *The Life of Hector Berlioz: As Written by Himself in His Letters and Memoirs*, translated by Katherine F. Boult (New York: E. P. Dutton, 1903), 64.

3. Ibid., 65.

4. Ibid., 66.

5. Ibid., 78–79.

6. Ibid., 81.

7. Ibid., 87.

8. Debussy, *Debussy on Music*, 211–214.

9. Erik Satie, *A Mammal's Notebook: Collected Writings of Erik Satie*, ed. Ornella Volta, trans. Antony Melville (London: Atlas Press, 1996), 121.

10. Erik Satie, *The Writings of Erik Satie*, ed. and trans. Nigel Wilkins (London: Eulenburg Books, 1980), 93.

11. David Grayson, "Debussy on Stage," in *The Cambridge Companion to Debussy*, ed. Simon Trezise (Cambridge: Cambridge University Press, 2003), 63.

12. Edmond Stoullig and Édouard Noël, *Les Annales du théâtre et de la musique* (Paris, 1883), quoted in J. G. Prod'homme, "Claude Achille Debussy," trans. Marguerite Barton, *Musical Quarterly* 4, no. 4 (October 1918): 555–571.

13. Berlioz too, after winning the prize in 1830, did everything possible to avoid going to Rome so as not to disrupt his love affair with Camille Moke. He appealed to the minister of the interior but was rejected despite the support of Spontini, Meyerbeer, and other important musicians; and despite a medical certificate alleging that his high-strung temperament and fragile nerves would find the Roman climate unwholesome.

14. Nichols, *Debussy Remembered*, 21–23. The quotes in the following three paragraphs are from this source.

15. Ibid.

16. Edmond Stoullig and Édouard Noël, *Les Annales du théâtre et de la musique* (Paris, 1884), quoted in Prod'homme, "Claude Achille Debussy," 555–571.

17. Nichols, *Debussy Remembered*, 21–23.

18. Arthur B. Wenk, *Claude Debussy and Twentieth-Century Music* (Boston: Twayne, 1983), 21–23.

19. Nichols, *Debussy Remembered*, 24–25.

20. Debussy, *Debussy on Music*, 211–214.

21. The pines of the Villa Borghese were memorialized in the first movement of Ottorino Respighi's orchestral suite *The Pines of Rome*. The fountain in the gardens of the Villa Medici was similarly honored in the last movement of Respighi's *The Fountains of Rome*. The "waste fields" of the Villa Borghese have since become one of the largest and most popular public parks in Rome.

22. Berlioz, *Life*, 147.

23. Debussy, *Debussy on Music*, 211–112.

24. Ibid., 212.

25. Ibid., 213.

26. François Lesure and Roger Nichols, eds., *Debussy Letters*, trans. Roger Nichols (Cambridge, MA: Harvard University Press, 1987), 5.

27. Roger Nichols, *The Life of Debussy* (Cambridge: Cambridge University Press, 1998), 34.

28. Debussy, *Debussy on Music*, 213.

29. Lesure and Nichols, *Debussy Letters*, 5.

30. Ibid., 8.

31. Ibid., 10–11.

32. Ibid., 10.

33. Lockspeiser, *Debussy*, 1:84.

34. Lesure and Nichols, *Debussy Letters*, 14–15.

35. Ibid., 14.

36. Margaret G. Cobb and Richard Miller, "Claude Debussy to Claudius and Gustave Popelin: Nine Unpublished Letters," *19th-Century Music* 13, no. 1 (Summer 1929): 39–48.

37. Ibid.

38. Ibid.

39. Ibid.

40. Lockspeiser, *Debussy*, 1:85.

41. Nichols, *The Life of Debussy*, 30.

42. Lesure and Nichols, *Debussy Letters*, 8.

43. Ibid., 13.

44. Ibid., 13.

45. Ibid., 15.

46. Ibid., 13.

47. Charles Baudelaire, *Paris Spleen*, trans. Keith Waldrop (Middletown, CT: Wesleyan University Press, 2009).

48. Nichols, *The Life of Debussy*, 34.

49. Lesure and Nichols, *Debussy Letters*, 13.

50. Ibid., 20–21.

51. Ibid., 20.

52. Debussy, *Debussy on Music*, 50n.

53. Ibid., 50n.

54. Ibid., 50n.

55. Stefan Jarocinski, *Debussy: Impressionism and Symbolism*, trans. Rollo Myers (London: Eulenburg, 1976).

56. Ibid., 13.

57. Lesure and Nichols, *Debussy Letters*, 22.

58. Lockspeiser, *Debussy*, 1:76.

Chapter 3: Debussy and the French Poets (1880–1891)

1. James Huneker, *Bedouins* (New York: Charles Scribner's Sons, 1920).

2. Jack Sullivan, *New World Symphonies: How American Culture Changed European Music* (New Haven, CT: Yale University Press, 1999), 66.

3. Jean Moréas, *Symbolist Manifesto* (1886).

4. Robert T. Nealy, "Endymion in France: A Brief Survey of French Symbolist Poetry," in *Les Mardis: Stéphane Mallarmé and the Artists of His Circle*, exhibition catalog (Lawrence: University of Kansas Museum of Art, 1966), 26.

5. Philip Stephan, *Paul Verlaine and the Decadence: 1882–90* (Manchester: University of Manchester Press, 1974), 2.

6. James L. Connelly, "The World of Mallarmé's Circle: The Historical Ambiance, 1870–1914," in *Les Mardis: Stéphane Mallarmé and the Artists of His Circle*, 12.

7. Ibid., 12.

8. Arthur Wenk, *Debussy and the Poets* (Berkeley and Los Angeles: University of California Press, 1976), 23–24.

9. Ibid., 35.

10. Sandrine Piau, interview by Michael Quinn, *Gramophone* (September 2003).

11. From Banville's "Petit Traité de Poésie Français" (Paris, 1888), quoted in Wenk, *Debussy and the Poets*, 10; author's translation.

12. Paul Verlaine, "Clair de lune"; author's translation.

Chapter 4: The Tyranny of Richard Wagner

1. Claude Debussy, "*Parsifal* and the Société des Grandes Auditions de France," *Gil Blas*, April 6, 1903; trans. B. Langdon Davies, "Richard Wagner," in *Monsieur Croche*, 130.

2. "French Hatred of Germany," *New York Times*, May 6, 1887.

3. Debussy's attendance on that night was a supposition made in Dietschy, *A Portrait of Claude Debussy*, 48.

4. "The Death Roll Swelling; Terrible Results of the Opera Comique Fire," *New York Times*, May 27, 1887.

5. Romain Rolland, *Musicians of To-day*, trans. Mary Blaiklock (New York: Henry Holt, 1914), 251.

6. Leon Botstein, "Paris in the 1860s: The Origins of Impressionism," concert notes for the American Symphony Orchestra (1994).

7. Edward H. House, "Wagner and Tannhäuser in Paris, 1861," *New England Magazine* (1891), http://users.gelgacom.net/wagnerlibrary/articles/. House's account and Wagner's are the basis of the *Tannhäuser* episode.

8. Richard Wagner, "A Report on the Production of 'Tannhäuser' in Paris," trans. William Ashton Ellis, in T*he Theatre: Richard Wagner's Prose Works*, vol. 3 (1894), http://users.gelcacom.net/wagnerlibrary/prose/index.htm.

9. "Letters from Judith Gautier to Chalmers Clifton," ed. Elaine Brody, *French Review* 58, no. 5 (April 1985): 670–674.

10. Botstein, "Paris in the 1860s."

11. Steven Huebner, "Debussy, Wagner, and *Le roi Arthus*," concert notes for the American Symphony Orchestra (2001).

12. Josiah Fisk, ed., *Composers on Music: Eight Centuries of Writings*, 2nd ed. (Boston: Northeastern University Press, 1997), 148.

13. Christopher John Murray, ed., *Encyclopedia of the Romantic Era, 1760–1850* (Chicago: Fitzroy Dearborn, 2004), 1202.

14. Kuno Francke, *Social Forces in German Literature* (New York: Henry Holt, 1897).

15. Daniel Coit Oilman, Harry Thurston Peck, and Frank Moore Colby, eds., *The New International Encyclopedia*, vol. 14 (New York: Dodd, Mead, 1905).

16. Béla Bartók, *Béla Bartók Essays*, ed. Benjamin Suchoff (London: Faber & Faber, 1976), 505.

17. Dietschy, *A Portrait of Claude Debussy*, 27.

18. Ibid., 53.

19. Lockspeiser, *Debussy*, 1: Appendix B (conversations with Guiraud, 1889–90).

20. Dietschy, *A Portrait of Claude Debussy*, 53.

21. Lesure and Nichols, *Debussy Letters*, 45.

22. Claude Debussy, *Monsieur Croche, the Dilettante Hater*, trans. B. N. Langdon Davies (New York: Viking Press, 1928), 132.

23. Debussy, *Debussy on Music*, 66–67.

24. Ibid., 229.

25. Ibid., 74.

26. Lockspeiser, *Debussy*, 1:96–97.

27. Debussy, *Debussy on Music*, 243.

28. Ibid., 83.

Chapter 5: Transitions (1887–1890)

1. Claude Debussy, *Monsieur Croche, antidilettante* (Paris: Les Bibliophiles Fantaisistes, 1921), 49; author's translation.

2. Nichols, *Debussy Remembered*, 158–163.

3. Vallas, *Claude Debussy*, 70.

4. William W. Austin, ed., *Debussy: Prelude to "The Afternoon of a Faun"* (New York: W. W. Norton, 1970), 7.

5. Ernest Newman, "The Development of Debussy," *Musical Times* 59 (May 1, 1918): 199–203.

6. Vallas, *Claude Debussy*, 68.

7. Sullivan, *New World Symphonies*, 63–64, 68.

8. Lockspeiser, *Debussy*, 2:140.

9. Sullivan, *New World Symphonies*, 63.

10. Robert Orledge, *Debussy and the Theatre* (Cambridge: Cambridge University Press, 1982), 103.

11. The T. S. Eliot quotes come from Eliot's 1948 Library of Congress lecture and his subsequent article, "From Poe to Valéry," republished in Eliot, *To Criticize the Critic and Other Writings* (Lincoln: University of Nebraska Press, 1992), 27–41.

12. Edgar Allan Poe, "The Philosophy of Composition," *Graham's Magazine*, April 1846.

13. Edgar Allan Poe, "The Raven," *American Review*, February 1845.

14. Dante Gabriel Rossetti, "The Blessed Damozel," *The Germ*, February 1850.

15. Dietschy, *A Portrait of Claude Debussy*, 48–49.

16. Newman, "The Development of Debussy."

17. Wenk, *Claude Debussy and Twentieth-Century Music*, 26–30.

18. John R. Clevenger, "Debussy's Rome Cantatas," in *Debussy and His World*, ed. Jane F. Fulcher (Princeton, NJ: Princeton University Press, 2001), 10.

19. Orledge, *Debussy and the Theatre*, 41.

20. Vallas, *Claude Debussy*, 81.

21. Dietschy, *A Portrait of Claude Debussy*, 65.

Chapter 6: In the Shadow of Eiffel's Tower

1. Debussy, *SIM*, February 15, 1913; in Debussy, *Debussy on Music*, 278.

2. "The Great French Show," *New York Times*, May 19, 1889.

3. Ibid.

4. Debussy, *Debussy on Music*, 278–79.

5. Annegret Fauser, *Musical Encounters at the 1889 Paris World's Fair* (Rochester, NY: University of Rochester Press, 2005), 189.

6. Wenk, *Claude Debussy and Twentieth-Century Music*, 51.

7. Lesure and Nichols, *Debussy Letters*, 76.

8. Wenk, *Claude Debussy and Twentieth-Century Music*.

9. Henri Quittard, quoted in "The French Press and Debussy," *Musical Times* 59 (May 1, 1918).

10. Lawrence Gilman, *Debussy's Pelléas et Mélisande* (New York: G. Schirmer, 1907), chapter 1.

11. Nichols, *Debussy Remembered*, 7.

12. Debussy, *Debussy on Music*, 277.

13. Nichols, *Debussy Remembered*, 129.

14. Gilman, *Debussy's Pelléas*, chapter 1.

15. Nichols, *Debussy Remembered*, 134.

16. Debussy, *Debussy on Music*, 20.

17. Gilman, *Debussy's Pelléas*, chapter 1.

18. Sullivan, *New World Symphonies*, 67.

19. Nichols, *Debussy Remembered*, 5.

20. Philip H. Goepp, *Symphonies and Their Meaning: Third Series* (Philadelphia: J. B. Lippincott, 1913), chapter 9.

Chapter 7: New Friends, New Directions (1890–1893)

1. Narcisse Lebeau, "Souvenirs de Debussy"; in Nichols, *Debussy Remembered*, 40.

2. Ibid., 31.

3. Lesure and Nichols, *Debussy Letters*, 34.

4. Nichols, *Debussy Remembered*, 42.

5. He leased the apartment in June 1891, according to the Centre de Documentation Claude Debussy. Most biographers say he took the apartment in 1892.

6. Victor I. Seroff, *Debussy: Musician of France* (New York: Putnam, 1956; reprint, Freeport, NY: Books for Libraries Press, 1970), 355–358. An article by Seroff, "A Footnote on Debussy's 'Gaby,'" was first published in the *Saturday Review*, January 25, 1959. It was based on information about Gaby that came to light with the publication of an article by Henri Pellerin, founder and president of the Association Le Pays d'Auge. Pellerin, a historian, knew Gaby when she lived in Orbec late in her life, and his account revealed much new information. Seroff discovered Pellerin's article after publishing his own Debussy biography in 1956; he included his "Footnote" in the 1970 edition. It should be noted that Seroff wrote several biographies and was sometimes accused of factual carelessness.

7. Ibid.

8. Nichols, *Debussy Remembered*, 32–34.

9. Roger Nichols, *The Life of Debussy*, 61.

10. Nichols, *Debussy Remembered*, 32–34.

11. Seroff, *Debussy: Musician of France*, 355–358.

12. Lockspeiser, *Debussy*, 1:103–107.

13. Dietschy, *A Portrait of Claude Debussy*, 50.

14. Nichols, *Debussy Remembered*, 36.

15. "Goes Home Without a Bride; Prince Poniatowski Once More Sets Sail for Paris," *New York Times*, June 7, 1894.

16. *San Francisco Examiner*, [ca. 1895], http://www.sfgenealogy.com/sf/history/hbchd2.htm.

17. "Goes Home Without a Bride."

18. Lesure and Nichols, *Debussy Letters*, 37.

19. Ibid., 39.

20. Nichols, *Debussy Remembered*, 38–39.

21. Ninths are complex chords with an outer span of nine notes, which is one note more than an octave.

22. Satie, *A Mammal's Notebook*, 106.

23. Alan M. Gillmor, *Erik Satie* (Boston: Twayne, 1988), xix.

24. Robert Orledge, *Satie Remembered*, trans. Roger Nichols (London: Faber & Faber, 1995), 28.

25. Ibid., 24.

26. Parts of the Chat Noir description are drawn from Elizabeth Robins Pennell, *Nights* (Philadelphia: J. H. Lippincott, 1916). Pennell, an American journalist, wrote a memoir of her days and nights spent in Rome, Venice, and Paris, accompanied by her husband, the illustrator Joseph Pennell, in the late nineteenth century. Parts of her book were written on assignment for the *Atlantic Monthly*.

27. Orledge, *Satie Remembered*, 25.

28. Satie, *A Mammal's Notebook*, 122.

29. Ibid., 123.

30. Orledge, *Satie Remembered*, 29.

31. Mary E. Davis, *Erik Satie* (London: Reaktion Books, 2007), 55.

32. An interval of the fourth is defined as two notes separated by four half-tones—for example, C to the F above it, or E-flat to the A-flat above. An augmented fourth is separated by five half-tones—C to F-sharp, or E-flat to A-natural.

33. Dietschy, *A Portrait of Claude Debussy*, 75.

Chapter 8: Maeterlinck (1891–1893)

1. Debussy, *New York Times*, June 26, 1910.

2. Lesure and Nichols, *Debussy Letters*, 41.

3. Ibid., 43.

4. Ibid., 43n.

5. William Lyon Phelps, "An Estimate of Maeterlinck," *North American Review* 213 (January 1921).

6. John Russell Brown, ed., *The Oxford Illustrated History of Theatre* (Oxford: Oxford University Press, 2001), 357.

7. Montrose J. Moses, *Maurice Maeterlinck: A Study* (New York: Duffield, 1911), 94.

8. Wenk, *Claude Debussy and Twentieth-Century Music*, 36.

9. Maurice Maeterlinck, *Princess Maleine*, trans. Richard Hovey (New York: Dodd Mead, 1920), 9. Quotes are from Hovey's introduction, "Modern Symbolism and Maurice Maeterlinck."

10. Ibid., 194–195.

11. Gillian Opstad, *Debussy's Mélisande: The Lives of Georgette Leblanc, Mary Garden and Maggie Teyte* (Woodbridge: Boydell Press, 2009), 13.

12. Ibid., 15.

13. Debussy, *Debussy on Music*, 76.

14. Lesure and Nichols, *Debussy Letters*, 44.

15. Ibid., 46.

16. Ibid., 47.

17. Nichols, *Debussy Remembered*, 13.

18. Ibid., 10.

19. Debussy, *Debussy on Music*, 76n.

20. Lesure and Nichols, *Debussy Letters*, 51.

21. Lesure and Nichols, *Debussy Letters*, 51–52.

22. Ibid., 56.

23. Durand's catalog at that time included works by Franck, Saint-Saëns, and d'Indy, the early operas of Wagner, and much more. In the early 1890s, Durand published Debussy's early piano works, including *Petite Suite*, the two "Arabesques," and the two "Romances." Jacques Durand, the son of August Durand, a founder of the publishing company, was already a friend of Debussy and was soon to succeed his father as publisher.

24. Lesure and Nichols, *Debussy Letters*, 59.

25. Ibid., 60–61.

Chapter 9: The Debussy Festival (1893–1894)

1. Maurice Kufferath, review of Debussy's String Quartet for the *Guide Musical*, March 4, 1894; in Vallas, *Claude Debussy*, 98–99.

2. Dietschy, *A Portrait of Claude Debussy*, 78.

3. H. P. Clive, *Pierre Louÿs, 1870–1925: A Biography* (Oxford: Clarendon Press, 1978), 17. This book is the source of much of the material on Louÿs.

4. Ibid., 119–120.

5. Jacqueline M. Charette, ed. and trans., *Claude Debussy Through His Letters* (New York: Vantage Press, 1990), 31–32.

6. Ibid., 35.

7. Vallas, *Claude Debussy*, 90–91.

8. Ibid., 93.

9. Ibid., 94.

10. Ibid., 92.

11. David J. Code, "Debussy's String Quartet in the Brussels Salon of 'La Libre Esthetique,'" *19th-Century Music* 30, no. 3 (Spring 2007): 257–287.

12. Lesure and Nichols, *Debussy Letters*, 65.

13. Ibid., 64.

14. Dietschy, *A Portrait of Claude Debussy*, 87.

15. Ibid., 89.

16. Ibid., 89.

17. Ibid., 88.

18. Nichols, *Debussy Remembered*, 43–44.

19. Ibid., 44.

20. Code, "Debussy's String Quartet."

21. Lesure and Nichols, *Debussy Letters*, 67–68.

22. Nichols, *Debussy Remembered*, 44.

23. Ibid., 45.

24. Ibid., 45.

25. Dietschy, *A Portrait of Claude Debussy*, 89.

26. Nichols, *Debussy Remembered*, 46–47, emphasis added.

Chapter 10: Mallarmé and the Paris Salons (1890–1893)

1. Aved Poorten, *Testament d'un musicien* (Paris, 1890); in James Ross, "Music in the French Salon," in *French Music Since Berlioz*, ed. Richard Langham Smith and Caroline Potter (Aldershot: Ashgate, 2006), 93.

2. Ross, "Music in the French Salon," 91.

3. Klaus Berger, "Mallarmé and the Visual Arts," in *Les Mardis: Stéphane Mallarmé and the Artists of His Circle* (Lawrence: University of Kansas Museum of Art, 1966), 51.

4. Francis Grierson, *Parisian Portraits* (New York: John Lane, 1913), 94.

5. Rosemary Lloyd, *Mallarmé: The Poet and His Circle* (Ithaca, NY: Cornell University Press, 1999), 178.

6. Grierson, *Parisian Portraits*, 85.

7. Jules Huret, *Echo de Paris* (1891), quoted in Wenk, *Debussy and the Poets*, 242.

8. Lloyd, *Mallarmé*, 179.

9. Arthur Symons, *The Symbolist Movement in Literature* (New York: E. F. Dutton, 1919), 185.

10. Grierson, *Parisian Portraits*, 88.

11. Lloyd, *Mallarmé*, 180.

12. Ibid., 149.

13. Ibid.

14. Ibid.

15. Rollo Myers, "Augusta Holmès: A Meteoric Career," *Musical Quarterly* 53, no. 3 (June 1967): 365–376.

16. Debussy, *Debussy on Music*, 114.

17. Myers, "Augusta Holmès."

18. Lloyd, *Mallarmé*, 152.

19. Wenk, *Claude Debussy and Twentieth-Century Music*, 36.

20. Symons, *The Symbolist Movement*, 180–181.

21. Lockspeiser, *Debussy*, 1:150.

22. Quote found in Charles Rosen, "Mallarmé the Magnificent," *New York Review of Books*, May 20, 1999, http://www.nybooks.com/articles/archives/1999/may/20/mallarme-the-magnificent/.

23. Symons, *The Symbolist Movement*, 181.

24. Paul Valéry, in *Leonardo, Poe, Mallarmé*, trans. M. Cowley and J. R. Lawler (London: Routledge, 1972), quoted in Elizabeth McCombie, introduction to *Stéphane Mallarmé: Collected Poems and Other Verse*, trans. E. H. Blackmore and A. M. Blackmore (Oxford: Oxford World's Classics, 2006), ix.

25. Lloyd, *Mallarmé*, 152.

26. Ibid., 148.

27. William W. Austin, "The History of the Poem and the Music," in *Debussy: Prelude to "The Afternoon of a Faun,"* ed. William W. Austin (New York: Norton Critical Series, 1970), 11.

Chapter 11: The Faun

1. Pierre Boulez, *Notes of an Apprenticeship*, trans. Herbert Weinstock (New York: Knopf, 1968), 345.

2. Lockspeiser, *Debussy*, 1:152.

3. William W. Austin, ed., *Debussy: Prelude to "The Afternoon of a Faun"* (New York: Norton Critical Series, 1970), 4.

4. Lockspeiser, *Debussy*, 1:153–154.

5. Ibid., 1:154.

6. Ibid., 1:156.

7. Austin, *Debussy: Prelude*, 13.

8. Ibid., 12.

9. Lloyd, *Mallarmé*, 154.

10. Austin, *Debussy: Prelude*, 13.

11. Ibid., 13.

12. Lloyd, *Mallarmé*, 154.

13. Boulez, *Notes of an Apprenticeship*, 344.

14. Austin, *Debussy: Prelude*, 85.

15. Ibid., 13–14.

16. Boulez, *Notes of an Apprenticeship*, 344–345.

17. Austin, *Debussy: Prelude*, 146.

18. Vallas, *Claude Debussy*, 104.

19. Ibid.

20. Ibid., 104–105.

21. Cecilia Dunoyer, *Marguerite Long: A Life in French Music, 1874–1966* (Bloomington: Indiana University Press, 1993), 98.

22. Austin, *Debussy: Prelude*, 147–148.

23. Ibid., 150.

24. Vallas, *Claude Debussy*, 103–104.

25. Lockspeiser, *Debussy*, 1:158.

26. Vallas, *Claude Debussy*, 106.

Chapter 12: Mélisande (1894–1898)

1. Debussy, letter to Pierre Louÿs, February 23, 1895; in Lesure and Nichols, *Debussy Letters*, 77.

2. Claude Debussy and Maurice Maeterlinck, *Pelléas et Mélisande*, French-English libretto, trans. Henry Grafton Chapman (New York: G. Schirmer, 1907).

3. Lesure and Nichols, *Debussy Letters*, 54–55.

4. Orledge, *Debussy and the Theatre*, 52.

5. Vallas, *Claude Debussy*, 107.

6. Lesure and Nichols, *Debussy Letters*, 62.

7. Ibid., 70.

8. Ibid., 72.

9. Charette, *Claude Debussy Through His Letters*, 29.

10. Lesure and Nichols, *Debussy Letters*, 73.

11. Ibid., 75.

12. Nichols, *Debussy Remembered*, 11.

13. Lesure and Nichols, *Debussy Letters*, 76.

14. Dietschy, *A Portrait of Claude Debussy*, 94.

15. Lesure and Nichols, *Debussy Letters*, 80.

16. Ibid., 80–81.

17. Ibid., 80.

18. Arthur Hartmann, *Claude Debussy as I Knew Him, and Other Writings of Arthur Hartmann*, Samuel Hsu, Sidney Grolnic, and Mark Peters, eds. (Rochester, NY: University of Rochester Press, 2003), 254. In 1929, Hartmann, an American violinist who befriended Debussy before the war, purchased three letters written by Debussy to Pierre Louÿs. The letter quoted here was one of them.

19. Lesure and Nichols, *Debussy Letters*, 82.

20. Oscar Thompson, *Debussy, Man and Artist* (New York: Tudor, 1940), 123n. Mauclair's comments, according to a footnote, were published in "the souvenir program for the Debussy festival at the time of the dedication of the [Debussy] monument in the Bois de Boulogne."

21. Orledge, *Debussy and the Theatre*, 57.

22. Dietschy, *A Portrait of Claude Debussy*, 96.

23. Orledge, *Debussy and the Theatre*, 58.

24. Vallas, *Claude Debussy*, 106.

Chapter 13: *Songs of Bilitis* (1894–1898)

1. M. D. Calvocoressi, "Claude Debussy," *Musical Times* (February 1, 1908): 81–82.

2. Pierre Louÿs, *The Songs of Bilitis*, trans. Alvah C. Bessie (Mineola, NY: Dover, 2010).

3. H. P. Clive, *Pierre Louys: 1870–1925* (Oxford: Clarendon Press, 1978), 110–111. Most sources give the number of poems in *Bilitis* as 146; Clive says the first edition had 93 poems and was augmented to 146 for the revised edition published in 1898. Of the 146, three were claimed to be epitaphs.

4. Ibid., 112.

5. André Gide, *If It Die*, trans. Dorothy Bussy (New York: Vintage Books, 2001), 250. The autobiography was written in French in 1919.

6. Ibid., 256.

7. Ibid., 254–255.

8. Ibid., 268.

9. Lockspeiser, *Debussy*, 1:175.

10. Gide, *If It Die*, 282.

11. David Grayson, "Bilitis and Tanagra: Afternoons with Nude Women," in *Debussy and His World*, ed. Jane E. Fulcher (Princeton, NJ: Princeton University Press, 2001), 119.

12. Ibid., 119.

13. Henri de Régnier, *Lettres à André Gide (1891–1911)* (Geneva: Librairie Droz, and Paris: Librairie Minard, 1972). This version of the dedication is found in a footnote on page 78, with reference to a letter from Régnier to Gide written July 21, 1894.

14. Edward Lockspeiser, "Neuf Lettres de Pierre Louÿs à Debussy (1894–1898)," *Revue de Musicologie* 48 (July–December 1962): 61–70; author's translation.

15. Orledge, *Debussy and the Theatre*, 260.

16. Ibid., 261.

17. Ibid.

18. Lockspeiser, *Debussy*, 1:178.

19. Ibid.

20. Grayson, "Bilitis and Tanagra," 120.

21. Louis Laloy, "Remarks on Debussy," *Le Mercure musical*, March 1, 1906; quoted in Deborah Priest, ed. and trans., *Louis Laloy (1874–1944) on Debussy, Ravel, and Stravinsky* (Aldershot: Ashgate, 1999), 78–79.

22. Vallas, *Claude Debussy*, 109.

23. Ibid., 110.

24. An interval of a third consists of two notes which are three or four semitones apart—for example, C and the E above it, or D and the F above it. Parallel thirds are chords, each comprising an interval of a third, that move in parallel motion, upward or downward. The result is "harmonious" in a way that parallel seconds or fourths are not.

25. Vallas, *Claude Debussy*, 110.

26. Nichols, *Debussy Remembered*, 57.

27. Vallas, *Claude Debussy*, 109.

28. Clive, *Pierre Louÿs*, 170.

Chapter 14: Claude in Love, or The Hearts of Artists (1890s)

1. Dietschy, *A Portrait of Claude Debussy*, ix.

2. Nichols, *Debussy Remembered*, 59–60.

3. George Copeland, "Debussy, the Man I Knew," *Atlantic Monthly*, January 1955, 31–38: "He was by way of being a genius, a noise-maker, an impressionist, a symbolist, a modernist, a libertine, and a recluse—all at one and the same time."

4. Cobb, "Claude Debussy to Claudius and Gustave Popelin," 39–48.

5. Lesure and Nichols, *Debussy Letters*, 31–33.

6. Lockspeiser, *Debussy*, 1:183.

7. Nichols, *Debussy Remembered*, 33–34.

8. Dietschy, *A Portrait of Claude Debussy*, 96.

9. Ibid.

10. Nichols, *Debussy Remembered*, 33–34.

11. Dietschy, *A Portrait of Claude Debussy*, 96.

12. Nichols, *Debussy Remembered*, 33–34.

13. Lesure and Nichols, *Debussy Letters*, 88–89.

14. Some accounts of the incident say that Gaby shot herself, or tried to, but there is no evidence of any shots being fired.

15. Lesure and Nichols, *Debussy Letters*, 88–89.

16. Seroff, *Debussy: Musician of France*, 355–358.

17. Lesure and Nichols, *Debussy Letters*, 93.

18. Seroff, *Debussy: Musician of France*, 355–358.

19. Lesure and Nichols, *Debussy Letters*, 94–95.

20. Lockspeiser, *Debussy*, 1:166–167.

21. Lesure and Nichols, *Debussy Letters*, 97n.

22. Dietschy, *A Portrait of Claude Debussy*, 101.

23. Lesure and Nichols, *Debussy Letters*, 97.

24. Dietschy, *A Portrait of Claude Debussy*, 102.

25. The two songs Debussy wrote were "Dieu! qu'il la fait bon regarder!" and "Yver, vous n'estes qu'un vilain." Debussy added a third *Chanson*, "Quand j'ay ouy le tabourin," ten years later. Written for unaccompanied chorus in four-part harmony, the church modes and counterpoint give the songs a distinctly medieval sound.

26. Nichols, *Debussy Remembered*, 52.

27. Ibid., 53.

28. Dietschy, *A Portrait of Claude Debussy*, 105.

29. Lesure and Nichols, *Debussy Letters*, 98.

30. Ibid., 100–101.

31. Ibid., 103.

32. Seroff, *Debussy: Musician of France*, 355–358.

33. Ibid., inscription quote; author's translation.

34. Clive, *Pierre Louÿs*, 158.

35. Lesure and Nichols, *Debussy Letters*, 103–104.

36. Dietschy, *A Portrait of Claude Debussy*, 105–106.

37. Lesure and Nichols, *Debussy Letters*, 105.

38. Ibid., 105–106.

39. Nichols, *Debussy Remembered*, 128–129.

40. Ibid., 114.

Chapter 15: *Nocturnes* (1899–1901)

1. Olin Downes, concert review, *New York Times*, October 22, 1930.

2. Nichols, *Debussy Remembered*, 57.

3. Lesure and Nichols, *Debussy Letters*, 38.

4. Ibid., 74–75.

5. Someone sitting for a portrait asked Whistler how he can paint in such a dark room. His answer is often quoted and is found in many literary sources with minor text variations.

6. Lesure and Nichols, *Debussy Letters*, 73.

7. Ibid., 93.

8. Charette, *Claude Debussy Through His Letters*, 31–32.

9. Lesure and Nichols, *Debussy Letters*, 100.

10. The translation of this quote is from the Los Angeles Philharmonic program notes, http://www.laphil.com/philpedia/music/nocturnes-claude-debussy.

11. Lesure and Nichols, *Debussy Letters*, 117.

12. Lockspeiser, *Debussy*, 1:104.

13. Downes, review, October 22, 1930.

14. Nichols, *Debussy Remembered*, 113.

15. Boulez, *Notes of an Apprenticeship*, 347.

Chapter 16: *Pelléas* (1902)

1. Lawrence Gilman, *Pelléas et Mélisande: A Guide to the Opera* (New York: G. Schirmer, 1907).

2. Charette, *Claude Debussy Through His Letters*, 34.

3. Dietschy, *A Portrait of Claude Debussy*, 111n.

4. Georgette Leblanc, *Souvenirs: My Life with Maeterlinck*, trans. Janet Flanner (New York: E. P. Dutton, 1932), 168–170.

5. Opstad, *Debussy's Mélisande*, 34.

6. Ibid., 37.

7. Ibid., 36.

8. Ibid., 37.

9. Leblanc, *Souvenirs*, 172–173.

10. Ibid., 174.

11. Ibid., 175.

12. Lesure and Nichols, *Debussy Letters*, 110.

13. Michael T. R. B. Turnbull, *Mary Garden* (Portland, OR: Amadeus Press, 1997), 18–20.

14. Ibid., 20–22.

15. Mary Garden and Louis Leopold Biancolli, *Mary Garden's Story* (New York: Simon & Schuster, 1951), 61–62.

16. Nichols, *Debussy Remembered*, 66–67.

17. Garden and Biancolli, *Mary Garden's Story*, 62.

18. Nichols, *Debussy Remembered*, 66–67.

19. Garden and Biancolli, *Mary Garden's Story*, 62.

20. Nichols, *Debussy Remembered*, 66–67.

21. Garden and Biancolli, *Mary Garden's Story*, 62–63.

22. Ibid., 66.

23. Claude Debussy and Maurice Maeterlinck, *Pelléas et Mélisande*, Act 3, Scene 1.

24. Garden and Biancolli, *Mary Garden's Story*, 67.

25. Ibid., 64–65.

26. Turnbull, *Mary Garden*, 31.

27. Garden and Biancolli, *Mary Garden's Story*, 68–69.

28. Lesure and Nichols, *Debussy Letters*, 123.

29. Nichols, *Debussy Remembered*, 81–82.

30. Ibid., 67.

31. Dietschy, *A Portrait of Claude Debussy*, 113.

32. Vallas, *Claude Debussy*, 123.

33. Dietschy, *A Portrait of Claude Debussy*, 114.

34. Nichols, *Debussy Remembered*, 67.

35. Lesure and Nichols, *Debussy Letters*, 124.

36. Nichols, *Debussy Remembered*, 67.

37. Garden and Biancolli, *Mary Garden's Story*, 73.

38. Nichols, *Debussy Remembered*, 82.

39. Dietschy, *A Portrait of Claude Debussy*, 114–115.

40. Garden and Biancolli, *Mary Garden's Story*, 70.

41. Michael Rose, *The Birth of an Opera* (New York: W. W. Norton, 2013), 310.

42. Garden and Biancolli, *Mary Garden's Story*, 70.

43. Ibid., 70–71.

44. Vallas, *Claude Debussy*, 125.

45. Turnbull, *Mary Garden*, 33.

46. Nichols, *Debussy Remembered*, 83–88.

47. Vallas, *Claude Debussy*, 125n.

48. Nichols, *Debussy Remembered*, 83.

49. Debussy, *Debussy on Music*, 226–227.

50. Orledge, *Debussy and the Theatre*, 64.

51. Ibid., 64.

52. Nichols, *Debussy Remembered*, 83–88.

53. Ibid., 83–88.

Chapter 17: *Pelléas* and the French Spirit

1. Debussy, "Why I Wrote *Pelléas*," April 1902; in Debussy, *Debussy on Music*, 74–75.

2. Dietschy, *A Portrait of Claude Debussy*, 117.

3. Lawrence Gilman, *Pelléas et Mélisande: A Guide to the Opera* (New York: G. Schirmer, 1907); Project Gutenberg, http://www.gutenberg.org/ebooks/16488.

4. Dietschy, *A Portrait of Claude Debussy*, 121–122.

5. Ibid., 118.

6. Vallas, *Claude Debussy*, 126–128.

7. Dietschy, *A Portrait of Claude Debussy*, 120.

8. Vallas, *Claude Debussy*, 130.

9. Lesure and Nichols, *Debussy Letters*, 126.

10. Vallas, *Claude Debussy*, 144–145.

11. Jann Pasler, "A Sociology of the Apaches: 'Sacred Battalion' for *Pelléas*," in *Berlioz and Debussy: Sources, Contexts and Legacies*, ed. Barbara L. Kelly and Kerry Murphy (Aldershot: Ashgate, 2007), 165. Much of the information about the Apaches is drawn from this essay.

12. Ibid.

13. Vallas, *Claude Debussy*, 130.

14. Ibid., 131.

15. Gilman, *Pelléas*.

16. Romain Rolland, *Musicians of To-day*, trans. Mary Blaiklock (New York: Henry Holt, 1915). Rolland's essay on Debussy provides the fabric of the several paragraphs in which Rolland is credited. Project Gutenberg, http://www.gutenberg.org/ebooks/16467.

17. Ibid.

18. Ibid.

19. Quoted in Gilman, *Pelléas*.

20. Rolland, *Musicians of To-day*. The Rousseau quotations come from his *Lettre sur la musique française* (1753).

21. Rolland, *Musicians of To-day*.

22. Gilman, *Pelléas*.

23. Ibid.

24. Rolland, *Musicians of To-day*.

25. Ibid.

Chapter 18: Women and the Sea (1902–1904)

1. J. G. Prod'homme, "Claude Achille Debussy" [obituary], *Musical Quarterly* 4, no. 4 (October 1918): 555–571.

2. Nichols, *Debussy Remembered*, 126–127.

3. Garden and Biancolli, *Mary Garden's Story*, 76.

4. Nichols, *Debussy Remembered*, 136–137.

5. Lesure and Nichols, *Debussy Letters*, 107.

6. From *Images* to the end of his life, almost all of Debussy's music was published by Durand.

7. Lesure and Nichols, *Debussy Letters*, 141–142.

8. Dietschy, *A Portrait of Claude Debussy*, 128.

9. Garden and Biancolli, *Mary Garden's Story*, 75.

10. Ibid., 78.

11. Ibid., 80.

12. Nichols, *Debussy Remembered*, 200.

13. Dietschy, *A Portrait of Claude Debussy*, 129–130.

14. Ibid., 132–133.

15. Lesure and Nichols, *Debussy Letters*, 147–148.

16. Ibid., 148.

17. Dietschy, *A Portrait of Claude Debussy*, 134.

18. Henri Borgeaud, ed., *Correspondance de Claude Debussy et Pierre Louÿs* (Paris: Librairie José Corti, 1945); author's translation.

342NOTES

19. Clive, *Pierre Louÿs*, 181; author's translation.
20. Garden and Biancolli, *Mary Garden's Story*, 81–84.

Chapter 19: Ease, Unease, Disease (1904–1908)

1. Debussy, "Why I Wrote Pelléas," April 1902; in Debussy, *Debussy on Music*, 75.
2. Dietschy, *A Portrait of Claude Debussy*, 135n.
3. Elliott Antokoletz and Marianne Wheeldon, eds., *Rethinking Debussy* (Oxford: Oxford University Press, 2011). Most of the information about the composer's income presented here and elsewhere in these chapters is from the chapter by Denis Herlin, "An Artist High and Low, or Debussy and Money," trans. Vincent Giroud.
4. A few years after moving there, Debussy's house number was changed to 80 avenue du Bois de Boulogne. In 1929, the avenue became avenue Foch, named after Ferdinand Foch, a French hero of the First World War. Avenue Foch, where palaces fight for elbow room among larger apartment buildings, is said to be one of the most exclusive and expensive residential streets in the world.
5. Hartmann, *Claude Debussy as I Knew Him*, 106.
6. Simon Tresize, ed., *The Cambridge Companion to Debussy* (Cambridge: Cambridge University Press, 2003), 108.
7. Laloy's was the first French biography of Debussy and the first to be considered authoritative, especially because of Laloy's personal relationship with the composer and the brilliance of his descriptions and analyses of the music. An earlier book-length biography, by Louise Liebich, was published in England in 1908; it is full of inaccuracies and premature conclusions about Debussy's work and life.
8. Deborah Priest, ed. and trans., *Louis Laloy (1874–1944) on Debussy, Ravel, and Stravinsky* (Aldershot: Ashgate, 1999), 191–192.
9. Ibid., 194.
10. Ibid., 201.
11. Ibid., 196.
12. Ibid., 195.
13. Charette, *Claude Debussy Through His Letters*, 153.
14. Lockspeiser, *Debussy*, 2:255.

Chapter 20: Debussy and the Modern Piano

1. Paul Roberts, *Images: The Piano Music of Claude Debussy* (Portland, OR: Amadeus Press, 1996), 5.
2. Boulez, *Notes of an Apprenticeship*, 349–350.
3. Lesure and Nichols, *Debussy Letters*, 155.
4. Marguerite Long, *At the Piano with Debussy*, trans. O. S. Ellis (London: J. M. Dent and Sons, 1972), 16.

5. Hartmann, *Claude Debussy as I Knew Him*, 79.

6. Long, *At the Piano with Debussy*, 22.

7. Ibid., 22, 18–19.

8. Guido Gatti, "The Piano Works of Claude Debussy," *Musical Quarterly* 7, no. 3 (July 1921): 419–420.

9. Alfred Cortot, *The Piano Music of Claude Debussy*, trans. Violet Edgell (London: J. & W. Chester, 1922), 11.

10. Lesure and Nichols, *Debussy Letters*, 136.

11. Gatti, "The Piano Works," 421.

12. Long, *At the Piano with Debussy*, 14.

13. Priest, *Louis Laloy*, 94.

14. Ibid., 79.

15. Roberts, *Images*, 204.

16. Ibid., 204–205.

17. Gatti, "The Piano Works," 436.

18. Priest, *Louis Laloy*, 96.

19. Centre de Documentation Claude Debussy, http://www.debussy.fr/encd/bio/bio5_03-09.php.

20. Siglind Bruhn, *Images and Ideas in Modern French Piano Music: The Extramusical Subtext in Piano Works by Debussy, Ravel, and Messiaen* (Hillsdale, NY: Pendragon Press, 1997), 5.

21. Ibid., 69.

22. Ibid., 118.

23. Roberts, *Images*, chapters 9 and 10.

24. Bruhn, *Images and Ideas in Modern French Piano Music*, 8–11.

25. Even later, after his surreal ballet *Parade* and his severely sober *Socrate*, Satie promoted himself, tongue in cheek, as a composer of *musique d'ameublement*—"furniture music." By this, he meant music that was not meant to be listened to—music to be played at theater intermissions while playgoers chatted, or music for hotel lobbies, where it wouldn't be any more noticed than the chairs or potted palms. In other words, it was music with little inherent value. As cunningly self-deprecating as the concept was, in this too he was a precursor. By the 1960s, Muzak was ubiquitous in hotels, stores, and corporate offices; it was not meant to be listened to but to distract from harsh noises, to influence purchasing patterns, to stimulate workers, or to substitute for live musicians in noisy restaurants. Satie is still with us.

26. Ornella Volta, *Satie Seen Through His Letters*, trans. Michael Bullock (London: Marion Boyars, 1989), 146–147.

27. Maurice Ravel, *A Ravel Reader*, compiled and ed. Arbie Orenstein (New York: Columbia University Press, 1990), 56.

28. The concert also featured several works by other composers, including Debussy's *Clarinet Rhapsody*.

29. Pierre-Daniel Templier, *Erik Satie*, trans. Elena L. French and David S. French (Cambridge: Massachusetts Institute of Technology Press, 1969), 32–33.

30. Ibid., 147.

31. Ravel, *A Ravel Reader*, 350.

32. In a 1928 lecture, Ravel again reiterated that Satie "had an appreciable effect" on Debussy and himself. But, wary of raising Satie's monument too high, Ravel offered that while Satie "may, perhaps, never have wrought out of his own discoveries a single complete work of art," he planted an "indispensable seed" which was "nourished in better surroundings"—i.e., the fertile soil of composers like Debussy and Ravel. Ravel, *A Ravel Reader*, 45.

33. Charette, *Claude Debussy Through His Letters*, 72–73.

Chapter 21: The Sorry, Starry Stage (1908–1913)

1. Jane F. Fulcher, ed., *Debussy and His World* (Princeton, NJ: Princeton University Press, 2001), 2.

2. Lockspeiser, *Debussy*, 2:118.

3. Ibid., 2:118–119.

4. Ibid., 2:119.

5. Nichols, *Debussy Remembered*, 217.

6. Ibid., 219.

7. Georges Jean-Aubry, "Some Recollections of Debussy," *Musical Times* 59 (May 1, 1918): 205.

8. Nichols, *Debussy Remembered*, 217–218.

9. Though Bax calls the host organization the "Music Club," Debussy told Durand it was the "Society of English Composers." Georges Jean-Aubry mentioned in his Debussy obituary in the *Musical Times* that the reception was given by "the Society of British Composers, the Playgoers', and the Concert-goers' Clubs." Coincidentally, during the same month, Jean Sibelius met Debussy in London, where the Finnish composer was similarly honored at the Music Club, attended by Arnold Bax.

10. Nichols, *Debussy Remembered*, 222–223.

11. Lockspeiser, *Debussy*, 2:123.

12. Filson Young, *More Mastersingers: Studies in the Art of Music* (New York: Henry Holt, 1911), 275–283.

13. Lesure and Nichols, *Debussy Letters*, 229–230.

14. T. S. Eliot, *From Poe to Valéry* (New York: Harcourt, Brace, 1948).

15. Debussy, *Debussy on Music*, 242.

16. Lockspeiser, *Debussy*, 2:145–146.

17. Orledge, *Debussy and the Theatre*, 110.

18. Charette, *Claude Debussy Through His Letters*, 167.

19. Orledge, *Debussy and the Theatre*, 110.

20. Charette, *Claude Debussy Through His Letters*, 91.

21. Ibid., 93.

22. Julie McQuinn, "Exploring the Erotic in Debussy's Music," in *The Cambridge Companion to Debussy*, ed. Simon Trevise (Cambridge: Cambridge University Press, 2003), 135.

23. Debussy, *Debussy on Music*, 247–248.

24. Orledge, *Debussy and the Theatre*, 219.

25. Gabriele D'Annunzio, libretto, trans. David Cox, booklet, *Le Martyre de Saint Sébastien*, London Symphony Chorus and Orchestra, Michael Tilson Thomas, conductor; Leslie Caron, narrator; Ann Murray, mezzo-soprano; Sylvia McNair, soprano (Sony Classical CD SK 48240, 1991).

26. Orledge, *Debussy and the Theatre*, 221.

27. Long, *At the Piano with Debussy*, 104.

28. Ibid., 102.

29. Geoffrey Norris, "Debussy: Playing with Colour," *Gramophone*, July 2012; http://www.gramophone.co.uk/feature/debussy-playing-with-colour.

30. Nichols, *Debussy Remembered*, 224–231. This and the following paragraphs are drawn from Vittorio Gui's article, "Debussy in Italy," first published in *Musical Opinion* (January 1939 and February 1939).

31. Ibid. This and the preceding paragraphs are drawn from Gui's article.

32. Charette, *Claude Debussy Through His Letters*, 168.

33. Lockspeiser, *Debussy*, 1:59.

34. Ibid., 2:254–261. From a translation of Falla's essay (ibid., Appendix B, "Manuel de Falla on Debussy") written for the journal *La Revue musicale*, December 1920, a famous issue devoted to Debussy's work, which also included musical tributes written for the occasion by Falla, Satie, Dukas, Ravel, Stravinsky, and others. Falla's guitar piece, "Homenaja," is especially moving.

35. Ibid. This and the preceding paragraphs are from Falla's essay.

36. Orledge, *Debussy and the Theatre*, 134.

37. Ibid., 135.

38. The opera is also known as *The Maid of Pskov*. Diaghilev rechristened it *Ivan the Terrible*, for reasons any theatrical producer can tell you.

39. John Martin, "City Ballet Gives New Robbins Work," *New York Times*, May 15, 1953.

40. John McGinness, "Vaslav Nijinsky's Notes for 'Jeux'," *Musical Quarterly* 88, no. 4 (Winter 2005): pp. 556–589.

41. Debussy, *Debussy on Music*, 291.

42. Lesure and Nichols, *Debussy Letters*, 263.

43. Ibid., 261–262.

44. Several versions of the scenario for *Jeux* exist (including the one in Debussy's published score), probably because of choreographic changes made during rehearsals. This description is based on the account by Adolphe Julien, who actually saw the ballet. Hanna Jarvinen, "Critical Silence: The Unseemly Games of Love in *Jeux* (1913)," *Journal of the Society for Dance Research* 27, no. 2 (Winter 2009): 199–226.

45. Orledge, *Debussy and the Theatre*, 168.

46. Jarvinen, "Critical Silence."

47. Orledge, *Debussy and the Theatre*, 171.

48. Ibid., 172.

49. Anthony Tommasini, "Shocking or Subtle, Still Radical," *New York Times*, September 18, 2012.

50. Ibid.

51. Andrew Clements, "Debussy: *Jeux*," *Guardian*, February 22, 2001.

52. Hartmann, *Claude Debussy as I Knew Him*, 15.

Chapter 22: War and Suffering (1913–1916)

1. Debussy, letter to D. E. Inghelbrecht, September 20, 1915; in *Debussy's Letters to Inghelbrecht: The Story of a Musical Friendship*, annotated Margaret G. Cobb, trans. Richard Miller (Rochester, NY: University of Rochester Press, 2005).

2. Debussy, letter to Jacques Durand, June 8, 1916; in Charette, *Claude Debussy Through His Letters*, 183.

3. Ibid., 132.

4. Ibid., 133.

5. Ibid.

6. Ibid., 133–134.

7. Ibid., 134–135.

8. Nichols, *The Life of Debussy*, 150.

9. Nichols, *Debussy Remembered*, 234–235.

10. Ibid., 232.

11. Ibid., 233–234.

12. Debussy, *Debussy on Music*, 317–320.

13. Lockspeiser, *Debussy*, 2:205.

14. Ibid., 2:205.

15. Debussy, "Noël des enfants qui n'ont plus de maison" (Paris: Durand, 1915); author's translation. The child of the song calls for vengeance not just for the children of France but also for "the little Belgians, the little Serbs, and the little Polish children too."

16. *Debussy's Letters to Inghelbrecht*, 59.

17. In a letter, Debussy refers to the "poisonous vapors" that Luther's hymn represents. Lesure and Nichols, *Debussy Letters*, 299.

18. Charette, *Claude Debussy Through His Letters*, 178.

19. *Debussy's Letters to Inghelbrecht*, 69.

20. Lesure and Nichols, *Debussy Letters*, 301.

21. Ibid., 302.

22. Vallas, *Claude Debussy*, 131.

23. Priest, *Louis Laloy*, 236n.

24. Charette, *Claude Debussy Through His Letters*, 155.

25. Carol A. Hess, *Sacred Passions: The Life and Music of Manuel de Falla* (Oxford: Oxford University Press, 2005), 54.

26. Boulez, *Notes of an Apprenticeship*, 354.

27. Lesure and Nichols, *Debussy Letters*, 300.

28. Long, *At the Piano with Debussy*, 41.

29. Cortot, *The Piano Music of Debussy*, 22.

30. Marianne Wheeldon, *Debussy's Late Style* (Bloomington: Indiana University Press, 2009), 136.

31. Lesure and Nichols, *Debussy Letters*, 301.

32. Vallas, *Claude Debussy*, 259.

33. Cortot, *The Piano Music of Debussy*, 23.

34. Lesure and Nichols, *Debussy Letters*, 300.

35. Charette, *Claude Debussy Through His Letters*, 148.

36. Ibid., 182.

37. Ibid., 149–150.

38. *Debussy's Letters to Inghelbrecht*, 81.

39. Charette, *Claude Debussy Through His Letters*, 150–151.

40. Ibid., 151.

41. Ibid., 151–152.

42. Centre de Documentation Claude Debussy, http://www.debussy.fr/encd/bio/bio7_15-18.php.

43. Orledge, *Debussy and the Theatre*, 102.

44. *Debussy's Letters to Inghelbrecht*, 83.

45. Orledge, *Debussy and the Theatre*, 102.

46. Charette, *Claude Debussy Through His Letters*, 152–153.

47. Ibid., 153–154.

48. *Debussy's Letters to Inghelbrecht*, 85.

49. Andrew Clements, *Guardian*, June 15, 2014, http://www.theguardian.com/music/2014/jun/15/fall-house-usher.

Chapter 23: Too Many Keys (1917–1918)

1. Debussy, letter to Robert Godet, September 4, 1916; in Charette, *Claude Debussy Through His Letters*, 152.

2. Revivals of *Parade* in peacetime allowed a kinder critical interpretation. It can now be called a triumphant preview of Dada and surrealism and a giddy masterpiece of the new French modernism.

3. Volta, *Satie Seen Through His Letters*, 132–133. The epithets are seen in the court documents.

4. Steven Moore Whiting, *Satie the Bohemian: From Cabaret to Concert Hall* (Oxford: Oxford University Press, 1999), 490.

5. Volta, *Satie Seen Through His Letters*, 148.

6. Lesure and Nichols, *Debussy Letters*, 324.

7. Lockspeiser, *Debussy*, 2:219.

8. Ibid., 2:220.

9. Long, *At the Piano with Debussy*, 8–9.

10. Ibid., 9.

11. Ibid., 46.

12. Lesure and Nichols, *Debussy Letters*, 332–333.

13. In March 1917, Debussy wrote a little piano piece for his coal merchant, who had supplied the family during a particularly cold and fuel-starved winter. The piece was called "Les Soirs illuminés," from a line by Baudelaire—"Les soirs illuminés par l'ardeur du charbon" (The evenings illuminated by the glow of coal).

14. Dietschy, *A Portrait of Claude Debussy*, 188.

15. Ibid., 188.

16. Robert Orledge, *Satie the Composer* (Cambridge: Cambridge University Press, 1990), 66.

17. The cannon acquired the name "Paris gun"; it was built for Paris and used nowhere else. The huge weapon was entrenched in the Ardennes Forest, seventy-five miles northeast of the capital. Official papers found after the war revealed its immensity. The cannon barrels were fitted with tubes 112 feet long, with a caliber of 210mm. The shells, weighing 234 pounds and packed with TNT, had a trajectory that reached an altitude of twenty-six miles; they were airborne for three minutes at a peak speed of 5,400 feet per second before reaching their target. The Paris gun was never found; it was presumably destroyed by the Germans before the war's end.

18. Nichols, *Debussy Remembered*, 246.

19. Lesure and Nichols, *Debussy Letters*, 335–336.

20. Prod'homme, "Claude Achille Debussy."

21. Vallas, *Claude Debussy*, 271.

22. Ibid., 272–273.

23. Nichols, *Debussy Remembered*, 248.

24. Hartmann, *Claude Debussy as I Knew Him*, 147.

Appendix A: People Passing Through

1. Seroff, *Debussy: Musician of France*, 355–358.

2. Klára Móricz, *Jewish Identities: Nationalism, Racism, and Utopianism in Twentieth-Century Music* (Oakland: University of California Press, 2008), 106.

3. Information about Edward H. House is derived from James L. Huffman, *A Yankee in Meiji Japan* (Lanham, MD: Rowman & Littlefield, 2003).

4. Much of the information on Louÿs is derived from H. P. Clive, *Pierre Louys: 1870–1925* (Oxford: Clarendon Press, 1978).

5. Poniatowski's Standard Electric Company and partners enlisted the Fred Locke Multipart Porcelain Insulators company to produce, for the new power lines, porcelain insulators to carry 40,000 volts after GE, Westinghouse, and Stanley Electric had already told them that such insulators were impossible or impractical to build; see http://fredlocke.insulators.info/Porcelain_Insulators/Multipart_History/Multipart_Styles/Multipart_p3.htm. Other information about Poniatowski's Western ventures comes from the *New York Times*, October 13, 1897; Gray Brechin, *Imperial San Francisco: Urban Power, Earthly Ruin* (Oakland: University of California Press, 2006); and http://www.energy-net.org.

6. Obituary for Prince André Poniatowski, *New York Times*, March 18, 1954.

7. Author's translation.

8. Mary McAuliffe, *Dawn of the Belle Epoque* (Lanham, MD: Rowman & Littlefield, 2011).

BIBLIOGRAPHY

Antokoletz, Elliott, and Marianne Wheeldon, eds. *Rethinking Debussy*. Oxford: Oxford University Press, 2011.

Austin, William W., ed. *Debussy: Prelude to "The Afternoon of a Faun."* New York: W. W. Norton, 1970.

Bartók, Béla. *Béla Bartók Essays*. Selected and edited by Benjamin Suchoff. London: Faber & Faber, 1976.

Baudelaire, Charles. *Paris Spleen*. Translated by Keith Waldrop. Middletown, CT: Wesleyan University Press, 2009.

Berger, Klaus. "Mallarmé and the Visual Arts." Chapter in *Les Mardis: Stéphane Mallarmé*.

Berlioz, Hector. *The Life of Hector Berlioz: As Written by Himself in His Letters and Memoirs*. Translated by Katherine F. Boult. New York: Dutton, 1903.

Borgeaud, Henri, ed. *Correspondance de Claude Debussy et Pierre Louÿs*. Paris: Librairie José Corti, 1945.

Botstein, Leon. "Paris in the 1860s: The Origins of Impressionism." Concert notes for the American Symphony Orchestra, 1994.

Boulez, Pierre. *Notes of an Apprenticeship*. Translated by Herbert Weinstock. New York: Knopf, 1968.

Brechin, Gray. *Imperial San Francisco: Urban Power, Earthly Ruin*. Oakland: University of California Press, 2006.

Brown, John Russell, ed. *The Oxford Illustrated History of the Theatre*. Oxford: Oxford University Press, 2001.

Bruhn, Siglind. *Images and Ideas in Modern French Piano Music: The Extramusical Subtext in Piano Works by Debussy, Ravel, and Messiaen*. Hillsdale, NY: Pendragon, 1997.

Calvocoressi, M. D. "Claude Debussy." *Musical Times* 49, February 1, 1908.

Centre de Documentation Claude Debussy. www.debussy.fr.

Charette, Jacqueline M., ed. and trans. *Claude Debussy Through His Letters*. New York: Vantage Press, 1990.

Clements, Andrew. "Debussy: *Jeux*." *Guardian*, February 22, 2001. http://www.theguardian.com/culture/2001/feb/23/classicalmusicandopera.

———. "Usher House / The Fall of the House of Usher." Review of two operas based on Poe, a new one by Gordon Getty and a reconstruction of Debussy's score by Robert Orledge, performed in Cardiff, Wales. *Guardian*, June 15, 2014. http://www.theguardian.com/music/2014/jun/15/fall-house-usher.

Clevenger, John R. "Debussy's Rome Cantatas." Chapter in Fulcher, *Debussy and His World*.

Clive, H. P. *Pierre Louÿs, 1870–1925: A Biography*. Oxford: Clarendon Press, 1978.

Cobb, Margaret G., and Richard Miller. "Claude Debussy to Claudius and Gustave Popelin: Nine Unpublished Letters." *19th-Century Music* 13, no. 1 (Summer 1989).

Code, David J. "Debussy's String Quartet in the Brussels Salon of 'La Libre Esthetique.'" *19th-Century Music* 30, no. 3 (Spring 2007).

Connelly, James L. "The World of Mallarmé's Circle; The Historical Ambience: 1870–1914." Chapter in *Les Mardis: Stéphane Mallarmé*.

Copeland, George. "Debussy, the Man I Knew." *Atlantic Monthly*, January 1955.

Cortot, Albert. *The Piano Music of Claude Debussy*. Translated by Violet Edgell. London: J. & W. Chester, 1922.

D'Annunzio, Gabriele. *Le Martyre de Saint-Sébastien*. Libretto translated by David Cox. From album notes for Sony Classical recording, SK 48240. Sony, 1993.

Davis, Mary E. *Erik Satie*. London: Reaktion, 2007.

Debussy, Claude. *Claude Debussy Through His Letters*. See Charette.

———. *Debussy Letters*. See Lesure and Nichols.

———. *Debussy on Music*. Translated and edited by Richard Langham Smith. New York: Knopf, 1977.

———. *Debussy's Letters to Inghelbrecht: The Story of a Musical Friendship*. Annotated by Margaret G. Cobb; translated by Richard Miller. Rochester, NY: University of Rochester Press, 2005.

———. *Monsieur Croche, antidilettante*. Paris: Les Bibliophiles Fantaisistes, 1921.

———. *Monsieur Croche, the Dilettante Hater*. Translated by B. N. Langdon Davies. New York: Lear, 1928.

Debussy, Claude, and Maurice Maeterlinck. *Pelléas et Mélisande* [score]. Libretto translated by Henry Grafton Chapman. New York: G. Schirmer, 1907.

Dietschy, Marcel. *A Portrait of Claude Debussy*. Edited and translated by William Ashbrook and Margaret G. Cobb. Oxford: Clarendon Press, 1990.

Downes, Olin. "Stokowski Triumphs." *New York Times*, October 22, 1930.

Duchesneau, Michel. *L'avant-garde musicale et ses sociétés à Paris de 1871 à 1939*. Sprimont: Editions Mardaga, 1999.

Dunoyer, Cecilia. *Marguerite Long: A Life in French Music, 1874–1966*. Bloomington: Indiana University Press, 1993.

Eliot, T. S. "From Poe to Valéry." New York: Harcourt, Brace, 1948. Republished in Eliot, *To Criticize the Critic and Other Writings*. Lincoln: University of Nebraska Press, 1992.

Fauser, Annegret. *Musical Encounters at the 1889 Paris World's Fair*. Rochester, NY: University of Rochester Press, 2005.

Fisk, Josiah, ed. *Composers on Music: Eight Centuries of Writings*. Boston: Northeastern University Press, 1997.

Francke, Kuno. *Social Forces in German Literature*. New York: Henry Holt, 1897.

Fulcher, Jane F., ed. *Debussy and His World*. Princeton, NJ: Princeton University Press, 2001.

Garden, Mary, and Louis Biancolli. *Mary Garden's Story*. New York: Simon & Schuster, 1951.

Gatti, Guido. "Piano Works of Claude Debussy." *Musical Quarterly* 7, no. 3 (July 1921).

Gautier, Judith. "Letters from Judith Gautier to Chalmers Clifton." Edited by Elaine Brody. *French Review*, April 1985.

Gibbons, William. "Debussy as Storyteller: Narrative Expansion in the *Trois Chansons de Bilitis*." *Current Musicology*, no. 85 (Spring 2008).

Gide, André. *If It Die*. Translated by Dorothy Bussy. New York: Vintage Books, 2001.

Gillmor, Alan M. *Erik Satie*. Boston: Twayne, 1988.

Gilman, Lawrence. "Claude Debussy." *Century*, May to October 1918.

———. *Debussy's Pelléas et Mélisande: A Guide to the Opera*. New York: G. Schirmer, 1907. http://www.gutenberg.org/ebooks/16488.

Goepp, Philip H. *Symphonies and Their Meaning: Third Series*. Philadelphia: J. B. Lippincott, 1913.

Grayson, David. "Bilitis and Tanagra: Afternoons with Nude Women." Chapter in Fulcher, *Debussy and His World*.

———. "Debussy on Stage." Chapter in Trezise, *The Cambridge Companion to Debussy*.

Grierson, Francis. *Parisian Portraits*. New York: John Lane, 1913.

Hartmann, Arthur. *Claude Debussy as I Knew Him, and Other Writings of Arthur Hartmann*. Samuel Hsu, Sidney Grolnic, and Mark Peters, eds. Rochester, NY: University of Rochester Press, 2003.

Herlin, Denis. "An Artist High and Low, or Debussy and Money." Translated by Vincent Giroud. Chapter in Antokoletz and Wheeldon, *Rethinking Debussy*.

Hess, Carol A. *Sacred Passions: The Life and Music of Manuel de Falla*. Oxford: Oxford University Press, 2005.

House, Edward H. "Wagner and 'Tannhäuser' in Paris." *New England Magazine* 4, issue 4 (1891). http://users.belgacom.net/wagnerlibrary/articles/.

Hovey, Richard. "Symbolism and Maurice Maeterlinck." First published in *The Plays of Maurice Maeterlinck*. Chicago: Herbert S. Stone, 1894.

Huebner, Steven. "Debussy, Wagner, and *Le roi Arthus*." Concert notes for the American Symphony Orchestra (2001).

Huffman, James L. *A Yankee in Meiji Japan: The Crusading Journalist Edward H. House*. Lanham, MD: Rowman & Littlefield, 2003.

Huneker, James. *Bedouins*. New York: Scribner, 1920.

Jacobs, Robert L. "Wagner and Judith Gautier." *Music & Letters* 18, no. 2 (April 1937).

Jarocinski, Stefan. *Debussy: Impressionism and Symbolism*. Translated by Rollo Myers. London: Eulenburg, 1976.

Jarvinen, Hanna. "Critical Silence: The Unseemly Games of Love in *Jeux* (1913)." *Dance Research: Journal of the Society for Dance Research* 27, no. 2 (Winter 2009).

Jean-Aubry, Georges. "Some Recollections of Debussy." *Musical Times* 59 (May 1, 1918).

Johnstone, Arthur. *Musical Criticisms*. Manchester, UK: University Press, 1905.

Kelly, Barbara L., and Kerry Murphy, eds. *Berlioz and Debussy: Sources, Contexts, and Legacies*. Aldershot: Ashgate, 2007.

Kerman, Joseph, ed. *Music at the Turn of the Century: A 19th-Century Music Reader*. Oakland: University of California Press, 1990.

Laloy, Louis. *Louis Laloy (1874–1944) on Debussy, Ravel, and Stravinsky*. Translated and annotated by Deborah Priest. Aldershot: Ashgate, 1999.

Leblanc, Georgette. *Souvenirs: My Life with Maeterlinck*. Translated by Janet Flanner. New York: E. P. Dutton, 1932.

Les Mardis: Stéphane Mallarmé and the Artists of His Circle. Collection of essays published in an exhibition catalogue. Lawrence: University of Kansas Museum of Art, 1965.

Lesure, François, and Roger Nichols, eds. *Debussy Letters*. Translated by Roger Nichols. Cambridge, MA: Harvard University Press, 1987.

Lloyd, Rosemary. *Mallarmé: The Poet and His Circle*. Ithaca, NY: Cornell University Press, 1999.

Lockspeiser, Edward. *Debussy: His Life and Mind*. 2 vols. Cambridge: Cambridge University Press, 1978.

———. "Neuf Lettres de Pierre Louÿs à Debussy (1894–1898)." *Revue de Musicologie*, July–December 1962.

———. "New Letters of Debussy." *Musical Times* 97, no. 1362 (August 1956).

Long, Marguerite. *At the Piano with Debussy*. Translated by O. S. Ellis. London: J. M. Dent, 1972.

Louÿs, Pierre. *The Songs of Bilitis*. Translated by Alvah C. Bessie. Mineola, NY: Dover, 2010.

Maeterlinck, Maurice. *Princess Maleine*. Translated by Richard Hovey. New York: Dodd Mead, 1920.

Mallarmé, Stéphane. *Collected Poems and Other Verse*. Translated by E. H. Blackmore and A. M. Blackmore. Oxford: Oxford World's Classics, 2006.

Martin, John. "City Ballet Gives New Robbins Work." [Ballet *Afternoon of a Faun*.] *New York Times*, May 15, 1953.

McAuliffe, Mary. *Dawn of the Belle Epoque: The Paris of Monet, Zola, Bernhardt, Eiffel, Debussy, Clemenceau, and Their Friends*. Lanham, MD: Rowman & Littlefield, 2011.

McGinness, John. "Vaslav Nijinsky's Notes for *Jeux*." *Musical Quarterly* 88, no. 4 (Winter 2005).

McQuinn, Julie. "Exploring the Erotic in Debussy's Music." Chapter in Trezise, *The Cambridge Companion to Debussy*.

Moréas, Jean. "Symbolist Manifesto." Translated by C. Liszt. http://www.mutablesound.com/home/?p=2165.

Móricz, Klára. *Jewish Identities: Nationalism, Racism, and Utopianism in Twentieth-Century Music*. Oakland: University of California Press, 2008.

Moses, Montrose J. *Maurice Maeterlinck: A Study*. New York: Duffield, 1911.

Murray, Christopher John, ed. *Encyclopedia of the Romantic Era, 1760–1850*. Chicago: Fitzroy Dearborn, 2004.

Myers, Rollo. "Augusta Holmès: A Meteoric Career." *Musical Quarterly* 53, no. 3 (June 1967).

Nealy, Robert T. "Endymion in France: A Brief Survey of French Symbolist Poetry." Chapter in *Les Mardis: Stéphane Mallarmé*.

New International Encyclopedia, vol. 14. Edited by Daniel Coit Oilman, Harry Thurston Peck, and Frank Moore Colby. New York: Dodd Mead, 1905.

Newman, Ernest. "The Development of Debussy." *Musical Times* 59, May 1, 1918.

New York Times. "Boston Orchestra Pays Last Visit." [First New York performance of *La Mer*.] March 22, 1907.

———. "The Death Roll Swelling: Terrible Results of the Opéra-Comique Fire." May 27, 1887.

———. "Debussy Discusses Music and His Work." [Interview.] June 26, 1910.

———. "D'Indy Conducts More French Music." [*Nocturnes*.] December 10, 1905.

———. "First Hearing Here of Debussy's Opera." [First New York performance of *Pelléas*.] February 20, 1908.

———. "French Hatred of Germany." May 6, 1887.

———. "French Talk and Gossip: The Money Lost in *Lohengrin*." May 8, 1887.

———. "Goes Home Without a Bride; Prince Poniatowski Once More Sets Sail for Paris." June 7, 1894.

———. "The Great French Show." [Paris International Exposition.] May 19, 1889.

———. "*Monna Vanna* as Opera; Maeterlinck Insists on Having His Wife Play Title Part at Comique." August 23, 1908.

———. "The Musical World—Opera, Concert, Recital." [*Pelléas* in New York.] February 23, 1908.

———. "The New York Symphony." [*Faune* and "Fêtes."] January 20, 1907.

———. "The New York Symphony Orchestra Plays." [First New York performance of *Prélude à "L'Après-midi d'un faune"*.] November 13, 1905.

———. Obituary for Prince André Poniatowski, March 18, 1954.

———. "Only One Topic in Paris; Public Interest in the Fire and How It Started." May 29, 1887.

———. "Prince Poniatowski's Investments." October 13, 1897.

———. "Princess Poniatowski Dead." August 7, 1911.

Nichols, Roger. *Debussy Remembered*. Portland, OR: Amadeus Press, 1992.

———. *The Life of Debussy*. Cambridge: Cambridge University Press, 1998.

———. *Ravel Remembered*. London: Faber & Faber, 1987.

Norris, Geoffrey. "Debussy: Playing with Colour." *Gramophone*, July 2012. http://www .gramophone.co.uk/feature/debussy-playing-with-colour.

Opstad, Gillian. *Debussy's Mélisande: The Lives of Georgette Leblanc, Mary Garden, and Maggie Teyte*. Woodbridge, Suffolk: Boydell Press, 2009.

Orledge, Robert. *Debussy and the Theatre*. Cambridge: Cambridge University Press, 1982.

———. "Debussy's *House of Usher* Revisited." *Musical Quarterly* 62, no. 4 (October 1976).

———. *Satie Remembered*. Translated by Roger Nichols. London: Faber & Faber, 1995.

———. *Satie the Composer*. Cambridge: Cambridge University Press, 1990.

Pasler, Jann. "A Sociology of the Apaches: 'Sacred Battalion' for *Pelléas*." Chapter in Kelly and Murphy, *Berlioz and Debussy*.

Pennell, Elizabeth Robins. *Nights*. Philadelphia: J. H. Lippincott, 1916.

Phelps, William Lyon. "An Estimate of Maeterlinck." *North American Review* 213 (January 1921).

Prod'homme, J. G. "Claude Achille Debussy." Translated by Marguerite Barton. *Musical Quarterly* 4, no. 4 (October 1918).

Pritchard, Jane, ed. *Diaghilev and the Ballets Russes, 1909–1929: When Art Danced With Music*. London: Victoria and Albert Museum / Washington: National Gallery of Art, 2010.

Poe, Edgar Allan. "The Philosophy of Composition." *Graham's Magazine*, April 1846.

———. "The Poetic Principle." *Home Journal*, August 31, 1850.

———. "The Raven." *American Review*, February 1845.

Quinn, Michael. Interview with Sandrine Piau. *Gramophone*, September 2003.

Quittard, M. Henri. Quote from *Le Figaro*, in "The French Press and Debussy." *Musical Times* 59 (May 1, 1918).

Ravel, Maurice. *A Ravel Reader: Correspondence, Articles, Interviews*. Compiled and edited by Arbie Orenstein. New York: Columbia University Press, 1990.

Régnier, Henri de. *Lettres à André Gide (1891–1911)*. Geneva: Librairie Droz / Paris: Librairie Minard, 1972.

Robb, Graham. *Rimbaud*. New York: W. W. Norton, 2000.

Roberts, Paul. *Claude Debussy*. London: Phaedon, 2008.

———. *Images: The Piano Music of Claude Debussy*. Portland, OR: Amadeus Press, 1996.

Rolland, Romain. *Musicians of To-day*. Translated by Mary Blaiklock. New York: Henry Holt, 1914. http://www.gutenberg.org/ebooks/16467.

Rose, Michael. *The Birth of an Opera*. New York: W. W. Norton, 2013.

Rosen, Charles. "Mallarmé the Magnificent." *New York Review of Books*, May 20, 1999.

Ross, James. "Music in the French Salon." Chapter in *French Music Since Berlioz*, edited by Richard Langham Smith and Caroline Potter. Aldershot: Ashgate, 2006.

Rossetti, Dante Gabriel. "The Blessed Damosel." *The Germ*, 1850.

Rousseau, Jean-Jacques. *Lettre sur la musique française* (1753). Quoted in Rolland, *Musicians of To-day*.

Rumph, Stephen. "Debussy's *Trois Chansons de Bilitis*: Song, Opera, and the Death of the Subject." *Journal of Musicology* 12, no. 4 (Autumn 1994).

Satie, Erik. *A Mammal's Notebook: Collected Writings of Erik Satie*. Edited by Ornella Volta; translated by Antony Melville. London: Atlas Press, 1996.

———. *The Writings of Erik Satie*. Edited and translated by Nigel Wilkins. London: Eulenburg, 1980.

Seroff, Victor I. "A Footnote on Debussy's 'Gaby.'" *Saturday Review*, January 25, 1959. Republished in Seroff, *Debussy, Musician of France*. Freeport, NY: Books for Libraries Press, 1970.

Stephan, Philip. *Paul Verlaine and the Decadence: 1882–90*. Manchester, UK: University of Manchester Press, 1974.

Sullivan, Jack. *New World Symphonies: How American Culture Changed European Music*. New Haven, CT: Yale University Press, 1999.

Symons, Arthur. *The Symbolist Movement in Literature*. New York: E. F. Dutton, 1919.

Templier, Pierre-Daniel. *Erik Satie*. Translated by Elena L. French and David S. French. Cambridge: Massachusetts Institute of Technology Press, 1969.

Thompson, Oscar. *Debussy, Man and Artist*. New York: Tudor, 1940.

Tommasini, Anthony. "The Greatest." [Debussy is the fifth greatest classical composer in history.] *New York Times*, January 21, 2011.

———. "Shocking or Subtle, Still Radical." [*Jeux*.] *New York Times*, September 18, 2012.

Trevitt, John. "Debussy Inconnu: The Later Vocal and the Instrumental Music." *Musical Times* 114, no. 1568 (October 1973).

Trezise, Simon, ed. *The Cambridge Companion to Debussy*. Cambridge: Cambridge University Press, 2003.

Turnbull, Michael T. R. B. *Mary Garden*. Portland, OR: Amadeus Press, 1997.

Vallas, Léon. *Claude Debussy: His Life and Works*. Translated by Maire O'Brien and Grace O'Brien. New York: Dover, 1973.

Verlaine, Paul. *Selected Poems*. Translated by Martin Sorrell. New York: Oxford World's Classics, 2009.

Volta, Ornella. *Satie Seen Through His Letters*. Translated by Michael Bullock. London: Marion Boyars, 1989.

Wagner, Richard. "A Report on the Production of 'Tannhäuser' in Paris." Translated by William Ashton Ellis. In *The Theatre: Richard Wagner's Prose Works*, vol. 3 (1894). http://users.belgacom.net/wagnerlibrary/prose/index.htm.

Wenk, Arthur B. *Claude Debussy and Twentieth-Century Music*. Boston: Twayne, 1983.

———. *Debussy and the Poets*. Berkeley: University of California Press, 1976.

Wheeldon, Marianne. *Debussy's Late Style*. Bloomington: Indiana University Press, 2009.

Whiting, Steven Moore. *Satie the Bohemian: From Cabaret to Concert Hall*. Oxford: Oxford University Press, 1999.

Young, Filson. *More Mastersingers: Studies in the Art of Music*. New York: Henry Holt, 1911.

ACKNOWLEDGMENTS

From my initial conception, I wanted this book to portray Debussy, his friends, and his colleagues as colorful, complex people rather than faceless historical figures. To accomplish that, I had at hand four essential books—a treasury of English translations of Debussy's letters and journal articles, as well as memoirs and miscellany written by many who knew him well. I am immensely grateful to the individuals who granted the permissions I needed to quote these books as liberally as I have done, so as to facilitate authenticity rather than paraphrase. Specifically, I want to reiterate my thanks to Roger Nichols, for his *Debussy Remembered* and his translation of *Debussy Letters*; to Jacqueline Charette, editor and translator of *Claude Debussy Through His Letters*; and, for *Debussy on Music*, to Allison Jakobovic at Random House/Knopf and Ariane Michaloux at Editions Gallimard.

In the course of my research and writing, dozens of writers and scholars contributed significantly to my understanding of Debussy's life and music and of the significance of his social and historical milieu. Among the most important to my work were the books of the biographers Louis Laloy, Léon Vallas, Edward Lockspeiser, and Marcel Dietschy; the eminent musicologists François Lesure and Robert Orledge; the writers H. P. Clive, David Grayson, Denis Herlin, Rosemary Lloyd, Gillian Opstad, Paul Roberts, Jack Sullivan, and Arthur B. Wenk; and many others. Dr Erik Assarsson helped me assess Debussy's cancer and treatment when I found little information in the historical record. In their classrooms, professors Julian Onderdonk and Mark Rimple of West Chester University broadened my understanding of the musical period now known as the Modern era.

I am grateful to Victoria Pryor for generously finding time to tutor me in some of the finer points of non-fiction writing. I wasn't sure I could write this book, but she was. Several people read my manuscript or parts of it, at various stages, and made helpful suggestions for improvements; special thanks go to Harris Chaiklin, Elaine Terranova, Rebecca Field, Vincent Craig, Mardie Zehner, and Liz Ladd. With cheerful diligence, Rosalie Dietz and her staff at the Malvern Public Library found all the books I needed, most of them obscure and long out of print, in Pennsylvania's integrated library system. Thanks, too, to Pamela Fried for her help in navigating the permissions process.

It isn't easy to get a book published these days, if it ever was, and this volume might never have tasted printer's ink without two people to whom I silently offer thanks on a daily basis: my friend Jan Garrigan and my agent Al Zuckerman. Many thanks go to John Cerullo, at Amadeus Press, for taking a chance on a first-time author; to Jessica Burr for her expert guidance and her patience; and to Barbara Norton and Jessica for their thorough, respectful, judicious editing.

Thanks to Shimon Waldfogel for his encouragement and his unflagging confidence in me. Thanks to my children, Larry Snyder and Tanya Snyder, for their love and support and for giving me four beautiful grandchildren while I was busy writing my book. And *tusen takk* to Carol, my wife, who dispenses affection, inspiration, and irrefutable common sense at all the right moments in just the right portions.

Finally, I am grateful to my parents, who passed from my life twenty years ago. My mother, Lillian, was an amateur painter who taught me to cherish beauty in nature, in art, in whatever form it takes. My father, Eli, a Sunday morning violinist, gave me music, which nourishes my soul.

INDEX